Photoperiodic regulation of insect and molluscan hormones

Photoperiodic regulation of insect and molluscan hormones

Ciba Foundation symposium 104

1984

Pitman

London

© Ciba Foundation 1984

ISBN 0 272 79751 0

Published in April 1984 by Pitman Publishing Ltd, 128 Long Acre, London WC2E 9AN, UK
Distributed in North America by CIBA Pharmaceutical Company (Medical Education Division),
P.O. Box 12832, Newark, NJ 07101, USA

Suggested series entry for library catalogues:
Ciba Foundation symposia

Ciba Foundation symposium 104
viii + 298 pages, 77 figures, 4 tables

British Library Cataloguing in publication data:

Photoperiodic regulation of insect and
    molluscan hormones.—(CIBA Foundation
    symposium; no. 104)
    1. Photoperiodism   2. Insects—Physiology
    I. Porter, Ruth   II. Collins, Geralyn M.
    III. Series
    595.7′019153   QL495

Printed in Great Britain at The Pitman Press, Bath

Contents

Participants

M. F. BOWEN   Department of Biology, University of North Carolina at Chapel Hill, Wilson Hall 046A, Chapel Hill, North Carolina 27514, USA

H. BRADLEY   Parasitology Unit, Department of Zoology, University of Edinburgh, West Mains Road, Edinburgh EH9 3JT, UK

J. BRADY   Department of Pure and Applied Biology, Imperial College at Silwood Park, Ascot, Berkshire SL5 7PY, UK

G. M. CHIPPENDALE   Department of Entomology, 1–87 Agriculture Building, University of Missouri—Columbia, Columbia, Missouri 65211, USA

D. L. DENLINGER   Department of Entomology, The Ohio State University, 1735 Neil Avenue, Columbus, Ohio 43210, USA

H-J. FERENZ   Fachbereich Biologie (7), University of Oldenburg, Postfach 25 03, D-2900 Oldenburg, Federal Republic of Germany

J. M. GIEBULTOWICZ   Department of Zoology, University of Washington, Seattle, Washington 98195, USA

L. I. GILBERT   Department of Biology, The University of North Carolina at Chapel Hill, Wilson Hall 046A, Chapel Hill, North Carolina 27514, USA

G. J. GOLDSWORTHY   Department of Zoology, University of Hull, Hull HU6 7RX, UK

J. HARDIE   ARC Insect Physiology Group, Department of Pure and Applied Biology, Imperial College at Silwood Park, Ascot, Berkshire SL5 7PY, UK

M. HODKOVÁ   Institute of Entomology, Czechoslovak Academy of Science, Vinicna 7, 128 00 Prague 2, Czechoslovakia

H. ISHIZAKI   Biological Institute, Faculty of Science, Nagoya University, Furocho, Chikusa-ku, Nagoya, Japan

J. JOOSSE   Biological Laboratory, Vrije Universiteit, De Boelelaan 1087, PO Box 7161, 1007 MC Amsterdam, The Netherlands

P. LANKINEN   Department of Genetics, University of Oulu, Linnanmaa, SF 90570, Oulu 57, Finland

A. D. LEES   Department of Pure and Applied Biology, Imperial College at Silwood Park, Ascot, Berkshire SL5 7PY, UK

S. MASAKI   Laboratory of Entomology, Faculty of Agriculture, Hirosaki University, Hirosaki 036, Aomori, Japan

W. MORDUE (*Chairman*)   Department of Zoology, University of Aberdeen, Tillydrone Avenue, Aberdeen AB9 2TN, UK

T. L. PAGE   Department of General Biology, Vanderbilt University, Nashville, Tennessee 37235, USA

C. S. PITTENDRIGH   Hopkins Marine Station, Stanford University, Pacific Grove, California 93950, USA

S. E. REYNOLDS   School of Biological Sciences, University of Bath, Claverton Down, Bath BA2 7AY, UK

B. ROBERTS   Department of Zoology, Monash University, Clayton, Victoria 3168, Australia

D. S. SAUNDERS   Department of Zoology, University of Edinburgh, West Mains Road, Edinburgh EH9 3JT, UK

P. G. SOKOLOVE   Department of Biological Sciences, University of Maryland Baltimore County (UMBC), 5401 Wilkens Avenue, Catonsville, Maryland 21228, USA

C. G. H. STEEL   Department of Biology, York University, 4700 Keele Street, Downsview, Ontario M3J 1P3, Canada

J. W. TRUMAN   Department of Zoology, NJ-15, University of Washington, Seattle, Washington 98195, USA

A. VEERMAN   Laboratory of Experimental Entomology, University of Amsterdam, Kruislaan 302, 1098 SM Amsterdam, The Netherlands

Chairman's introduction

WILLIAM MORDUE

Department of Zoology, University of Aberdeen, Tillydrone Avenue, Aberdeen AB9 2TN, UK

1984 Photoperiodic regulation of insect and molluscan hormones. Pitman, London (Ciba Foundation symposium 104), p 1

The participants at this symposium are an intriguing mix of people, with similar research problems which are being approached in very different ways. The idea behind this meeting, suggested initially by David Saunders, was to bring together people working on insect or molluscan photoperiodic clocks and on hormones to see if we could find any common ground. Several people here work in both areas, but most of us are at one or other end of the spectrum. I hope that we can find some common points of synthesis as we hear about work on circadian and photoperiodic rhythms in insects, arachnids (mites) and molluscs. Perhaps we can in the next few days become even closer in our understanding of the interface between perception of environmental cues, in this case photoperiodic changes, and the initiation or the inhibition of an endocrine-controlled event. The transduction mechanism between perception of the stimuli and a change in an endocrine-controlled event is, for me, a particular fascination. For most of the organisms that we shall be considering, the only real manifestation that we have available to indicate that the animal has perceived a photoperiodic response is some developmental or physiological event that we can monitor.

My own work tends to be on neurosecretions but I shall try to set an example, as a good chairman should, of not being preoccupied only with my own particular interests, so that we can hope to see some gelling together of the two major aspects of this symposium.

Introduction: the links between 'wet' and 'dry' physiology

DAVID S. SAUNDERS

Department of Zoology, University of Edinburgh, West Mains Road, Edinburgh, EH9 2JT, UK

1984 Photoperiodic regulation of insect and molluscan hormones. Pitman, London (Ciba Foundation symposium 104), p 2–6

By way of introduction I should first say something about our varied definitions of the words 'photoperiodism' and 'photoperiodic'. In this symposium we shall be dealing with photoperiodism in its widest possible sense, to include rhythmic and clock-like phenomena that are entrained or regulated by the daily light cycle, as well as photoperiodism in its strictest sense—as a seasonal phenomenon regulating annual cycles of reproduction, polymorphism, etc. If we kept strictly to this latter aspect, we would have to exclude circadian phenomena. But, as we shall see, some theories about photoperiodic time-measurement are based on circadian rhythmicity, and if we are to understand anything about the wiring patterns of the 'clock' in the insect or molluscan brain, this wider treatment is essential.

Fig. 1 shows the essence of the problem of photoperiodism, as depicted in A. S. Danilevskii's book (1965) on seasonal development in insects. This figure shows the changes in photoperiod with the months of the year, at different latitudes. The seasonal changes in photoperiod proceed with mathematical accuracy, and thus provide very good ('noise-free') time cues that both plants and animals can use to govern their seasonal activity. For example, in London at a latitude of 50 °N, the photoperiod in the depth of winter is about 8 h. At the equinox the photoperiod is, not surprisingly, 12 h of dark and 12 h of light at all latitudes. At the height of summer in London we have about 16 h of light, but a biologically effective photoperiod of 17.5 to 18 h if the twilight 'zones' are included. Some people at this symposium are from Chapel Hill, North Carolina (35 °N), where day-lengths show an annual range from about 10 to 14.5 h; another participant (Pekka Lankinen) works within the Arctic circle (65 °N) where days range from 4 h in the winter to continuous illumination in midsummer. Organisms have evolved a wide variety of responses to such differences, here the most important being a longer critical day-length at higher latitudes.

2

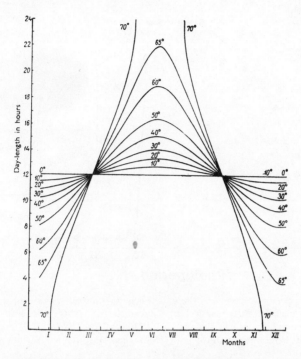

FIG. 1. The seasonal changes in day-length at different latitudes in the northern hemisphere (from Danilevskii 1965).

Fig. 2 shows the 'clock' end of the problem. It illustrates the sharp photoperiodic response curve of *Pyrrhocoris apterus*, the red or Linden bug. Such a curve is typical for a 'long-day' species with a winter diapause. It is obtained by exposing populations of the insect to different *static* photoperiods at the time when the insect is sensitive to photoperiod—in this case during the 4th and 5th (final) nymphal instars. The proportion of the insects that go into diapause at each photoperiod is then obtained. Females of *P. apterus* have an ovarian or reproductive diapause, and it is a simple matter to discover, by dissection, whether the ovaries have developed or not. If the ovaries have remained small, as at short day-length (8 to 15 h), the insects are deemed to be in diapause. If the insects become reproductive and their ovaries full of mature eggs, as at long day-length (16+ h), they are counted as being in a non-diapause state. In Fig. 2 there is a typical and remarkably precise critical day-length between 15 h and 16 h of light, below which all bugs enter a firm ovarian diapause. Day-lengths shorter than the minimum day-length that they encounter in their natural environment (~8 h) produce a weaker diapause response. The ecologically important switch mechanism between long days

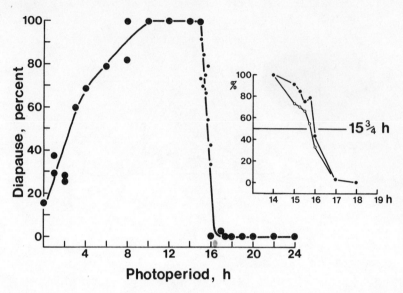

FIG. 2. Photoperiodic responses of the linden bug, *Pyrrhocoris apterus*: induction of ovarian diapause as a function of day-length. Large and small data points show results from different experiments. *Inset:* Data for bugs maintained for 21 days (closed circles) or 28 days (open circles) at photoperiods close to the critical value (15.75 h per 24). Total number of bugs = 470 (from Saunders 1983).

and short days is clearly a product of natural selection and implies that the organism is able to measure either day-length, or night-length, or some more complex combination of the two.

Fig. 3 shows what I consider to be the minimal requirements for the photoperiodic regulation of diapause. The light : dark cycle is perceived by a photoreceptor, which tells the animal whether it is day or night. This information is fed through to a clock, whose job is to do the measuring: i.e. it differentiates between a long day and a short day or, commonly, between a long night and a short night. A decision is then made at some stage in the organism's development, which diverts the 'information' about night-length, via hormonal mechanisms, down two pathways: development or diapause. Yet this is not the whole story because the sensitive period for photoperiodism often occurs much earlier than the appearance of the hormonal effectors. For example, in flesh flies (*Sarcophaga spp.*) the diapause occurs in the pupal instar, but the insect is sensitive to photoperiod during its embryonic and early larval stages; i.e. photoperiodic sensitivity comes to an end long before pupal diapause supervenes in the insect's life-cycle. During the sensitive period, one long day or one long night is not sufficient: the animal needs to accumulate and to integrate a *number* of long or short photoperiods. The

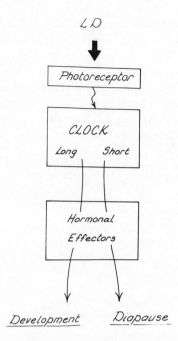

FIG. 3. Schematic representation of the minimal chain of events involved in photoperiodic regulation of the hormones controlling diapause or development.

whole problem seems to involve the transduction of environmental information (long or short day or night) by the 'clock', the accumulation and storage of this information in the central nervous system (about which little is known), and the ultimate transmission of this stored information into the hormonal system which decides whether the animal goes into diapause or not. At this symposium we shall have people talking about all levels: photoreceptors; clocks, and how they differentiate between short and long days; the transmission of information from the clock to the endocrine effectors; and the ultimate hormonal regulation of diapause induction, maintenance and termination.

The clock and the hormonal approaches have been quite separate until now. People working on the clock 'end' of photoperiodism have tended, because of the enormous difficulties of the subject, to regard the insect as a 'black box' whose net response to light is assessable experimentally. This has encouraged model building to explain how time-measurement is achieved, and we shall be hearing, for example, about circadian models, hour-glass models, internal and external coincidence, and other formal approaches to the problem. At the other end of the scale, endocrinologists have tended to accept photoperiodism as merely an unexplained discrimination between long and short days, and to postulate, for example, that long-days facilitate release or synthesis of the hormones necessary for development. Searching questions about how long and short days are differentiated by the insect have tended not to be considered by this group. Michael Menaker has called the clock-work aspects of the subject *'dry physiology'* and the hormones *'wet physiology'*. Our job here is to draw the two approaches and the two groups of investigators together. Over the next few days I am confident that progress will be made in this direction.

REFERENCES

Danilevskii AS 1965 Photoperiodism and seasonal development of insects. 1st English edn. Oliver & Boyd, Edinburgh

Saunders DS 1983 A diapause induction-termination asymmetry in the photoperiodic responses of the linden bug, *Pyrrhocoris apterus*, and an effect of near-critical photoperiods on development. J Insect Physiol 29:399-405

Unity and diversity in insect photoperiodism

SINZO MASAKI

Laboratory of Entomology, Faculty of Agriculture, Hirosaki University, Hirosaki 036, Aomori, Japan

Abstract. The universal occurrence of photoperiodism in insects is due to convergent evolution. The neuroendocrine system, playing the central role in the photoperiodic response, gives diversified terminal expressions of adaptive significance. The response curve reflects the distributions of individual threshold photoperiods in three different ranges corresponding to the minimum number of dark and light hours that are presumably required for the time-measuring function and the genetic time-scale (critical photoperiod). Variations of the photoperiodic response curve can be derived from graded shifts of these distributions. There are, however, some unusual response curves that do not fit this model. Resonance tests suggest two different types for the photoperiodic clock mechanism: the hour-glass and the circadian oscillator. For the latter, the possibility cannot be ruled out that the observed periodicity is due to the interference by the circadian organization and not to the oscillatory nature of the timer itself. In any case, the long-night effect is similarly reversed by light breaks, and various modes of the response to night interruption may be ascribed to variations in the duration and light sensitivity of the two separate stages in the dark reaction. The possible existence of pre-adaptation to seasonal photoperiodism is suggested by the response of hybrids between the temperate and tropical forms of ground crickets.

1984 Photoperiodic regulation of insect and molluscan hormones. Pitman, London (Ciba Foundation symposium 104), p 7–25

This review is a cursory glance at unity and diversity in insect photoperiodism, an approach that is a feasible, though perhaps biased, way of drawing a quick sketch of the many diversified photoperiodic phenomena in insects. The large body of published work on insect photoperiodism, accumulated since the first experiments over 50 years ago, has been thoroughly reviewed recently (Beck 1980, Saunders 1982, Tyshchenko 1977), providing ample material for discussion on any special problem in this field. I have relied on these excellent reviews for background information, and have omitted detailed references for rather general statements.

7

Multiple origins of photoperiodism

Photoperiodism as a means of seasonal adaptation is one of the most remarkable examples of convergent evolution, being universal in both animals and plants. Moreover, the ways in which various organisms respond to photoperiod are so similar that methods invented by botanists have been effectively used to analyse formal properties of the clock machinery in insects and mites. This similarity is probably due to adaptational and functional necessities rather than to the direct common ancestry of the photoperiodic clocks themselves.

The same may be true even in closely related species. The two species of ground cricket in northern Japan, *Pteronemobius mikado* and *Pteronemobius nigrofasciatus*, regulate nymphal growth by responses of the short-day type, and they regulate egg diapause by responses of the long-day type (Masaki 1978). These species are more closely related to tropical species than to each other: the former to *Pteronemobius taprobanensis* and the latter to *Pteronemobius fascipes*. I examined these tropical forms and found only slight, if any, sensitivity to photoperiod: they extend north to the subtropical islands of Japan where they show responses of the long-day type to control nymphal growth, in contrast to the responses of the short-day type shown by the temperate species.

As crickets are believed to be of tropical origin, this geographic pattern suggests that the photoperiodic responses of the two temperate species have evolved independently of each other. Similar examples can be found in many other groups of species. The reason for such convergence is obvious. Day-length is the most accurate seasonal cue ever available for any organism that is both sensitive to light and capable of measuring time.

Convergence of insects in photoperiodism might have been enhanced also by their physiological endowments. In any photoperiodic response, the insect must perform at least the following sequence of functions: reception of photoperiodic signals; measurement of light or dark time; transduction and summation of the photoperiodic information; control of neural and endocrine outputs; and manifestation of the terminal, or final, responses. Only the neuroendocrine system is capable of taking the central part in this sequence. Moreover, the photoperiodic receptor itself is extra-retinal and located in the brain, with the possible exception of *Pterostichus nigrita* (Ferenz 1975). Kono et al (1983) have recently discovered organelles that are suspected to be light-sensitive in giant glial cells and in perineurium cells of the brain of *Pieris rapae*.

Diversity in terminal expression of photoperiodism

Since the neuroendocrine system controls and integrates various developmental and metabolic phenomena, it can express photoperiodic influences in various ways: diapause responses (induction, termination, preprogramming of intensity, selection of alternative stages for diapause); growth responses (rate of growth, number of moults, timing of adult differentiation); morphological responses (seasonal forms, wing forms, other less dramatic structural or colour variations); behavioural responses (tactic movements, flight and migration, aggregation, cocooning, selection of oviposition sites); and sex-determining responses (mode of reproduction, sex ratio).

Only a few examples of previously little-known responses will be cited here. *Aedes togoi* (Nagasaki population) undergoes diapause at either one of two widely separated stages of development, depending on the larval photoperiod within the short-day range: at the egg stage in LD 12:12 (12 h light:12 h dark) and at the fourth larval instar in LD 10:14 (Mogi 1981). In *Chelonus inanitus* the ratio of females to males among the progeny increases from 0.66 in LD 14:10 to 1.11 in LD 12:12 (Rechav 1978), while in *Polistes chinensis* the production of male progeny by foundresses is promoted by short day-lengths (Suzuki 1981).

Most terminal expressions of photoperiodic response are closely linked to the neuroendocrine mechanism of diapause and, together with biochemical adjustments not listed above, form the diapause syndrome. In *Diatraea grandiosella*, for example, the sequence of complicated and highly adaptive behaviour before diapause can be elicited by administering a mimic of juvenile hormone (Chippendale 1978). In *Oncopeltus fasciatus*, a switch from diapause and migratory flight to mating and oviposition is invoked by environmental factors, including photoperiod, and this switch corresponds well with the changing titre of juvenile hormone (Rankin 1978). The photoperiodic control of seasonal polyphenism and ovarian diapause in *Polygonia c-aureum* are both mediated by the median neurosecretory cells in the pars intercerebralis (Fukuda & Endo 1966, Endo 1972). However, photoperiodic responses are not always included in the diapause syndrome. For example, many univoltine species of cricket obligatorily enter diapause only at the egg stage, and yet they control nymphal growth in response to photoperiod (Masaki 1978).

The neuroendocrine system coordinates responses to various endogenous and exogenous stimuli. Possibly through this process, or in some other way, most of the photoperiodic expressions listed above are subject to modification by environmental factors such as temperature, food, population density, etc. In the complex chain of events that culminates in various terminal expressions, the photoperiod-receptive site and pigments and the formal properties of photoperiodic time-measurement have been the subjects of pioneering studies. The direct endocrine control of some terminal expressions has been elucidated to a certain extent. However, the link between these events, i.e. the transduction of the photoperiodic cue into the neuroendocrine output, is still missing, though some suggestions have been made. For example, Saunders (1982) related the different patterns of accumulation and release of secretory granules by the median neurosecretory cells in short-day and long-day larvae of *Pieris rapae* (Kono 1975) to the photoperiodic information storage.

Variability of photoperiodic response curves

Various expressions of photoperiodism may show similar or dissimilar response curves, the most common of which are long-day types such as those found in diapause induction of many species that are active in summer and dormant in winter (Fig. 1). Mirror-images of those responses are short-day types, of which only several examples are known.

At first sight, there seem to be several different types of response curve (Fig. 1, upper panel). However, most photoperiodic response curves can be viewed as cumulative distributions of individual thresholds in three different

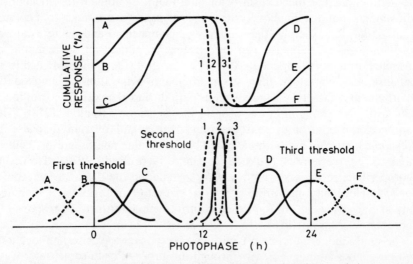

FIG. 1. Upper panel: Photoperiodic responses of long-day type plotted as cumulative percentage responses. Curves except for BD and CD are all known to occur. Broken lines show shifts in critical photoperiod. Lower panel: Corresponding distributions of individual thresholds. Broken curves at <0 h and >24 h represent non-existent hypothetical distributions just to show that graded shifts in threshold distribution produce various photoperiodic response curves.

ranges of photoperiod (lower panel). The first and third thresholds in Fig. 1 might be related to the minimum number, respectively, of light and dark hours required for photoperiodic time-measurement. The second threshold is the so-called critical photoperiod—a genetic time-scale dividing 'long' from 'short' photoperiods. This is less variable than the others, owing to natural selection, for the accurate timing of diapause, etc. Various photoperiodic response curves are derived by shifting these threshold distributions. There are, however, some strange response curves that do not fit the three-threshold model (Fig. 2). Presumably, the left-hand curves in Fig. 2 are the results of an absence or a relaxation of natural selection for the critical photoperiod.

The photoperiodic response is also characterized by the temporal pattern,

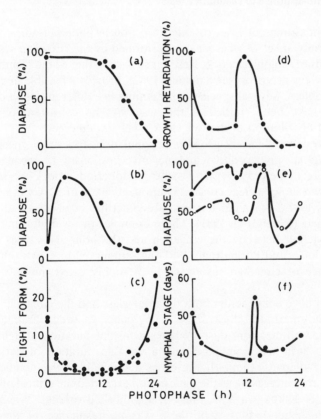

FIG. 2. Unusual examples of photoperiodic response: (a) *Choristoneura fumiferana* (Harvey 1957); (b) *Tetranychus telarius* (Bengston 1965); (c) *Callosobruchus maculatus* (Utida 1969); (d) *Agrotis ypsilon* (Goryshin & Akhmedov 1971); (e) *Bombyx mori* larvae kept as eggs at 25 °C (closed circles) or 16 °C (open circles) in constant dark (DD) (Sumimoto 1974); (f) *Pteronemobius nigrofasciatus* (R. Igarashi & S. Masaki, unpublished results).

as defined by the arrangement of the sensitive and responsive stages in the life-cycle. Once again, insects show diversity in this respect. The time-interval between the two stages is variable from species to species and, in extreme cases, the photoperiodic information is transmitted from one generation to the next. Further complication occurs when different ranges of photoperiod are required in successive stages to elicit the response. The temporal pattern represents the genetic programme of the 'storage' and 'release' of photoperiodic information, which is one of the important unknown aspects of insect photoperiodism.

Diversity in response to resonance tests

As time-measurement is an essential function in photoperiodism, the question naturally arises of whether it is performed by the circadian system or by other kinds of biological clock. Resonance tests, either of the Nanda-Hamner or the Bünsow protocol (see Saunders 1982), provide a feasible first approach to this problem. Several species, representing five different insect orders and Acarina, have been studied in this way, but no consistent phylogenetic pattern of distribution of the two clock types has emerged.

Moreover, two different geographic populations of a single species, *Pterostichus nigrita*, give positive and negative responses to resonance tests, respectively (Thiele 1977). The same photoperiodic clock of *Sarcophaga argyrostoma* shows a clear circadian periodicity at 20 or 22 °C but not at 16 °C (Saunders 1982). A similar temperature effect has been observed in *Drosophila auraria* (Pittendrigh 1981). These examples throw doubt on the reality of a distinction between the circadian and the hour-glass types of photoperiodic clock, and Pittendrigh (1981) has attempted to explain the absence or presence of circadian resonance by a sophisticated multiple oscillator model.

I myself have come across both the hour-glass and the circadian responses of the photoperiodic clock. *Plodia interpunctella* seems to measure the photoperiodic time from dusk. When a constant duration of light, ranging from 4 to 24 h, was combined with a variable duration of darkness, the percentage diapause similarly varied as a function of the number of dark hours, sharply increasing as the dark period exceeded the critical night-length of 13.5 h (S. Kikukawa & S. Masaki, unpublished results). When the dark period was extended to 90 h, there was no resonance of the diapause response, at least at 25 °C (Takeda & Masaki 1976). On the other hand, the wing-form response of *Pteronemobius fascipes* showed a beautiful circadian periodicity in light regimes of the Bünsow protocol, with cycles of LD 12:36 or 12:84.

How is a circadian component involved?

In the cricket's wing-form response, the 'free-running' rhythm of the photo-periodic clock was shorter than 24 h, as indicated by the response phases advanced on the third and fourth days in constant darkness compared with those on the first and second days (S. Masaki & R. Igarashi, unpublished results). This was in accordance with the free-running rhythm of locomotor activity (Y. Watari & S. Masaki, unpublished results).

As deuterium oxide (heavy water, D_2O) is known to lengthen the circadian period in a wide variety of organisms, we also examined its influence on the cricket's critical photoperiod. Neither 10% nor 20% D_2O gave any significant result. The critical photoperiod was between 12 and 12.5 h, being similar to that in the control groups (Fig. 3). This did not, however, disprove the involvement of a circadian component in the photoperiodic clock, because D_2O at these concentrations did not affect the free-running rhythm of locomotor activity (S. Masaki & Y. Watari, unpublished results).

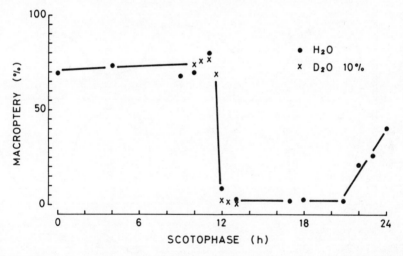

FIG. 3. Effect of deuterium oxide (D_2O) on the photoperiodic wing-form determination in *Pteronemobius fascipes* fed on dry insect feed. Crosses: 10% D_2O given as water supply. Circles: H_2O control.

Night-interruption experiments provided a further opportunity to compare the cricket's photoperiodic clock and its rhythm of activity. When an interruption in early night was followed by a dark period shorter than the critical length, the long-winged form predominated (see Fig. 5, c-1, below). Probably, the interrupting pulse had reset the clock. On the other hand, the activity rhythm was phase-set by the main light:dark transition, and no phase-shift by night interruption was observed (Y. Watari & S. Masaki, unpublished results).

The photoperiodic clock of the cricket certainly shows a circadian resonance, and yet its identity is still in doubt. The related temperate species, *Pteronemobius nigrofasciatus*, poses a related question. This cricket has three different photoperiodic responses: egg diapause, wing form and nymphal development. When the cricket was subjected to light:dark schedules of the Bünsow protocol, the first two responses—diapause and macroptery—showed clear circadian periodicity, but the nymphal development, expressed in terms of the mean development time, did not. Nevertheless, the statistical variance of development time increased and decreased in a circadian fashion (Fig. 4).

The circadian increase in the variance might be a reflection of some unfavourable disturbing effect of out-of-phase light signals on the circadian organization but not on the time-measuring system itself. There is a general

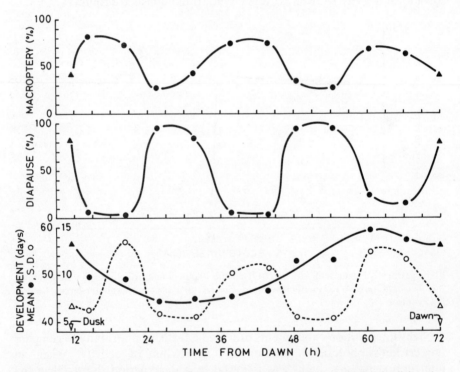

FIG. 4. Resonance responses to a Bünsow protocol (LD 11.5 : 60.5, 1.4h interrupting light pulse, 26 °C) in *Pteronemobius nigrofasciatus*. Horizontal axis indicates the time of onset of interrupting light pulse (S. Masaki & R. Igarashi, unpublished results). Solid line, mean development time; dotted line, variance in development time (1 SD).

tendency for the variance in development rate to increase when insects are exposed to various kinds of environmental stresses. An abnormal light cycle is one such stress.

If we extend this interpretation to the other two responses which, at first sight, so strongly support the direct involvement of a circadian component, a quite different picture emerges. The photoperiodic clock itself may be an hour-glass, and an extended night would induce egg diapause and short-wing development. However, the effector functions would be impeded when the circadian organization of the general physiology is disturbed by light cycles far from modulo τ (the free-running period). Circadian periodicity would then appear in the terminal expression, but it might be a manifestation of the circadian organization itself and not of the kinetics of photoperiodic time-measurement. There is as yet no conclusive evidence to exclude either the circadian or the hour-glass hypothesis. The 'hour-glass timer–oscillator-counter' model recently proposed by Vaz Nunes & Veerman (1982) seems to give a new line of approach to photoperiodic time-measurement.

Similarity in the response to night interruption

Irrespective of whether oscillatory or hour-glass, all the tested cases of photoperiodic response are highly sensitive to night interruption, and the long-night effect is reversed by light breaks. There are two peaks of such an effect, one occurring soon after dusk (peak A) and the other before dawn (peak B) (Saunders 1982). The response pattern is considerably variable among different species, as indicated by the relative sizes of the two peaks. In extreme cases, either A or B alone persists. Even the same species may show different patterns of response depending on the experimental conditions (Fig. 5).

Presumably, peaks A and B represent two distinct light-sensitive stages equivalent to stages 1 and 3 recognized for the *Megoura viciae* clock (Lees 1973). When the two stages (A and B) are separated by a period of light insensitivity, the response is bimodal (Fig. 5, a-1 and b-1). However, if the dark period after night interruption exceeds the critical length for diapause induction, the short-day effect is exerted and peak A does not appear (Fig. 5, a-2). When stage A is very closely followed by stage B, or the intervening light-insensitive stage is very short, only one wide plateau of response may occur (Fig. 5, c-1). Even in such a case, stages A and B can be distinguished by using a brief (10 min) interrupting light that is perceived only in stage B (Fig. 5, c-2). Conversely, in *Mamestra brassicae*, a 1 h interruption gives peak B alone, but when a 3 h pulse is used peak A also appears (b-1, b-2).

Various response curves to night interruption can thus be derived from

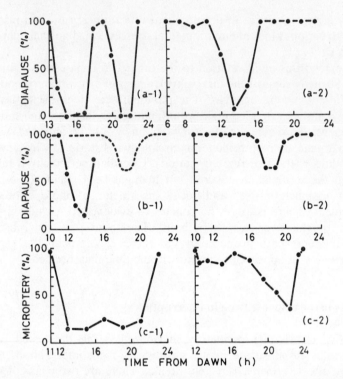

FIG. 5. Night-interruption effects under different experimental conditions. Data points are plotted against the time of onset of interrupting light pulse. (a) *Hyphantria cunea* (1) LD 13:11, 1 h interruption; (2) LD 6:18, 1.5 h interruption (S. Masaki & M. Takeda, unpublished results). (b) *Mamestra brassicae* (1) LD 10:14, 3-h pulse-scanned from hour 11 to 15 (solid line); (2) LD 10:14, 1-h pulse-scanned throughout the scotophase. This result is replotted as the broken line in (1), for comparison (Furunishi et al 1982). (c) *Pteronemobius fascipes* (1) LD 11:13, 1 h interruption; (2) LD 12:12, 10 min interruption (Y. Watari & S. Masaki, unpublished results).

variations in the duration and the light sensitivity of the two stages in the course of dark-time measurement. The common feature in the response suggests that the same principle of time-measurement is operating. Although some recent models of photoperiodic clock are based on hypothetically quantified reactions in light and darkness, students of photoperiodism have been rather reluctant to follow the kinetics closely since the last intensive study by Lees (1973). One of the reasons for this is probably the difficulty in the formal analysis owing to interference by the circadian system. In such analysis, the light and dark components of the cycle must be varied independently of each other. This is possible only in a typical hour-glass example such as the *Megoura* clock. In other cases, the circadian interference would hamper the expression of the time-measuring response as the light:dark cycle deviates from a 24 h duration.

Some evolutionary problems

Photoperiodism comprises complicated physiological processes even in each of its component functions. This highly complex system of adaptation can hardly be formed by only a single step of genetic change. As in many other cases of major evolutionary change, photoperiodism would have been established through progressive modification of pre-existing physiological endowments.

Tyshchenko (1977) presented seven hypothetical steps in the evolution of photoperiodism: (1) direct response to light; (2) appearance of exogenous circadian rhythms; (3) establishment of endogenous circadian rhythms; (4) integration of circadian rhythms; (5) photoperiodic regulation of physiological functions; (6) acquisition of photoperiodic memory function; and (7) transmission of photoperiodic information through generations. He assumes that quantitative responses such as continuous control of growth appear at step 5, and that qualitative responses such as discrete diapause or morph determination appear at step 6.

At step 4, various oscillators should have definite phase-relations to the driving oscillator or to one another. Environmental modification of such phase-relationships would have a favourable or an unfavourable impact on various aspects of physiology. The establishment of step 4 would therefore tend to invoke natural selection, leading to step 5. Photoperiodism should then be an unavoidable evolutionary consequence of circadian organization, if we accept the multiple oscillator theory (Pittendrigh 1981).

Another possible course of evolution is suggested by the results of crossing experiments between the temperate strain Nara (N) of *Pteronemobius nigrofasciatus* and the tropical strain Bali (B) of *Pteronemobius fascipes*. The temperate form programmes its egg diapause in response to the maternal photoperiod while the tropical form virtually lacks egg diapause. When they were crossed, the incidence of egg diapause was affected by both parental genotypes, but the critical photoperiod—defined as the mid-point in the critical range of the response curve—seemed to be a maternal character. In F1 (N♀ × B♂) or backcross (N × NB) progeny, the critical photoperiod was close to the temperate duration of 14 h. In backcross (BN × N) eggs, the critical photoperiod was shorter, between 12 and 13 h (A. Nagase, unpublished; see p 21).

Although the Bali stock does not show any diapause response, it seems to have genes that affect the critical photoperiod. It might have a photoperiodic clock with a short critical photoperiod that is used for some other purpose. This stock showed, in fact, a slight wing-form response to photoperiod, and produced some long-winged adults only in photoperiods of 13 h and longer (S. Masaki & A. Nagase, unpublished results). Therefore, the critical photoperiod can exist before an effector mechanism (egg diapause) has been established. From this I am tempted to suppose further that an hour-glass, such as the hatching timer of *Metrioptera hime* (Arai 1979), might also be homologous to the photoperiodic clock and might be pre-adapted to seasonal photoperiodism. If such a timer occurs universally, it would provide a basis for convergent evolution of photoperiodism in insects.

Acknowledgements

Studies on *Pteronemobius* spp. were supported by grants 411806, 520903 and 56105006 from the Ministry of Education, Science and Culture, Japan. I am grateful to my former and present graduate students, Makio Takeda, Shigeru Kikukawa, Ritsuko Igarashi, Atsushi Nagase and Yasuhiko Watari, who worked with me at various stages of this research. This is contribution No. 94 from the Laboratory of Entomology, Hirosaki University.

REFERENCES

Arai T 1979 Effects of light-on and light-off on the hatching time in *Metrioptera hime* Furukawa (Orthoptera: Tettigoniidae). Kontyû 47:66-77
Beck SD 1980 Insect photoperiodism, 2nd edn. Academic Press, New York
Bengston M 1965 Overwintering behaviour of *Tetranychus telarius* (L.) in the Stanthorpe district, Queensland. Queensl J Agric Anim Sci 22:170-176
Chippendale GM 1978 Behavior associated with the larval diapause of the southwestern corn borer, *Diatraea grandiosella*: probable involvement of juvenile hormone. Ann Entomol Soc Am 71:901-905
Endo K 1972 Activation of the corpora allata in relation to ovarian maturation in the seasonal forms of the butterfly, *Polygonia c-aureum* L. Dev Growth Differ 14:263-274
Ferenz H-J 1975 Photoperiodic and hormonal control of reproduction in male beetles, *Pterostichus nigrita*. J Insect Physiol 21:331-341
Fukuda S, Endo K 1966 Hormonal control of seasonal forms in the butterfly *Polygonia c-aureum* L. Proc Jpn Acad 42:1082-1087
Furunishi S, Masaki S, Hashimoto Y, Suzuki M 1982 Diapause responses to photoperiod and night interruption in *Mamestra brassicae* (Lepidoptera: Noctuidae). Appl Entomol Zool 17:398-409
Goryshin NI, Akhmedov RM 1971 Fotoperiod i temperatura kak faktory v razvitii sovki *Agrotis ypsilon* (Lepidoptera, Noctuidae). Zool Zh 50:56-66
Harvey GT 1957 The occurrence and nature of diapause-free development in the spruce budworm *Choristoneura fumiferana* (Clem.) (Lepidoptera: Tortricidae). Can J Zool 35:549-572

Kono Y 1975 Daily changes of neurosecretory type II cell structure of *Pieris* larvae entrained by short and long days. J Insect Physiol 21:249-264

Kono Y, Kobayashi M, Claret J 1983 A putative photoreceptor-organelle in insect brain glial cell. Appl Entomol Zool 18:116-121

Lees AD 1973 Photoperiodic time measurement in the aphid *Megoura viciae*. J Insect Physiol 19:2279-2316

Masaki S 1978 Seasonal and latitudinal adaptations in the life cycles of crickets. In: Dingle H (ed) Evolution of insect migration and diapause. Springer, New York, p 72-100

Mogi M 1981 Studies on *Aedes togoi* (Diptera: Culicidae). 1: Alternative diapause in the Nagasaki strain. J Med Entomol 18:477-480

Pittendrigh CS 1981 Circadian organization and the photoperiodic phenomena. In: Follett BK, Follett DE (eds) Biological clocks in seasonal reproductive cycles. Wright, Bristol, p 1-35

Rankin MA 1978 Hormonal control of insect migratory behaviour. In: Dingle H (ed) Evolution of insect migration and diapause. Springer, New York, p 5-32

Rechav Y 1978 Biological and ecological studies of the parasitoid *Chelonus inanitus* (Hym.: Braconidae) in Israel. IV: Oviposition, host preferences and sex ratio. Entomophaga 23:95-102

Saunders DS 1982 Insect clocks, 2nd edn. Pergamon Press, Oxford

Sumimoto K 1974 Studies on the developmental physiology of the silkworm *Bombyx mori* in controlled environment. I: Effect of larval photoperiod on the induction of embryonic diapause under nutritional conditions of artificial diet. Environ Control Biol 12:109-116 [Japanese]

Suzuki T 1981 Effect of photoperiod on male egg production by foundresses of *Polistes chinensis antennalis* Perez (Hymenoptera, Vespidae). Jpn J Ecol 31:347-351

Takeda M, Masaki S 1976 Photoperiodic control of larval development in *Plodia interpunctella*. Proceedings of the joint United States–Japan seminar on stored product insects. Manhattan, Kansas, p 186-201

Thiele HU 1977 Differences in measurement of day-length and photoperiodism in two stocks from subarctic and temperate climates in the carabid beetle *Pterostichus nigrita* F. Oecologia (Berl) 30:349-365

Tyshchenko VP 1977 Fiziologiya fotoperiodizma nasekomykh. Tr Vses Entomol Ova 59:1-155

Utida S 1969 Photoperiod as a factor inducing the flight form in the population of the southern cowpea weevil, *Callosobruchus maculatus*. Jpn J Appl Entomol Zool 13:129-134

Vaz Nunes M, Veerman A 1982 Photoperiodic time measurement in the spider mite *Tetranychus urticae*: a novel concept. J Insect Physiol 28:1041-1053

DISCUSSION

Gilbert: In your experiments with deuterium oxide, is the D_2O fed to the crickets or injected?

Masaki: It is fed. We feed the crickets on a dry diet and give them a water supply in a small bottle.

Pittendrigh: But surely the crickets can generate a lot of metabolic water from their dry food, and the heavy water will be only a small proportion of their total water?

Masaki: Even if the crickets produce a lot of metabolic water, they cannot survive on it alone. If the water supply is removed, the crickets will die within one or two days, so they apparently do drink the water.

Pittendrigh: Was it correct that you found no effect of D_2O on either the rhythm or the time-measurement?

Masaki: We found no influence of 10 and 20% D_2O either on the free-running rhythm of locomotor activity or on the critical photoperiod for wing-form determination. We intend to examine the effect of a higher concentration of D_2O on the locomotor activity. If there is any effect, then we can start again to study its influence on the critical photoperiod.

Denlinger: D_2O has a very impressive effect on *Sarcophaga* (Rockey & Denlinger 1983). When we incorporate 20% D_2O into the larval diet we can completely obliterate the diapause response. This effect does not appear in constant darkness, so we are certain that we are not interfering with the animal's capacity for diapause. We envisage that the light-sensitive phase of the circadian oscillation is being shifted. With D_2O we eliminate the perception of short days, and hence no diapause appears.

Masaki: We would expect D_2O to increase the critical night-length, at least in the case of external coincidence, which is suggested by Dr Saunders for *Sarcophaga argyrostoma* (Saunders 1979). Your observation seems to suggest another effect. If the sensitive period is shifted, by D_2O, to the later stage of development, the number of short-day cycles seen by the maggots decreases and, accordingly, the incidence of diapause is lowered. This possibility can be tested by extending the shifted sensitive stage by a low temperature.

Beck (1980) also did an experiment with D_2O and the corn borer *Ostrinia nubilalis*. I plotted his data and found no clear influence on the critical photoperiod. What I saw was a general decrease in the incidence of diapause by D_2O.

Sokolove: Have you done any experiments on thermoperiod and temperature cycles to see their effect on behavioural rhythm?

Masaki: I have not done any thermoperiodic experiments on behaviour. However, in the ground cricket, the wing-form response is not affected by thermoperiod (R. Igarashi, unpublished work). In the Indian meal moth *Plodia interpunctella* we have found a very clear thermoperiodic response (Masaki & Kikukawa 1981).

Sokolove: One could, in principle, use thermoperiod to drive a behavioural rhythm, and then use light-pulses to probe various phases of the activity cycle to see whether there is any relationship between the behavioural 'clock' and the sensitive period of the 'photoperiodic clock'.

Masaki: It seems worthwhile to try such experiments. One way to discriminate between circadian interference and photoperiodic time-measurement is to give temperature and light cycles in various phase-relationships.

Mordue: If the tropical and subtropical species of cricket that do not respond to photophase are moved to a temperate environment, do they start responding; do they have the mechanism for measuring photoperiod?

Masaki: I have not attempted a large-scale temperature experiment. A temperature of 25°C is the most favourable one for this animal. If crickets are reared at 20°C, the survival rate is very low and so it is very difficult to see the influence of temperature on this species. Although the tropical species does not show any diapause response, I would suggest that it has the mechanism for measuring photoperiod and that it pre-adapts itself to evolve a photoperiodic control of diapause.

Pittendrigh: In your crossing experiments on the tropical strain of *Pteronemobius fascipes* from Bali (B) and the temperate strain of *Pteronemobius nigrofasciatus* from Nara (N), you concluded that the critical day-length for the F1 hybrid was different from that for the pure Nara strain. This suggested to you that the Bali genes were affecting the time-measuring system. But this does not necessarily follow. The problem reminds me of ours (Pittendrigh & Minis 1971) many years ago with *Pectinophora* (the pink bollworm). Perhaps, as with *Pectinophora*, the whole curve of % diapause versus photoperiod has been depressed in the F1 hybrid crickets.

Masaki: But the % of diapause in the cross N♀ × B♂ was lower than in the cross (B × N)♀ × N♂, yet the critical photoperiod was longer. So the shift in the critical photoperiod is not a simple superficial influence of a decreasing diapause percentage. I do not define the critical photoperiod by the 50% incidence of diapause but by the mid-point in the descending slope of the photoperiod response curve. This probably corresponds to the median value; see Fig. 1 below and also p 10.

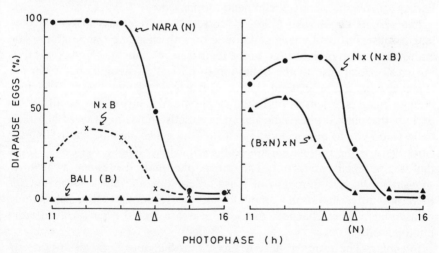

FIG. 1. (*Masaki*) Percentage of diapause eggs as a function of the photophase of parent generations in various crosses between *Pteronemobius fascipes* from Bali (B), Indonesia, and *P. nigrofasciatus* from Nara (N), Japan. In hybrids the female stock is named first. Arrow on abscissa indicates the mid-point in the critical range of photoperiod for each cross, except for the Bali stock which lacks a diapause response (A. Nagase & S. Masaki, unpublished work).

Pittendrigh: So is it correct that the critical day-length has changed in the F1, compared with Nara?

Masaki: I don't think that the slight difference in the critical photoperiod between N and N × B, or N × (N × B), is real. As I described in my paper, the critical photoperiod is a maternal character because diapause is expressed at the egg stage, and is primarily determined by females, depending on the photoperiod.

Steel: Is there a way of confirming that these differences in critical photoperiod are significant? You have described an approximately 30 min or less difference in apparent critical day-length between N and N × B, or N × (N × B), when you define critical day-length as 50% diapause. However, you showed that the transition between short-day and long-day responses in the response curve occurs over a range of 90 min. Hence, I wonder how important a 30 min change in 50% response really is.

Masaki: If you test a sufficient number of photophases in the critical range and obtain a distribution curve as shown in Fig. 1 (p 10), a conventional statistical method can be used to assess the significance of differences in the critical photoperiod among different crosses. Of course, correction should be made for the proportion of those individuals not responding to photoperiod. In any case, my hypothesis of the existence of critical photoperiod before the evolution of diapause is only one of several possible hypotheses.

Mordue: Does the problem lie in the measuring of diapause induction? Perhaps this is the wrong phenomenon to measure.

Pittendrigh: Danilevskii (1965) discussed the differences in critical day-lengths observed with changing latitude or with changing temperature. The entire curve is often depressed as the temperature changes. One takes, arbitrarily, 50% diapause as the definition of critical day-length, but I am not convinced that this reflects any change at all in the clock mechanism. What may be happening is a depression in the amplitude of the response to all photoperiods that may be being measured in exactly the same way as before. I understood you to be concluding that the Bali genes must be controlling the clock because the Bali parent affects the critical day-length, but I don't think that is a necessary argument. The critical photoperiod (defined as 50% response) is surely different. But it isn't clear that the clock mechanism is therefore different. If the amplitude of the response to the same time-measurement were changed, the 50% response would occur at a different photoperiod.

Reynolds: The problem here is surely that diapause is an all-or-none response and that a proportion of the population is becoming incapable of showing that response. In that case, one ought to measure the critical day-length for 50% diapause induction in *that proportion* of the population that is susceptible. The trouble is, of course, we do not know *which* insects are susceptible!

Mordue: Another problem is that one has to measure a developmental event that is several steps removed from the initial perception of the signal.

Reynolds: Although diapause itself is an all-or-none response, does any one mother produce only diapause eggs?

Masaki: No; she can produce both diapause and non-diapause eggs.

Reynolds: In that case, one ought to have an easier experimental approach because here the response is quantitative in individual responding insects.

Masaki: It would be very interesting to use animals that showed a quantitative response, for example, in diapause intensity, developmental rate or continuous morphometric variation.

Reynolds: Is ovarian diapause in *Pyrrhocoris apterus* also an all-or-none response, Dr Saunders?

Saunders: Yes (Saunders 1983).

Masaki: Does the duration of ovarian diapause vary as a function of photoperiod?

Saunders: I haven't looked at that.

Brady: In relation to this problem, what effect does D_2O have on critical photoperiod? If it does have an effect, how can one distinguish between that and a simple amplitude response?

Saunders: There is some work by Brenner & Engelmann (1973) on resonance experiments, using the flowering plant *Chenopodium rubrum*. They showed that with 10% D_2O the whole resonance effect was shifted along the time axis, i.e. the free-running period (τ value) was lengthened, which is what one would expect from a circadian photoperiodic clock treated with D_2O.

Pittendrigh: I was intrigued by Professor Masaki's results showing the diversity of photoperiodic responses in the cricket: some responded in an orthodox way to night interruptions and others did not. But, of course, not all the responses need be controlled by the same clock. Professor Ishizaki's research group (see this volume) have demonstrated, unequivocally, separate pacemakers in the brain and in the prothoracic glands themselves, both directly coupled to light. If these two oscillators should prove to have different periods and different phase-response curves, one can easily imagine changing phase relationships between the brain and the prothoracic glands, with photoperiod.

Chippendale: There has been a great increase in studies on insect photoperiodism over the last few years. Most of these studies have been done on insects that have one or more cycles per year; very few studies have been done on insects that take more than one year to complete their life-cycle. Do you have any comments about the role of photoperiod in insects, such as periodical cicadas, which take 13 or 17 years to complete their life-cycle?

Masaki: It is difficult to answer this because of the paucity of data. Univoltine species are not basically different in this respect from multivoltine species. But with a period of 13 years or more, as in the periodical cicadas, the story may be quite different; there must be some mechanism for counting years, but this is unknown at present, and its study would take a very long time!

Bowen: I am fascinated by the degree of phenotypic plasticity that can be obtained by changing environmental signals. Professor Masaki described many kinds of external morphologies whose expression varies, depending on what photoperiod the animals experience. Is anything known about the internal morphology, specifically the neuronal circuitry, in this respect? I know that post-embryonic neuronal changes occur in insects. Is it possible that the photoperiod to which an insect is exposed could change the neuronal patterning in the central nervous system, and could this explain some of the results that we see?

Truman: The structure of the nervous system is very hard to untangle, and is more like a haystack than a black box! Recently developed dye techniques have allowed people to begin to examine the morphology of particular neural elements that have definable behavioural functions. I do not yet know of any concrete evidence that relates to photoperiodism from this work.

Pittendrigh: In the cat, Randall (1981) showed that the size of a somatosensory receptive field was controlled by photoperiod.

Bowen: It is interesting to note here that Konopka's clock mutants possess neurosecretory cells which are displaced relative to the wild type (Konopka & Wells 1980).

Truman: Another interesting study is on neurons that control song in the zebra finch (Gurney 1981). Neurons in the region of the brain involved with song grow their dendrites in response to androgens. Thus, their dendritic fields would expand or contract, depending on the season. The photoperiod, through its effects on androgen secretion, would therefore control the form of these cells.

Bowen: In Florida, a single species of katydid produces two different calling songs at different seasons (Whitesell & Walker 1979). The response is photoperiodically dependent and may be an example of environmentally determined neuronal patterning.

REFERENCES

Beck SD 1980 Insect photoperiodism. Academic Press, New York
Brenner W, Engelmann W 1973 Heavy water slows down the photoperiodic timing of flower induction in *Chenopodium rubrum*. Z Naturforsch 28C:356

Danilevskii AS 1965 Photoperiodism and seasonal development in insects. Oliver & Boyd, Edinburgh

Gurney ME 1981 Hormonal control of cell form and number in the zebra finch song system. J Neuroscience 1:658-673

Konopka RJ, Wells S 1980 Drosophila clock mutations affect the morphology of a brain neurosecretory cell group. J Neurobiol 11:411-417

Masaki S, Kikukawa S 1981 The diapause clock in a moth: response to temperature signals. In: Follett BK, Follet DE (eds) Biological clocks in seasonal reproductive cycles. Wright, Bristol, p 101-112

Pittendrigh CS, Minis DH 1971 The photoperiodic time-measurement in *Pectinophora gossypiella* and its relation to the circadian system in that species. In: Menaker M (ed) Biochronometry. National Academy of Sciences, USA, p 212-250

Randall W 1981 A complex seasonal rhythm controlled by photoperiod. J Comp Physiol 142:227-235

Rockey SJ, Denlinger DL 1983 Deuterium oxide alters pupal diapause response in the flesh fly, *Sarcophaga crassipalpis*. Physiol Entomol, in press

Saunders DS 1979 External coincidence and the photoinducible phase in the *Sarcophaga* photoperiodic clock. J Comp Physiol 132:179-189

Saunders DS 1983 A diapause induction-termination asymmetry in the photoperiodic responses of the linden bug, *Pyrrhocoris apterus*, and an effect of near-critical photoperiods on development. J Insect Physiol 29:399-405

Whitesell JJ, Walker TJ 1979 Photoperiodically-determined dimorphic calling songs in a katydid (*Neoconocephalus triops*). Nature (Lond) 274:887-888

The circadian component in photoperiodic induction

C. S. PITTENDRIGH, J. ELLIOTT and T. TAKAMURA

Hopkins Marine Station of Stanford University, Pacific Grove, California 93950, USA

Abstract. A variety of experimental protocols demonstrates that there is a circadian component in the photoperiodic responses of organisms. Since photoperiodic induction occurs in only some entrained steady states of the circadian system, the mechanisms of entrainment are reviewed here and are related to models of the circadian involvement in photoperiodism. Special attention is devoted to the multi-oscillator nature of circadian systems and to the impact of photoperiod on the temporal sequence of events within the system.

1984 Photoperiodic regulation of insect and molluscan hormones. Pitman, London (Ciba Foundation symposium 104), p 26–47

The chequered history of 'Bünning's hypothesis'

It is now 47 years since Erwin Bünning published his remarkable insight—then almost entirely an intuitive guess—that 'endogenous daily rhythms' played some causal role in the photoperiodic control of flowering. It is important to recognize this very general proposition as the real contribution in Bünning's (1936) paper and not to confound its merits with the clear shortcomings of his more specific model of *how* it is involved (see Pittendrigh & Minis 1964). Bünning's hypothesis failed to attract much support outside Germany for a couple of decades and was certainly overshadowed in the US for several years by the discovery of phytochrome by S. B. Hendricks, H. A. Borthwick & M. W. Parker. Unlike 'rhythm', phytochrome was a molecule, and the spontaneous dark reversion of phytochrome from its far-red to red form offered an attractive model (Hendricks 1960, 1963) for the time-measurement implicit in photoperiodic induction. Phytochrome continued to be a distraction in this way at least until 1965 when Hendricks and Borthwick themselves (see Cumming et al 1965) had to abandon that molecule as a potential photoperiodic clock. It is remarkable that this continued until 1965, since Nanda & Hamner had published an unequivocal demonstration of the validity of Bünning's general proposition as far back as 1959; and their results had been discussed intensively (and evidently with feeling on both sides) at the Botanical Congress in Montreal that year. It is interesting that in a biographical memoir many years later Hendricks says of Borthwick that he was never much attracted by the rhythm approach—rhythm was 'only a word' (Natl Acad Sci Biographical Memoirs). I suspect that this attitude is still rather widespread; that juvenile hormone, prothoracicotropic hormone and ecdysone titres seem a more attractive framework for explanation precisely because of their tangible concreteness. Nevertheless, there is a circadian component in the photoperiodic responses of very many organisms (indeed the great majority) and the analysis of photoperiodism cannot ignore it.

Fig. 1 summarizes the outcome of the Nanda-Hamner protocol applied to a wide variety of organisms. A short photoperiod (e.g. 8 h) that is non-inductive in a 24 h day becomes inductive when the cycle length (T) is increased by extending the duration of darkness. Indeed several different cycle-lengths, all of which are defined by $T = n\tau + k$, are photoperiodically inductive; τ is a circadian period (close to 24 h). The phenomenological result is clear: circadian periodicity is involved in the photoperiodic response of the tested species. At least three other widely used experimental protocols (see Saunders 1976) yield additional evidence testifying to the validity of Bünning's 'general proposition'. None of them alone, however, informs us how circadian oscillations are involved: all they tell us is that the circadian component in photoperiodic induction involves the system's entrainment (phase-shifting) responses to light. Some understanding of those responses is therefore a prerequisite for evaluation of all the experimental results in this field (see Pittendrigh & Minis 1964, Pittendrigh 1966).

The entrainment of circadian pacemakers

Current understanding of the entrainment of circadian systems focuses on the *phase-response curves* of the pacemaking oscillation that drives them. The phase-shift ($\Delta\phi$) caused by a standardized brief light pulse is characteristic, in its sign (delay or advance) and magnitude, of the pacemaker's phase (ϕ) exposed to the pulse. The phase-response curve describing this dependence [$\Delta\phi_n(\phi_n)$] is remarkably similar (Fig. 2) in its general form for all circadian pacemakers studied: (1) the half-cycle (subjective night) that normally coincides with darkness in nature is always much more responsive to light than the other half-cycle (subjective day); and (2) the early subjective night is always characterized by delay responses and the later subjective night by advances. Both of these universal phase-response-curve features are analytical necessities (Daan & Pittendrigh 1976, Pittendrigh 1981a). In the only

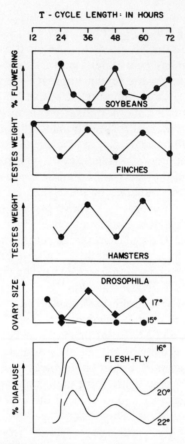

FIG. 1. A sample of Nanda-Hamner transects. Each panel plots a changing photoperiodic response (percentage flowering, testis weight etc.) as a function of the length, in hours (*T*), of the entraining light:dark cycle. The duration of the photoperiod (light pulse) is held constant in each panel. The response rises and falls (modulo ~24h) as a function of *T*. (From Pittendrigh 1981a). Temperature for the lower two panels is in °C.

case (*Drosophila*) where the kinetics of pacemaker phase-shifts has been adequately studied, the full response (even a 12 h shift) has been shown to develop nearly instantaneously (Pittendrigh 1974, 1981a).

It is convenient to distinguish two 'mechanisms' by which light:dark cycles can entrain circadian pacemakers. In both, the action of the light in each cycle is to change the oscillator's period (τ) by an amount equal to $\tau - T$, where T is the period of the light cycle. In one mechanism a brief light pulse (seconds or minutes) causes a discrete phase-shift ($\Delta\phi$) whose sign and magnitude are defined by $\tau - T$. This *discrete entrainment* is illustrated in Fig. 3, which is

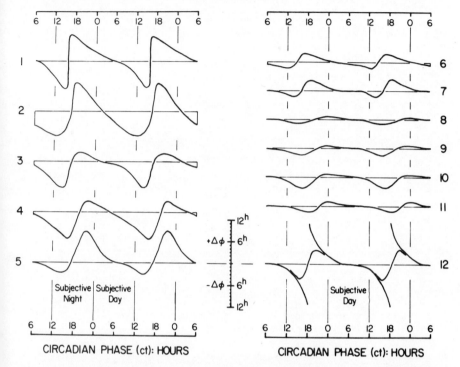

FIG. 2. Phase-response curves for light-pulses from a diversity of organisms, unicellular species, plant, insect and vertebrate, based on data from various sources. (1) *Sarcophaga* (fly); pulse = 3 h, 100 lux; (2) *Coleus* (green plant); pulse = 4 h, 13 000 lux; (3) *Leucophaea* (cockroach); pulse = 6 h, 50 000 lux; (4) *Euglena* (unicellular); pulse = 4 h, 1000 lux; (5) *Gonyaulax* (unicellular); pulse = 3 h, intensity unknown; (6) *Anopheles* (mosquito); pulse = 1 h, 70 lux; (7) *Mesocricetus* (hamster); pulse = 0.25 h, 100 lux; (8) *Peromyscus leucopus* (deer mouse); pulse = 0.25 h, 100 lux; (9) *Peromyscus maniculatus* (deer mouse); pulse = 0.25 h, 100 lux; (10) *Mus musculus* (house mouse); pulse = 0.25 h, 100 lux; (11) *Taphozous* (bat); pulse = 0.25 h, 100 lux; and (12) *Drosophila pseudoobscura* (fruitfly); pulse = 0.25 h (Type 0 phase-response curve) and 1 ms (Type 1 phase-response curve).

based on *Drosophila pseudoobscura*, where τ happens to be 24 h. When the period (T) of the light cycle is 27 h, the pulse (~ 50 lux for 15 min) falls, in steady state, on the pacemaker phase (ϕ), where the $\Delta\phi$ response is a 3 h delay; when T is 21 h it falls at a very different phase, where the response is a 3 h advance. When a circadian pacemaker's period and phase-response curve (for some brief light pulse) are known it is easy to illuminate almost any selected phase of its cycle by adjusting the period (T) of a cycle of such pulses. The simplicity of this discrete mechanism makes it just as easy to predict the phase-relation of pacemaker to more complex light cycles involving two pulses per cycle; this corresponds with the natural conditions for night-active

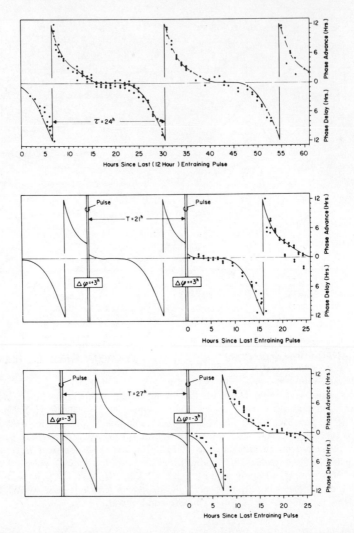

FIG. 3. The time-course of the free-running and entrained pacemaker is assayed by a succession of $\Delta\phi$ responses. Top trace: the pacemaker free-running for three cycles in constant dark (DD) after release from LD 12:12 (12 h light:12 h dark). Middle and lower traces plot the predicted pacemaker time-course in relation to 15 min pulses recurring at $T = 21$-h and 27-h intervals. After release from entrainment, the phase of the pacemaker is assayed (by the second-pulse technique) relative to the last-seen entraining pulse.

animals which see two 'pulses' of light each day, one at sunset and another at dawn. In this case the entrained steady state is reached when the sum of the two phase-shifts is equal to $\tau - T$ (see Pittendrigh 1981b).

The second entrainment 'mechanism' involves longer light pulses ('photo-periods') in each cycle and thus corresponds with the natural situation for day-active organisms. At the beginning of a long photoperiod the pacemaker experiences the same abrupt phase-shift effected by a brief pulse; and as the light continues it modulates the angular velocity of the oscillator, speeding it up in the late subjective night and early day, then slowing it in the late subjective day. This deceleration increases and, if the intensity is high enough and the photoperiod long enough (>9h in *Drosophila*), it becomes total arrest at the beginning of the subjective night. Thus, for nearly all naturally occurring photoperiods, entrainment in nature is effected by a daily arrest of the pacemaking oscillation towards the end of the light and a renewal of motion at the beginning of darkness each night. As day-length increases in the first half of the year, dawn illuminates progressively earlier phases in the oscillator's late subjective night, and as winter approaches the reverse sequence ensues (Fig. 4).

Entrainment and 'external coincidence' models of photoperiodic induction

Table 1 lists the many classes of model so far advanced to account for the circadian element in photoperiodism. The brevity of this paper happily precludes any attempt to explain, let alone evaluate, all of them. In one case ('resonance effect', see below p 36) the circadian system does not necessarily execute the photoperiodic time-measurement itself, but its proximity to resonance with the light cycle ($T \simeq \tau$) affects the magnitude of the

TABLE 1 Classes of model for the circadian component in photoperiodism

---

I: Non-clock role for the circadian system
  The 'resonance' effect. Magnitude of the photoperiodic response depends on the circadian system's proximity to 'resonance' (i.e. when T (period of light-cycle) is equal to τ (period of circadian system).

II: A 'clock' role for the circadian system
  (a) 'External coincidence'. Photoperiodic induction occurs only when some photo-inducible phase (ϕ_i) of the circadian system coincides with light:

      (i) ϕ_i is a pacemaker phase
    or (ii) ϕ_i is a phase in a slave-oscillation

  (b) 'Internal coincidence'. Photoperiodic induction occurs only when critical phases in two separate oscillators (x and y), internal to the circadian system, coincide in time:

      (i) x and y are mutually coupled oscillators in a 'complex pacemaker'
      (ii) x and y are separate (uncoupled) light-sensitive oscillators
      (iii) x and y are pacemaker and slave
    or (iv) x and y are two slaves

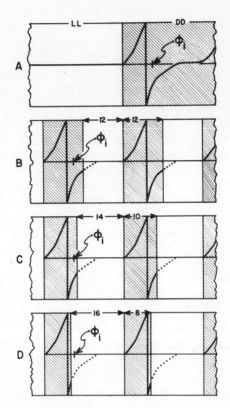

FIG. 4. (*Drosophila pseudoobscura*). A, Constant light (LL) suppresses the *Drosophila* oscillation; on transfer to constant dark (DD) it resumes its motion starting from circadian time (CT) 12 h. B, C and D. Photoperiods of 12 or more hours similarly stop the oscillation which starts afresh from CT:12 h with the onset of darkness each night. The light at dawn falls further back into the late subjective night as photoperiod increases. For illustrative purposes ϕ_i has been represented as occurring at CT:21 h: it is not illuminated by photoperiods of 12- and 14-h duration; a 16-h photoperiod illuminates it.

response to the time-measurement. In all the other hypotheses (models) listed in Table 1 the circadian system is itself responsible for discriminating between longer and shorter days. They fall into two very arbitrary groups that are not even mutually exclusive. The first—usually dubbed 'external coincidence'—includes Bünning's original (1936) formulation of photophil and scotophil halves of the circadian cycle and the somewhat more explicit formulation by Pittendrigh & Minis in 1964. Photoperiodic induction occurs only when some specific phase (ϕ_i) in the scotophil half of the circadian cycle coincides with light; a photochemical reaction that requires this coincidence initiates the chain of events leading to the photoperiodic response. In a sense this model is necessarily true and trivial: there are of course some phases of the system's circadian cycle that coincide with light only under longer photoperiods and for the most part they occur in the late subjective night (Fig. 4). This 'model' accommodates most of the results from all the experimental protocols that yield evidence of a circadian component in photoperiodism because, for the most part, it is little more than a redescription of them.

Its principal merit is its implicit emphasis on the phase-shifting behaviour of the system—on the coincidence of light with some crucial phase(s) of the circadian cycle where a particular $\Delta\phi$ response occurs. This is what led Pittendrigh & Minis (1964) to design the 'T-experiment' protocol: long-day effects can be brought about by very brief pulses in cycles whose frequency (period) is such as to ensure the coincidence of that brief pulse with some specific circadian phase. It also provides a satisfactory explanation (Pittendrigh & Minis 1971) of Hillman's (1964) otherwise perplexing results from experiments using two pulses per cycle, separated by 11 and 13 h intervals: the photoperiodic responses of *Lemna perpusilla* here are precisely what one would have predicted from an external coincidence model. And more recently Saunders (1976) finds 'external coincidence' wholly adequate for an understanding of the circadian component in the photoperiodic response of *Sarcophaga* spp., as does Elliott (1981) for hamsters.

In summary, the 'external coincidence' idea, combined with an understanding of entrainment mechanisms, is useful in predicting and explaining the photoperiodic effectiveness of various exotic experimental light cycles but it offers no further insight into what makes some entrained steady states inductive and others not. Moreover, it seems incompetent—without major additional assumptions—to account, even in a formal way, for several important phenomena. These include: (1) the substitution of thermoperiod for photoperiod; (2) the temperature-dependence of critical day-length in several insects; and (3) phase-response curves of the *Pectinophora gossypiella* type. The mere existence of circadian surfaces, let alone their detail, also seems difficult to explain in terms of external coincidence.

The multi-oscillator nature of circadian organization: 'internal coincidence' models of photoperiodic induction

A quite distinct type of model for the photoperiodic time-measurement was introduced independently by Pittendrigh (1960, 1972, 1981a) and Tyshchenko (1966) and is based on increasingly clear evidence that circadian systems comprise many oscillations whose mutual phase-relations could well be altered by a change in photoperiod. It is important to emphasize at the outset that these 'internal coincidence' models are not to be thought of as exclusive alternatives to 'external coincidence'; like the latter their rationale is that photoperiodic induction occurs only in some entrained steady states of the system. The merit of external coincidence is its focus on the entrainment mechanism; the focus of internal coincidence is on changing temporal order (phase-relation of constituent oscillators) in a multi-oscillator circadian system.

There is now strong evidence that the pacemaker of vertebrate circadian systems is a complex of two mutually coupled oscillators, one of which (E) is entrained principally by evening light and the other (M) by morning light (Pittendrigh 1974, Daan & Pittendrigh 1976). As sundown and dawn come close together in summer, the phase-relation between the constituent oscillators is reduced. Fig. 5 summarizes some of the recent experiments in our laboratory (J. A. Elliott & C. S. Pittendrigh 1983, unpublished) which show that the hamster's phase-response curve (which tracks the pacemaker's time-course) is markedly affected by photoperiod: on short days the phase-response curve's 'dead zone' (nearly no response to light) is narrow and its amplitude is great: brief pulses can elicit phase-shifts as large as 12 h. But, as photoperiod lengthens, the dead zone becomes longer and its amplitude is reduced: clearly the physical state of the pacemaking system itself is being profoundly changed by photoperiod and the data suggest that this change includes the phase-relation between evening and morning oscillators.

A related set of possibilities arises when an animal has several anatomically separated (non-redundant) pacemakers coupled to the light : dark cycle. We now know of three such cases. In one of these (the sparrow) the pineal, and still other oscillators (which are detected after pinealectomy), are all coupled to the environmental light : dark cycle (Takahashi & Menaker 1982). Unless they all have precisely the same period (τ) and phase-response curve their mutual phase-relations will probably change as photoperiod changes. The second example comes from the invertebrates that interest us here. In some beautiful recent experiments on *Samia cynthia ricini*, Mizoguchi & Ishizaki (1982) show that in addition to the light-sensitive pacemaker in the brain (that times the release of prothoracicotropic hormone) there is another, quite separate, light-coupled circadian clock in the prothoracic glands themselves. The common occurrence of extraocular pathways (intracellular pigments) that couple circadian pacemakers to light suggests that the sparrow and *Samia* may well be just the beginning: that we will find that a multiplicity of light-entrained oscillators in a single system is more the rule than the exception. The third established case makes a specially interesting additional point: in *D. pseudoobscura* there are two light-coupled, circadian pacemakers in the adult brain that differ markedly in their periods and phase-response curves: one, with τ very close to 24 h, drives the eclosion rhythm and has a Type-0 phase-response curve; a second drives the locomotion rhythm and has

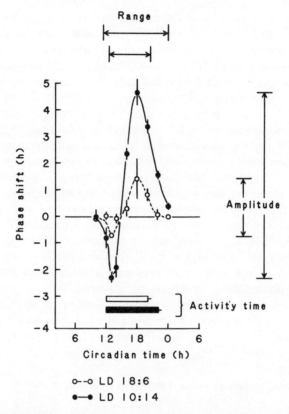

FIG. 5. Photoperiod-dependence of the hamster's phase-response curve. Each point plots the mean ± SEM for a group of 3–5 hamsters pulsed with light (15 min) at the indicated circadian time (CT) on the tenth cycle of a period of constant dark (DD) after release from entrainment to the light: dark (LD) cycle. Open symbols—long photoperiod (LD 18:6); closed symbols—short photoperiod (LD 10:14). Bars represent the duration of nocturnal wheel-running (mean ± SEM) with onset of activity designated at CT 12 h. Following the short photoperiod (LD 10:14) phase-shift responses ($\Delta\phi \geqslant 0.5$ h) occur over a broader range of the circadian cycle (the 'dead zone' is reduced), and the phase-response curve has a larger amplitude than it does following entrainment to a long photoperiod (LD 18:6). The decreased range and amplitude of the phase-response curve after LD 18:6 is correlated with a reduction in the fraction of the cycle devoted to wheel-running activity (activity time) and both observations reflect the photoperiod-dependence of the state of a complex circadian pacemaker (decrease in 'Ψ_{EM}'). In the hamster photoperiod-induced change in the physiological state of the pacemaker may lie at the basis of photoperiodic time-measurement (J. A. Elliott & C. S. Pittendrigh, unpublished).

τ close to 23 h and a Type-1 phase-response curve (Engelmann & Mack 1978, and C. S. Pittendrigh, unpublished confirmation). There is no doubt that the phase-relation of these two pacemakers depends on photoperiod.

Multicellular systems also include circadian oscillations which are not themselves directly entrained by light but, rather, act as slaves to the light-sensitive pacemaking oscillation. *Homo sapiens* (Aschoff et al 1967) and *Drosophila pseudoobscura* (Pittendrigh 1981a) provide well studied examples. One of us (Pittendrigh 1981a) has recently suggested that the temporal sequence of events in an animal circadian system is probably based on a series of slave oscillations driven by a common pacemaker. If the slaves differ in their natural frequencies, or in the strength of their coupling to the pacemaker, they will have different steady-state phase-relations to it and, hence, to each other. These phase differences (open to evolution by adjustment of slave parameters) are the basis of the temporal programme. Computer simulations of such a 'circadian programme', show that its temporal sequence is subject to significant change as photoperiod lengthens or shortens and, in so doing, changes pacemaker waveform: the various slave oscillations in the system respond differentially to the pacemaker's seasonal changes.

The multiplicity of light-coupled oscillators, and of slaves driven by them, makes seasonal change in the temporal fine-structure of a circadian system inevitable as photoperiod lengthens or shortens. And there are several different possible ways (as the details in Table 1 reflect) in which the changing phase-relations internal to the system could be used as a 'clock' to recognize a critical day-length.

A non-clock role for the circadian component in photoperiodism

Earlier we noted briefly that the circadian component in photoperiodic responses may have nothing to do with the time-measurement at all, as Vaz Nunes & Veerman (1982) have recently emphasized in an important analysis of spider-mite photoperiodism. This possibility was first noted (Pittendrigh 1966) in a re-analysis of Beck's data (1962) for *Ostrinia*; it was argued that while the data did indeed favour (though not prove*) an hour-glass time-measurement of the critical 10 h night-length, the magnitude of the response at all photoperiods was dependent on how close the length of the light cycle (T) was to 24 h—i.e. to resonance with a circadian system. This approach was later extended (Pittendrigh 1972) to predict, successfully, the existence of the so-called extended circadian surfaces that Saunders (1976) then found in *Nasonia* spp. and *Sarcophaga* spp. These circadian surfaces appear, to us, intractable to explanation in terms of either hour-glass or external coinci-

---

* S. Skopik (personal communication) has recently shown that *Ostrinia's* hour-glass behaviour is, as in several other insects, temperature-dependent.

dence models of the photoperiodic time-measurement unless some resonance effect is added as a modulation of that measurement. On the other hand, it has been shown (Pittendrigh 1981a) that the mutual phase-relations of constituent oscillations in a circadian system will vary systematically with change in photoperiod and cycle length and so yield a circadian surface. Thus an internal coincidence approach to the circadian component in photoperiodic induction appears competent to yield either photoperiodic time-measurement, or a resonance function, or both.

Summary and perspective

The last 25 years have yielded abundant proof that there is indeed a circadian component in the photoperiodic responses of a great many very different organisms; but we still lack any sure understanding of what that component is. We are not even sure it is always (indeed ever!) the clock that effects the photoperiodic time-measurement; in some species it may be the clock, and elsewhere not; and even when it does serve to measure photoperiod we cannot be sure it always does so in the same way. Moreover there is growing empirical support for our own intuitive preference that extensive convergent evolution probably underlies the phenomenological similarities between different taxa. It is not beside the point that soybeans, flies and hamsters all give a positive response to a Nanda-Hamner protocol: there is surely a circadian component to the photoperiodic induction of flowering, insect diapause and mammalian testicular recrudescence; but there is very little chance that the similarity is more than mere convergence! And the same caveat applies even within those invertebrate groups that interest us here. Saunders (1976) has already emphasized strong differences between *Sarcophaga* spp. and *Nasonia* spp.; the differences between *Pieris* spp. (Danilevskii 1957) and other lepidoptera in the effect of temperature on critical day-length seem fundamental to us and not explainable by minor variation on a common mechanism. We are also much impressed by the great dissimilarities between the behaviour of *Drosophila littoralis* that Dr Lankinen (see this volume) has reported and our own findings (T. Takamura & C. S. Pittendrigh, unpublished) for *Drosophila auraria*. Fig. 6 contrasts our findings with these others (see Lankinen & Lumme, this volume). It is not even clear that the diversity of individual photoperiodic responses within the same insect are all based on the same strategy for measuring photoperiod. Professor Sinzo Masaki first drew my attention to this important point; his research group found night interruptions to be effective in some of the several photoperiodic responses of one species of *Pteronemobius* but not in others. Prompted by this important

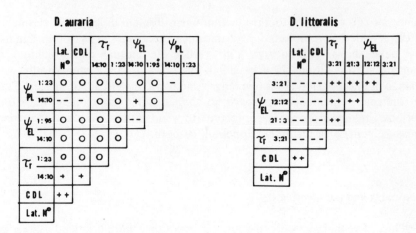

FIG. 6. Significant correlation (or its absence) of circadian system features in the photoperiodic responses in *Drosophila littoralis* (see Lankinen & Lumme, this volume) and *D. auraria* (T. Takamura & C. S. Pittendrigh, unpublished). 0, no correlation; + and ++, weak and strong positive correlation; — and --, weak and strong negative correlation. Lat $N°$ = geographic races from North to South. CDL = critical day length. τ_R = period of free-running rhythm (after specified light:dark regimes). Ψ_{EL} = phase relation of eclosion peak to light—the earlier, the more negative (for specified LD regimes). Ψ_{PL} = phase relation of pacemaker (assayed by phase-response curve) to light—the earlier, the more negative (for specified LD regimes). Critical day-length varies systematically with latitude in both species, as expected. In *D. littoralis* all assayed features of the circadian system (τ_R and Ψ_{EL}) are strongly correlated (positively or negatively) with critical day-length in a way that is amenable to explanation by 'external coincidence'. This is not so in *D. auraria*.

observation we are finding somewhat similar results in *D. auraria* (T. Takamura, K. Elliott & C. S. Pittendrigh, unpublished).

Our own inclination is to emphasize the attractive set of possibilities lumped under the rubric of 'internal coincidence' not as an exclusive alternative but as a supplement to 'external coincidence'. Every observation about photoperiodic induction that we know of can be accommodated by 'internal coincidence'. That is, of course, at once both its strength and weakness. While it is surely correct to emphasize that the internal temporal structure of a multi-oscillator circadian system will, almost necessarily, change with a change in day-length, it is just as necessary to emphasize the nearly insuperable difficulties in attempting to discriminate among the rich array of possibilities by using the purely formal arguments that have characterized the field so far.

Yet our formal efforts have not been pointless, and neither do they lack any future. Indeed, our still embryonic understanding of the multi-oscillator structure of the circadian system is the proper and necessary framework for the pursuit of neuroendocrine detail. Tamarkin et al (1976) and Goldman et

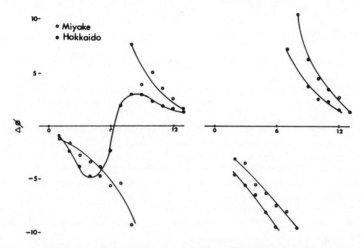

FIG. 7. Phase-response curves for two geographic races of *Drosophila auraria* in Japan. Miyake, southern; Hokkaido, northern. *Left:* 15 min, 50 lux pulses. Hokkaido has a Type-1 (weak resetting) phase-response curve; Miyake has a Type-0 (strong resetting) curve. *Right:* 60 min, 50 lux pulses. Both races now show Type-0 phase-response curves. In both panels there is a clear phase-difference between the races: the Hokkaido phase-response curve lies to the left of Miyake—it is closer to the last-seen photoperiod. The strains differ in their 'subjective light intensities'. Abscissae scales are in hours.

al (1982) have given us important leadership here in their analysis of hamster photoperiodism: the effect of standard melatonin injections is quite remarkably dependent on the phase of the circadian system at the time of injection. And closer to home we have the classic demonstrations from J. W. Truman's & H. Ishizaki's laboratories (see papers in this volume) that in saturniid moths three different hormones (prothoracicotropic hormone, ecdysone and eclosion hormone) are all under strict circadian control. So while it is clear that purely formal circadian studies have a limited future it is equally sure that the time has passed when a preference for the concrete permits one to dismiss 'rhythm' as 'just a word'. Someone could have a fine time were *Samia cynthia ricini* (or some other large and easily cultured saturniid) to have a series of geographic races like those we and our Finnish colleagues are currently exploiting in *Drosophila* spp. One could combine neuroendocrine analyses with a study of how (if at all) the circadian system systematically co-varies with latitudinal change in critical day-length.

Acknowledgements

Work reported in this paper was supported by grants from the National Institutes of Health (GM 28803-02), the National Science Foundation (PCM-811304) and National Aeronautics and Space Administration (NAG 2-122) to C. S. Pittendrigh.

REFERENCES

Aschoff J, Gerecke U, Wever R 1967 Desynchronization of human circadian rhythms. Jpn J Physiol 17:450-457

Beck SD 1962 Photoperiodic induction of diapause in an insect. Biol Bull (Woods Hole) 122:1-12

Bünning E 1936 Die endonome Tagesperiodik als Grundlage der photoperiodischen Reaktion. Ber Dtsch Bot Ges 54:590-607

Cumming BG, Hendricks SB, Borthwick HA 1965 Rhythmic flowering responses and phytochrome changes in a selection of *Chenopodium rubrum*. Can J Bot 43:825-853

Daan S, Pittendrigh CS 1976 A functional analysis of circadian pacemakers in noctural rodents. II: The variability of phase response curves. J Comp Physiol 106:253-266

Danilevskii AS 1957 Photoperiodism as a factor in the formation of geographical races of insects. Entomol Obozr 36:6-27

Elliott JA 1981 Circadian rhythms, entrainment and photoperiodism in the Syrian hamster. In: Follett BK, Follett DE (eds) Biological clocks in seasonal reproductive cycles. Wright, Bristol, p 203–217

Engelmann W, Mack J 1978 Different oscillators control the circadian rhythm of eclosion and activity in *Drosophila*. J Comp Physiol 127:229-237

Goldman BD, Carter DS, Hall VD, Roychoudhury P, Yellon SM 1982 Physiology of pineal melatonin in three hamster species. In: Klein DC (ed) Melatonin rhythm generating system: developmental aspects (Steamboat Springs Symposium). Karger, Basel, p 210-231

Hendricks SB 1960 Rates of change of phytochrome as an essential factor determining photoperiodism in plants. Cold Spring Harbor Symp Quant Biol 25:245-248

Hendricks SB 1963 Metabolic control of timing. Science (Wash DC) 141:21-27

Hillman WS 1964 Endogenous circadian rhythms and the response of *Lemna perpusilla* to skeleton photoperiods. Am Nat 98:323-328

Mizoguchi A, Ishizaki H 1982 Prothoracic glands of the saturniid moth *Samia cynthia ricini* possess a circadian clock controlling gut purge timing. Proc Natl Acad Sci USA 79:2726-2730

Nanda KK, Hamner KC 1959 Photoperiodic cycles of different lengths in relation to flowering in *Biloxi* soybean. Planta (Berl) 53:45-52

Pittendrigh CS 1960 Circadian rhythms and circadian organization of living systems. Cold Spring Harbor Symp Quant Biol 25:159-182

Pittendrigh CS 1966 The circadian oscillation in *Drosophila pseudoobscura* pupae: a model for the photoperiodic clock. Z Pflanzenphysiol 54:275-307

Pittendrigh CS 1972 Circadian surfaces and the diversity of possible roles of circadian organization in photoperiodic induction. Proc Natl Acad Sci USA 69:2734-2737

Pittendrigh CS 1974 Circadian oscillations in cells and the circadian organization of multicellular systems. In: Schmitt FO, Worden FG (eds) The neurosciences: third study program. MIT Press, Cambridge, Mass, p 437-458

Pittendrigh CS 1981a Circadian organization and the photoperiodic phenomena. In: Follett BK, Follett DE (eds) Biological clocks in seasonal reproductive cycles. Wright, Bristol, p 1-35

Pittendrigh CS 1981b Circadian systems: entrainment. In: Aschoff J (ed) Handbook of behavioral neurobiology, vol 4: biological rhythms. Plenum, New York, p 95-124

Pittendrigh CS, Minis DH 1964 The entrainment of circadian oscillations by light and their role as photoperiod clocks. Am Nat 98:261-294

Pittendrigh CS, Minis DH 1971 The photoperiodic time-measurement in *Pectinophora gossypiella* and its relation to the circadian system in that species. In: Menaker M (ed) Biochronometry. National Academy of Sciences, Washington DC, p 212–250

Saunders DS 1976 Insect clocks, 1st edn. Pergamon Press, London

Takahashi J, Menaker M 1982 Entrainment of the circadian system of the house sparrow: a population of oscillators in pinealectomized birds. J Comp Physiol 146:245-253

Tamarkin L, Westrom WK, Hamill AI, Goldman BD 1976 Effect of melatonin on the reproductive systems of male and female hamsters: a diurnal rhythm in sensitivity to melatonin. Endocrinology 99:1534-1541

Tyshchenko VP 1966 Two-oscillatory model of the physiological mechanism of insect photoperiodic reaction. Zh Obshch Biol 33:21-31

Vaz Nunes M, Veerman A 1982 External coincidence and photoperiodic time measurement in the spider mite *Tetranychus urticae*. J Insect Physiol 28:143-154

DISCUSSION

Hodková: In many insects—for example, adults of *Pyrrhocoris apterus* (Hodek 1971), adults of *Psylla pyricola* (McMullen & Jong 1976), and mature larvae of *Molophilus ater* (Coulson et al 1976)—the photoperiodic response is lost with the completion of diapause development. Do you think that, for example, periods of oscillations may be changed during diapause development? Perhaps the photoperiodic entrainment of the post-diapause oscillations by any photoperiod results in the phase relationships, which do not allow diapause.

Pittendrigh: That is one of several possible explanations but I have no particular preference for it. Perhaps the pacemakers in the system become uncoupled from the light, as they do in *Sarcophaga* pupae.

Saunders: Yes; that is certainly one interpretation of the *Sarcophaga* data. David Denlinger and I might argue about when the sensitive period comes to an end; this seems to be different in different species. In *Sarcophaga argyrostoma* the sensitive period seems to go on into the wandering stage but the pupae are certainly not photoperiodic (Saunders 1979).

Hodková: So, after the completion of diapause development, the photoperiodic clock that mediates photoperiodic responses need not be entrained by light, although it is very probable that various circadian activities can still be entrained.

Pittendrigh: That is entirely possible.

Chippendale: You mentioned the importance of taking into account differences in temperature, and thermoperiod, especially in the resonance experiment on *Drosophila* species (Pittendrigh 1981, unpublished results). How important is it to study temperature cycles in the absence of photoperiodic cues? You mentioned data on the southwestern corn borer, which we study. Kikukawa (1983), as part of his doctoral study, has extended our work with thermoperiodic effects in the corn borer and has shown a thermoperiodic response curve for diapause induction in constant darkness; the response is suppressed in constant light. The critical thermoperiod is not sharply defined, but it is considerably longer than the critical photoperiod.

Pittendrigh: One would indeed expect that in constant light the pacemaker would be damped out; so one would obtain no response because one cannot entrain a non-existing oscillation. The difference between constant light and constant dark, therefore, does not trouble me. If the phase relationships among constituent oscillations in a circadian system are changed by a change in the photoperiod, they should also be changed by a change in thermoperiod; but the critical thermoperiod for obtaining those changes remains unpredictable, so it is not surprising that the critical thermoperiod is somewhat different from the critical photoperiod.

Reynolds: Are you saying that the population of rhythms entrained by thermoperiod is not necessarily the same as the population of rhythms entrained by photoperiod?

Pittendrigh: No; I am assuming, for the moment: (1) that only one pacemaking oscillation is involved; (2) that its wave-form is changed by change in photoperiod; (3) that a diversity of slave oscillations driven by the pacemaker respond differentially to change in pacemaker wave-form and, hence, are subject to changing mutual phase-relations as photoperiod lengthens or shortens; and (4) that change in thermoperiod also affects pacemaker wave-form and, hence, the mutual phase-relations among slaves. However, it is by no means necessary that the thermoperiod and photoperiod that effect induction, by establishing some critical set of slave phase-relationships, will have the same duration.

Sokolove: Even small temperature changes in a thermoperiodic experiment might affect the output from the photochemical receptor. One typically assumes that there is a receptor for photoperiod; one could equally well assume that there is a receptor for temperature, and easily construct an external coincidence model to explain the data from thermoperiodic experiments.

Saunders: In our original discussions about the use of thermoperiodism, 10 or 12 years ago, we were trying to use thermoperiod to mimic photoperiod in the sense that thermoperiod might be a tool for distinguishing internal from external coincidence (Saunders 1973). What about the opposite? Supposing you found a species in which you could not obtain a thermoperiodic response curve but for which thermoperiods given in conjunction with photoperiods would allow you to predict the shift of the light-sensitive phase from the dark to the light by phase-delaying or phase-advancing. Would that not be some evidence for external coincidence? I have found these results with *Sarcophaga* (D.S. Saunders, unpublished data, 1983).

Pittendrigh: It would depend on whether it was an external coincidence based on a pacemaker or on a slave, and in this case it sounds like you are dealing with a slave.

Saunders: But that doesn't rule out a photosensitive phase.

Pittendrigh: I agree.

Bowen: You have said that organisms appear to consist of a multiplicity of oscillators, and you warned about the danger of using the output of one rhythm to predict the behaviour of another. Yet this is what has been done for years in the study of photoperiodic induction.

Pittendrigh: I agree; and it is what Dorothy Minis and I (Pittendrigh & Minis 1964) initially advocated 20 years ago. We were, I think correct in doing so; the study of *some* circadian rhythm (concurrently with photoperiodic induction) is certainly better than studying none. The current practice has shortcomings as well as advantages; and we clearly do need new approaches.

Bowen: Could you therefore suggest some new approaches?

Pittendrigh: Different species may have different mechanisms. I see great advantages in concentrating on some single species that: (1) like *Samia*, is large enough to permit neuroendocrine analysis; (2) like *Samia*, has an easily assayed circadian system; (3) unlike *Samia*, has a wide range of latitudinal races with different critical day-lengths; and (4) like *Drosophila*, is readily amenable to change (by selection or chemical mutagenesis) in the genetic basis of the photoperiodic response.

Truman: I am not sure that geographical variation is essential in the analysis of endocrine mechanisms.

Pittendrigh: It is not essential but it is desirable. Ideally there would be some genetic variation in the system, and the easiest way to obtain that is to examine different geographical races.

Brady: But I understood you to say earlier (p 22) that the differences in critical photoperiod in the geographical races of Danilevskii were an effect of differences in amplitude of the circadian rhythm, and not an effect of critical photoperiod *per se*?

Pittendrigh: Yes, but I still want to analyse them.

Saunders: But surely there are now clear data on the geographical effects on critical day-length (Bradshaw 1976; Eertmoed 1978)?

Pittendrigh: Danilevskii (1965) gave examples of cases where temperature or latitude changed the photoperiodic response curves to the left or right, without a change in their amplitudes, but he also described some examples of change in amplitude, and those are the difficult ones to explain.

Gilbert: You implied that neuroendocrinological studies on *Drosophila* are likely to be difficult, but they can nevertheless be done if sufficient care is exercised. It is vital to attempt such work if it would help to merge the two disciplines of clocks and hormones.

Mordue: Some of this work has been done with mutants. By using temperature shocks in *Drosophila* one can mimic many developmental phenomena. For example, Rauschenbach et al (1983a,b) elicited the production of juvenile hormone esterase by the use of temperature shocks.

Gilbert: Yes. The proteins produced after heat-shock treatment of

Drosophila seem to be identical to the ecdysteroid-induced proteins in *Drosophila* (Ireland et al 1982).

Pittendrigh: Professor Ishizaki's group (this volume), in studying the neuroendocrinology of the gut-purge rhythm in *Samia*, have demonstrated a remarkably strong circadian control of the timing of release of both prothoracicotropic hormone (PTTH) and ecdysone. The temporal relationships between the PTTH and the ecdysone are fascinating, and their work is a beautiful example of the way in which knowledge of circadian physiology can be usefully employed in endocrinological analyses.

Gilbert: What would you say is the major question in your field at this moment?

Pittendrigh: The time-measurement, as such, has always been the focus of my interests in this field. When I began, in 1952, my working hypothesis was that what we now call circadian rhythms reflected the existence of clock-like oscillations in cells. That hypothesis, prompted by the then recent discovery of time-compensated sun-orientation in animals, was, however, at variance with several published claims that the period of circadian rhythms was, like other cellular processes, temperature-dependent. When we reinvestigated the issue we found that the circadian oscillation had a (clock-like) temperature-compensated period. That feature of circadian oscillations is now known to be universal and remains a focus of my interest.

Equally challenging is the problem of the time constants involved. How can any contemporary molecular model cope with the time constants involved in an oscillator whose period is 24h—or, for that matter, 350 days? One recent discovery in this field may well become seminal in pursuing photoperiodic time-measurements. Kyriacou and Hall (1980), using Konopka's (Konopka & Benzer 1971) clock mutants in *Drosophila melanogaster*, have studied the love-song of male fruit flies. It consists of a high-frequency (ms range) wing vibration that is frequency-modulated by a second oscillator whose period is ~50s. In the mutant whose circadian period is down (from 24h) to 19h the period of the song-modulating oscillation is also reduced (to ~35s), and in the mutant with a circadian period of 29h it is increased to ~65s. Moreover, the period (in seconds) of the song-modulating oscillation is temperature-compensated like circadian oscillations. This is exciting: one and the same gene product is affecting time-constants in both the second and the daily range.

Reynolds: Do you think that finding a gene product that affects the periodicity of the clock would necessarily help you to find out the nature of the clock? Surely this is as non-specific a clue as the ablation of certain parts of the brain?

Pittendrigh: I agree. Nevertheless the 'new genetics' could well *help* to solve the problem. For example, if we had monoclonal antibodies to the clock-locus (*per*) in *D. melanogaster* we could make great strides in localizing the pacemaker.

Roberts: In insects that undergo metamorphosis, the operational cells in the pupal brain may not be the same as those in the larval brain. The adult brain's operational cells may be different again. Interpretation of, say, results on larval behaviour may not relate directly to those on pupal diapause or on adult behaviour, so caution should be observed.

Truman: But one should qualify that statement. Work on *Manduca sexta* and *Drosophila* has shown that many neurons are conserved during metamorphosis (Truman et al 1983, Technau & Heisenberg 1982). The same cells just change their function as they go from larva, to pupa, to adult. It is true that a large number of cells is added to the brain, especially to the optic and the olfactory lobes. But in higher insects the optic lobes are not involved in photoperiodic or circadian time-keeping. These functions occur in more internal regions of the brain, where there is a lot of cell conservatism, and not a complete cellular replacement from the larval to the adult stage.

Brady: There is also evidence of clocks in insects doing different things in pupae and in adults, and of their doing so with different periods; for example in mosquitoes (Jones & Reiter 1975).

Truman: In *Manduca* we now have evidence (Truman, this volume) for two distinct clocks, in two separate regions of the animal, controlling essentially the same rhythm.

Brady: Professor Pittendrigh mentioned in his paper some results on continuous injection of melatonin in free-running hamsters. I understood that the duration of the melatonin injection directly affected the photoperiodic response, or did it directly affect the development of the gonads? Are you implying that the melatonin is equivalent to the clock itself, rather than to its output?

Pittendrigh: No. Incidentally, I am not sure these results have yet been published in full, but they are at least outlined in Goldman et al (1982). Goldman finds—quite contrary to earlier indications he had published—that what is important in the photoperiodic control of gonad size in hamsters is the absolute duration (in hours) of melatonin levels above some critical threshold. He can control this by the injection of exogenous melatonin. His crucial observation is that a given duration of melatonin injection is effective *irrespective of the phase of the circadian system* through which the melatonin-'pulse' lasts. Clearly the circadian system itself is, therefore, not responsible for measuring the duration of the melatonin signal; some other 'clock' does that. The circadian system is, however, involved in the overall system in nature: its function is to transduce the duration of darkness (reciprocal of photoperiod) into the duration of increased melatonin.

Truman: So are you saying that there is another step between the melatonin detection and the development of the gonads?

Pittendrigh: The circadian system is a step between the light and the clock, and is not itself the clock.

Truman: Is the melatonin acting directly on the gonads?

Pittendrigh: No, unless the clock is in the gonads, which I doubt.

Mordue: The melatonin could be working indirectly through the median eminence and anterior pituitary.

Pittendrigh: The crucial observation is that a particular ($\sim$12h) duration of melatonin injection is photoperiodically effective irrespective of the phase of the circadian system.

Brady: In rats, if melatonin is measured in light:dark cycles it is exactly driven by the light, with virtually a square-wave formation (Klein 1974).

Pittendrigh: Yes; and that is compatible with my proposition that the role of the circadian system is to transduce the duration of light into the duration of the presence of melatonin. It is this duration that the clock 'sees', and the clock is apparently not circadian.

Hardie: I have some results that may be of interest to people studying clock mechanisms. Perhaps the most intensely investigated clock of the hour-glass type is the one that Tony Lees has been working on for many years, in the aphid species *Megoura viciae* (Lees 1973). In the life-cycle of a different aphid species, the black-bean aphid, *Aphis fabae*, there is an interesting winged morph, which is a migrant form (see Hardie, this volume). This aphid uses both a winter host and a summer host plant, so in the autumn it has to migrate from the summer host to the winter host. The winged form is determined by photoperiod: short days induce its appearance. The final, adult form of this individual is not fully determined until about four days after birth. If it is transferred to long days during this malleable period, then the adult will develop as a wingless or apterous form or as an intermediate form between winged and apterous (see Hardie, this volume). I did resonance experiments on this photoperiodic response and plotted the percentage of insects that were apterized against the length of scotophase into which they were transferred immediately after birth; photophase was 12h in duration. At 15°C, I obtained a classical hour-glass response curve; but at 20°C the curve showed a definite circadian component. So not all aphids show strictly hour-glass types of response to resonance experiments.

REFERENCES

Bradshaw WE 1976 Geography of photoperiodic response in a diapausing mosquito. Nature (Lond) 262:384-386

Coulson JC, Horobin JC, Butterfield J, Smith GRJ 1976 The maintenance of annual life-cycles in two species of Tipulidae (Diptera); a field study relating development, temperature and altitude. J Anim Ecol 45:215-233

Danilevskii AS 1965 Photoperiodism and seasonal development in insects. Oliver & Boyd, Edinburgh

Eertmoed GE 1978 Embryonic diapause in the psocid, *Peripsocus quadri-fasciatus*: photoperiod, temperature, ontogeny and geographical variation. Physiol Entomol 3:197-206

Goldman BD, Carter DS, Hall UD, Roychoudhury P, Yellon SM 1982 Physiology of pineal melatonin in three hamster species. In: Klein DC (ed) Melatonin rhythm generating system: developmental aspects. (Steamboat Springs Symposium) Karger, Basel, p 210-231

Hodek I 1971 Termination of adult diapause in *Pyrrhocoris apterus* (Heteroptera: Pyrrhocoridae) in the field. Entomol Exp Appl 14:212-222

Ireland RC, Berger EM, Sirotkin K, Yund MA, Osterbur D, Fristrom J 1982 Ecdysterone induces the transcription of four heat shock genes in *Drosophila* S3 cells and imaginal discs. Dev Biol 93:498-507

Jones MDR, Reiter P 1975 Entrainment of pupation and adult activity rhythms during development in the mosquito *Anopheles gambiae*. Nature (Lond) 254:242-244

Kikukawa S 1983 Geographical adaptations and seasonal time measurement of the southwestern corn borer, *Diatraea grandiosella*. PhD thesis, University of Missouri

Klein DC 1974 Circadian rhythms in indole metabolism in the rat pineal gland. In: Schmitt FO, Worden FG (eds) Neurosciences: a third study program. MIT Press, Cambridge, Massachusetts, p 509-515

Konopka R, Benzer S 1971 Clock mutants of *Drosophila melanogaster*. Proc Natl Acad Sci USA 68:2112-2116

Kyriacou CP, Hall JC 1980 Circadian rhythm mutations in *Drosophila melanogaster* affect short-term fluctuations in the male's courtship song. Proc Natl Acad Sci USA 77:6729-6733

Lees AD 1973 Photoperiodic time measurement in the aphid *Megoura viciae*. J Insect Physiol 19:2279-2316

McMullen RD, Jong C 1976 Factors affecting induction and termination of diapause in pear psylla (Homoptera: Psyllidae). Can Entomol 108:1001-1005

Pittendrigh CS 1981 Circadian organization and the photoperiodic phenomena. In: Follett BK, Follett DE (eds) Biological clocks in seasonal reproductive cycles. Wright, Bristol, p 1-35

Pittendrigh CS, Minis DH 1964 The entrainment of circadian oscillations by light and their role as photoperiodic clocks. Am Nat 98:261-294

Rauschenbach IY, Lukashina NS, Korochkin LI 1983a The genetics of esterases in *Drosophila*. VII: The genetic control of the activity level of the JH-esterase and heat-resistance in *Drosophila virilis* under high temperature. Biochem Genet 21:253-265

Rauschenbach IY, Lukashina NS, Korochkin LI 1983b The genetics of esterases in *Drosophila*. VIII: The gene regulating the activity of JH-esterase in *Drosophila virilis*. Biochem Genet, in press

Saunders DS 1973 Thermoperiodic control of diapause in an insect: theory of internal coincidence. Science (Wash DC) 181:358-360

Saunders DS 1979 The circadian eclosion rhythm in *Sarcophaga argyrostoma*: delineation of the responsive period for entrainment. Physiol Entomol 4:263-274

Technau G, Heisenberg M 1982 Neural reorganization during metamorphosis of the corpora pedunculata in *Drosophila melanogaster*. Nature (Lond) 295:405-407

Truman JW, Levine RB, Weeks JC 1983 Reorganization of the nervous system during metamorphosis of the moth *Manduca sexta*. In: Balls M, Bownes M (eds) Metamorphosis. Cambridge University Press, Cambridge (Br Soc Dev Biol Symp 8), in press

Photoperiod reception in spider mites: photoreceptor, clock and counter

A. VEERMAN and M. VAZ NUNES

Laboratory of Experimental Entomology, University of Amsterdam, Kruislaan 302, 1098 SM Amsterdam, The Netherlands

Abstract. Photoperiodic induction of diapause in the spider mite *Tetranychus urticae* (class Arachnida) is a two-step process, comprising photoperiodic time-measurement and the summation of a number of successive photoperiodic cycles. A theoretical model has been developed, consisting of separate 'clock' and 'counter' mechanisms, which accurately describes the photoperiodic responses obtained with *T. urticae* in highly diverse light:dark regimes, based on diel as well as non-diel photoperiods, both with and without light interruptions of the dark. This so-called 'hour-glass timer–oscillator counter' model also accounts for the influence of the circadian system on the photoperiodic reaction: the model is based on the assumption that the circadian system is not involved in photoperiodic time-measurement but exerts an inhibitory effect on induction in certain regimes, in which the circadian system is not 'at resonance' with the external light:dark cycle. The photoreceptor for the photoperiodic reaction is thought to be a rhodopsin-like pigment; this is suggested by mutant studies and nutritional studies with spider mites and predatory mites, which show that carotenoids or vitamin A are essential for photoperiodic induction of diapause in these mites.

1984 Photoperiodic regulation of insect and molluscan hormones. Pitman, London (Ciba Foundation symposium 104), p 48–64

Despite extensive research over past decades, the regulation of photoperiodic responses in insects and mites is still poorly understood at a physiological level. Progress has been made in the study of the effector part—the humoral mechanisms involved in the regulation of diapause in various insects—but the way in which photoperiod controls neuroendocrine centres in the brain is still largely unknown. Attention has been directed mainly at photoperiodic time-measurement, but it is now generally recognized that photoperiodic induction is a two-step process, comprising both time-measurement and the summation of the photoperiodic information contained in a number of successive photoperiodic cycles (for reviews, see Beck 1980, Saunders 1981, 1982). The responses measured are the integrated result of both processes—the first being the qualitative distinction between long and short nights, and the second being the quantitative summation of a number of inductive events. As stated by Saunders (1981), the nature of this stored information and its translation into endocrine events is one of the central problems in insect photoperiodism.

In this paper, photoperiodic induction of diapause in the two-spotted spider mite, *Tetranychus urticae* (an arachnid of the order Acari), is explained on the basis of a theoretical model consisting of both a 'clock' and a 'counter' mechanism; tests of the validity of the model are shown for some highly diverse photoperiodic regimes.

The hour-glass timer–oscillator counter model

Because of their smallness, mites are not very suitable objects for the study of the effector part of the photoperiodic mechanism, but work with spider mites and predatory mites has provided information on the receptor part, including the photoreceptor, the clock and the counter. Working with spider mites offers several advantages: they are small and therefore easy to keep and rear in large numbers; the diapause state (only the females may undergo a facultative reproductive diapause, induced by short-day photoperiods during the immature stages) is immediately recognizable by the orange colour of the diapausing mites; and they show very sharp responses to various photoperiodic regimes (Veerman 1977a,b). In the course of our work we have also found a marked influence of the circadian system on the photoperiodic reaction in these mites (Veerman & Vaz Nunes 1980).

At first we tried to explain photoperiodic induction of diapause in spider mites on the basis of models that have been developed for the photoperiodic clock in some insect species (Vaz Nunes & Veerman 1979a,b, 1982a). However, when it proved impossible to explain certain experiments with spider mites in terms of these models, in which time-measurement is assumed to be a function of one or two circadian oscillations, we chose to develop another model, based on a different assumption about the role of the circadian system in photoperiodic induction. We elaborated the suggestion made by Pittendrigh (1972) that, irrespective of the actual mechanism used for night-length measurement, the success with which time-measurement is effected may depend on the proximity of the circadian system to 'resonance' with the entraining light:dark cycle. In other words, apart from its possible role in photoperiodic time-measurement, the circadian system may also exert an influence on other parts of the complex mechanism leading from photoperiod perception to the expression of a photoperiodic response. Depending on how the circadian system is attuned to the external light:dark cycle, it may or may not interfere with the further processing of the clock's output, the accumulation of the daily bits of photoperiodic 'information'. These considerations led us to propose what we have called the 'hour-glass timer–oscillator counter' model (Vaz Nunes & Veerman 1982b), a theoretical model devised to test: (1) whether photoperiodic induction in *T. urticae* can be explained as the combined result of 'hour-glass' time-measurement and the accumulation, by a simple counter mechanism, of the output of this hour-glass clock; and (2) whether the influence of the circadian system on photoperiodic induction may be understood as a 'resonance' effect, expressed as an inhibition of the summation process that is performed by the photoperiodic counter. Experimental data providing the basis for the model as well as details of its operation are discussed later in this paper.

The photoreceptor

For perceiving photoperiod, insects and mites presumably possess some kind of photoreceptor, which is thought to form an integral part of the photoperiodic clock (e.g. Lees 1981). The location of the photoreceptor and the nature of its pigment(s) have received particular attention (Beck 1980, Saunders 1982), and the two mite species we have chosen to study have provided information about the pigment(s).

By studying the induction of diapause in several pigment-mutants of *T. urticae*, which show various defects in their carotenoid metabolism (Veerman 1974), we obtained the first indications that β-carotene might be necessary for photoperiodic induction (Veerman & Helle 1978). Diapause incidence in albino mutants was significantly lower than in the wild-type, when the mites were reared under diapause-promoting short days. Various crosses between albino and wild-type showed that a high incidence of diapause in albino mites was realized only when the albino daughters came from hybrid, phenotypically wild-type mothers. Apparently, a maternal effect was responsible for complete induction. We explained these results by assuming that small amounts of carotenoids, deposited by the hybrid females in their eggs, are sufficient to allow photoperiodic induction to proceed normally in their albino offspring, which are not able to obtain β-carotene from their food themselves (Veerman 1980).

More direct evidence of the involvement of carotenoids in the photoperiodic reaction was obtained in feeding experiments with the predatory mite *Amblyseius potentillae*. Diapause induction in response to short days was normal in mites fed on the eggs of fully pigmented wild-type *T. urticae*; no response to photoperiod was found in mites fed on the eggs of carotenoid-deficient albino spider mites. The response to photoperiod in the latter could be restored, however, by adding an oily solution of β-carotene to the egg diet (Van Zon et al 1981).

Recently we found that the pollen of broad bean (*Vicia faba*) also constitutes a carotenoid-free diet for *A. potentillae*. The predatory mites develop and reproduce normally on the pollen diet, but they no longer respond to short photoperiods. Supplementation of the pollen diet with various pure pigments showed that only vitamin A and carotenoids with pro-vitamin A function are capable of restoring the photoperiodic response in predatory mites that have been deprived of carotenoids for one generation or more (Veerman et al 1983). Apparently, vitamin A is essential for the photoperiodic reaction in these mites, and it may well function as the photoreceptor pigment in the form of a rhodopsin-like protein complex. Since *A. potentillae* is an eyeless mite, it follows also that photoperiodic photoreception occurs extraretinally, possibly by direct photostimulation of neurons in the central nervous system. The action spectrum, determined by Lees (1953) for photoperiodic induction of diapause in the fruit-tree red spider mite, *Panonychus ulmi*, could also imply that, in at least some mite species, a rhodopsin-like pigment functions as the photoreceptor for the photoperiodic clock.

The clock

There are several reasons why we chose to test the hypothesis that photoperiodic time-measurement in *T. urticae* may be described according to hour-glass kinetics, one reason being that the results of a number of experiments with spider mites could not be reconciled with any of the more explicit circadian clock models. More importantly, however, for a proper test of the assumption that the influence of the circadian system on photoperiodic induction is restricted to a 'resonance' effect, is that time-measurement itself should not be assumed to be a function of the circadian system. For a theoretical analysis, both possible functions of the circadian system—time-measurement and a more general physiological effect on the photoperiodic counter—should be treated separately. Still another reason is that, to discriminate between the hypotheses that photoperiodic clocks are either oscillators or hour-glasses, well defined—and thus testable—models of either type are a prerequisite. Several oscillator-based models have been described (Beck 1980, Pittendrigh 1981, Saunders 1982); to make comparisons possible we thought it necessary to develop an hour-glass timer, the formal properties of which are expressed in mathematical terms. We based our hour-glass clock on the non-mathematical hour-glass model developed by Lees (1973, 1981) for the aphid *Megoura viciae*, in which hour-glass time-measurement has been firmly established.

Since it is likely that time-measurement is the outcome of a complex of light and dark reactions, the kinetics of the hour-glass clock were designed to consist of light increase and decrease as well as dark increase and decrease reactions; time-measurement is thought to be accomplished when a certain stage in the reaction sequence is reached, a short-night or long-night measurement being dependent on whether this stage, called H^*, falls in the light (H_L^*) or dark (H_D^*) respectively (Fig. 1).

We are aware that these reactions as well as their kinetics are completely

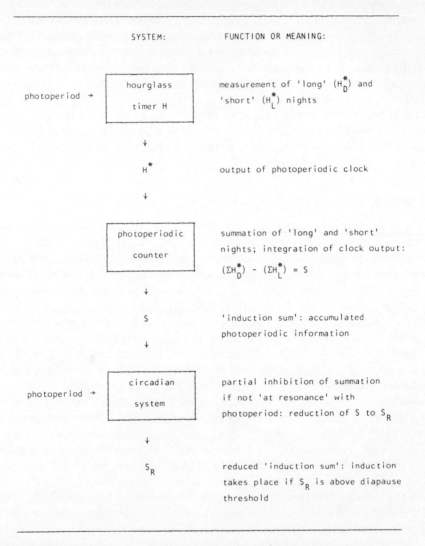

FIG. 1. Schematic representation of the operation of the 'hour-glass timer–oscillator counter' model for photoperiodic induction of diapause in the spider mite *Tetranychus urticae*.

theoretical; to obtain a testable hypothesis, however, this approach seems to us the best available. The complexity of the kinetics of the hour-glass model may well reflect the complexity of the as yet unknown mechanism of photoperiodic time-measurement in these mites; on the other hand, it would be a misconception to expect the hour-glass to be more than a formal clock mechanism, describing how any sequence of light and darkness may lead to the measurement of either a 'short' night or a 'long' night.

A detailed description of the operation of the hour-glass timer has been given elsewhere (Vaz Nunes & Veerman 1982b); some examples of its application to various photoperiodic regimes, in combined operation with the photoperiodic counter, are given below.

The counter

The presence of some kind of photoperiodic counter mechanism in *T. urticae* is inferred from experimental data, which show that the percentage incidence of diapause in the population increases with an increasing number of long nights experienced by the developmental stages that are sensitive to the photoperiod (Veerman 1977a). Other experiments, in which various sequences of short-day (long-night) cycles were followed by long-day (short-night) cycles or by continuous darkness, demonstrated that long-day photoperiods exert an effect on induction as well, of about equal strength as that of short-day photoperiods, but working in the opposite direction: the inductive effect of a sequence of short-day cycles can be diminished or cancelled completely by a following sequence of long-day cycles (Veerman 1977a).

From these experiments we may conclude that the most simple model conceivable for a photoperiodic counter mechanism—that is, one that adds up only long nights—is not valid for *T. urticae*: apparently both long nights and short nights are accumulated, albeit with opposite effects of about equal strengths. Therefore the operation of the photoperiodic counter in *T. urticae* is expressed as:

$$(\Sigma H_D^*) - (\Sigma H_L^*) = S,$$

S being the 'induction sum', the sum of photoperiodic information accumulated during the sensitive period of the mites (Fig. 1). If at the end of the inductive period S surpasses a certain minimum value, the 'diapause threshold', diapause is expected to occur.

As explained above, the model was meant to test the hypothesis that the circadian influence on photoperiodic induction might consist solely of an inhibitory effect on the summation and integration of the output of the photoperiodic clock, exerted in regimes in which the circadian system is not 'at resonance' with the external light:dark cycle. However, the effect of light:dark regimes on the complete multioscillator circadian system is not readily analysable. Therefore, to quantify the 'resonance' effect, we looked at the behaviour of a single, well defined circadian oscillation, whose phase-resetting can be calculated for the most widely divergent photoperiodic regimes (Vaz Nunes 1981, Vaz Nunes & Veerman 1982a). We assumed that inhibition of the summation reaction might be expected when certain circadian phases of the oscillation are illuminated, which for a proper course of the summation reaction should occur in darkness. These 'wrong phases' of the oscillation were found to comprise the complete 'subjective night'; trials of a predictive model, based on the idea that inhibition of the summation reaction depends on the phase-relationship between the oscillation and the driving light cycle, showed that the degree of inhibition is a function of the circadian phases of the subjective night that are illuminated (Vaz Nunes & Veerman 1982b).

A schematic representation of the operation of the complete 'hour-glass timer–oscillator counter' model is shown in Fig. 1. It should be realized, however, that the scheme gives a step-wise account of the sequence of calculations only; in the animal the operation of the clock, the counter and the circadian influence on the counter are not sequential processes, but all elements operate in each cycle. In other words, the reduction of S to S_R (Fig. 1) is supposed to take place step by step in each photoperiodic cycle during the whole sensitive period, and not all at once at the end of the induction process, as the scheme might suggest. In those regimes where the phase-relationship between the circadian oscillation and the external light:dark cycle is 'correct' (when the oscillation and the external regime are 'at resonance') the induction sum is not reduced, and $S = S_R$.

Results and discussion

The probability that the 'hour-glass timer–oscillator counter' model gives a correct description of the kinetics of the photoperiodic mechanism becomes greater the more experiments can be accurately described by the model. Therefore it is necessary to test the validity of the model in as many different photoperiodic regimes as possible. Model-predicted and experimentally observed incidences of diapause are shown here for four regimes which have been widely used for the analysis of photoperiodic time-measurement:

(a) symmetrical 'skeleton' photoperiods, consisting of two one-hour pulses of light in each 24-h cycle (Fig. 2);

(b) asymmetrical 'skeleton' photoperiods (night-interruption experiments with a one-hour light pulse 'scanning' through the night) (Fig. 3);

(c) a 'resonance' experiment with a constant photophase of 2 h and a variable scotophase (Fig. 4);

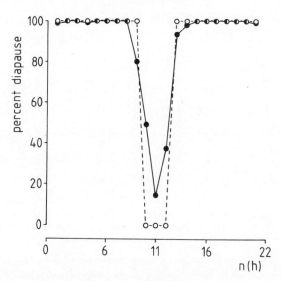

FIG. 2. Effect of symmetrical 'skeleton' photoperiods [regimes with two one-hour pulses of light per cycle, which can be expressed in the general form of LD (*light*:dark) $1:n:1:(22-n)$] on diapause induction in *T. urticae* (closed circles). Open circles: diapause incidences predicted by the 'hour-glass timer–oscillator counter' model. Abscissa (*n* hours) indicates the time between the two pulses of light in a 24 h cycle.

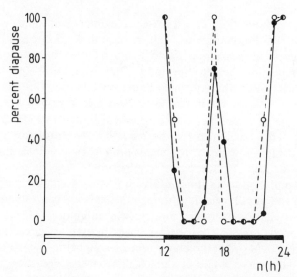

FIG. 3. Effect of one-hour night-interruptions in LD $12:12$ (asymmetrical 'skeleton' photo-periods) on diapause induction in *T. urticae* (closed circles). Open circles: diapause incidences predicted by the 'hour-glass timer–oscillator counter' model. Abscissa (*n* hours) indicates the time from the start of the main photophase in a 24h cycle.

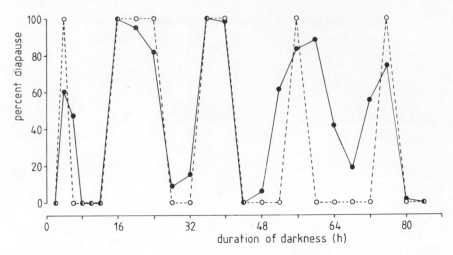

FIG. 4. Diapause induction in *T. urticae* in a 'resonance' experiment with a constant photophase of 2 h and a variable scotophase (closed circles). Open circles: diapause incidences predicted by the 'hour-glass timer–oscillator counter' model. (From Vaz Nunes & Veerman 1982b.)

and (d) a night-interruption experiment in which a one-hour light pulse is used to probe for light sensitivity in a very long night, in this case, 52 h (Fig. 5).

The figures show that in all cases (regimes with and without light interruptions, based on diel as well as non-diel photoperiods) the fit is remarkably good; in fact, it appears to be much better than that obtained with any other model for the photoperiodic clock (see Vaz Nunes & Veerman 1979a, 1982a). Also, the 'normal' photoperiodic response curve can be described accurately by the model (Vaz Nunes & Veerman 1982b).

The outcome of experiments like those presented in Figs. 2–5 has often been interpreted as evidence for the circadian nature of the photoperiodic clock. Our results show that this conclusion may be premature: the outcome of the various types of photoperiodic experiments can be explained just as well by a combination of hour-glass time-measurement and a circadian influence on the photoperiodic counter mechanism. According to the 'hour-glass timer–oscillator counter' model, the inhibition of the summation reaction depends on the phase-relationship between a circadian oscillation and the driving light cycle, the phase-relationship being 'incorrect' when light falls in the subjective night of the oscillation. As greatly varying phase-relationships ('correct' as well as 'incorrect') may occur even in cycles based on the same period length (e.g. in night-interruption experiments), it follows that 'resonance' does not depend solely on the period-length of the driving cycle. In this respect our conception of 'resonance' differs from the original

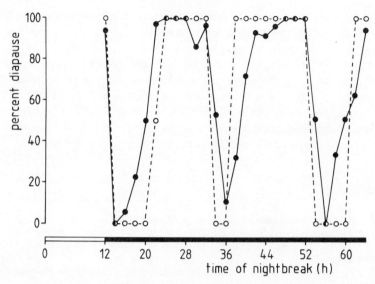

FIG. 5. Night-interruption experiment with *T. urticae* showing the effect of a one-hour pulse of light scanning a very long night of 52 h duration (closed circles). Open circles: diapause incidences predicted by the 'hour-glass timer–oscillator counter' model. (From Vaz Nunes & Veerman 1982b.)

view, according to which the circadian system is 'at resonance' with the driving light cycle if the period T of the external cycle is close to the free-running period τ (or modulo τ) of the endogenous oscillation(s) (Pittendrigh 1972).

In Figs. 2–5 predictions are shown for 0, 50 and 100% diapause. We would like to stress here that in principle the model predictions are of an all-or-none character, depending on whether the value of S_R in a given regime is above the diapause threshold or not. However, diapause determinations are based not on single mites but on a population sample, and it is well known that diapause thresholds may show greater or less variation within a species or population (e.g. Saunders 1981). Therefore we have introduced an upper and lower value for the diapause threshold in *T. urticae* and have interpreted any value of S_R found to lie between these thresholds as a prediction for an incidence of 50% diapause (Vaz Nunes & Veerman 1982b).

According to the 'hour-glass timer–oscillator counter' model, photoperiodic induction in *T. urticae* may be understood as the combined effect of hour-glass time-measurement, accumulation of photoperiodic information and the influence of the circadian system on the summation process. As shown above, this interpretation is supported by the results obtained in experiments with spider mites based on the most widely varying photoperiodic regimes. An important question is the extent to which similarities in photoperiodic responses of different species of arthropods are the result of convergent evolution, or whether various elements of the induction mechanism, like the photoreceptor, the clock and the counter, have a common physiological basis. In this respect it is of interest that the spider mite model also proves to be applicable to some insect species (Vaz Nunes 1983). As long as a direct approach to the study of photoperiodic induction in insects and mites is not feasible, model studies seem to be the obvious means for a comparative analysis of the mechanism of photoperiodic induction.

REFERENCES

Beck SD 1980 Insect photoperiodism, 2nd edn. Academic Press, New York

Lees AD 1953 Environmental factors controlling the evocation and termination of diapause in the fruit tree red spider mite *Metatetranychus ulmi* Koch (Acarina: Tetranychidae). Ann Appl Biol 40:449-486

Lees AD 1973 Photoperiodic time measurement in the aphid *Megoura viciae*. J Insect Physiol 19:2279-2316

Lees AD 1981 Action spectra for the photoperiodic control of polymorphism in the aphid *Megoura viciae*. J Insect Physiol 27:761-771

Pittendrigh CS 1972 Circadian surfaces and the diversity of circadian organization in photoperiodic induction. Proc Natl Acad Sci USA 69:2734-2737

Pittendrigh CS 1981 Circadian organization and the photoperiodic phenomena. In: Follett BK, Follett DE (eds) Biological clocks in seasonal reproductive cycles. Wright, Bristol, p 1-35

Saunders DS 1981 Insect photoperiodism—the clock and the counter: a review. Physiol Entomol 6:99-116

Saunders DS 1982 Insect clocks, 2nd edn. Pergamon Press, Oxford

Van Zon AQ, Overmeer WPJ, Veerman A 1981 Carotenoids function in photoperiodic induction of diapause in a predacious mite. Science (Wash DC) 213:1131-1133

Vaz Nunes M 1981 A 'simple clock' approach of circadian rhythms: an easy way to predict the clock's singularity. J Theor Biol 92:227-239

Vaz Nunes M 1983 Photoperiodic time measurement in the spider mite *Tetranychus urticae* Koch. PhD thesis, University of Amsterdam

Vaz Nunes M, Veerman A 1979a Photoperiodic time measurement in spider mites. I: Development of a two interval timers model. J Comp Physiol 134:203-217

Vaz Nunes M, Veerman A 1979b Photoperiodic time measurement in spider mites. II: Effects of skeleton photoperiods. J Comp Physiol 134:219-226

Vaz Nunes M, Veerman A 1982a External coincidence and photoperiodic time measurement in the spider mite *Tetranychus urticae*. J Insect Physiol 28:143-154

Vaz Nunes M, Veerman A 1982b Photoperiodic time measurement in the spider mite *Tetranychus urticae*: a novel concept. J Insect Physiol 28:1041-1053

Veerman A 1974 Carotenoid metabolism in *Tetranychus urticae* Koch (Acari: Tetranychidae). Comp Biochem Physiol 47B:101-116

Veerman A 1977a Aspects of the induction of diapause in a laboratory strain of the mite *Tetranychus urticae*. J Insect Physiol 23:703-711

Veerman A 1977b Photoperiodic termination of diapause in spider mites. Nature (Lond) 266:526-527

Veerman A 1980 Functional involvement of carotenoids in photoperiodic induction of diapause in the spider mite, *Tetranychus urticae*. Physiol Entomol 5:291-300

Veerman A, Helle W 1978 Evidence for the functional involvement of carotenoids in the photoperiodic reaction of spider mites. Nature (Lond) 275:234

Veerman A, Vaz Nunes M 1980 Circadian rhythmicity participates in the photoperiodic determination of diapause in spider mites. Nature (Lond) 287:140-141

Veerman A, Overmeer WPJ, Van Zon AQ, De Boer JM, De Waard ER, Huisman HO 1983 Vitamin A is essential for photoperiodic induction of diapause in an eyeless mite. Nature (Lond) 302:248-249

DISCUSSION

Sokolove: Could you explain in greater detail about how the resonance effect of the circadian system works?

Veerman: We have tried to keep the model as simple as possible, and we just look at the phase resetting behaviour of one circadian oscillator. Then, for each regime, we determine whether the subjective night is illuminated or not. If it is not illuminated, there is no inhibition, but if some light falls in the subjective night, inhibition is to be expected, the strength of this inhibition being dependent on the circadian phases of the subjective night that are illuminated.

Pittendrigh: In that sense one is almost considering two clocks. The resonance affects the time measurement because the critical issue is whether the light is falling in the subjective night or not. That is a coincidence clock.

Veerman: No; not necessarily. The way we express it, the circadian system reduces the expression of the response by an effect on the counter mechanism. For instance, even in regimes where, as a result of the resonance effect, a maximal reduction of the induction sum is to be expected, we still get full diapause if the reduced induction sum remains above a certain threshold, and this depends on the number of cycles counted by the mites during their sensitive stages. So the circadian system modulates the expression of the response but does not itself function as the clock.

Steel: Do you have any evidence for a direct link between the carotenoids and the photoreceptor? I presume there can be a number of interpretations of how carotenoid deficiency affects diapause induction, without supposing that the carotenoids comprise the photoreceptor?

Veerman: All the evidence we have up to now for spider mites is genetic evidence from work with the albino mutants (Veerman 1980). We have other indirect evidence from feeding experiments with predator mites (Van Zon et al 1981, Veerman et al 1983) and with the parasitoid wasp *Apanteles glomeratus* (unpublished work). With the wasp it is its host, the caterpillar, that takes up the vitamin A from the diet, after which the wasp larva obtains its supply of vitamin A probably from the haemolymph of the host. We do not yet have any more direct evidence for the link between vitamin A and the photoreceptor.

Chippendale: Since you found that photoperiodic sensitivity was restored after you fed carotenoids to the depleted mite and wasp, it might be possible to follow their tissue distribution, perhaps by using labelled carotenoids.

Mordue: The timing of this replacement therapy may be relevant here. Do they have to feed for days, hours or weeks?

Veerman: We have not followed the distribution of the carotenoids, but it should be possible to do so using labelled carotenoids or labelled vitamin A. As regards the timing of the replacement, the predacious mites have to be reared for at least one generation on a carotenoid-deficient diet before the response to the photoperiod disappears. In the next generation we start to feed them on a diet supplemented with vitamin A or β-carotene. In that generation we then measure the photoperiodic response. The wasps show a complete loss of the ability to diapause in response to carotenoid deprivation, even in the first generation; feeding the second generation on a vitamin A-supplemented diet restores the photoperiodic reaction. So in both cases feeding takes several days.

Reynolds: Do you have an action spectrum for the photoperiodic response in *Tetranychus*?

Veerman: No, not yet.

Truman: Work on photoperiodism always faces the problem of establishing the site of the photoreceptor. Lesion experiments provide a gross estimate of its location, but the precise cellular site of the photoreceptor is still unknown. The use of radiolabelled carotenoids may help here. In animals that have been depleted of their carotenoids, a small supplement might selectively reach the very cells involved in the photoperiodic response.

Veerman: There are indications that in spider mites carotenoids are indeed channelled preferentially to the photoperiodic photoreceptors instead of being used for body pigmentation. We found a maternal effect in crossing experiments between albino and wild-type spider mites, from which we concluded that small amounts of carotenoids in the eggs are already sufficient to allow a normal photoperiodic reaction in the fully grown spider mites. It could be worthwhile to follow this up in dietary studies using radiolabelled carotenoids.

Mordue: But that was a very small amount of carotenoid relative to the size of the adult.

Veerman: Well, as you saw for the predacious mites, we mix the pigments with the diet, and how much they take up is difficult to determine.

Brady: What happens in *Pectinophora*? Is it correct that eggs are entrained before there is any detectable photoreceptive pigment?

Pittendrigh: No; it is the other way around; we had a photoperiodic effect in *Pectinophora* (Pittendrigh & Minis 1971) with monochromatic red light that would not entrain any of the rhythms that we looked at. Frank & Zimmerman (1969) obtained some results on virtually carotenoid-free *Drosophila* and they found no effect on the pacemaker's response (phase-shift) to light signals.

Truman: Yes, but they were able to study it for only one generation.

Goldsworthy: I understand that you recognize a diapause mite by its becoming pigmented. It is possible to have a diapause mite that is non-pigmented? Can you differentiate between a requirement of pigment for diapause and a requirement for the photoreceptor?

Veerman: Diapause in wild-type mites is easily recognizable by the orange pigmentation, but I have also observed yellow and albino mites that are in diapause. It is possible to recognize even the albino mites as being in diapause because they are smaller than the summer forms (due to the absence of gut contents and the reduced size of the ovaries) and because their behaviour is different: they do not feed and do not lay eggs. So we do have several criteria, even for the non-pigmented mites, to help us to differentiate the diapausing ones. In answer to your second question, in the genetic experiments that I mentioned before, we saw that the pigment requirement for the photoreceptor is much smaller than for eye-spot and body pigmentation.

Giebultowicz: Was the haemolymph of the wasp larvae also different in colour or was it just the cocoons that differed?

Veerman: I don't know yet. We would have to open up the caterpillars to look at the parasitoid larvae; these are still preliminary experiments. However, it is not unlikely that the carotenoids are present in the haemolymph of the larvae at a certain time before they use them for spinning their cocoons.

Masaki: Does temperature produce any diapause response in the albino mites? If you were to search for a temperature response it would be possible to test whether the pigment participates in the diapause induction mechanism itself or only in the photoperiodic reception.

Veerman: We have several strains of the albino mites, and all are very labile in the sense that highly variable percentages of diapause are found in each strain under identical rearing conditions. Almost all our experiments have been done at 18–19°C. However, lowering the temperature in continuous darkness has no inducing effect on the wild-type strain. But I have not looked specifically for a temperature effect in the albinos.

Bowen: It is possible to determine whether the pigment is involved in the hour-glass component or in the circadian component of time-measurement, or both?

Veerman: On the present evidence it is not possible to say how the pigment is involved in photoperiodic photoreception. Even on the basis of action spectra for diapause induction it would still be difficult, I am afraid, to identify the photoreceptor pigment, let alone to discriminate between its possible function in the clock or in the circadian component of the induction mechanism. A combination of pigments might be involved. However, I do believe that a rhodopsin-like pigment is involved because we have now found the same response in several species.

Saunders: On what grounds did you reject internal coincidence and external coincidence models, or any circadian models, for time-measurement in the clock mechanism?

Veerman: We have tested the external coincidence model extensively (Vaz Nunes & Veerman 1982). Internal coincidence models are more difficult to test. We tried the internal coincidence model of Tyshchenko (1966) and it didn't work for a number of symmetrical 'skeleton' photoperiods (unpublished work).

Saunders: At what point did the external coincidence model fail so that you abandoned it?

Veerman: The external coincidence model went a long way towards explaining our results. But the model failed with some of the interruption experiments with extended nights: for example, in one with the diapause peaks at 10 h apart (unpublished work), as well as with symmetrical 'skeleton' photoperiods with one-hour pulses of light. In addition, diapause induction in continuous darkness remains a problem.

Pittendrigh: In your modelling you have had to invent the shape of the phase-response curve because you did not know what it really was. My own experience with modelling is that the detailed behaviour of the system is very sensitive to the shape and amplitude of the phase-response curve. So it may be unwise to abandon external coincidence on the basis of the behaviour of an unknown phase-response curve.

Veerman: Even if we could have taken a phase-response curve for, say, a locomotor rhythm, as your own paper (this volume) showed, it would remain to be seen whether it could be used to test the external coincidence model.

Pittendrigh: I agree; but surely the negative evidence is rather weak.

Veerman: We tried to model phase-response curves with various shapes and looked for the best fit to explain all our results, but we failed with a number of these experiments, and that made us look for another hypothesis.

Gilbert: In many photoperiodic studies the end point is the percentage of animals that undergo diapause. What about the quality of the diapause? What is the 'depth' of the diapause as affected by the number of hours of light and dark?

Veerman: We've not done those experiments yet.

Denlinger: In *Manduca sexta*, the duration of diapause strictly depends on how many short days are received by the animals. If they have received short days throughout embryonic and larval life they all go into diapause, but it is a very short diapause. If they receive just a few short days at the end of larval life, not so many of them enter diapause, but those that do enter have a very long diapause (Denlinger & Bradfield 1981). It may well be naive to consider only the all-or-none nature of diapause. There is often a continuum between diapause and non-diapause.

Mordue: It is an interesting general point that people working on clocks and on hormones may both be looking at different black boxes. The 'clock' people may be looking at the endocrine system simply as a black box and minimizing the importance of qualitative responses. The endocrinologists may tend to believe that there is a set of neuronal mechanisms, which simply transduce the signal, and that the hormone release is either turned on or not. We should not just be considering all-or-none responses but whole sets of quantitative and qualitative differences too; both are capable of being subjected to fine tuning.

Page: Could you educate me about how oscillator and hour-glass models are involved in photoperiodic time-measurement? I believe that Beck (1974a,b, 1976, 1980) has a model that could explain all photoperiodic response curves of various organisms if one adjusts the kinetics of the oscillators in the appropriate way. How does his model relate to yours? How much manipulation of the kinetics of your model is necessary for it to fit other insects?

Veerman: As a matter of fact we began our work on the photoperiodic clock with an attempt to apply Beck's model, the dual system theory, to our spider mites (Vaz Nunes & Veerman 1979), but it did not work for them. By adjusting his model, which resulted in two hour-glasses instead of two oscillators functioning as the clock, we could get it to work, but only for experiments based on 24h cycles. We had to abandon both of these models as soon as we found the resonance effect in these spider mites. There is therefore no connection between Beck's model and the one we are using now. In order to explain data from insects by our own model we have to determine a number of measurements for the hour-glass kinetics from the normal photoperiodic response curve and, preferably, from one or two night-interruption experiments also. We can then calculate the expected response for other experiments. For the calculation of the resonance effect we need a phase-response curve. The free-running period (τ) of the oscillation involved in the resonance effect is taken preferably from resonance experiments: it is, for instance, about 20h for *Tetranychus* and about 24h for *Sarcophaga*. The counter may show differences also. It is difficult to analyse the various components separately because when measuring a photoperiodic response we can measure only diapause or non-diapause in a population sample.

Truman: The responses of the spider mites and predacious mites and the wasps to constant darkness was always non-diapause. It is interesting that this response to constant darkness mimics that shown by carotenoid-free animals.

Veerman: Actually, with carotenoid-containing diets or, in the case of the spider mites, in the wild-type strain, we always find 0% diapause in continuous darkness. This makes it possible to use these species for this kind of work. It would be difficult if they gave 100% diapause in total darkness.

Pittendrigh: Yet *Pectinophora* does this (Pittendrigh & Minis 1971).

Veerman: Yes; this might be an essential difference!

REFERENCES

Beck SD 1974a Photoperiodic determination of insect development and diapause. I: Oscillators, hourglasses, and a determination model. J Comp Physiol 90:275-295

Beck SD 1974b Photoperiodic determination of insect development and diapause. II: The determination gate in a theoretical model. J Comp Physiol 90:297-310

Beck SD 1976 Photoperiodic determination of insect development and diapause. V: Diapause, circadian rhythms, and phase response curves, according to the dual system theory. J Comp Physiol 107:97-111

Beck SD 1980 Insect photoperiodism, 2nd edn. Academic Press, New York

Denlinger DL, Bradfield JY 1981 Duration of pupal diapause in the tobacco hornworm is determined by number of short days received by the larva. J Exp Biol 91:331-337

Frank KD, Zimmerman WF 1969 Action spectra for phase shifts of a circadian rhythm in *Drosophila*. Science (Wash DC) 163:688-689

Pittendrigh CS, Minis DH 1971 The photoperiodic time-measurement in *Pectinophora gossypiella* and its relation to the circadian system in that species. In: Menaker M (ed) Biochronometry. National Academy of Sciences, USA, p 212-250

Tyshchenko VP 1966 Two-oscillatory model of the physiological mechanism of insect photoperiodic reaction. Zh Obshch Biol 27:209-222 [Russian]

Van Zon AQ, Overmeer WPJ, Veerman A 1981 Carotenoids function in photoperiodic induction of diapause in a predacious mite. Science (Wash DC) 213:1131-1133

Vaz Nunes M, Veerman A 1979 Photoperiodic time measurement in spider mites. I: Development of a two interval timers model. J Comp Physiol 134:203-217

Vaz Nunes M, Veerman A 1982 External coincidence and photoperiodic time measurement in the spider mite, *Tetranychus urticae*. J Insect Physiol 28:143-154

Veerman A 1980 Functional involvement of carotenoids in photoperiodic induction of diapause in the spider mite *Tetranychus urticae*. Physiol Entomol 5:291-300

Veerman A, Overmeer WPJ, Van Zon AQ, De Boer JM, De Waard ER, Huisman HO 1983 Vitamin A is essential for photoperiodic induction of diapause in an eyeless mite. Nature (Lond) 302:248-249

Long-night summation and programming of pupal diapause in the flesh-fly, *Sarcophaga argyrostoma*

DAVID S. SAUNDERS and HELEN BRADLEY

Department of Zoology, University of Edinburgh, West Mains Road, Edinburgh EH9 3JT, UK

Abstract. In the ovoviviparous flesh-fly, *Sarcophaga argyrostoma*, the photoperiodic 'sensitive period' begins in the intrauterine embryo and continues to the young third instar larva, but sensitivity declines during this period and ends by the time the post-feeding or wandering larva enters the soil. During the sensitive period the larvae 'add up' inductive long nights in a temperature-compensated fashion, and the final incidence of pupal diapause depends on an interaction between the number of long nights experienced and the length of the sensitive period. Lengthening the sensitive period by temporary starvation of young larvae thus increases pupal diapause, whereas shortening the sensitive period by premature extraction of larvae from their food, or overcrowding, lowers it. Delaying puparium formation by crowding or by wet treatment of photoperiodically insensitive wandering larvae, however, also lowers diapause incidence. Selection for fast and slow larval development, mainly affecting the duration of the post-sensitive period, has similar effects on diapause. In a speculative attempt to explain how photoperiodic 'information' is stored within the central nervous system, to be used on a much later occasion, it is suggested that an unknown 'diapause titre' accumulates within the larval brain which ultimately prevents prothoracicotropic hormone release or ecdysteroid synthesis in the diapausing pupa.

1984 Photoperiodic regulation of insect and molluscan hormones. Pitman, London (Ciba Foundation symposium 104), p 65–89

In common with many other insects that inhabit higher latitudes, the ovoviviparous flesh flies (*Sarcophaga* spp.) have evolved a seasonally appropriate strategy in which successive generations of active flies appear in the summer, but the winter months are passed in a state of diapause. Also in common with these other species, the seasonal switch from the continuously developing to the diapausing pathway is controlled by photoperiod (day-length and/or night-length) which uniquely provides the organism with an accurate and reliable indicator of the passing seasons.

The minimal requirements for such a regulatory mechanism must be a photoreceptor, a 'clock' to measure day- or night-length, and an ultimate (endocrine) effector; all these components probably reside in the cerebral component of the nervous system (Truman 1971).

The clock in *Sarcophaga argyrostoma* begins to function in the intrauterine embryo, and is maximally sensitive to photoperiod during embryogenesis and larval development through to the early third instar (Denlinger 1971, Saunders 1981a). The resulting diapause, on the other hand, occurs in the pupa, after pupal apolysis and head eversion, but before the differentiation of the pharate adult (Fraenkel & Hsiao 1968). The phenomenon of diapause induction must therefore involve a chain of events spanning the greater part of embryonic and post-embryonic development and several important changes in behaviour—larviposition, two larval moults, larval wandering, entering the soil, puparium formation, and pupation—much of which is regulated by the endocrine activities of the brain—ring gland axis (prothoracicotropic hormone, ecdysone, juvenile hormone), which is also thought to be interrupted at diapause (Denlinger 1981). The whole process, therefore, probably involves a 'programming' of the cerebral neuroendocrine system by photoperiod, in which seasonal information acquired early in development is stored and integrated within the central nervous system to be used on a much later occasion. The nature of this storage is one of the more important unresolved problems associated with the seasonal cycles of breeding and dormancy in insects. This paper describes in formal terms some of the events in this chain, referred to collectively as the photoperiodic 'counter', and speculates on their possible endocrine basis.

The 'clock' and the 'counter'

Properties of the clock

The photoperiodic response curve for *S. argyrostoma* (Fig. 1a) is typical for a long-day species, with all individuals developing without arrest when the larvae are reared at photoperiods longer than 15.5 h, but with the majority of pupae entering a firm diapause when photoperiods are shorter than 14.5 h. Exposure of larvae to abnormal cycles in which the light and dark periods are independently varied, however, shows that the dark period is of central importance to the timing mechanism: the clock measures a critical night-length of about 9.5 h, with much less regard to the length of the 'day'. This can be seen, for example, in regimes containing 16 h of light (a 'long-day' in a 24 h cycle) which induce diapause once the dark period exceeds 9.5 h (Fig. 1b).

An extensive analysis of the photoperiodic clock in a wide range of natural and abnormal light cycles (Saunders 1973, 1981b) has suggested that time-measurement is a function of the insect's circadian system. Furthermore, a cybernetic approach to the entrainment of the circadian system by light pulses and cycles, using the pupal eclosion rhythm as 'hands of the clock' (Saunders 1978, 1981b), has revealed a close parallel between eclosion and photoperiodism. This approach has also revealed short-night effects (=development) when a particular circadian phase (called circadian time, Ct 21.5) is illuminated, but long-night effects (=diapause) when Ct 21.5 falls in the dark. Although there are many unresolved problems, the results of these studies suggest that the *Sarcophaga* clock conforms most closely to the 'external coincidence' model of Pittendrigh (1972). In normal 24 h cycles (Fig. 1c) this model suggests that the circadian oscillators which make up the clock are phase-set to Ct 12 at the end of the light period, regardless of its length once it exceeds about 10 h. Consequently the discrimination between short and long nights depends on the illumination or non-illumination of a restricted photo-inducible phase (ϕ_i), at Ct 21.5, by the light at dawn. The most critical test of this model is the so-called *T*-experiment in which 1 h pulses of light are provided in light:dark (LD) cycles from 21.5 to 30.5 h duration (within the range of entrainment of the system). This experiment demonstrates that diapause avoidance is only obtained when ϕ_i coincides exactly with the short light pulses; in all other regimes diapause incidence remains high (Fig. 1d).

Properties of the counter

The measurement of a long night by the clock is only part of the process of diapause induction: the larvae also need to experience a sequence of long nights during their 'sensitive period' (embryo to third-stage feeding larva) before the pupa is committed to diapause. The essential features of this mechanism were observed when cultures of larvae, produced by adult flies maintained at 25 °C and in continuous light, were raised in long nights (LD 10 : 14 h) and a range of temperatures (16 to 26 °C) (Saunders 1971). Those larvae raised at high temperature (26 °C) all became non-diapausing pupae (Fig. 2a), whereas those raised at low temperature (16 to 18 °C) all entered diapause. At intermediate temperatures (20 to 24 °C), however, the first larvae to form puparia developed without arrest, whereas the last to do so entered pupal diapause. This observation led to the concept of the 'counter' mechanism which proposes that the accumulation of long nights is a more highly temperature-compensated process ($Q_{10} = 1.4$) than is the length of the larval sensitive period ($Q_{10} = 2.7$). Consequently, at high temperatures the larvae come to the end of their sensitive period before experiencing a critical *number* of long nights, whereas at low temperatures the critical number has

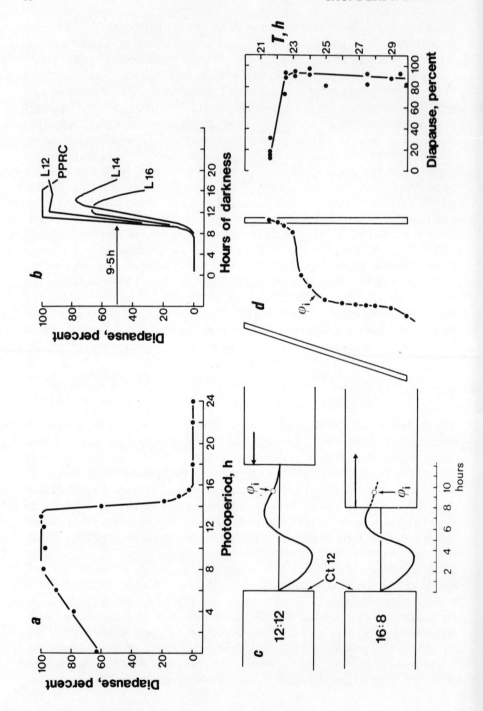

already been experienced before the sensitive period ends. The fact that summation is temperature-compensated comes as no surprise if the mechanism is part of an entrained circadian system; and similar temperature-compensated summation phenomena have been shown to operate in a range of other insects (Goryshin & Tyshchenko 1974, Saunders 1981a), sometimes accumulating long nights, sometimes short nights, and sometimes both.

The photoperiodic mechanism in *S. argyrostoma*, involving clock and counter, is thus an autumnal system evolved to regulate the appearance of the diapause state. Embryos and larvae produced late in the season 'add up' successive long nights once the dark period exceeds about $9\frac{1}{2}$ h, and then enter diapause as pupae. Since the sensitive period comes to an end before puparium formation, photoperiod is not involved in the processes of diapause maintenance or termination.

Gibbs's model for long-night summation: the diapause titre

Gibbs (1975) proposed a model for the photoperiodic counter (Fig. 2c) in which the summation of long nights is seen as the accumulation of an unknown 'diapause titre', perhaps in discrete 'information packets', which ultimately prevents the release of an ecdysiotropic signal from the pupal brain. Thus, at the end of the sensitive period the stored information, in the form of the diapause titre, is compared with an internal and presumably inherited threshold: if it exceeds that value the pupa enters diapause, if not, the pupa develops. A similar model, called the 'memory link', has been proposed by Goryshin & Tyshchenko (1974) for a number of species that show temperature-compensated summation of long or short nights.

FIG. 1. Aspects of the photoperiodic clock in *Sarcophaga argyrostoma*. (**a**) Photoperiodic response curve for induction of pupal diapause (data from Saunders 1971). (**b**) The effect of night-length on diapause induction at constant photophase (L = 12, 14 and 16 h), compared with similar data from the photoperiodic response curve (PPRC). Note the critical night-length (about 9.5 h), even with a photophase of 16 h, which is a 'long day' in natural photoperiods (data from Saunders 1973). (**c**) The 'external coincidence' model for the photoperiodic clock. The circadian oscillation(s) which make up the clock (the time-course of which is shown by a curve derived from a phase-response curve for the pupal eclosion rhythm exposed to 1 h pulses of light) is phase-set by 'lights off' to a circadian time (Ct 12) characteristic of the start of the subjective night, regardless of the length of the light pulse (12 or 16 h). The photo-inducible phase (ϕ_i) lies 9.5 h (the critical night-length) later. Consequently, in LD 12:12 (a long night) it falls in the dark (= diapause induction), whereas in LD 16:8 (a short night) it is illuminated by the light at dawn (= non-diapause). (**d**) The '*T*-test'. *Left-hand panel:* computer predictions of the phase relationship between ϕ_i and the light pulse in photocycles containing 1 h of light and ranging from $T = 21$ to $T = 30$. *Right-hand panel:* Diapause incidence in the same regimes, showing high diapause when ϕ_i falls in the dark, but low diapause (= development) when it is illuminated by the pulse (data from Saunders 1981b).

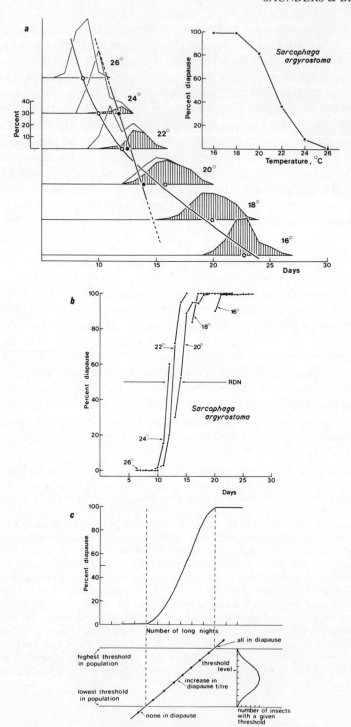

These models do not identify the nature of the stored information, and we have only circumstantial evidence for its existence. Indeed, the phenomenon could equally well be described by a decrease in a 'titre' which promotes development; or even perhaps by the summation of long nights signalling a change in neural firing patterns (see Gainer 1972). Nevertheless, the models serve to systematize and explain a body of data; they also offer testable predictions. One such prediction is that shortening the sensitive period and therefore restricting the number of long nights experienced should reduce the incidence of diapause, whereas lengthening the sensitive period should increase it. Such tests have been attempted before (Saunders 1975, Droop 1975), but this paper now presents new and more extensive data (H. Bradley, unpublished work, 1983).

Experimental lengthening and shortening of the larval sensitive period

In natural conditions larvae of *S. argyrostoma* feed in a cluster within a carcass, but then leave their food and disperse into drier sites for puparium formation. Feeding larvae are therefore crowded and wet, whilst wandering post-fed larvae are solitary and dry. For this reason, attempts to alter the duration of larval development by physical means (other than temperature) were directed separately at the feeding and post-feeding stages. All experiments were performed in temperature and photoperiodic conditions in which the final incidence of pupal diapause in the control cultures was less than 'saturated' (i.e. 40–60%); this allowed for both increase and decrease in diapause.

Manipulation of the length of the feeding stages

Larvae deposited by flies kept in continuous light (LL) at 25 °C were cultured in long nights (LD 12 : 12) at 17 °C; in these conditions the control cultures gave a final diapause incidence of about 40%. In experimental cultures, the length of the feeding period was altered by removing young larvae from their

---

FIG. 2. The photoperiodic 'counter' in *S. argyrostoma*. (a) Incidence of pupal diapause in cultures raised in long nights (LD 10 : 14) at temperatures ranging from 26 to 16 °C. Polygons show percentage puparium formation per day; the shaded areas show the proportion of pupae entering diapause. For explanation see text (data from Saunders 1971). (b) Diapause incidence as a function of the number of long nights experienced during the larval sensitive period, at a range of constant temperatures (26 to 16 °C). RDN, the 'required day number' (days to 50% diapause). (c) A theoretical model to account for the summation of long nights by the photoperiodic counter (from Gibbs 1975).

food and starving them for 1, 2 or 3 days before replacing them in culture conditions.

One day of starvation, commencing on the day of larviposition (day 0), lengthened larval life and delayed puparium formation by about one day, from a mean of 11.1 days in the control to 12.2 days in the experimental insects (Fig. 3). A similar period of starvation, commencing 24 h later (day 1), had no similar delaying effect, perhaps because the larvae had already fed for 24 h and therefore had a nutritional reserve. Starvation on day 2, however, had the dramatic effect of splitting the distribution of puparium formation into two clear peaks separated by 6 days. The interpretation of this result is that the first peak comprised the young third-instar larvae that had reached the 'critical size or weight' necessary for puparium formation (Shaaya & Levensbrook 1982), whereas those in the second peak had not, and these required a further period of feeding before competence to form a puparium was achieved. By day 3 the bimodal response to a one-day period of starvation had disappeared, but similar bimodalities were observed with groups of larvae starved for 2 or 3 days, starting on day 3 (Fig. 3).

As with earlier observations on the temporal pattern of diapause production (Fig. 2a) it was observed that the first larvae to form puparia developed without arrest whilst the later ones entered diapause. Similarly, in the bimodal distributions, the first peaks contained only developing individuals, whereas nearly all the diapausing pupae were confined to the second peak (Fig. 3). When all peaks were treated separately, there was a clear positive correlation ($r = +0.95$) between the mean length of larval development (larviposition-to-puparium formation) and the incidence of pupal diapause.

In another series of experiments the feeding period was shortened by the premature removal of post-'critical weight' third instar larvae from their food (Fig. 4). With this technique, manual extraction of larvae 1 to 6 days earlier than the start of wandering in the control culture caused a systematic shortening of the larval period from about 17 to 9 days. Once again there was a clear linear relationship ($r = +0.98$) between the mean length of larval development and diapause incidence.

The effect of density during the larval feeding period was investigated in cultures set up at 17°C, LD 12 : 12, in groups of 100, 300, 500, 700 and 1000 larvae in a measured amount of food; all post-feeding larvae were then kept in groups of 100 in dry sawdust to avoid the modifying effects of wet and crowding during the subsequent dispersal phase. This experiment (Fig. 5) showed a systematic shortening of the developmental period with larval density from 13.4 days in groups of 100 to 10.8 days in groups of 1000, an effect brought about either by a reduced intake of food per larva, or by increased excretory material or increased temperature within the more crowded cultures. Once again, however, there was a positive relationship

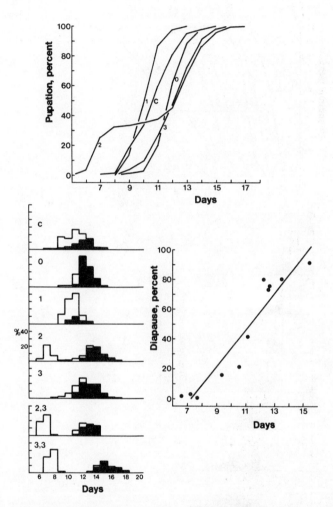

FIG. 3. The effects of temporary starvation of young feeding larvae of *S. argyrostoma* on the length of larval development and pupal diapause incidence. Adult flies maintained at 25 °C, in constant light; larval cultures at 17 °C, LD 12:12. *Top panel:* cumulative percent puparium formation. *Lower left:* incidence of non-diapause pupae (open histograms) and diapause pupae (closed histograms) per day. 0—larvae starved for one day starting on day 0; 1—starved one day starting day 1; 2—starved one day starting day 2; 3—starved one day starting day 3; 2,3—starved for two days starting on day 3; 3,3—starved for three days starting on day 3. C—unstarved control culture. *Lower right:* relationship between mean duration of larval development (number of long nights) and diapause incidence ($y = 12.26x - 89.04$; $r = 0.95$).

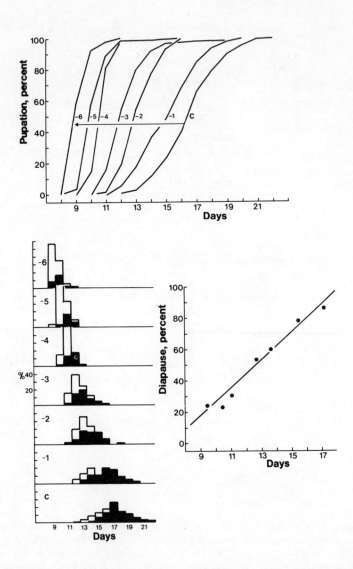

FIG. 4. The effects of premature extraction of young third instar larvae from their food on pupal diapause incidence. Adult flies at 25 °C, constant light; larvae at 17 °C, LD 12 : 12. Panels as in Fig. 3. C—control culture; −1 to −6—larvae extracted 1 to 6 days before larvae in the control culture initiated wandering behaviour. *Lower right:* relationship between the number of long nights and diapause incidence ($y = 8.98x − 64.42$; $r = 0.98$).

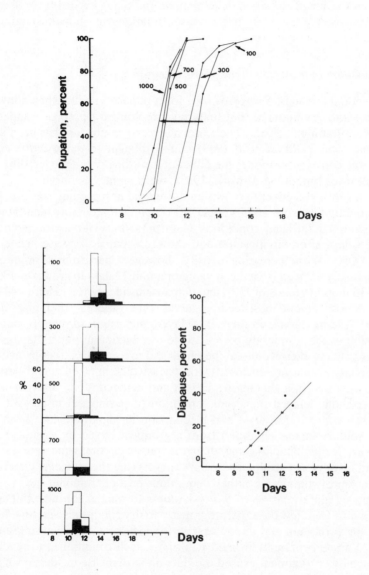

FIG. 5. The effects of larval density during the feeding phase on the incidence of pupal diapause. Adult flies at 25 °C, constant light; larvae at 17 °C, LD 12:12. Panels as in Fig. 3. *Lower right:* relationship between number of long nights and diapause incidence ($y = 10.1x - 92.5$; $r = 0.84$). 100 to 1000—numbers of larvae within measured amounts of food.

between the length of larval development and diapause incidence (Fig. 5c). This is assumed here to be a causal relationship, notwithstanding the uncertainties noted above.

Manipulation of the length of the post-feeding stage

Post-feeding larvae of S. *argyrostoma* form puparia rapidly when allowed to disperse into dry material, but undergo a prolonged period of wandering if kept wet or at high density. The effect of excessive moisture has been known for some time (Ohtaki et al 1968) and is thought to delay the release of prothoracicotropic hormone; the effect of crowding was discovered by J. M. Giebultowicz (unpublished work, 1980), working in Edinburgh.

Fig. 6 shows the effect of crowding during the post-feeding stage on larvae deposited by flies kept at 25 °C, LD 12:12, and subsequently maintained (in dry sawdust) in the same conditions. Control (solitary) larvae formed puparia about 8 days after larviposition and showed a pupal diapause incidence of about 90%. With increasing density, however, puparium formation was progressively delayed (to a mean value of about 12 days in groups of 100, and about 15 days in groups of 150), and diapause incidence fell to about 40–50%. High density among post-feeding larvae thus differed from high density among feeding larvae in that it delayed puparium formation, and this extension of the wandering period led to a reduction in pupal diapause.

These effects of crowding can be mimicked to a certain extent by agitation: solitary larvae that are enclosed with dry sawdust in 50 ml round-bottomed flasks, mounted in a shaking waterbath and agitated at 100 movements per minute, show delayed puparium formation (experimental insects 8.6 days, unshaken controls 7.8 days) and a reduction in pupal diapause from 97 to 53%. Solitary larvae separated from a group of larvae by a gauze screen, however, formed puparia and diapause pupae at the same rate as those without an adjacent group. These data suggest that the crowding effect is one of mechanical stimulation rather than odour or a pheromone.

Allowing mature larvae of S. *argyrostoma* to wander into wet rather than dry sawdust for a few days, before transfer to dry conditions, led to a delay in puparium formation and an increase in the incidence of diapause (Saunders 1975). Larvae eventually formed puparia in such conditions, however, and prolonged wet treatment caused a reduction in diapause incidence similar to that observed for excessive crowding in the dry. Preliminary data (H. Bradley, unpublished work, 1983) suggest that early post-feeding larvae are not able to react to crowded conditions whilst wet, but that they can do so after dispersal. This makes 'biological sense' in that larvae *are* crowded and wet whilst in their food, becoming solitary and dry only after dispersal to pupation sites.

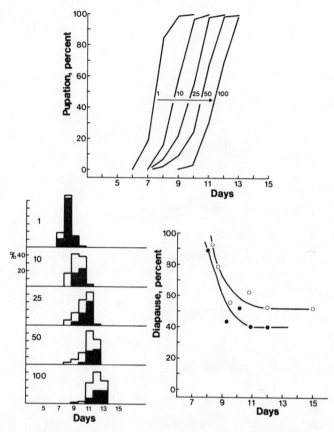

FIG. 6. The effects of larval density (crowding) during the post-feeding or wandering phase. Panels as in Fig. 3. Adults and larvae at 25 °C, LD 12:12. 1 to 100—numbers of mature larvae per small glass jar (in dry sawdust).

Selection for 'fast' and 'slow' developmental strains and its effect on diapause induction

A 'stock' population of flies was maintained as adults and larvae at 25 °C under constant light. From a single breeding population, fast developers were selected by breeding from about 30 to 50 of the first larvae to form puparia, and slow developers were selected by breeding from a similar number of the last to form puparia. Selection was continued for 12 to 13 generations by the same procedure. Although details of this selection experiment will be described elsewhere, suffice it to say that two strains had diverged within very few generations, the 'fast' ones producing (at 25 °C, LL) a highly synchronized pattern of puparium formation 3 to 4 days earlier than the 'slow' ones

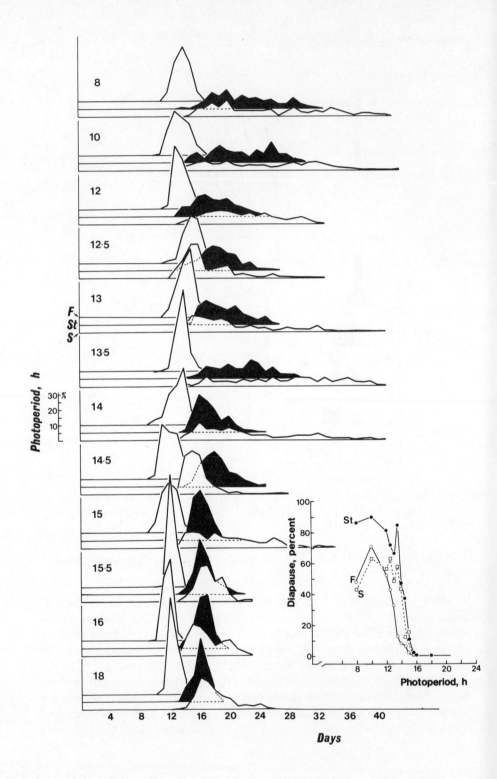

which showed a delayed pupation pattern with a long negative skew. Since 'fast,' 'slow' and 'stock' larvae all appeared to leave their food on the same day of culture, selection seems to have altered the duration of the post-feeding or wandering stage, perhaps by dealing the release of prothoracico-tropic hormone necessary for puparium formation.

The three strains were then raised at 17 °C in light cycles ranging from LD 8:16 to 18:6. The patterns of puparium formation (Fig. 7) showed a systematic shortening of the larval period with increasing photoperiod in all three strains, consistent with earlier results with the 'stock' strain (Saunders 1976). The most dramatic shortening occurred at the critical night-length (LD 14.5:9.5) with marked reductions in the lengths of the tails in the 'stock' and 'slow' strains.

Puparia derived from this experiment were then kept at 20 °C and in the dark for a further 10 days, and were then opened to ascertain the diapause status of the pupae or pharate adults within them. According to Gibbs's simple 'counter' hypothesis (see above) which suggested that larvae were photoperiodically sensitive up to puparium formation, the 'fast' strain with its shorter larval life was expected to show less diapause than the 'stock' strain (in long nights), whereas the 'slow' strain, with its delayed puparium formation, was expected to show more. The results (Fig. 7) showed that selection for larval developmental speed in a diapause-free environment (25 °C, LL) did affect the incidence of diapause in long nights, but not in this simple fashion. For example, the 'fast' strain showed a reduction in diapause over the 'stock' strain in all photoperiods from LD 8:16 to 12:12 and also showed a shift in the critical photoperiod to shorter values, as expected; but the 'slow' strain, too, showed a reduction in diapause incidence in long nights (but no shifted critical value). Possible reasons for this are outlined below in a modified counter hypothesis.

Formal properties of the photoperiodic 'counter' in *Sarcophaga argyrostoma*

The present results necessitate a slight but important reappraisal of the simple counter model of Gibbs (1975), as outlined above. In this early version the period of development from embryogenesis to puparium formation was regarded as the photoperiodic sensitive period, and all three larval instars were thought to be equally sensitive. The present results, however, strongly

FIG. 7. The rate of larval development (oviposition to puparium formation) in three strains of *S. argyrostoma* ('fast', *F*; 'stock', *St*; and 'slow', *S*) selected for time of puparium formation at 25 °C, in constant light. *Inset:* the incidence of pupal diapause of *F*, *St* and *S* at 17 °C and photoperiods from LD 8:16 to LD 18:6.

suggest that the sensitive period comes to an end soon after the onset of wandering behaviour, and that sensitivity to long nights declines from a maximum in embryos and young feeding larvae to the point at which it ceases. Late post-feeding larvae—which are normally subterranean—are then virtually insensitive to photoperiod. The results also show that alterations to the length of larval development have different diapause-inducing effects on sensitive and post-sensitive larvae. In the former, for example, a lengthening of development (by temporary starvation) increases the number of long nights 'seen' and increases diapause, whereas a shortening of development (by premature extraction) decreases the number of long nights 'seen', and reduces diapause. In larvae in the post-sensitive period, however, delays in puparium formation may, in certain circumstances, *reduce* the final incidence of diapause. These effects will now be examined in greater detail.

Lengthening or shortening larval development by temporary starvation (Fig. 3), which affects young, highly sensitive, feeding larvae, has particularly strong effects as evidenced by the slope of the regression (12.26). Premature extraction of third-instar feeding larvae from their meat (Fig. 4), which affects older, less sensitive larvae, on the other hand, has less strong effects (slope 8.98). Crowding in the feeding stages, which maximally affects older third-instar larvae, has even weaker effects on diapause incidence (Fig. 5), whilst delaying the start of wandering for a day or two in wet sawdust (Saunders 1975) has weaker effects still. These observations point to a declining influence of long nights as development proceeds. Once post-feeding or wandering behaviour has commenced and the sensitive period ends, however, any delay in puparium formation by crowding or prolonged wet treatment then causes a drop in diapause incidence, as though the mechanism accumulating long nights had gone into 'reverse'.

Results from the selection for 'fast' and 'slow' developmental rates are also consistent with this interpretation. For example, the shorter larval period of the 'fast' strain results in less diapause in all inductive photoperiods, a result probably consistent with the curtailment of the sensitive period. Prolonged extension of the post-feeding stage, as in the 'slow' strain, however, leads to a reduction in pupal diapause because, as in gross overcrowding and protracted wet treatment, puparium formation is delayed beyond the end of photoperiodic sensitivity.

In terms of the putative 'diapause titre', these results could be explained thus: every time a long night is measured by the clock (i.e., when ϕ_i falls in the dark) some 'quantum' of long-night information is produced and stored. More diapause titre is produced and stored early in the sensitive period than later, and the amount stored steadily declines during the period from the embryo to the end of the sensitive period. Soon after wandering behaviour commences, however, the larva is no longer sensitive to photoperiod, no further diapause titre is produced or stored, and any delay in puparium formation (by crowding, prolonged wet treatment, or protracted wandering as in the 'slow' strain) results in a drop in the titre of stored information, perhaps because of catabolism or 'breakdown'. If the titre then falls below the individual threshold, the pupa fails to enter diapause and it develops without arrest.

Endocrine control of pupal diapause in *Sarcophaga* spp: a case of negative feedback?

What little is known about the endocrinology of diapause in *Sarcophaga* spp. suggests that the titre of ecdysteroids in the haemolymph of diapausing pupae remains low whilst that in non-diapausing pupae shows a dramatic rise associated with pharate adult development (Ohtaki & Takahashi 1972, Denlinger 1981); diapause is therefore a result of a below-threshold titre of moulting hormone. This view is supported by the observation that injection of diapausing pupae with 20-hydroxyecdysone causes a resumption of development (Gibbs 1976, Zdarek & Denlinger 1975). Although direct observations on prothoracicotropic hormone (PTTH) are lacking in *Sarcophaga*, these results are taken to show that the release of this hormone from the brain is interrupted in the diapausing animal. In short, exposure of *Sarcophaga* to a train of long nights during the embryonic and larval sensitive period somehow prevents PTTH release (and therefore subsequent ecdysone synthesis) in the diapausing pupa.

This temporary cessation of endocrine activity which constitutes the diapause state might be the result of negative feedback. The most likely site for such control is at the PTTH neurosecretory cells or neurohaemal organ (Saunders 1981a); but since the prothoracic glands of diapausing *Manduca sexta* pupae become refractory to activation by PTTH (Bowen et al 1984), the ring gland could be another. Such feedback inhibition could involve ecdysteroids (Steel 1975, 1978) or PTTH itself. Alternatively, regulation of PTTH release could involve juvenile hormones (Nijhout & Williams 1974, Hiruma et al 1978), perhaps by complex interactions. Although direct evidence for such regulatory processes in pupal diapause is currently lacking, three observations made during the period just before the onset of diapause may support the idea. These are: Ohtaki & Takahashi's (1972) observation of a higher titre of ecdysteroids in the haemolymph of diapause-destined *Sarcophaga peregrina* at puparium formation; Walker & Denlinger's (1980) observation of a high (and cyclical) titre of juvenile hormone in diapause-programmed *Sarcophaga crassipalpis*, which lasted for at least 5 days after puparium formation and was absent in non-diapause flies; and the observation by M. F. Bowen (personal communication 1983) that *in vitro* release of juvenile hormone III (but not juvenile hormone I) by the corpora allata of *M. sexta* presents different timing profiles in short- and long-day fifth-instar larvae. The first suggests the possibility of steroid feedback, the second and the third a possible role for juvenile hormone in the regulation of pupal diapause. Furthermore, although immediate regulation of pupal diapause may involve such agencies, it is also easy to propose a scheme ultimately controlled by an elevated (or lowered) 'diapause titre' within the long-night or diapause-destined brain, thereby linking down-stream endocrine events with 'up-stream' phenomena associated with the clock and the counter.

Evidence for an accumulated 'diapause titre', however, is currently restricted to the type of formal analysis reported in this paper. More direct evidence is lacking. For example, implantation of brains from short-night (development-destined) wandering larvae of *S. argyrostoma* into long-night (diapause-destined) recipients caused a high proportion of the latter to alter their diapause programme. Implantation of long-night brains into short-night larvae, on the other hand, failed to induce diapause (Giebultowicz & Saunders 1983). This result, which is similar to that obtained earlier for *Mamestra brassicae* (Yagi & Honda 1977), and more recently for *M. sexta* (M. F. Bowen & D. S. Saunders, unpublished work 1983) clearly demonstrates a qualitative endocrine difference between short- and long-night brains at the end of the sensitive period. Although this result appears to exclude a circulating humoral agent or 'diapause hormone', it does not exclude material (i.e. a 'diapause titre') accumulating entirely within the brain and then regulating known humoral components of the cerebral neuroendocrine system.

A detailed knowledge of the timings, titres, and inter-relationships between PTTH, ecdysteroids and juvenoids, in both long- and short-night larvae, together with a demonstration of possible biochemical differences between long- and short-night brains, are important prerequisites for further progress. Only then can concrete and testable models for diapause regulation, and for the transmission of photoperiodic information from the clock, be proposed.

Acknowledgements

The work described in this paper was supported at various times by the Science & Engineering Research Council (S.E.R.C.) and the Nuffield Foundation. Helen Bradley was maintained by an S.E.R.C. studentship. We also wish to thank Kathleen Rothwell for technical assistance, and Drs W. E. Bollenbacher and M. F. Bowen for their critical reading of the manuscript.

REFERENCES

Bowen MF, Bollenbacher WE, Gilbert LI 1984 *In vitro* studies on the role of the brain and prothoracic glands in the pupal diapause of *Manduca sexta*. J Exp Biol, in press

Denlinger DL 1971 Embryonic determination of pupal diapause in the flesh fly *Sarcophaga crassipalpis*. J Insect Physiol 17:1815-1822

Denlinger DL 1981 Hormonal and metabolic aspects of pupal diapause in Diptera. Entomol Gen 7:245-259

Droop B 1975 The effects of altering the length of larval development, at a constant temperature, on photoperiodic induction of diapause in *Sarcophaga argyrostoma*. BSc thesis, University of Edinburgh

Fraenkel G, Hsiao C 1968 Manifestations of a pupal diapause in two species of flies, *Sarcophaga argyrostoma* and *S. bullata*. J Insect Physiol 14:689-705

Gainer H 1972 Effects of experimentally induced diapause on the electrophysiology and protein synthesis of identified molluscan neurones. Brain Res 39:387-402

Gibbs D 1975 Reversal of pupal diapause in *Sarcophaga argyrostoma* by temperature shifts after puparium formation. J Insect Physiol 21:1179-1186

Gibbs D 1976 The initiation of adult development in *Sarcophaga argyrostoma* by β-ecdysone. J Insect Physiol 22:1195-1200

Giebultowicz JM, Saunders DS 1983 Evidence for the neuro-hormonal basis of commitment to pupal diapause in larvae of *Sarcophaga argyrostoma*. Experientia (Basel) 39:194-196

Goryshin NI, Tyshchenko VP 1974 The place of the memory link in the mechanism of photoperiodic reaction in insects. Zh Obshch Biol 35:518-530 [Russian]

Hiruma K, Yagi S, Agui N 1978 Action of juvenile hormone on the cerebral neurosecretory cells of *Mamestra brassicae in vivo* and *in vitro*. Appl Entomol Zool 13:149-157

Nijhout HF, Williams CM 1974 Control of moulting and metamorphosis in the tobacco hornworm, *Manduca sexta* (L.): cessation of juvenile hormone secretion as a trigger for pupation. J Exp Biol 61:493-501

Ohtaki T, Takahashi M 1972 Induction and termination of pupal diapause in relation to the change of ecdysone titer in the flesh fly, *Sarcophaga peregrina*. Jpn J Med Sci Biol 25:369-376

Ohtaki T, Milkman RD, Williams CM 1968 Dynamics of ecdysone secretion and action in the fleshfly *Sarcophaga peregrina*. Biol Bull (Woods Hole) 135:322-334

Pittendrigh CS 1972 Circadian surfaces and the diversity of possible roles of circadian organization in photoperiodic induction. Proc Natl Acad Sci USA 69:2734-2737

Saunders DS 1971 The temperature-compensated photoperiodic clock 'programming' development and pupal diapause in the flesh-fly, *Sarcophaga argyrostoma*. J Insect Physiol 17:801-812

Saunders DS 1973 The photoperiodic clock in the flesh fly, *Sarcophaga argyrostoma*. J Insect Physiol 19:1941-1954

Saunders DS 1975 Manipulation of the length of the sensitive period, and the induction of pupal diapause in the fleshfly, *Sarcophaga argyrostoma*. J Entomol Ser A Physiol Behav 50:107-118

Saunders D S 1976 The circadian eclosion rhythm in *Sarcophaga argyrostoma*: some comparisons with the photoperiodic clock. J Comp Physiol 110:111-133

Saunders DS 1978 An experimental and theoretical analysis of photoperiodic induction in the flesh-fly, *Sarcophaga argyrostoma*. J Comp Physiol 124:75-95

Saunders DS 1981a Insect photoperiodism: the clock and the counter. Physiol Entomol 6:99-116

Saunders DS 1981b Insect photoperiodism: entrainment as a basis for time measurement. In: Follett BK, Follett DE (eds) Biological clocks in seasonal reproductive cycles. Wright, Bristol, p 67-81

Shaaya E, Levensbrook L 1982 The effects of starvation and 20-hydroxyecdysone on feeding and pupariation of early 3rd instar *Calliphora vicina* larvae. J Insect Physiol 28:683-688

Steel CGH 1975 A neuroendocrine feedback mechanism in the insect moulting cycle. Nature (Lond) 253:267-269
Steel CGH 1978 Nervous and hormonal regulation of neurosecretory cells in the insect brain. In: Gaillard P, Boer HH (eds) Comparative endocrinology. Elsevier, Amsterdam, p 327-330
Truman JW 1971 The role of the brain in the ecdysis rhythm of silkmoths: comparison with the photoperiodic termination of diapause. In: Menaker M (ed) Biochronometry. National Academy of Sciences, Washington DC, p 483-504
Walker GP, Denlinger DL 1980 Juvenile hormone and moulting hormone titres in diapause and non-diapause destined flesh flies. J Insect Physiol 26:661-664
Yagi S, Honda T 1977 Endocrinological studies on pupal diapause of cabbage armyworm, *Mamestra brassicae* L. 1: Critical period of brain hormone secretion for metamorphosis. Jpn J Appl Entomol Zool 21:90-93 [Japanese, English summary]
Zdarek J, Denlinger DL 1975 Action of ecdysoids, juvenoids, and non-hormonal agents on termination of pupal diapause in the flesh fly. J Insect Physiol 21:1193-1202

DISCUSSION

Truman: Are all long nights equivalent for the purpose of the animal's adding them up?

Saunders: All these experiments have been done with a 12h-long night. I have done some others with a 14h-long night and I can't see any difference in the number of long nights required to induce diapause, but we have not systematically looked at this.

Pittendrigh: But in your earlier work, wasn't there a suggestion that the number of days to diapause varied with the photoperiod?

Saunders: Yes; in *Nasonia vitripennis* there is evidence of such a difference between short and long days (Saunders 1966). In *Sarcophaga argyrostoma* the length of the sensitive period, as measured conveniently by the number of days to puparium formation, is also photoperiodically dependent, but again the difference is between long and short days and not within short days/long nights themselves. This is quite separate from whether the animals are programmed for diapause or not. Diapause-destined larvae will pupariate later than development-destined larvae but the difference is independent of the diapause stage: if the experiments are done at 25°C, after the embryos have previously been exposed to long days when there is no diapause in the system, short-day larvae will still take longer to form puparia than long-day larvae (Saunders 1976).

Hodková: I have also investigated the effect of starvation on diapause induction by short-day photoperiods in *Pyrrhocoris apterus* adults (M. Hodková, unpublished work) (see also p 91). I compared females that were either fed or starved after transfer from long days to short days. In the starved females, one week at short days was sufficient for diapause induction. This was indicated by the absence of oviposition, even when females received food after one week of starvation. But if the females received food immediately after the transfer from long days they needed about two weeks of short-day photoperiods to induce diapause. I interpreted this to mean that, in an animal that is fed and ovipositing, a certain number of short photoperiods have less effect than in an animal that has its ovarian development inhibited by starvation. Perhaps the reproductive activity may have a feedback effect on the photoperiodic response.

Saunders: In *P. apterus* the laying of eggs is directly dependent on taking a meal. The advantage of these *S. argyrostoma* larvae is that they are all eating. One could criticize the present experiments because if the animals are pulled out early from their food, or if they are pupating early, like the overcrowded ones, they have had less food than the ones that go on into diapause. The weaker interpretation, perhaps, is that diapause depends on how much food they have had, but I believe it depends on the number of cycles that they have seen in culture.

Mordue: It is somewhat confusing that with exactly similar experiments one can manipulate the development of a number of insects that do not normally exhibit diapause. *Tenebrio* larvae, of a certain weight when removed from culture, will pupate very rapidly. Animals of exactly the same weight left in culture will carry on feeding and produce, subsequently, bigger pupae and adults. This is nothing at all to do with photoperiod. The phenomena of starvation, facultative and obligatory feeding and their interrelationships with the endocrine system are quite complex.

Saunders: Shaaya & Levensbrook (1982) have looked at *Calliphora vicina* and they claim to pinpoint the minimum weight of the third-instar larva as 17 mg; below this weight larvae cannot pupate, and above it they can. There is also a weight or size phenomenon in *Manduca*.

Roberts: It is known that *Sarcophaga* has to be on the food for a minimum of 3–12 h in the third instar for pupariation to occur. If this period of feeding is not allowed the larvae die.

Gilbert: Bodenstein (1943) did that with *Drosophila* 40 years ago!

Masaki: I believe you have explained the temperature effect on diapause induction and the critical photoperiod by your photoperiodic counter theory (Saunders 1971). But today you have said that the diapause-inducing effect of short days is reversed by extending the wandering period after the sensitive stage. If the animal is kept at a lower temperature, the wandering stage becomes long. So the reversing effect should also be increased, and this might compensate for the temperature effect on the critical photoperiod.

Saunders: At the end of the sensitive period, when you take the final wandering larva, or even as late as after puparium formation, if you reduce the temperature you can increase the amount of diapause, and if you increase the temperature at that stage you can decrease the amount of diapause (Gibbs

1975). This can be continued until the time at which the animal is committed to diapause, which may be just hours before pupation itself. It remains malleable right to the end, but one has passed the photoperiodic sensitive period; the animal can apparently no longer respond to long nights.

Denlinger: A whole sequence of developmental events needs to be fulfilled before diapause is reached. The diapause programme is very easily reversed by tricks such as high temperature but the insect cannot easily be shunted in the direction of diapause.

Masaki: Is there any tendency for diapause-destined larvae to prolong the wandering stage?

Saunders: Yes.

Masaki: So if you select those larvae that have a long larval stage, is there a possibility that you are selecting for a stronger tendency for diapause?

Saunders: Yes, although the data did not suggest that; there was less diapause. David Denlinger and I have had a long-running battle about the cause of this delay in puparium formation.

Denlinger: Yes. I argue that this delay is a part of the diapause system, and that these larvae are slower *because* they are going to enter diapause. David Saunders argues that it is independent.

Saunders: I consider it to be independent because I now have much evidence that when larvae are bred under absolutely non-diapausing conditions (i.e. embryos in constant light, at 25°C, and larvae at different photoperiods and also at 25°C), the length of time between larviposition and puparium formation is photoperiodically dependent. In other words, with short days (long nights) they take longer to form puparia than at long days or short nights, and the change is quite abrupt and at the critical day-length. So I see length of development as an independent photoperiodic response (Saunders 1976).

Denlinger: But since *Sarcophaga crassipalpis* has a much narrower sensitive period, it is not quite relevant for comparison with *S. argyrostoma*, of course.

Giebultowicz: There could be other explanations than the leaking out of a diapause titre for the reduced diapause seen after a very long wandering stage. This phenomenon is seen only in animals that were 'weakly' committed for diapause (in short days but high temperature). Conditions that would not ensure that the animals survived diapause, such as wet environment or loss of storage materials due to prolonged wandering, could influence the endocrine system to switch to non-diapause development.

Saunders: I am not happy with that explanation because one might find that the animals that fail to go into diapause because of a failure to find a suitable pupation site would not survive anyway because winter is coming; even if they produced progeny they would probably all die out. I can see little selective advantage in either strategy. I regard this as just a physiological phenomenon that may tell us something about the inductive process.

Denlinger: They cannot successfully pupariate and pupate in a wet environment, so continuing to wander makes a lot of sense.

Saunders: S. argyrostoma larvae *will* form puparia and pupate and emerge in the wet, and they have no diapause; diapause incidence is often reduced to below 10% in some of our wet cultures.

Roberts: As Dr Denlinger said, *Sarcophaga* spp. cannot successfully pupariate in a wet environment (Ohtaki 1966). Ohtaki concluded that the wet environment caused the prothoracic glands to stop secreting the ecdysteroids necessary for initiating and completing pupariation. In contrast, I have found from *in vitro* culture of ring glands (unpublished work) that ecdysone is indeed being produced, in fact at its highest possible level. High levels of haemolymph ecdysteroids were also recorded by radioimmunoassay, and they were oscillating strongly and were excreted. The animal appears to be trying to avoid 'drowning' and is extremely active, i.e. wandering.

Saunders: That is not strictly in agreement with the original work of Ohtaki et al (1968) though, is it?

Roberts: No. S.L. Wentworth and I have just finished some work on wet treatment of *Sarcophaga* spp. At the ecdysteroid peak for pupariation you only need a little 'blip' of ecdysteroid compared to the control. For example, larvae maintained in wet conditions required 70% less ecdysteroid for pupariation to occur.

Saunders: So what holds up pupariation?

Roberts: The ecdysteroids are being secreted. We have assayed the water for ecdysteroids and were amazed to see that ecdysteroids were secreted at a very high and constant rate over a 120h period.

Denlinger: We are convinced that the delay may be related to cyclic AMP. If a fly larva, at the time it leaves the food, is given an injection of cholera toxin (an activator of adenylate cyclase), or cyclic AMP derivatives, it will continue to wander for many weeks and will fail to pupariate. This, interestingly, occurs only in short-day (diapause-destined) flies. The long-day flies do not respond to cyclic AMP by extending their wandering period. Perhaps cyclic AMP levels are high in these short-day flies and normally drop, before being elevated again before puparium formation. But the long-day flies have a different profile; probably the cyclic AMP levels have dropped already before the animal starts wandering, so that it is no longer sensitive to a boost in cyclic AMP.

Gilbert: What would the cyclic AMP be doing?

Denlinger: We can't say for sure. Its concentrations are high in the ring glands but not in the brain (unpublished work). A fall in cyclic AMP may be important for stimulation of its release. Your own work has indicated that the cyclic AMP level in the prothoracic gland of *Manduca sexta* drops before the ecdysone level rises. That drop may be highly significant, and if it did not occur, the prothoracic glands might not be stimulated to release ecdysone.

Gilbert: Wendy Smith in my lab has demonstrated a good correlation between cyclic AMP and steroidogenesis in the prothoracic gland of *Manduca sexta* (W. Smith, L.I. Gilbert & W.E. Bollenbacher, unpublished results). One of the problems we have in comparing *Manduca* with *Sarcophaga* is that the *Manduca* brain has one of the most potent adenylate cyclases demonstrated in any animal (D. Sheridan, W. Combest and L.I. Gilbert, unpublished results). Yet you are saying that the cyclic AMP level in the brain of *Sarcophaga* doesn't seem to be very high.

Denlinger: I think that cyclic AMP in *Sarcophaga* is important in stimulating the prothoracic glands but that the stimulation involves both a rise and a fall in cyclic AMP. In certain cell cultures (e.g. Wang et al 1978) a precedent for this has been obtained: the cyclic nucleotide must be removed from the culture before the response is elicited.

Gilbert: Well, one of the tenets of endocrinology is that one must get rid of the stimulating substance very quickly; otherwise it's not an efficient modulator of cellular activity.

Joosse: I can summarize what we know about cyclic AMP and the functioning of neuroendocrine cells. Cyclic AMP plays a role in the release of peptides by exocytosis. When dibutyryl cyclic AMP is added to certain types of neuroendocrine systems, particularly the ovulation hormone system of *Lymnaea stagnalis*, this induces firing of these systems which continues as long as the dibutyryl cyclic AMP is present. It is easy to get a hormone released in this way, and what comes free is exactly the same as what is released in the normal way (E. W. Roubos & W. P. M. Geraerts, personal communication).

Sokolove: But that is exocytotic release of a peptide hormone, not necessarily steroidogenesis.

Joosse: Yes. This does not concern steroidogenesis.

Reynolds: We should remember that hormones other than ecdysteroids are needed for puparium formation in blowflies (Fraenkel 1975). Apparently, two peptides control the retraction of the anterior segments of the larva and the tanning of the larval cuticle. The precise timing of puparium formation probably depends on the secretion of these hormones, rather than on the ecdysteroid titre.

REFERENCES

Bodenstein D 1943 Hormones and tissue competence in the development of *Drosophila*. Biol Bull (Woods Hole) 84:34-58

Fraenkel G 1975 Interactions between ecdysone, bursicon, and other endocrines during puparium formation and adult emergence in flies. Am Zool (Suppl) 15:29-48

Gibbs D 1975 Reversal of pupal diapause in *Sarcophaga argyrostoma* by temperature shifts after puparium formation. J Insect Physiol 21:1179-1186

Ohtaki T 1966 On the delayed pupariation of the fleshfly *Sarcophaga peregrina*. Jpn J Med Sci Biol 19:97-104

Ohtaki T, Milkman RD, Williams CM 1968 Dynamics of ecdysone secretion and action in the fleshfly *Sarcophaga peregrina*. Biol Bull (Woods Hole) 135:322-334

Saunders DS 1966 Larval diapause of maternal origin. II: The effect of photoperiod and temperature on *Nasonia vitripennis*. J Insect Physiol 12:569-581

Saunders DS 1971 The temperature compensated photoperiodic clock 'programming' development and pupal diapause in the flesh-fly *Sarcophaga argyrostoma*. J Insect Physiol 17:801-812

Saunders DS 1976 The circadian eclosion rhythm in *Sarcophaga argyrostoma*: some comparisons with the photoperiodic clock. J Comp Physiol 110:111-133

Shaaya E, Levensbrook L 1982 The effects of starvation and 20-hydroxyecdysone on feeding and pupariation of early 3rd instar *Calliphora vicina* larvae. J Insect Physiol 28:683-688

Wang T, Sheppard JR, Foker JE 1978 Rise and fall of cyclic AMP required for onset of lymphocyte DNA synthesis. Science (Wash DC) 201:155-157

General discussion

Effect of temperature on the photoperiodic clock in *Megoura viciae*

Lees: I would like to mention some recent work which bears on the nature of the photoperiodic clock in *Megoura viciae*. At 15 °C, nights longer than the critical length of 9.5 h promote production of oviparae whereas shorter nights induce virginoparae production. At 20 °C, however, the effect of long nights is largely abolished. In a resonance experiment, using an intermediate temperature of 18 °C and a range of dark periods up to 76 h, I found that some aphids still responded by producing oviparae while others did not. Nevertheless, there was no evidence of periodic maxima or minima at circadian intervals, even though the system was finely balanced. This suggests (as previous evidence has done) that the *Megoura* clock is of the hour-glass type.

More recently, I have been looking at the effect of temperature (particularly low temperature) on the scotophase—the part of the cycle particularly concerned with time measurement. Experimental temperatures were given during the first 4 h of the scotophase in a 24 h cycle and, after returning the aphids to 15 °C, I measured the critical night-length. At −3 °C, which the aphids survive, the critical night-length was found to be 12 h; that is, during the 4 h of chilling the clock had lost 2.5 h. The delay is progressively less at higher temperatures and reaches zero at +3 to +6 °C. There is almost complete temperature compensation between 6 and 20 °C.

An interesting feature is that if the same temperatures are given during hours 4–8 of the scotophase instead of during hours 1–4, an exactly similar timing delay is produced, even though previous work (Lees 1973) has shown that light interruptions early and late in the scotophase have entirely different effects. The response to light at these low temperatures is also instructive. At −3 °C, a 4-h light exposure is not perceived at all; that is, its effect is equivalent to 4 h of darkness at this temperature. This means that the scotophase clock is still running steadily, albeit slowly. The photoreceptor system can therefore be put out of action without stopping the clock. I have always thought of the receptor as forming part of the timing mechanism, but am now beginning to wonder whether it is somewhat separate from it.

Steel: How long were the animals kept under those regimes?

Lees: For six cycles, immediately after birth.

Steel: Is that the minimum necessary to elicit these responses?

Lees: No; it is rather more than the threshold number of cycles, which is about four. In relation to this, I agree with David Saunders (this volume) that the counter mechanism is very important.

Pittendrigh: Is the temperature-dependence of the clock mechanism a wholly new result on *Megoura* or has it been seen before?

Lees: I have not done any low-temperature experiments before. In the older work (Lees 1963), constant temperatures between 10 and 25 °C were applied during the whole of the short-day cycle. I found that within the 10—20 °C range the response is virtually temperature-compensated, the critical night-length increasing by no more than 30 min per 10 °C rise in temperature. Of course, at the lower end of the temperature scale, if the test is applied to scotophase chilling only, the critical night-length must *decrease* by many hours for a 10 °C rise in temperature (say from −3 to +7 °C.).

Pittendrigh: Is the direction of the temperature-dependence similar to the temperature-dependence of critical night-length in the classical descriptions of Danilevskii (1965)?

Lees: Danilevskii (1965) and his colleagues, working mainly with constant and medium-to-high temperatures, found that the direction was usually the same but varied greatly according to the species. For example, compensation was almost perfect in *Pieris brassicae* whereas in the moth *Acronycta rumicis* the critical night-length increased by as much as 3 h per 10 °C rise in temperature between 15 and 25 °C. It seems that temperature is here affecting components other than the rate of the scotophase clock.

Long- and short-day effects on diapause induction in *Pyrrhocoris apterus*

Hodková: Some of my endocrinological work may also be of interest to those who work on photoperiodic clocks. I have studied the regulation of the corpus allatum by the brain in adult females of *Pyrrhocoris apterus*. The next link in the chain of pathways is the ovary, which is stimulated by juvenile hormone release from the corpus allatum. Under short-day photoperiods, the brain inhibits the corpus allatum from the pars intercerebralis, and juvenile hormone is not produced. Under long-day conditions, this inhibition does not exist and juvenile hormone is produced. If the nerves between the brain and the corpus allatum are cut, juvenile hormone is produced under both photoperiods. Short-day brains can be changed to long-day brains, and *vice versa*, simply by transfer of animals from one photoperiod to another (part A in Fig. 1). As several photoperiods are needed to produce this change, we can speak about the accumulation of photoperiodic information. But we cannot speak here about retention of photoperiodic information because the brain usually behaves according to the ambient photoperiod. An exception to this is illustrated if the complexes of brain and corpus allatum, originating from short-day

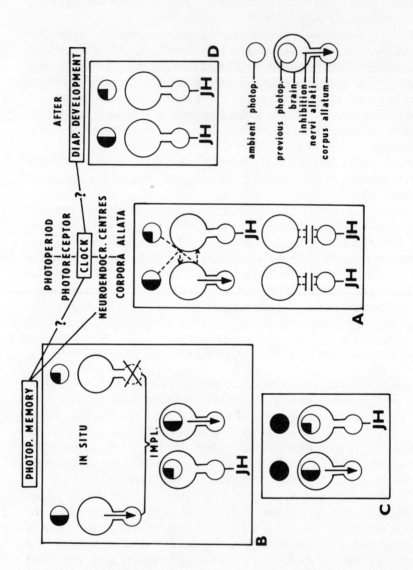

FIG. 1 (*Hodková*) Photoperiodic regulation of corpus allatum in relation to adult diapause of *Pyrrhocoris apterus*. (Modified after Hodková 1976, 1977, 1979, 1982.)

animals, are transplanted to long-day allatectomized animals (or *vice versa*). The animals always behave according to the photoperiod to which the donor was exposed (part B in Fig. 1). Unoperated animals transferred into continuous darkness behave according to the previous photoperiodic exposure (part C in Fig. 1). Thus, the photoperiodic information is retained somewhere in the brain of *P. apterus*, but we do not know how.

The phase of an overt rhythm can be transferred by transplanting the brain into a brainless animal. This has been shown, for example, in the eclosion rhythm of the silk moths *Hyalophora cecropia* and *Antheraea pernyi* (Truman 1972). The photoperiodic memory of the transplanted brain may manifest itself by the rhythm (e.g. eclosion rhythm) that may correspond in phase with the previous rhythm of the donor. In other words, if the brain from one animal, entrained by a certain photoperiod, is transplanted to the brainless host and then kept in continuous darkness, the eclosion gate should correspond to the gate that would have appeared in the donor.

Pittendrigh: So you can transplant the *phase* information, but there is no evidence from those experiments of Professor Truman that any information about the duration of the previous *photoperiod* can be transferred.

Hodková: Yes; the term 'phase memory' would be better than 'photoperiodic memory'. In the system that I am studying, the output is the inhibitory activity of the brain. Thus, an overt rhythm cannot be observed. It may be assumed that the presence or absence of inhibitory activity is controlled by phase relationships among unknown endogenous rhythms within the brain. Those phase relationships may be entrained by photoperiod and maintained even if the photoperiodic entrainment does not continue (in the host's body, Fig. 1B, or in continuous darkness, Fig. 1C). The retention of the photoperiodic information might be due to a clock activity. Alternatively, the retention may be controlled by the accumulation of an unknown factor such as 'diapause titre', about which Dr Saunders was speaking in connection with pupal diapause of *Sarcophaga argyrostoma* (Saunders & Bradley, this volume). To explain the retention of both short-day and long-day information in *P. apterus* it must be supposed that, in the brain that was excised and transferred to the host's body (part B, Fig. 1) or left *in situ* and transferred to continuous darkness (part C, Fig. 1), this factor is neither synthesized nor broken down.

The aphid *Megoura viciae*, transferred from a short-day to a long-day photoperiod, could not switch from oviparae production to virginoparae production if the clocks (areas of neuropile lateral to the medial neurosecretory cell groups) were removed (Steel & Lees 1977). So in that case, at least, the information about short days had to be retained without any relationship to the photoperiodic clock. I wonder whether, in *P. apterus*, both short-day and long-day responses could be maintained without any relationship to the clock system.

Another problem is the loss of photoperiodic response after completion of diapause development, by which I mean the process that is different from photoperiodic activation. If diapause is terminated by the transfer of the insect from short days to long days, the insect always remains responsive to photoperiod, and diapause can be reinduced by short days. So this insect belongs to part A of the scheme in Fig. 1. But if diapause is terminated by other means, for example by long exposure of the insect to low temperatures, the photoperiodic response is irreversibly lost and there is no inhibition of the corpus allatum under short days or long days (part D, Fig. 1). We don't know what is happening during diapause development but perhaps there is some change within the clock system. Perhaps study of the circadian clock in these two systems, i.e. before and after diapause development (parts A and D, Fig. 1), could clear up both the process of diapause development and the involvement of circadian components in diapause induction.

Saunders: Have you any evidence that diapause induction has a circadian basis in *P. apterus*?

Hodková: No, because I have not yet done experiments on the clock systems.

Saunders: I have tried some resonance experiments, and there doesn't seem to be much evidence for circadian rhythmicity in the photoperiodic response. My preliminary data also seem to suggest that *P. apterus* measures day-length, and not night-length.

Hodková: It should be possible to find a circadian activity (e.g. respiratory rhythm) that might depend on photoperiod.

Saunders: Yes; I tried recording oviposition rhythms but they were not at all clearly defined.

Masaki: If you expose this insect to long days, diapause is terminated. But, if you return the animals to short-day exposure, can diapause again be induced?

Hodková: Yes. If diapause is terminated by long days, i.e. by photoperiodic activation, the animals enter diapause again under short days. But if diapause is terminated e.g. by long cold exposure, i.e. by completion of diapause development, diapause is not reinduced by short-day exposure (Hodek 1983). The loss of the response to short days was always checked by the maintenance of oviposition at 25 °C.

Sokolove: Does that imply a reversible photoperiodic phenomenon?

Saunders: Yes; one can switch it backwards and forwards.

Mordue: If this insect lives only for a year, once it has had an exposure to cold it may treat that as a winter phase and behave as though its allotted span of time is over.

Hodková: From the ecological point of view one could say that this is a favourable adaptive mechanism because *P. apterus* can begin reproduction early in spring while the photoperiod is still short. In nature, *P. apterus* enters a long dormancy of at least seven months and lives, thus, slightly less than one year. If one breeds the insect in the laboratory at long days and 25 °C it starts oviposition early (7–10 days) after the beginning of the adult stage, which lasts for only 50–60 days, in addition to the larval stage of about one month.

Saunders: P. apterus is an interesting animal for many other reasons apart from having a diapause that one can re-induce several times by switching it from long days to short days. In my hands the critical day-length for diapause induction and the critical day-length for diapause termination are over one hour apart. This is the only animal I know of for which the critical day-lengths for induction and for termination are different (Saunders 1983).

Mordue: Are these *P. apterus* adults different from larvae of corn borers because they are not in the business of counting the number of either long or short days? Do they need to be exposed to only a small number of short days before an effect is elicited?

Hodková: In adult females transferred from long days, seven short days are sufficient for diapause induction in starved females, and about two weeks in fed females.

Mordue: In larval systems such as in blowflies and corn borers, very many short days have to be counted before the system responds, and the information has to be stored in some way. The *P. apterus* adults probably do not have the same sort of storage problem.

Pittendrigh: You are suggesting that the clock system can give a signal to induce diapause only if the animal has been in long days and then goes into short days. There are plenty of plants in which, similarly, the transition from long to short or from short to long days is necessary to get the signal.

Hodková: P. apterus needs no transition from long to short days to enter diapause; it spontaneously enters diapause if raised at short days from the egg or larval stage.

Lees: After diapause termination by low temperature in winter, could the insect be in an analogous condition to aphids in which there is some sort of inhibitor which prevents them from responding to short days? Nobody knows what this delaying factor is. In some aphids it can persist into late summer.

Hodková: My suggestion was that this may be something related to a biological clock system. A timer may be involved in the loss of photoperiodic response, as a long passage of time seems to be crucial for the loss of photoperiodic response. Low temperatures (5–10 °C, or even 15 °C) are important for the maintenance of the insect's vigour during diapause development rather than for the completion of diapause development itself (Hodek 1983). But the photoperiodic response is lost irreversibly in *P. apterus*. There may be more analogy between aphids and another Heteropteran, *Aelia acuminata*, where the photoperiodic response can disappear and reappear several times during life of an individual (Hodek 1983).

REFERENCES

Danilevskii AS 1965 Photoperiodism and seasonal development of insects. Oliver & Boyd, Edinburgh

Hodek I 1983 Role of environmental factors and endogenous mechanisms in the seasonality of reproduction in insects diapausing as adults. In: Brown VK, Hodek I (eds) Diapause and life cycle strategies in insects. Junk Publishers, The Hague (III Int Congr Entomol, Kyoto, Japan, 1980) p 9-33

Hodková M 1976 Nervous inhibition of corpora allata by photoperiod in *Pyrrhocoris apterus*. Nature (Lond) 263:521-523

Hodková M 1977 Function of the neuroendocrine complex in diapausing *Pyrrhocoris apterus* females. J Insect Physiol 23:23-28

Hodková M 1979 Hormonal and nervous inhibition of reproduction by brain in diapausing females of *Pyrrhocoris apterus* L. (Hemiptera). Zool Jahrb Abt Allg Zool Physiol Tiere 83:126-136

Hodková M 1982 Interaction of feeding and photoperiod in regulation of the corpus allatum activity in females of *Pyrrhocoris apterus* L. (Hemiptera). Zool Jahrb Abt Allg Zool Physiol Tiere 86:477-488

Lees AD 1963 The role of photoperiod and temperature in the determination of parthenogenetic and sexual forms in the aphid *Megoura viciae* Buckton III. Further properties of the maternal switching mechanism in apterous aphids. J Insect Physiol 9:153-164

Lees AD 1973 Photoperiodic time measurement in the aphid *Megoura viciae*. J Insect Physiol 19:2279-2316

Saunders DS 1983 A diapause induction-termination asymmetry in the photoperiodic responses of the linden bug, *Pyrrhocoris apterus*, and an effect of near-critical photoperiods on development. J Insect Physiol 29:399-405

Steel CGH, Lees AD 1977 The role of neurosecretion in the photoperiodic control of polymorphism in the aphid *Megoura viciae*. J Exp Biol 67:117-135

Truman JW 1972 Circadian rhythms and physiology with special reference to neuroendocrine processes in insects. In: Circadian rhythmicity. Pudoc, Wageningen (Proc Int Symp Circadian Rhythmicity, Wageningen, 1971) p 111-135

Genetic analysis of geographical variation in photoperiodic diapause and pupal eclosion rhythm in *Drosophila littoralis*

PEKKA LANKINEN and JAAKKO LUMME

Department of Genetics, University of Oulu, Linnanmaa, SF-90570 Oulu 57, Finland

Abstract. The effects of photoperiod on reproductive diapause and the pupal eclosion rhythm were studied in several strains of *Drosophila littoralis* originating between latitudes 42 °N and 69 °N in Europe and Caucasus, USSR. The critical day-length for diapause varies latitudinally from 12 to 20 h ($r = 0.953$; $n = 33$). The timing of eclosion in diel light : dark cycles was studied, and maximal variation was found at LD 3 : 21 (3 h light : 21 h dark). The variation of eclosion medians (from 'lights off') was from 12 to 21 h, and was latitude-dependent ($r = -0.778$; $n = 53$). The period and phase of the free-running pupal eclosion rhythm were determined in 15 stocks. The inter-strain variation in period length ranged from 18.6 to 23.9 h, and was also correlated with latitude ($r = -0.681$; $n = 15$), but it was better correlated with critical day-length ($r = -0.727$; $n = 13$) and with time of eclosion at LD 3 : 21 ($r = 0.721$; $n = 13$). The variation in the phase of free-running rhythm of pupal eclosion was weakly latitude-dependent ($r = -0.484$; $n = 15$). Analysis of partial correlations revealed genetic linkage and perhaps a functional relationship between critical day-length and period length. Functional correlation was obvious between the timing of eclosion in the light : dark cycle and both the phase and the period of the free-running rhythm. Phase and period are not genetically linked. These results were confirmed by selecting against diapause in a hybrid stock: the pupal eclosion rhythm also changed.

1984 Photoperiodic regulation of insect and molluscan hormones. Pitman, London (Ciba Foundation symposium 104), p 97–114

When Bünning, half a century ago (1936), suggested that an endogenous circadian clock is involved in day-length measurement, he challenged generations of experimental biologists. So far, it has been demonstrated in several cases (but not in all) that photoperiodic time-measurement is based on a circadian system (e.g. Fig. 21 in Pittendrigh 1981). But Bünning explicitly proposed that the clock expressing itself in leaf movements, or in pupal eclosion rhythms, is the common pacemaker that hides behind photoperiod-

ism (the master clock hypothesis). This proposal has been tested by studying
different overt rhythms and the photoperiodic reaction in the same organisms
(Pittendrigh & Minis 1971, Truman 1971, Saunders 1981). The experiments
needed are often tedious. When several pacemakers drive different overt
rhythms in the same organism, components and complexes having different
period lengths can drift apart in some circumstances (as in free-running
humans; see Aschoff & Wever 1981) or can express themselves in different
developmental stages (eclosion rhythm and adult activity rhythm in *Drosophila pseudoobscura*; Engelmann & Mack 1978). The present study is an
extension of this idea. Instead of 'individuals', we are studying a whole widely
distributed species. We assume that if there is any genetic variation in the
separate time-measuring functions, then genetically separable components of
the system can perhaps 'drift apart' in the great evolutionary theatre.

As an afterthought, we are justifying the choice of subject (made irreversibly in 1976) as follows. The pupal eclosion rhythms of *D. pseudoobscura*
(e.g. Pittendrigh 1981) and *Drosophila melanogaster* (Smith & Konopka
1981) are among the best studied circadian rhythms. Unfortunately, these two
genetically well known species do not have photoperiodic responses. *Drosophila littoralis* was known to have a clearly definable photoperiodic
diapause, with a wide geographical variation in critical day-length (Lumme &
Oikarinen 1977). In the study of photoperiodism we appreciate the photoperiodic response so much that we decided to start a study on possible genetic
variation in the eclosion rhythm of *D. littoralis*, even if the first trials by the
'falling fly' device (Fig. 44 in Engelmann & Klemke 1983) had been a
catastrophe. To make *D. littoralis* competitive with its genetically better
known relatives, we recently started isolating mutants and constructing a gene
map in the merry 'Fly Room' spirit of T. H. Morgan. We now have about 25
localized genetic markers scattered over all chromosomes, and several
inversions to be used in future rhythm work. Konopka (1981) has made clear
the power of a genetic approach. However, the results presented here arise
from the 'pre-Morganian' period.

Genetic variation is a prerequisite for studying something genetically. Our
starting point was the latitudinal cline in critical day-length for the photoperiodic reproductive diapause. Here we shall present parallel latitudinal
clines in parameters that describe the pupal eclosion rhythm. The question is
whether the parallel clines are functionally or genetically related, or are
independent adaptations without a common physiological basis. We have
been trying to distinguish between these alternatives by two genetic methods.
First, we search for phenotypic correlations between the critical day-length
and the eclosion rhythm among diverse fly stocks. Secondly, two different
strains are crossed, and parallel and non-parallel changes are followed in
successive generations.

Materials and determination of the parameters of eclosion rhythm

The flies

The material consists of 53 stocks of *D. littoralis*, which originate from the following main areas: Finland (61.1–69.1 °N), 22 separate strains; Sweden (59.4 °N), eight strains from one population; Moscow, USSR (54.4 °N), two strains; Central Europe (Switzerland, Rumania, Yugoslavia, 43.9–47.3 °N), nine strains; and Caucasus, USSR (41.6–44.7 °N), 12 strains. Most of the fly stocks were founded by single females, and some of them have been full-sib inbred for 5–15 generations. Since capture (1967–1981) or arrival in our laboratory the strains have been kept in a windowless room in continuous light (LL) at 19 °C to prevent any selection from acting on diapause characteristics. For the present purpose, any random genetic drift can have only desirable consequences.

Determination of the photoperiodic reaction

In our routine, flies are raised in LL at 19 °C, and the emerged adults are collected every day and transferred to the light : dark cycles (fluorescent tubes, 16 ± 2 °C). Females are dissected at the age of three weeks, and those having small undeveloped ovaries are scored as being in diapause. *Critical day-length* is the estimated day-length where half the females are in diapause.

Monitoring the pupal eclosion rhythm, and defining its parameters

The emergence of adults is recorded by an automatic registration apparatus based on the 'falling ball'-principle (Lankinen & Lumme 1982; Fig. 45 in Engelmann & Klemke 1983). The larvae are raised in LL at 19 °C. Cohorts of about ten days of larvae are allowed to pupariate, and when the first flies emerge, the pupae are washed out from the plastic jar and loaded into the eclosionometer. This is then placed either in light : dark cycles or in a continuously dark (DD) box at the same temperature, 19 °C. Three parameters of the eclosion rhythm are used here. *The eclosion time in entraining light : dark cycles* (ψ_{LD}) is calculated as the median timing (from the 'lights off') of the eclosions summed hourly over the fourth and later days. On average, each ψ_{LD} is based on 2.2 independent repeats, 13.5 days of registration, and 690 emergences. *The free-running rhythm of eclosion* is initiated by transfer from LL to DD. *The period length of the free-running rhythm* (τ) is calculated from the timing of the third and later eclosion peaks (the first two days may show 'transients'; see Fig. 3, later). *The phase of eclosion in the free-running rhythm (ψ_{EL}) is* the estimated hour of the median of the 'first-day peak' from 'lights off', calculated back from the third and later days. Each estimate is based on an average of 11 independent repeats and 5000 emergences, and the free-running rhythms presented later (Figs. 3 and 6) are normalized distributions of direct hourly summations of the repeats. If ambient temperature regulation failed, the affected repeats were excluded from the results.

Geographical variation

Photoperiodic response

Six examples of photoperiodic curves are presented in Fig. 1. Of the 33 strains studied, 32 have a strong short-day diapause response. In the strain *Ticino 4*, the photoperiodic response is almost totally depressed (Fig. 1). A slight depression was also found in some strains from Caucasus, the maximum percentage of females in diapause being 60–95%. The latitudinal cline in critical day-length is depicted later in Fig. 4. The change of 1.3 h per 5° latitude is well in accordance with 'Danilevskii's rule' for long-day insects. Of the total variation found in critical day-length, 91% can be accounted for by latitude and the remaining 9% is 'local' plus error variation, values close to those published earlier for a smaller number of stocks (Lumme & Oikarinen 1977).

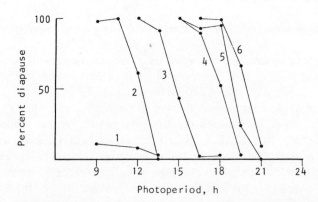

FIG. 1. The geographical variation of adult diapause in *Drosophila littoralis*. The diapause percentages are the proportions of females with undeveloped ovaries at the age of three weeks after eclosion at 16 °C. The strains originate from the following localities: 1, *Ticino 4* (46.2 °N); 2, *Batumi 1* (41.6 °N); 3, *Zürich* (47.3 °N); 4, *Paltamo 1* (64.3 °N); 5, *Inari 2* (68.8 °N); and 6, *Oulu 1* (65.0 °N).

Eclosion rhythm in entraining light : dark cycles

In Fig. 2 the mediams of eclosion distributions of four stocks are displayed as a function of day-length. The examples contain both extremes (earliest and latest), and two intermediate stocks. The inter-strain differences are obvious in all photoperiods. The width of the eclosion peaks is not visible (see Fig. 5, later, for examples of that), but they are at their narrowest when the median is just after 'lights on'.

The inter-strain differences are maximal in very short day-lengths, where eclosion is also closest to being normally distributed. Therefore, the diel eclosion rhythm was studied in all 53 strains at LD 3 : 21, and the medians of the peaks are presented below in Fig. 4 as a function of the latitude of origin. In this cline, 61% of the total variation is 'latitudinal' and 39% 'local' plus error.

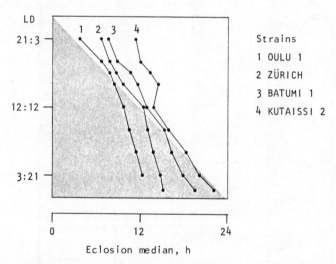

FIG. 2. The phase of eclosion medians as a function of photoperiod in four strains at 19 °C. Shaded area shows the period of dark. LD, light : dark cycle.

Parameters of the free-running eclosion rhythm

The normalized free-running eclosion rhythms of five stocks are presented in Fig. 3; (one further stock is shown later in Fig. 6). Genetic variation can be seen in the period length (τ) and also in the phase of emergence peaks (ψ_{EL}) of the rhythm. These parameters have been determined for 15 strains so far, and the geographical variation of τ is illustrated in Fig. 4. The proportion of latitudinal variation is 46%, the residual 54%. There is also genetic variation

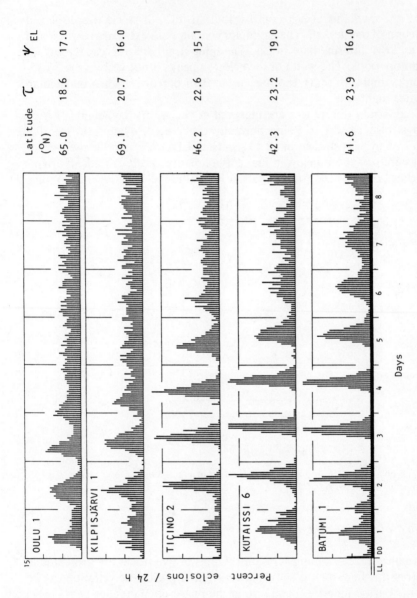

FIG. 3. The free-running rhythm of pupal eclosion. The distributions of eclosions are presented as normalized percentages over gliding intervals of 24 h. Temperature 19°C, rhythm initiated by LL/DD transfer. Latitude, period (τ) and phase (ψ_{EL}) of the free-running rhythm are tabulated.

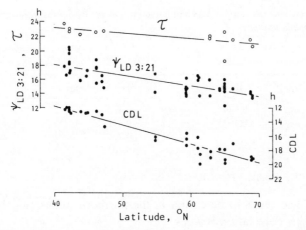

FIG. 4. The latitudinal clines of critical day-length (CDL, $y = 0.27x + 1.12$; $r = 0.953$; $n = 33$); median of eclosion at LD 3:21 ($\psi_{LD3:21}$, $y = -0.16x + 24.45$; $r = -0.778$; $n = 53$); and period of the free-running eclosion rhythm (τ, $y = -0.08x + 26.28$; $r = -0.681$; $n = 15$).

in the phase of emergence, but ψ_{EL} is the least latitude-dependent of the parameters studied. Of the variation in ψ_{EL}, 23% is explained by latitude, and the correlation is not significant ($n = 15$, $P < 0.1$). In the examples in Fig. 3 it is also apparent that the damping of the rhythm is a genetically governed variable, but this has not been analysed. Among the 15 stocks studied, there are also examples where rhythms that have a long τ are found to dampen rapidly; thus, the impression of a cline arising from Fig. 3 is somewhat misleading.

Phenotypic correlations between parameters of the time-measuring system

All four parameters measured, critical day-length, τ, ψ_{EL}, and $\psi_{LD3:21}$ show genetic variation among the strains studied. Three of them have a significant latitudinal cline. In Table 1 we present the pairwise correlations between all the parameters and latitude. These correlations are calculated on the basis of the 13 stocks of *D. littoralis* from which all the variables were determined. Table 1 also contains partial correlations between the variables of the time-measuring system after removal of the clinal latitudinal variation. The signs of the correlations indicate only the arbitrarily chosen directions of the variables. Towards the north, τ shortens, critical day-length lengthens (but the complement, critical night-length, shortens), and the eclosion peak in the light:dark cycle occurs earlier, i.e. $\psi_{LD3:21}$ shortens. The phase of eclosion in

TABLE 1 Correlations between latitude and parameters of the time-measuring system among 13 stocks of *Drosophila littoralis*

Variable	Primary correlations				Partial correlations, with the latitudinal variation removed		
	CDL	$\psi_{LD\,3:21}$	τ	ψ_{EL}	$\psi_{LD\,3:21}$	τ	ψ_{EL}
Latitude	0.961***	−0.749**	−0.649*	−0.412			
CDL		−0.764**	−0.727**	−0.391	−0.245	−0.492†	0.020
$\psi_{LD\,3:21}$			0.721**	0.701**		0.467	0.650*
τ				0.102			−0.238

*** $P < 0.001$; ** $P < 0.01$; * $P < 0.05$; † $P < 0.1$.

the free run also tends to be earlier in the northern stocks (ψ_{EL} has smaller values) but this correlation is weak.

All the correlations between latitude-dependent variables are significant, but this is only due to the parallel clines mentioned above. The part of Table 1 that contains the partial correlations between variables that have been 'purified' from the latitudinal variation is more interesting. The critical day-length is still correlated with the period length, τ, of the free-running rhythm (in the original values, τ was better correlated with critical day-length than with latitude.) This persistent correlation indicates that between these variables there is a deeper connection than only a parallel cline: it could be either a functional relationship or a genetic linkage disequilibrium. The correlation is not very strong, but τ explains 24% of the residual variation in critical day-length.

The other case worth mentioning is the correlation between the two separate measures of the phase of eclosion, ψ_{EL} and $\psi_{LD\,3:21}$. Of the latter (which is the reasonable choice as the dependent variable) 42% is explained by the variation in the former. Because the correlation between phase in the light : dark cycle and τ also deviates from zero, a three-variable regression between $\psi_{LD\,3:21}$ (dependent) versus τ and ψ_{EL} was calculated, and it explains 79% of the variation in $\psi_{LD\,3:21}$, i.e. 23% more than latitude in the 13 strains. The equation for this relationship is $\psi_{LD\,3:21} = 0.845\tau + 0.453\psi_{EL} - 0.001$ (all variables were 'purified' from the latitudinal variation). In this case, it seems reasonable to suggest that this correlation is functional, and not based on linkage disequilibrium.

Crossing analysis of the time-measuring system

All the parameters treated in this study are difficult to measure accurately; they all show standard deviations that are large in comparison with the

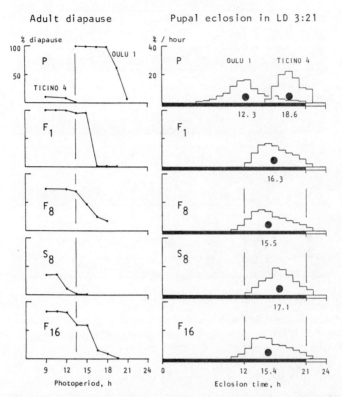

FIG. 5. Photoperiodic reaction curves (left) and pupal eclosion rhythm in LD 3:21 (right) in stocks *Oulu 1* and *Ticino 4*, in their F1 hybrid between *Ticino 4* females and *Oulu 1* males in control lines cultured in LL at 19 °C (F8 and F16), and in the Selection line started from F8 and cultured in LD 9:15 at 16°C for eight generations (S8). The medians of eclosion time of the entrained rhythm are indicated by a solid circle.

differences between means of different strains. Therefore, resolution in crossing experiments is a problem. We chose the stocks *Oulu 1* and *Ticino 4* for a crossing experiment because of the marked differences between them in the means of most parameters under study. The critical day-length of *Oulu 1* is 19.9 ± 0.8h; in *Ticino 4* there is no diapause. The difference in $\psi_{\mathrm{LD}\,3:21}$ is 6.3h (Fig. 5). The period of the free-running rhythm differs by 4.1h and the phase (ψ_{EL}) by 1.6h (Fig. 6). ψ_{EL} of *Oulu 1* is difficult to determine, and may be subject to interpretation. These stocks were crossed, and the next generations until F8 were raised in LL at 19 °C. This allows considerable recombination between presumed genetic loci that control separate aspects. The presumed location for the gene controlling critical day-length is the fourth chromosome (Lumme 1981). The fourth chromosome was checked to

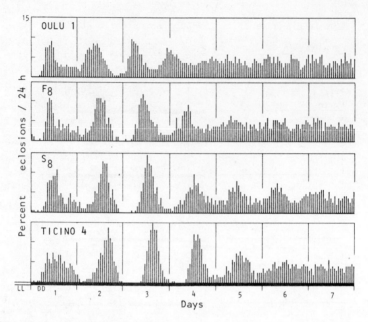

FIG. 6. The free-running rhythm of pupal eclosion in stocks Ticino 4 and Oulu 1, in their F8 hybrid generation and in *Selection* line after eight generations in LD 9:15 at 16 °C (S8). Other properties of this experimental material are presented in Fig. 5.

be *Standard* in both stocks. The stocks differed in whether or not they had a long inversion in the third chromosome, which is fused with the fourth in *D. littoralis*.

In the F8 generation the diapause and eclosion rhythm were found to be still segregating (Figs. 5 & 6). No selection or drift in any of the traits had happened. The hybrid population was then divided into selected line ($S_0 = F8$) and control line. The selected line was raised in LD 9:15 at 16 °C, which is intended to cause a rapid change in the photoperiodic response curve (Lumme & Pohjola 1980). The control line was continued in LL at 19 °C.

After eight generations the lines were studied again. No marked changes were detected in the control line (F16 in Fig. 5). In the selected line, the photoperiodic response curve was approaching that of *Ticino 4*, as intended. The phase of eclosion at LD 3:21 had changed by 1.6 h, but it was still 1.5 h earlier than in *Ticino 4*. However, this is a marked correlated response to the selection, when compared with the control. Similar changes can be seen in the parameters of the free-running rhythm, too. An accurate determination of τ and ψ_{EL} is impossible from the rhythm in F8, a consequence of genetic variation between individuals in a population rhythm (Fig. 6). This variation appears most conspicuously in the low amplitude of the rhythm. After selection, the amplitude is high again, which indicates that variation between individuals has diminished. The period length of the selected population is the same as in *Ticino 4*. The phase ψ_{EL} is 2.0 h earlier than in *Ticino 4*. It is worth mentioning that *Ticino 4* is a derivative of few individuals of a basic strain; and in another line (*Ticino 2* in Fig. 3), ψ_{EL} is 15.1, i.e. 3.5 h earlier than in *Ticino 4* (the τ values are identical).

Discussion

Stabilizing natural selection, which adjusts the end of the reproductive period in each local population along a latitudinal gradient of day-length and climate, has been discussed earlier (Lumme 1978). The resulting strict cline in critical day-lengths of the populations is, however, the only measure of the power of this selection in *D. littoralis*. The adaptive significance of the proper timing of eclosion early in the morning is apparently based on optimal humidity conditions and perhaps on minimal predation, as discussed in many papers on eclosion rhythms. The results presented here demonstrate that the populations of *D. littoralis* really are differentiated latitudinally, in effect so that flies of each local population tend to emerge at dawn in day-lengths that prevail in the season of eclosions. In day-lengths slightly longer than optimal, 'lights on' causes an instant eclosion, which could easily be explained as an adaptation to the constantly changing day-length. If we take the strictness of the cline in $\psi_{LD\,3:21}$ as a measure of the selection pressure (and response) we may conclude that the selection that adjusts eclosion is less stringent than the selection against badly timed reproduction.

The critical day-length for photoperiodic diapause and for the timing of eclosion in diel alternation of light and darkness are the final phenotypic variables exposed to selection. In the wild, flies hardly ever free-run. The properties of the free-running eclosion rhythm of *D. littoralis* do not tempt one to regard them as independently adaptive. However, there is a latitudinal cline in τ, even if the correlation of τ with latitude is slightly weaker than its correlations with critical day-length and $\psi_{LD\,3:21}$. We may conclude that τ is indirectly under natural selection, through its contributions to the final phenotypes. It should be mentioned that we have studied only two ecologically relevant time-measuring systems; undoubtedly there are others! Technical difficulties have prevented monitoring of adult activity rhythm and oviposition rhythm, which are the most obvious subjects for future study.

A genetically separable, non-linked factor participates in the genetic variation of the timing of eclosion, together with the factor that controls τ. It expresses itself as the phase of eclosion in free-running rhythm (ψ_{EL}). Because our experiments are not designed to solve the formal properties of the rhythm, we will not develop further the tempting analogy with the A and B oscillators of Pittendrigh (1981), but this certainly deserves experimental attention in the future.

The connection between τ and critical day-length may well be physiological, too. But in addition to the variable mechanism controlling τ, there must be another, genetically separable factor responsible for the final phenotype. Earlier studies of the cline in critical day-length have revealed that the major proportion of the variation is controlled by a gene locus called *Cdl* in the fourth chromosome (Lumme 1981). The most cautious hypothesis derived from the phenotypic correlations and the crossing and selection experiments presented here is that the factor which controls τ is genetically linked with *Cdl*, without any functional connection. The main evidence is that the eclosion rhythm changed readily when the diapause phenotype was selected. Also, the distribution of τ and critical day-length among our stocks indicates linkage, even if we assume that two genetically separated but physiologically cooperating factors control them.

Acknowledgements

We owe a debt to Wolfgang Engelmann for encouraging us in the germination period of this study.

REFERENCES

Aschoff J, Wever R 1981 The circadian system of man. In: Aschoff J (ed) Handbook of behavioral neurobiology, vol 4: biological rhythms. Plenum Press, New York, p 311-331

Bünning E 1936 Die endogene Tagesrhythmik als Grundlage der photoperiodischen Reaktion. Ber Dtsch Bot Ges 54:590-607

Engelmann W, Klemke W 1983 Biorhythmen. Quelle und Mayer, Heidelberg

Engelmann W, Mack J 1978 Different oscillators control the circadian rhythm of eclosion and activity in *Drosophila*. J Comp Physiol 127:229-237

Konopka RJ 1981 Genetics and development of circadian rhythms in invertebrates. In: Aschoff J (ed) Handbook of behavioral neurobiology, vol 4: biological rhythms. Plenum Press, New York, p 173-181

Lankinen P, Lumme J 1982 An improved apparatus for recording the eclosion rhythm in *Drosophila*. Drosophila Inf Serv 58:161-162

Lumme J 1978 Phenology and photoperiodic diapause in northern populations of *Drosphila*. In: Dingle H (ed) Evolution of insect migration and diapause. Springer, New York, p 145-170

Lumme J 1981 Localization of the genetic unit controlling the photoperiodic adult diapause in *Drosophila littoralis*. Hereditas 94:241-244

Lumme J, Oikarinen A 1977 The genetic basis of the geographically variable photoperiodic diapause in *Drosophila littoralis*. Hereditas 86:129-142

Lumme J, Pohjola L 1980 Selection against photoperiodic diapause started from monohybrid crosses in *Drosophila littoralis*. Hereditas 92:377-378

Pittendrigh CS 1981 Circadian organization and the photoperiodic phenonema. In: Follet BK, Follet DE (eds) Biological clocks in seasonal reproductive cycles. Wright, Bristol, p 1-35

Pittendrigh CS, Minis DH 1971 The photoperiodic time measurement in *Pectinophora gossypiella* and its relation to the circadian system in that species. In: Menaker M (ed) Biochronometry. National Academy of Sciences, Washington DC, p 212-250

Saunders DS 1981 Insect photoperiodism: entrainment within the circadian system as a basis for time measurement. In: Follet BK, Follet DE (eds) Biological clocks in seasonal reproductive cycles. Wright, Bristol, p 67-81

Smith RF, Konopka RJ 1981 Circadian clock phenotypes of chromosome aberrations with a breakpoint at the *per* locus. Mol Gen Genet 183:243-251

Truman JW 1971 The role of the brain in the ecdysis rhythm of silkmoths: comparison with the photoperiodic termination of diapause. In: Menaker M (ed) Biochronometry. National Academy of Sciences, Washington DC, p 483-504

DISCUSSION

Pittendrigh: Drosophila littoralis seems to differ considerably from other *Drosophila* species that I have come across, in that it shows this damping effect in constant darkness. We have seen no trace of this phenomenon in many other species of *Drosophila*, including some species from the Arctic circle.

Lankinen: We have also tested other species of *Drosophila* ourselves and have observed that they can free-run well, without damping, in constant darkness in our laboratory conditions. So our results on *D. littoralis* are not artificially produced as a result of our experimental methodology. In addition, a very northern species, *Drosophila subarctica*, is behaving just like the northern strains of *D. littoralis*. We also have another species, *Drosophila phalerata*, that has a wide geographical distribution and a photoperiodic diapause. It has the same kind of geographical variation in pupal eclosion rhythm as *D. littoralis* has; its northern populations have an earlier phase and a lower amplitude than the southern ones.

Brady: What is the adaptive or ecological significance of the correlation between the τ value and latitude?

Lankinen: The τ value of pupal eclosion rhythm is certainly not selected directly; the flies are not free-running in nature. But perhaps τ is expressing itself through other manifestations of rhythm, which may be under latitudinal selection.

Brady: Are there other examples of this type of geographical variation in τ?

Pittendrigh: Dr T. Takamura and I are currently trying, like Dr Lankinen, to clarify how—if at all—the circadian system effects the photoperiodic time-measurement in *Drosophila*. Like Dr Lankinen, we are exploiting the natural genetic variations in the system provided by a series of latitudinal races with different critical day-lengths. Our species is *D. auraria* from the Japanese island chain: as in *D. littoralis* (and other insects) the further north the species, the longer the critical day-length. There are both marked similarities and differences in our two sets of findings. The principal difference is that in all the *D. littoralis* races the circadian rhythm of eclosion rapidly damps out in darkness; this does not happen in *D. auraria* or any other *Drosophila* species so far studied. Dr Lankinen probably has a major new finding here: all his races came from much higher latitudes than ours. This novel feature of rapid damping in darkness may yet be typical of the high latitudes where daylight is *nearly* continuous in the breeding season. It will be interesting to find out how these far-northern strains behave in continuous dim illumination—perhaps they will not damp under such (more nearly natural) conditions. Among other differences between *D. littoralis* and *D. auraria* are geographical trends in the *apparent* period of the circadian rhythm. But I think it unwise to stress or to look for special meanings here. It is unreasonable to use the transients of a damping rhythm (in *D. littoralis*) as a measure of the pacemaker's period; the values we have for *D. auraria* are from a truly persisting rhythm, and are not really comparable. On the other hand, the data from both laboratories currently favour an external coincidence model for the time-measurement. So much remains to be done it is premature to consider too much detail at the moment.

Masaki: The damping of the rhythm in the northern strain reminds me of the hour-glass response to a resonance experiment on the subarctic carabid beetle (Thiele 1977a,b). In contrast, the central European carabid beetles show a circadian oscillation in their photoperiodic responses. There may be similar geographical tendencies among different species in the maintenance or damping rate of circadian rhythmicity.

Saunders: In Pflüger & Neumann's work (1971) on eclosion in *Clunis marinus*, the northerly strain (Tromsö) produced peaks of eclosion, and then damped, whereas the Normandy populations free-ran.

Pittendrigh: Have you done any resonance experiments with *D. littoralis*, Dr Lankinen?

Lankinen: Not yet, but we have very straightforward expectations about the results of such experiments, because we have these different τ values in pupal eclosion rhythm. We expect to be able to measure correlated periods for maximal diapause induction, too.

Pittendrigh: But if they damp out you may not get a resonance effect at all.

Lankinen: Yes, that may prove to be a problem, of course.

Veerman: We did some resonance experiments with a Russian strain of some spider mites from Leningrad (60°N), and they didn't damp out. We found sharp peaks and troughs, as in the Dutch strain (52°N), but τ was about 1 h shorter in this more northern population (unpublished results).

Masaki: If the period of the free-running rhythm is not the period of the pacemaker, Professor Pittendrigh, why can we call that pacemaker the master clock?

Pittendrigh: We do *not* think of the rhythm as the pacemaker. The rhythm (of eclosion events) is directly observed and therefore has a directly observed period (τ_R). To measure the period (τ_P) of the pacemaker driving the rhythm we have to make an elaborate set of measurements: we must measure the interval between successive phase-response curves (Fig. 17 in Pittendrigh 1981). This example is, incidentally, the only case (*Drosophila*) where a circadian pacemaker's period (as distinct from the rhythm it drives) has been measured. In *Drosophila* (and very probably elsewhere) the directly observed rhythm reflects the behaviour of a slave oscillator driven by the pacemaker (Pittendrigh 1981). Pacemaker and slave eventually assume a determinate phase-relation in darkness, so the period of the rhythm then does reflect the period of the pacemaker. But that phase-relation is changed (to a greater or lesser extent) by *any* entraining light:dark cycle. The result is that when the system enters darkness the period of the rhythm does *not*, initially, reflect that of the pacemaker: it reflects transients of the slave oscillator (advancing or delaying) as it regains its steady-state phase relation to the pacemaker. The few cycles of the *D. littoralis* rhythm that we see in darkness are almost surely transients and are not a reliable measure of the pacemaker's period.

Lankinen: This is true. That is why we studied free-running rhythm after transfer from constant light to constant darkness. In some cases it was still difficult to determine τ exactly because of the short duration of the steady-state rhythm.

Pittendrigh: It is possible, however, to measure the period of the pacemaker in other ways.

Association between wing shape and reception of light

Lankinen: We actually have some recent evidence that wings are receptors of light! We have measured the percentage of diapause at different day-lengths in a strain of *Drosophila littoralis* from Oulu for which critical day-length is very long. If wings or part of the wings or halteres are excised, the critical day-length appears to change, becoming 1.3 h shorter. It is not necessarily the damaging of the wing that is relevant to this effect because a similar shortening of critical day-length occurs in a mutant strain which was isolated from that strain, and has curled wings instead of normal straight wings (see Fig. 1).

Pittendrigh: I believe that someone in Morgan's lab long ago showed that the phototactic responses of *vestigial* (virtually no wings) mutants of *Drosophila melanogaster* were very different from those of wild-type *D. melanogaster*.

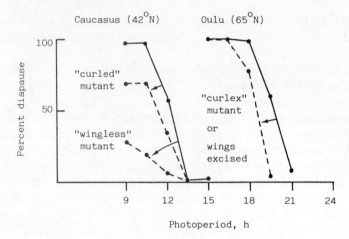

FIG. 1 (*Lankinen*) The effect of wing excision and wing mutation on photoperiodic diapause in two strains of *Drosophila littoralis* (P. Lankinen, unpublished work).

Lankinen: If no wings at all were present in *D. littoralis* there was, again, a change in the critical day-length. We have a strain from Caucasus with a critical day-length of 12 h and a 100% diapause response in short day-lengths. In the wingless mutant that has no wings and halteres at all, and which was isolated from that strain, we have found an almost complete absence of photoperiodic response.

Masaki: Is the pleiotropic effect exerted by the wingless gene?

Lankinen: Yes; this must be so. I am not saying, of course, that the wing is definitely the photoreceptor or even a part of the clock mechanism. Nevertheless, this possibility is real because the wings are not dead structures; they have many sensilla campaniformia (sensory organs), which are neurally connected to the thoracic ganglia. Through these connections the wings may have some direct or indirect effect on the hormonal balance of the endocrine system, whereby activation of the corpus allatum in the thorax is possibly the last step in switching on ovarian growth.

Steel: Are any other bodily structures—e.g. the legs—able to influence critical day-length?

Lankinen: I have not tested the legs, but I have cut the antennae, which have a much richer nerve supply, and this has practically no effect. However, cutting off the halteres, supplied by the same neural centres as the wings, have almost the same influence as the wings in this respect.

Steel: Of course, there may be endocrinological differences on either side of the critical day-lengths. Such excisions as you have described are certainly capable of altering the animal's endocrine milieu. It is interesting, however, that the wingless mutant also shows this phenomenon. One would like to know about the endocrinology of that mutant.

Lankinen: Yes. These results are very recent and I really don't know how to go further with them. The responses are definitely real.

Mordue: Are the wing polymorphisms in aphids or crickets related to such changes in critical day-length?

Lees: I have measured the critical night-length in alatae of *Megoura viciae* and it is almost exactly the same as in the apterous form (unpublished results).

Hardie: There was also some suggestion in the 1960s that antennae possessed light receptors (Booth 1963).

Lees: Yes; but that was not in connection with the photoperiodic response.

Sokolove: Could an effect of temperature on the critical day-length explain Dr Lankinen's results? The wing surface is quite an effective radiator and it might be changing the effective temperature seen by the photoperiodic system.

Lankinen: I doubt that as a suitable explanation because the mutant with curved wings shows this phenomenon and its wings have a similar surface area to non-mutant wings. Also, the halteres are not very big, but cutting them has a great effect.

Sokolove: We might also remember that animals can change their temperature by muscular activity as well as by radiative mechanisms. The weight being driven by the thoracic muscles that move the wings may indirectly affect the internal temperature of the animal. By changing the wing weight, one may be changing the frequency of wing beating and thus changing the temperature.

Sokolove: Do the wings not beat when they mate?

Lankinen: Not much in the culture-bottle conditions!

Saunders: Wouldn't one expect the temperature effect to work the opposite way around? If no wings are present, there is no flapping and no generation of heat; the animals are cooler and so one would expect the short-winged individuals to have more diapause rather than less.

Sokolove: No; because when the wings are cut off, the frequency of beating may well be faster and not slower.

Reynolds: This does happen. A fly with cut wings will show an increased frequency of thoracic muscle contractions (Pringle 1949). Nevertheless, it seems unlikely that the increased frequency of contraction could produce a very large temperature increase in animals that are as small as this.

Gilbert: It has been shown in the diapausing and non-diapausing Monarch (butterfly) that the rate of juvenile hormone (JH) breakdown is much greater in the flying insect (Lessman & Herman 1981).

Reynolds: I think you must be careful here. At least one wingless mutant of *Drosophila*, *apterous*[4], is also a JH mutant (Postlethwait et al 1976).

REFERENCES

Booth CO 1963 Photokinetic functions of aphid antennae. Nature (Lond) 197:265-266

Lessman CA, Herman WS 1981 Flight enhances juvenile hormone inactivation in *Danaus plexippus plexippus* (Lepidoptera:Danaidae). Experientia (Basel) 37:599-601

Pflüger W, Neumann D 1971 Die Stenerung einer gezeitenparallelen Schlüpfrhythmik nach dem Sanduhr-Prinzip. Oecologia (Berl) 7:262-266

Pittendrigh CS 1981 Circadian organization and the photoperiodic phenomena. In: Follett BK, Follett DE (eds) Biological clocks in seasonal reproductive cycles. Wright, Bristol, p 1-35

Postlethwait JH, Handler AM, Gray PW 1976 A genetic approach to the study of juvenile hormone control of vitellogenesis in *Drosophila melanogaster*. In: Gilbert LI (ed) The juvenile hormones. Academic Press, New York, p 449-469

Pringle JWS 1949 The excitation and contraction of the flight muscles of insects. J Physiol 108:226-232

Thiele H-U 1977 Differences in measurement of daylength and photoperiodism in two stocks from subarctic and temperate climates in the carabid beetle, *Pterostichus nigrita* F. Oecologia (Berl) 30:349-365

Neuronal organization of a circadian clock in the cockroach *Leucophaea maderae*

TERRY L. PAGE

Department of General Biology, Box 42, Station B, Vanderbilt University, Nashville, Tennessee 37235, USA

Abstract. The circadian clock that controls locomotor activity in the cockroach *Leucophaea maderae* is composed of two oscillators—one located in each optic lobe of the protocerebrum—that are mutually coupled via a neural pathway in the brain. Each oscillator receives information for entrainment by light solely via the compound eyes, and regulates locomotor activity via axons of the optic tract. Control of locomotor activity may be mediated by a damped secondary oscillator. In addition to the pathway that couples the driving oscillators in the optic lobes there appears to be a second mode of interaction between bilaterally distributed components of the system, which involves suppression of the expression of the contralateral oscillation. General features of the organization of this circadian system are also found in other groups of insects and in molluscs. The results reinforce the generally accepted view that circadian organization in multicellular organisms depends on a population of anatomically discrete circadian oscillators and on their coupling relationships within the individual.

1984 Photoperiodic regulation of insect and molluscan hormones. Pitman, London (Ciba Foundation symposium 104), p 115-135

Over the past two decades efforts to understand the anatomical organization of biological clocks have largely focused on the analysis of the timing systems that regulate daily (circadian) rhythms in behaviour. The experimental strategies used are invariably based on a conceptual model of the circadian system that consists of four functionally defined components. The model consists of a pacemaker that generates the primary timing cue, photoreceptors for entrainment, and two coupling pathways, one that mediates the flow of entrainment information from the photoreceptor to the pacemaker and a second that couples the pacemaker to the overt rhythm it controls. Two general questions have been the focus of the research prompted by this model. First, are there localizable anatomical correlates of these functionally defined elements? Second, to what extent is this 'minimal' model a complete representation of the circadian system?

Substantial progress has been made on both fronts. Although there are no instances in which pacemakers, photoreceptors for entrainment, or the coupling pathways have been linked to specific cells, much evidence indicates that restricted regions of the nervous and neuroendocrine systems can fulfil the functions of the various components. Pacemakers, photoreceptors and steps in the coupling pathways have been localized in various organisms. However, in the course of these experiments evidence has surfaced that indicates the model is incomplete as a representation of the circadian system in at least one significant way. Studies on diverse species show that within a single individual there may be several circadian oscillators, and that any one overt rhythm may be under the control of a pacemaking system that is composed of two or more oscillatory structures; furthermore, different overt rhythms may be under the control of separate pacemaking systems. Thus, temporal organization is derived from a population of discrete oscillators that in some cases are independent or in other instances interact via internal coupling pathways.

These principles are illustrated in the following pages, which summarize the results of efforts to describe the neural organization of the circadian system that controls locomotor activity in the cockroach. The initial discussion describes the localization of the site of pacemaking oscillation for the system, the photoreceptors for entrainment, and the initial step in the output pathway that couples the oscillator to the locomotor activity. Second, evidence for interactions between bilaterally redundant elements of the circadian system is considered. Finally, results that indicate the presence of damped, secondary oscillators in the output pathway are discussed.

Circadian organization in the cockroach

Photoreceptors for entrainment

Several studies have provided unequivocal evidence that the compound eyes of cockroaches (*Leucophaea maderae* and *Periplaneta americana*) are the sole sites of phototransduction for entrainment of the circadian rhythm of locomotor activity. Painting over the compound eyes (Roberts 1965) or surgical transection of the optic nerves (Nishiitsutsuji-Uwo & Pittendrigh 1968a) abolishes entrainment by light. The ocelli (simple eyes) are neither necessary nor sufficient for entrainment (Roberts 1965, Nishiitsutsuji-Uwo & Pittendrigh 1968a). Although the photoreceptors responsible for entrainment within the eye have not been identified, recent studies on *P. americana* have provided information on spectral sensitivity of the entrainment pathway (Mote & Black 1981), and experiments involving partial ablations of compound eyes in *L. maderae* indicate that within any one eye there are several photoreceptors involved in entrainment (T. L. Page, unpublished results).

The optic lobes—locus of the driving oscillation?

Nishiitsutsuji-Uwo & Pittendrigh (1968b) first discovered the importance of the optic lobes of the protocerebrum in the regulation of locomotor activity in the cockroach when they found that removal of these structures disrupted the rhythm of this activity in *Leucophaea maderae*. This observation has been confirmed for other cockroach species (*P. americana*—Roberts 1974, and *Blaberus fuscus*—Lukat & Weber 1979), and it has been shown that the loss of rhythmicity caused by optic lobe ablation persists indefinitely (Page 1983a). The results suggested the possibility that the optic lobes were the locus of the driving oscillation that controls the circadian rhythm of locomotor activity.

Optic-tract regeneration

Bilateral section of the optic tracts, thus isolating the optic lobe neurally from the midbrain, also disrupts the rhythm of locomotor activity (Nishiitsutsuji-Uwo & Pittendrigh 1968b); however, I recently discovered that when the optic lobes are left *in situ* the rhythm consistently reappears in 3–5 weeks (29 ± 6.2 days; mean $\pm$ SD; $n = 22$). Several lines of evidence indicate that the recovery of rhythmicity depends on the regeneration of neural connections between the optic lobe and the midbrain (Page 1983a). Histological examinations showed that structural regeneration had occurred in the brains of animals in which rhythmicity returned. Furthermore, if structural regeneration was blocked by the insertion of a glass barrier between the optic lobe and the midbrain, recovery of rhythmicity was prevented or slowed. Extracellular recording after optic-tract section showed recovery of light-evoked neural activity in the ventral nerve cord that was driven via the compound eyes, and the time-course of the recovery of this neural activity paralleled the recovery of behavioural rhythmicity. Therefore, structural and functional connections between the optic lobe and the midbrain do regenerate, with a time-course similar to that of rhythm recovery.

While these results reiterated the central importance of the optic lobes in the maintenance of the locomotor activity rhythm and further indicated that their effect was mediated by axons in the optic tract, they provided no new data on their functional role in sustaining rhythmicity. The conclusion that the optic lobes were the locus of the driving oscillation for the rhythm depended on the demonstration that these structures were not only necessary to sustain rhythmicity but also that they controlled the phase and the period of the locomotor activity rhythm.

Control of rhythm period and phase by the optic lobes

One aspect of the locomotor activity exhibited after nervous regeneration—the period of the free-running rhythm (τ)—has been of particular interest. The free-running period after recovery of the locomotor activity rhythm was found to be strongly correlated with the period of the pre-operative rhythm ($r = 0.87$) (Page 1983a). This result prompted a series of experiments in which the optic lobes were transplanted between individuals with substantially different free-running periods. For these experiments I used animals that had been raised from birth in 26 h (LD 13:13) or 22 h (LD 11:11) light cycles. The periods of the free-running rhythms of animals raised in the two conditions differ by over 1 h, and the period difference is maintained for at least 5 months after isolation in constant darkness (DD) (Page & Block 1980, Page 1982). In the experiments both optic lobes were exchanged between individuals that were free-running in DD (Page 1982, 1983a). Of 22 animals that received optic lobe transplants, 14 survived and, several weeks after surgery, these exhibited a clear circadian rhythm of locomotor activity (Fig. 1). The pre-operative period of the donor and the post-operative period of the host were strongly correlated ($r = 0.96$) although, on average, τ after regeneration was slightly longer than τ for the donor before surgery ($\overline{\Delta\tau} = 0.2 \pm 0.21$ h). These data showed that the transplantation of the optic lobes from one animal to another, whose own optic lobes had been removed, could both restore the rhythm of activity and impose the period of the donor animal's rhythm on the rhythm of the host.

I have used two approaches to demonstrate that the optic lobes control the phase as well as the period of the free-running rhythm of locomotor activity.

FIG. 1. Effects on locomotor activity of optic-lobe transplantation between groups of animals raised in LD 11:11 or LD 13:13. Activity was monitored by placing animals in leucite running wheels. Rotation of the wheel was sensed by a magnetic reed switch that was connected to an event recorder. Data for successive days were placed one set below the other in chronological order. Each record has been photographically duplicated to provide a 48 h time-base to aid in visual inspection of the data (12M, 12 midnight; CST, central standard time). (A) Locomotor activity records, showing restoration of rhythmicity after transplantation ('exchange'). The records begin with intact animals free-running in constant darkness. After 4 weeks the optic lobes were exchanged and, after several weeks of low activity, rhythmicity returned in both cases. (B) Plots of the free-running period of the activity rhythm after transplantation versus the period of the donor animal before surgery. Diagonal line shows the values expected if the pre- and post-operative periods were identical. Solid circles, data from transplants between groups; open circles, data from transplants within groups (data from Page 1982, 1983a).

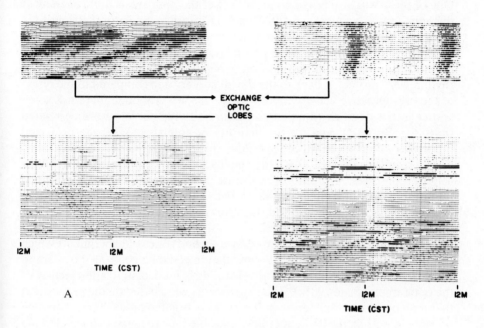

A

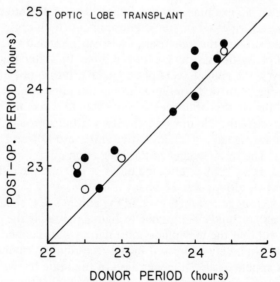

B

One of these was also based on the ability of the optic tracts to regenerate. If the optic lobe does contain a self-sustaining circadian oscillator that continues in motion during the period of regeneration, one would expect the phase of the locomotor activity rhythm to be conserved. In 19 animals in which the optic tracts were severed and allowed to regenerate, the onsets of the activity rhythm were projected back to the day of surgery and compared to the phase of the pre-operative activity rhythm (Page 1983a). Although there was some scatter in the data, rhythm phases before and after surgery were correlated ($r = 0.61$; $P < 0.01$), and for the majority of animals (13/19) the projected phase was within 4 h of the pre-operative rhythm phase on the day of surgery. These results suggested that: (a) the oscillation that controls locomotor activity continued in motion, in the neurally isolated optic lobe, with a free-running period similar to the period of the rhythm after regeneration; and (b) the oscillation conserved the information on the phase of the rhythm at the time of surgery (Page 1983a).

These conclusions were supported by a second series of experiments which demonstrated that the phase of the oscillation could be controlled by light to which the animal was exposed for several days immediately after section of the optic tracts (Page 1983a). The experiments were based on the proposition that if an oscillation did persist in the neurally isolated optic lobe it should be possible to entrain it with light cycles, since the lobe remained attached to the compound eye. To examine this possibility 20 animals were entrained to LD 12:12 and, after a period of stable entrainment, both optic tracts were cut. The day after surgery the light:dark cycle was phase-advanced by 6 h for 10 animals and phase-delayed by 6 h for the other 10. After 10 days on the new light:dark cycle the animals were placed in DD. If the optic lobe contained an entrainable oscillator that continued in motion after optic-tract section then the phase of the rhythm after regeneration should reflect the phase of the last light:dark cycle—the rhythms in the two groups would be expected to reappear on average about 20 days after entry into DD and to be about 12 h out of phase. The results matched this prediction quite well. On average, the rhythm recovered 20.2 days after the onset of DD and the difference in phase between the two groups was 12.5 h.

These results suggested that, even in the absence of a behavioural rhythm, an oscillation that could be entrained by light persisted in the neurally isolated optic lobe, and that the new phase information was retained after entry into DD and was ultimately expressed in the free-running rhythm of locomotor activity that appeared after regeneration of the optic tracts.

Another experimental approach to demonstrate that the optic lobes control the phase of the free-running activity rhythm has been the use of localized low-temperature pulses (Page 1981a). Localized cooling of the optic lobe was accomplished by positioning a cooled insect pin near one optic lobe of animals in which either the ipsilateral or the contralateral optic tract had been cut. Animals that were free-running in DD were removed from their activity monitors and either the intact or the neurally isolated optic lobe was cooled to about 7.5 °C for 6 h. Animals were then returned to the activity monitors and the phases of the pre- and post-pulse rhythms were compared. The results are illustrated in Fig. 2A,B. Cooling the intact optic lobe consistently caused an average phase shift of several hours ($\overline{\Delta\phi} = -7.1 \pm 1.9$ h, $n = 10$) while cooling the neurally isolated optic lobe had no effect on the phase of the free-running rhythm of locomotor activity ($\overline{\Delta\phi} = -0.6 \pm 0.8$ h, $n = 5$). Cooling the mid-brain also had no phase-shifting effect. The demonstration that low-tempera-ture pulses shifted the phase of the rhythm only when an intact optic lobe, rather than a neurally isolated optic lobe or the midbrain, was cooled provides a further indication that the optic lobes can regulate the phase of the activity rhythm.

In summary, it has been shown that: (a) integrity of the neural connections between the optic lobes and the midbrain of the protocerebrum is required for maintenance of the free-running rhythm of locomoter activity; (b) the optic lobes control the phase of the free-running activity rhythm; (c) the optic lobes control the period of the free-running activity rhythm; and (d) a circadian oscillation that can be phase-shifted by light persists in the neurally isolated optic lobe. The conclusion that the optic lobes contain a circadian pacemaker that controls the temporal distribution of locomotor activity in *Leucophaea maderae* via axons in the optic tract seems inescapable. Fur-thermore the periodic motion of the oscillator apparently continues in the absence of neural input from other central nervous system structures, although the data do not rule out the possibility that humoral factors originating outside the optic lobe may be necessary to sustain the oscillation.

Localization of pacemaker function within the optic lobe

The region within the optic lobe that controls the rhythm of locomotor activity has been further localized. After removal of one optic lobe, surgical or electrolytic lesions distal to the second optic chiasm or dorsal to the lobula have no effect on rhythmicity, while lesions in the ventral half of the lobe near the lobula frequently abolish the activity rhythm (Roberts 1974, Sokolove 1975, Page 1978). The results suggest that the cells responsible for generating the pacemaking oscillation have their somata and/or processes in this region of the optic lobe. Further work is necessary to determine whether one, a few, or many cells in the region comprise the oscillator, or whether the pace-making signal may be generated redundantly in several cells.

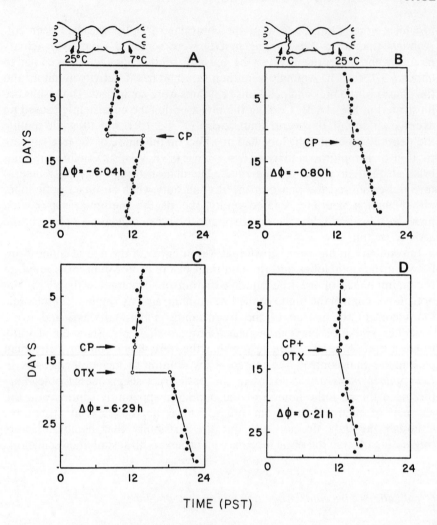

FIG. 2. Examples of data from animals treated with localized low-temperature pulses. Solid circles, time of activity onset for each day; open circles, projected phases of the rhythms before and after the pulse; lines are linear regressions; PST, Pacific standard time. Pulses were 6 h in duration and began at activity onset. In (A), the intact optic lobe of an animal with one sectioned optic tract was cooled (CP) to 7 °C while the neurally isolated optic lobe was maintained at 25 °C; in (B), the neurally isolated optic lobe was cooled while the intact lobe was maintained at 25 °C. Cooling the intact lobe caused a large phase delay ($\Delta\phi$) while cooling the neurally isolated lobe had little effect. C and D illustrate the effects of a low-temperature pulse to one lobe on the rhythm driven by the contralateral lobe: (C) the optic tract of the treated lobe was cut (OTX) 4 days after the pulse (CP), and the subsequent rhythm, driven by the untreated lobe, was phase-delayed by several hours; (D) the optic tract of the treated lobe was sectioned 0.5 h after the pulse, thus preventing the phase-shift in the rhythm.

Mutual coupling between optic-lobe oscillators

In early studies it was shown that unilateral ablation of the optic lobe or section of the optic tract did not abolish the rhythm of activity (Nishiitsutsuji-Uwo & Pittendrigh 1968b). This suggested that each optic lobe might contain an oscillator sufficient to drive the locomotor activity rhythm. This possibility raises two additional questions. First, if there are two optic-lobe pacemakers, are they functionally equivalent? Second, are the two pacemakers coupled, to ensure synchrony in the absence of temporal cues from the environment? Initial investigations involved a systematic study of the effects of unilateral optic-lobe ablation on the free-running rhythm of locomotor activity (Page et al 1977). The two optic lobes were found to be functionally redundant, at least as measured by the ability to maintain rhythmicity and average period in DD. However, ablation of either the right or the left optic lobe or section of one optic tract consistently led to a small but significant increase in τ ($\Delta\tau = 0.2 \pm 0.26$ h). On this basis we suggested that bilaterally distributed oscillators in the optic lobes were mutually coupled via the optic tracts and that the free-running period of the coupled pair (about 23.7 h) was shorter than the period of the individual oscillators (23.9 h).

Support for this interpretation was obtained in experiments using localized low-temperature pulses (Page 1981a, and see above), delivered to one optic lobe of intact animals. The treated lobe was removed at varying times after the pulse to assay the phase of the rhythm driven by the contralateral oscillator. If the treated lobe was removed 4 days after the pulse the subsequent rhythm (driven by the untreated lobe) was phase-delayed by several hours (Fig. 2C), but if the treated lobe was removed only 0.5 h after the pulse, the phase-shift in the contralateral lobe was prevented (Fig. 2D). The results indicated that the low-temperature pulse caused a phase-shift in the treated optic lobe (without directly affecting the phase of the contralateral pacemaker), which was subsequently transmitted to the oscillator in the contralateral optic lobe. It was also shown that cooling one optic lobe of an intact animal resulted in an average steady-state phase shift that was nearly 2 h less than the phase-shift obtained when the optic lobe contralateral to the pulse was neurally isolated by optic-tract section. This observation suggested that, after desynchronization of the two pacemakers, the return of the coupled system to a steady state involved a phase advance in the treated pacemaker as well as the phase delay in the pacemaker of the untreated optic lobe.

The notion that the two oscillators in the optic lobes were coupled was further reinforced by the finding that either one of the compound eyes was sufficient to entrain both oscillators. After isolation of one optic lobe from the ipsilateral compound eye by optic-nerve section, the oscillator in that optic

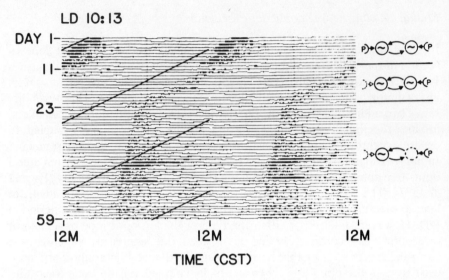

A

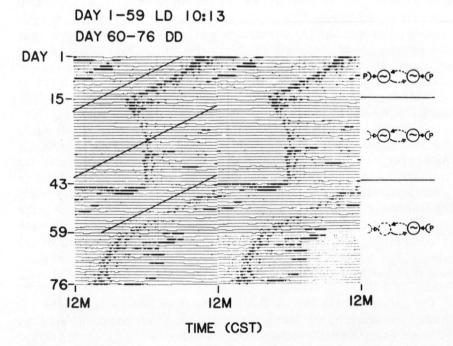

B

lobe could be phase-shifted by a delay in the light cycle (Page et al 1977) or could be entrained by a 23 h light : dark cycle (Page 1983b) (Fig. 3A).

Loss of mutual coupling after optic tract regeneration

Since the connections between the optic-lobe pacemaker and the midbrain structures that regulate activity can regenerate after optic-tract section or optic-lobe transplantation, the pathway that couples the two optic-lobe pacemakers may also be able to regenerate. Two types of experiment have suggested that this regeneration does not occur and, surprisingly, that an intact optic lobe can completely suppress the expression of an oscillator that has been forced to regenerate its output connections (Page 1983b).

One experiment made use of the fact that either compound eye can entrain both oscillators. One optic-lobe pacemaker was surgically isolated from its own (ipsilateral) compound eye by optic-nerve section. The entrainment of this pacemaker would then depend on the coupling between the two optic lobes (Page et al 1977, Page 1978). A 23 h light cycle (LD 10 : 13) was used to drive the contralateral optic lobe (still attached to its compound eye) at a period about 1 h less than the normal period of a single free-running oscillator. The question was whether the entrainment information transduced by the intact eye would be transmitted to the contralateral optic lobe after section and regeneration of one of the optic tracts. Results of such an experiment are shown in Fig. 3B. After optic tract section 110 days were allowed for regeneration, after which animals were placed in activity monitors

---

FIG. 3. Activity records of animals in a 23 h light : dark cycle (LD 10 : 13). The time of 'lights off' is indicated by the lines in the left half of the figure. To the right of the activity record is a schematic representation of the cockroach's circadian system. There are two oscillators (⊖), one located in each optic lobe. Each oscillator receives input from photoreceptors of the ipsilateral compound eye (P). The oscillators are also mutually coupled. (A) *Intact animal*. The record begins with the activity rhythm entrained by the light : dark cycle. Entrainment persists after Day 11 when the left optic lobe is isolated from any photoreceptive input via its compound eye by optic-nerve section. On Day 23 the right optic tract was severed, thus eliminating the right optic-lobe pacemaker. The subsequent rhythm began to free-run in the light : dark cycle, now driven by the left optic-lobe pacemaker only. The phase of the rhythm indicates that the left pacemaker had been entrained by the light cycle. (B) *Sectioned animal*. The right optic tract had been cut and allowed to regenerate (indicated by the dashed lines in the right-hand scheme). On Day 15 the left optic nerve was cut, thus eliminating the photoreceptors of the left eye. The rhythm began to free-run in the light : dark cycle (*cf.* A). There was no evidence of an entrained component to the activity. On Day 43 the left optic tract was cut, thus isolating the left pacemaker from the central nervous system. On the day after surgery an entrained rhythm began to appear, several hours out of phase with the prior free-running rhythm. On Day 59 the light : dark cycle was discontinued and the rhythm began to free-run.

in LD 10:13. The animals were entrained normally by the light cycle, and after two weeks the optic nerve of the intact optic lobe was severed. Invariably the animals began to free-run in the light:dark cycle, and there was no indication of an entrained (23 h) component to the locomotor activity. The results indicated that the entrainment information transduced by the intact eye was not reaching the contralateral pacemaker, which was free-running in the presence of the light:dark cycle, and that the lobe with a regenerated optic tract was unable to drive its own component of locomotor activity.

After 4 weeks the optic tract of the intact lobe was cut. In 5 of 6 animals a stably entrained rhythm of locomotor activity was apparent within a few (1–3) days of surgery. The phase difference between the entrained rhythm and the previously free-running rhythm was variable and depended on the phases of the light:dark cycle and the free-running rhythm at the time of surgery. When the cockroaches were placed in constant darkness, the rhythm began to free-run, indicating that activity was not simply being forced by the light:dark cycle. These data clearly indicated that entrainment information was not being transmitted via the regenerated optic tract to the intact pacemaker. Similar experiments also suggested that entrainment information was not transmitted in the other direction, from the intact to the regenerated optic lobe (T. L. Page, unpublished results). Thus, the data provided no indication that the coupling pathway between the optic lobes had regenerated. It was also of particular interest that the intact optic lobe appeared to suppress the expression of the pacemaker that had regenerated its output connections.

Results of experiments that involved transplantation of a single optic lobe led to similar conclusions (Page 1983b). In these experiments a single optic lobe was exchanged between animals that had been raised on either a 22 h or a 26 h light cycle. Regeneration of the coupling pathway between the remaining host optic lobe and the transplanted pacemaker would be expected to result in a major change in the free-running period of one or both optic-lobe pacemakers. In 13 transplants there was no substantial change in period after surgery and, thus, no indication of regeneration of the coupling pathway between the two pacemakers. However, neither was there any convincing evidence of the appearance of a second free-running component which might have been expected if a neural output from the transplanted lobe to the activity-regulating structure in the midbrain had regenerated without becoming recoupled to the contralateral pacemaker. This absence of a second component suggests that the intact (host) optic lobe was suppressing any expression of the transplanted pacemaker. That regeneration had occurred, at least in most animals, was demonstrated by section of the optic tract of the host optic lobe. After optic-tract section, 7 of 10 surviving animals exhibited a clear free-running rhythm of locomotor activity, beginning 1–3 days after surgery, with a period near that expected for a rhythm driven by the donor optic lobe. Phase differences between pre- and post-surgical rhythms were variable, ranging from 2–11 h.

These results indicated that the transplanted optic lobe had regenerated those connections with the midbrain that were necessary to drive the locomotor activity rhythm, but that the intact optic lobe had suppressed expression of the regenerated donor pacemaker. Only after the host pacemaker had been surgically disconnected from the midbrain was the transplanted lobe able to control locomotor activity.

Frequently in these experiments there was also evidence that the host optic lobe eventually regenerated its connections with the midbrain after optic-tract section. The regeneration was often reflected in the appearance of a modulated activity level with a periodicity that corresponded to the beat frequency of the two (host and donor) oscillators. The clearest example is shown in Fig. 4. The results indicated, after regeneration of both optic tracts, that each optic lobe can drive an independent component of the activity rhythm. As in previous experiments there was no indication of regeneration of an entrainment pathway between the two optic lobes.

These results suggest that although the pathway that couples each optic-lobe pacemaker to locomotor activity consistently regenerates after optic-tract section or optic-lobe transplantation, the entrainment pathway between the two optic lobes does not; therefore, these pathways are functionally distinct. Furthermore, an intact optic lobe can suppress the control of locomotor activity by a contralateral pacemaker that has been forced to regenerate its output connections. We do not yet know the mechanism and the pathway for this novel mode of interaction between bilaterally distributed elements of the circadian system. Suppression probably occurs at some point along the output pathway that couples each pacemaker to locomotor activity, rather than by a direct interaction between the two oscillators, since measurements of phase or period gave no indication that one pacemaker could influence the oscillation in the contralateral optic lobe (Page 1983b).

Organization of the output pathway

Several studies have been directed at describing the pathway by which the pacemaking system in the optic lobes is coupled to locomotor activity. A first step in the output pathway is via axons in the optic tracts (Page 1983a). The termination of the crucial cells has not been identified; however, lesions to the pars intercerebralis (Nishiitsutsuji-Uwo et al 1967) or section of the circum-oesophageal connectives (Roberts et al 1971) have been shown to disrupt the locomotor activity rhythm, suggesting that these structures are involved in coupling the pacemaker to the activity.

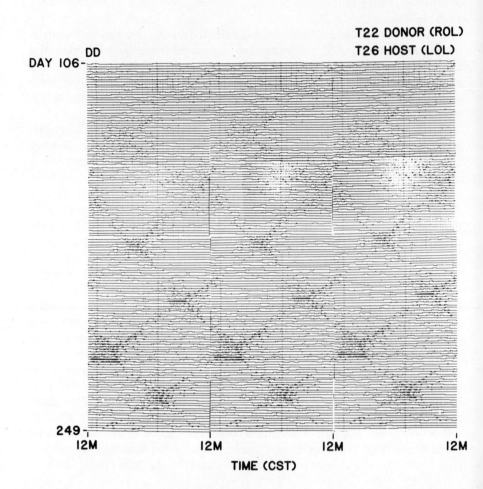

FIG. 4. Activity record in an animal with a unilateral optic-lobe transplant. The host animal had been raised from birth in LD 13:13 (T26) and the donor had been raised in LD 11:11 (T22). The right optic lobe (ROL) of the donor was transplanted. The host retained its left optic lobe (LOL). The record begins 106 days after transplantation and 33 days after section of the host optic tract; the record is 'triple-plotted', and shows 72 h across. Two clear components to the activity rhythm appear to be free-running independently. An increase in the activity level is evident when the two components come into phase, and activity is nearly eliminated when the components are in anti-phase.

Although animals are aperiodic in constant conditions after optic lobe ablation, a rhythm of locomotor activity is expressed in a temperature cycle (Page 1981b, and unpublished). Certain features of the rhythm suggest that the temperature cycle is acting through a damped oscillator. For example, the phase-angle difference between the temperature cycle and the rhythm depends on the period of the cycle as well as on the ratio of the duration of the warm phase to the cold phase. The results raise the possibility that the optic-lobe pacemaker regulates locomotor activity through a secondary, damped oscillator. Since, after regeneration of both optic tracts, the activity rhythm can be split into two distinct components with different free-running periods (Fig. 4) an oscillatory driven system must be composed of at least two, relatively independent oscillators. The simultaneous expression of two frequencies would be incompatible with the notion of a single secondary oscillator coupling both pacemakers to locomotor activity. Further work is necessary to localize the site of the secondary oscillator, to characterize its properties, and to confirm that it is a step in the output pathway by which the optic lobe normally regulates levels of locomotor activity.

Conclusions

The results of studies summarized here are schematically shown in Fig. 5. Circadian regulation of locomotor activity in *Leucophaea maderae* is derived from a bilaterally distributed pair of self-sustaining oscillators in the optic lobes of the protocerebrum. These oscillators receive light-entrainment information exclusively via the compound eyes. The output signal from each of the oscillators has two functionally distinct destinations. The first is to the oscillator in the contralateral optic lobe. This pathway mutually couples the two oscillators and provides a pathway by which light-entrainment information transduced by one compound eye is transmitted to the contralateral optic

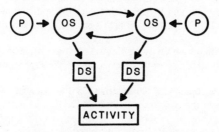

FIG. 5. Schematic model of the circadian timing system in *Leucophaea*. Two bilaterally paired driving oscillators (OS) are mutually coupled. Each receives input from photoreceptors (P) of the ipsilateral compound eye, and controls a driven system (DS) that regulates activity.

lobe. The second output pathway connects the pacemakers in the optic lobes to a 'driven system' in the midbrain that couples the pacemaking system to the locomotor activity. There is some evidence to suggest that this driven system may behave like a damped oscillator that can be driven either by temperature cycles or by the periodic output of the optic-lobe pacemaking system. Finally, there is an as yet unidentified pathway (not shown) by which the timing system on one side of the brain can suppress the expression of the contralateral oscillator.

The organization of circadian pacemaking systems that control behavioural rhymicity in other insects and in molluscs appears to be similar to the organization of the pacemaking system in the cockroach, although there are interesting differences in detail (Page 1981b,c). An important question is whether the circadian clocks involved in photoperiodic time-measurement are the same as, or structurally similar to, those that control circadian behaviour. At present the answer is uncertain, and a clear direction for future research will be the more detailed study of the anatomical and physiological basis of circadian clocks and their relationship to photoperiodic time-measurement.

Acknowledgements

This paper is dedicated to Colin S. Pittendrigh on the occasion of his 65th birthday. This work was supported by US Public Health Service–National Institutes of Health Grant GM 30039.

REFERENCES

Lukat R, Weber F 1979 The structure of locomotor activity in bilobectomized cockroaches (*Blaberus fuscus*). Experientia (Basel) 35:38-39

Mote ML, Black KR 1981 Action spectrum and threshold sensitivity of entrainment of circadian running activity in the cockroach *Periplaneta americana*. Photochem Photobiol 34:257-265

Nishiitsutsuji-Uwo J, Pittendrigh CS 1968a Central nervous system control of circadian rhythmicity in the cockroach. II: The pathway of light signals that entrains the rhythm. Z Vgl Physiol 58:1-13

Nishiitsutsuji-Uwo J, Pittendrigh CS 1968b Central nervous system control of circadian rhythmicity in the cockroach. III: The optic lobes, locus of the driving oscillation? Z Vgl Physiol 58:14-46

Nishiitsutsuji-Uwo J, Petropulos SF, Pittendrigh CS 1967 Central nervous system control of circadian rhythmicity in the cockroach. I: Role of the pars intercerebralis. Biol Bull (Woods Hole) 133:679-696

Page TL 1978 Interactions between bilaterally paired components of the cockroach circadian system. J Comp Physiol 124:225-236

Page TL 1981a Effects of localized low-temperature pulses on the cockroach circadian pacemaker. Am J Physiol 240:R144-R150

Page TL 1981b Localization of circadian pacemakers in insects. In: Follett BK, Follett DE (eds) Biological clocks in reproductive cycles. Wright, Bristol, p 113-124

Page TL 1981c Neural and endocrine control of circadian rhythms in invertebrates. In: Aschoff J (ed) Handbook of behavioral neurobiology. IV: Biological rhythms. Plenum, New York, p 145-172

Page TL 1982 Transplantation of the cockroach circadian pacemaker. Science (Wash DC) 216:73-75

Page TL 1983a Regeneration of the optic tracts and circadian pacemaker activity in the cockroach *Leucophaea maderae*. J Comp Physiol 152:231-240

Page TL 1983b Effects of optic tract regeneration on internal coupling in the circadian system of the cockroach. J Comp Physiol, in press

Page TL, Block GD 1980 Circadian rhythmicity in cockroaches: effects of early post-embryonic development and ageing. Physiol Entomol 5:271-281

Page TL, Caldarola PC, Pittendrigh CS 1977 Mutual entrainment of bilaterally distributed circadian pacemakers. Proc Natl Acad Sci USA 74:1277-1281

Roberts SK 1965 Photoreception and entrainment of cockroach activity rhythms. Science (Wash DC) 148:958-959

Roberts SK 1974 Circadian rhythms in cockroaches: effects of optic lobe lesions. J Comp Physiol 88:21-30

Roberts SK, Skopik SD, Driskill RJ 1971 Circadian rhythms in cockroaches: does brain hormone mediate the locomotor cycle? In: Menaker M (ed) Biochronometry. National Academy of Sciences, Washington DC, p 505-515

Sokolove PG 1975 Localization of the cockroach optic lobe circadian pacemaker with micro-lesions. Brain Res 87:13-21

DISCUSSION

Brady: Why do you suppose there is a damped oscillator in *Leucophaea maderae*? Surely, it is unlikely that if there is one it would not be manifest? In sparrows, for example, a free-running rhythm *is* obtained for a few days after removal of the pineal (Gaston & Menaker 1968).

Page: It is not easy to explain the phase-angle dependence on the period of the temperature cycle without some kind of an oscillatory structure. For me the simplest explanation is that there is an oscillator that is damped rapidly enough so that its peak, even on the first cycle after entry into constant conditions, doesn't go above some necessary threshold to trigger locomotor activity.

Truman: Besides the coupling, do you see any other differences between a regenerated optic lobe and an intact one with respect to its ability to advance or delay phase-shifts or in the number of transients that it shows?

Page: We have not looked at that.

Truman: What was the amplitude of the temperature cycle in the experiment that you described?

Page: It was 6°C. The low temperature was about 20°C and the high temperature was 26°C.

Mordue: Do the regenerated lobes continue to function normally?

Page: Yes; they continue to drive the locomotor activity rhythm indefinitely.

Giebultowicz: Do you think that two kinds of neurons could be involved, one of which is able to regenerate its processes while the other type cannot; or are they all of one type, and can only *some* connections regenerate?

Page: That is difficult to answer. Histological examination shows that after the optic tracts are cut the lateral neuropil of the midbrain bulges out. The optic lobe regrows into the neuropil and many regenerated nerve endings can be seen there. In the intact animal are other tracts that go across the optic lobe and terminate near the midline, but we have not yet found those regenerating in the sectioned animals. So it appears that some tracts regenerate and some do not. We have used a cobalt technique to get these results but we intend to try horseradish peroxidase in the future.

Goldsworthy: Could you describe the ultrastructural appearance of these regenerating nerve tracts? Do they contain neurosecretory droplets?

Page: I have not looked at this, but Beattie (1971) has found neurosecretory cells in the optic lobe of the cockroach, *Periplaneta americana*, located near the lamina. If these are located in the same place in *Leucophaea maderae* they certainly are not necessary for maintaining rhythmicity or for coupling pathways within the circadian system that I have described in my paper.

Goldsworthy: We (Highnam & Goldsworthy 1972) have sectioned neurosecretory tracts to the corpora cardiaca in the locust and observed that the regenerating axons seem to go around 'searching' for the corpora cardiaca. This sounds similar to what you have described for the cockroach and it would be nice to know whether those are neurosecretory axons.

Page: I find it curious that after we have sectioned the optic tract the rhythm of locomotor activity returns almost invariably, and so the regeneration of the particular pathway responsible is almost 100% successful. This suggests that the regenerating axons may not have to find particular postsynaptic cells. Once they are in the right area perhaps they release a neuromodulator or neurohormone, which can drive the rhythm.

Joosse: Huberman et al (1981) have found, in a great number of animal groups, a neuropeptide of molecular weight 1200 that depresses motor neuron activity in crayfish. The release of something similar could be induced in the species that you have studied. I believe that its concentration in the nervous system is very easy to determine.

Sokolove: Have you done any behavioural tests to indicate, aside from any entrainment response, whether the animal can still orient to a light source?

Page: I have looked at light-evoked neural activity in the cervical connectives, and that returns. But I haven't done a detailed behavioural analysis or looked to see whether cells that are physiologically identifiable can be found in the cervical connectives after regeneration.

Chippendale: What approaches does your research suggest might be appropriate for those of us who are interested in photoperiodic studies, and seasonal effects?

Page: Surgical lesions and transplantations can, it seems, yield a lot of information about the organization of the system, if they are done sufficiently carefully. It surprises me that this has not been attempted more in photoperiodic species, e.g. in crickets, where the surgery would be relatively easy. Work on crickets (e.g. Loher 1972) has shown that the organization of their circadian system is very similar to that in cockroaches. Williams (1969) has done some of these experiments on the silkmoth *Hyalaphora cecropia*, including brain transplantation, to localize the photoperiodic clock in that species.

Mordue: If you section the optic tracts in the cockroach, and then apply light flashes during the dark phase, does the pacemaker still respond, and does this treatment disrupt the continuous walking in the dark? Is the pacemaker receptive to these periods of light?

Page: I have not used these single light pulses to test the immediate effect on either the locomotor activity or the pacemaker, but it is clear that the pacemaker can be entrained by light cycles after regeneration. After a phase-shift of the light cycle, the activity rhythm will re-entrain with a relatively normal timecourse.

Brady: Something strange happens to the control of behaviour though, because when you cut the optic tracts and left them *in situ* there was virtually no activity for about a month; yet the activity restarted at the time when the rhythm restarted. So something complicated is happening between the command centres and the motor output.

Page: The response to removal of the optic lobe or section of the optic tract, in terms of locomotor activity level, is quite variable from one animal to the next. It is only after regeneration that one sees a clear patterning to the activity. Even then, the daily level of activity can vary widely, even within an individual. So I am cautious about trying to infer anything about the general physiological organization of the circadian system from the activity levels.

Pittendrigh: In some insects such as the desert-dwelling beetle, *Blaps* (Koehler & Fleissner 1978), it is clear (even without resort to surgery) that bilaterally distributed pacemakers are not mutually coupled. Each eye in *Blaps* contains an autonomous pacemaker. In nature they are exposed to a common light:dark cycle and therefore remain in synchrony. When the insect is transferred to constant darkness the two eyes free-run, but with different frequencies, and they rapidly become out of phase; they are not mutually coupled.

Page: Another potentially interesting tool is the ability to manipulate the free-running period in an animal by raising it on various light cycles. This may be useful in experiments to determine how the circadian system might be involved in photoperiodic time-measurement.

Denlinger: Does that work in any other system?

Page: As far as I know, similar effects have not been reported for any other system.

Pittendrigh: Klaus Hoffmann (1955) was the first to try these techniques; he raised lizards in various light cycles. It is interesting that the periods he used were well outside the limits of entrainment and therefore probably had no impact on the pacemaker. We tried similar techniques with mice and found after-effects that endured for more than 100 cycles; but they did eventually wear off (Pittendrigh & Daan 1976).

Page: The effects that Block and I have found persist longer than that—for the 10–12 months of the adult life-time of the cockroach; it seems to be a permanent change. When we use a 12:24 light:dark cycle, during post-embryonic development of the cockroaches, we also get an effect on the adult free-running period. Presumably, the period of this light cycle is outside the range of entrainment of the pacemaker in the nymph.

Reynolds: Is there some critical period during the animal's life for this entrainment?

Page: I hope to establish that in the near future. I would also like to examine the effects of other light cycles that might be ecologically more significant—for example, the effect of photoperiod on free-running period during development.

Pittendrigh: Your evidence so far seems to suggest that this long after-effect on rhythm period is something that can be done only to the nymph and not to the adult.

Page: That is true. If an animal is raised to adulthood in a 12:12 light:dark cycle and is then placed in a non-24h light cycle, the period of the oscillator is not affected to the extent that it is when the animal is exposed during development.

Goldsworthy: Cockroaches possess a supposedly hyperglycaemic hormone in their corpora cardiaca (Steele 1961). Is this related in any way to the rhythms you have been studying? Perhaps you are looking at a pacemaker that controls the release of such a hormone. As far as I know there is no established function for this hormone in cockroaches.

Page: This hormone is certainly not important for the rhythm of locomotor activity because one can remove the corpora cardiaca without losing the activity rhythm.

Goldsworthy: There is a danger there, because the axonal tracts to the corpora cardiaca can regenerate new endings and continue to release neuro-hormones (Goldsworthy et al 1972).

Page: It would depend on which group of secretory cells the hormone is coming from. John Brady (1967) has fairly completely removed the median neurosecretory cells of the pars intercerebralis of *Periplaneta americana* by lesioning the cell bodies, and that has no effect on the activity rhythm. There is not yet any evidence that a hormone is involved at any step along the way.

Brady: Cymborowski (1981) has published some work related to this. In rather simpler experiments than yours, he transplanted 'fast' and 'slow' brains in crickets, and immediately obtained fast-induced rhythms and slow-induced rhythms, without any regeneration. Presumably the optic lobes remained associated with the transplanted brains, so one can consider only the brain's output. Perhaps such work may lead to a connection between the hormonal and the non-hormonal sides of the controversy.

Page: It is a rather complicated story because if one sections the circumoesophageal connectives the rhythm is lost. Therefore any hormone that is released cannot be acting directly on the thorax to drive locomotor rhythmicity and must be acting on the brain. There is evidence now from *Drosophila* (Handler & Konopka 1979) as well as from the cricket *Acheta domesticus* (Cymborowski 1981) that the insect brain can release some diffusible factor that can regulate activity.

REFERENCES

Beattie TM 1971 Histology, histochemistry, and ultrastructure of neurosecretory cells in the optic lobe of the cockroach *Periplanta americana*. J Insect Physiol 17:1843-1855

Brady J 1967 Control of the circadian rhythm of activity in the cockroach. I: The role of the corpora cardiaca, brain and stress. J Exp Biol 47:153-163

Cymborowski B 1981 Transplantation of circadian pacemaker in the house cricket *Acheta domesticus* L. J Interdiscip Cycle Res 12:133-140

Gaston S, Menaker M 1968 Pineal function: the biological clock in the sparrow? Science (Wash DC) 160:1125-1127

Goldsworthy GJ, Johnson RA, Mordue W 1972 *In vivo* studies on the release of hormones from the corpora cardiaca of locusts. J Comp Physiol 79:85-96

Handler AM, Konopka RJ 1979 Transplantation of a circadian pacemaker in *Drosophila*. Nature (Lond) 279:236-238

Highnam KC, Goldsworthy GJ 1972 Regenerated corpora cardiaca and hyperglycemic factor in *Locusta migratoria*. Gen Comp Endocrinol 18:83-88

Hoffman K 1955 Aktivitatsregistrierungen bei frisch geschlüpften Eidechsen. Z Vgl Physiol 37:253-262

Huberman A, Aréchiga H, Arámburo C 1981 Search for the neurodepressing hormone in a stomatopod, *Squilla mantis*. Experientia (Basel) 37:51-52

Koehler WK, Fleissner G 1978 Internal desynchronization of bilaterally organized circadian oscillators in the visual system of insects. Nature (Lond) 274:708-710

Loher W 1972 Circadian control of stridulation in the cricket, *Teleogryllus commodus* Walker. J Comp Physiol 79:173-190

Pittendrigh CS, Daan S 1976 A functional analysis of circadian pacemakers in nocturnal rodents. I: The stability and lability of spontaneous frequency. J Comp Physiol 106:223-252

Steele JE 1961 Occurrence of a hyperglycaemic factor in the corpus cardiacum of an insect. Nature (Lond) 192:680-681

Williams CM 1969 Photoperiodism and the endocrine aspects of insect diapause. Symp Soc Exp Biol 23:285-300

Circadian-clock control of hormone secretion in *Samia cynthia ricini*

HIRONORI ISHIZAKI, AKIRA MIZOGUCHI and *MARIKO FUJISHITA

Biological Institute, Faculty of Science, Nagoya University, Furocho, Chikusa-ku, Nagoya, Japan (Present address: Department of Applied Biological Science, Faculty of Science and Technology, Science University of Tokyo, Japan)*

Abstract. A considerable developmental-stage-specific diversity exists in the circadian-clock control of the timing of hormone release during development of *Samia cynthia ricini*. The timing of prothoracicotropic hormone release, as inferred from neck-ligation experiments, is under circadian-clock control in larval–larval moulting and in larval–prepupal transition, but not in pupal cuticle formation. In the latter case prothoracicotropic hormone plays only a minor role in prothoracic gland activation; juvenile hormone and still another unknown factor, presumably neural, are concerned with the activation. This might be somehow related to the lack of circadian-clock control at this stage. For larval–prepupal transition, a clock residing in the prothoracic glands also controls the timing. This has been shown by transplanting prothoracic glands and applying various local illuminations to see their effects on gut-purge timing. The presence of the prothoracic gland clock was further supported by the fact that the phase-shifts of the onset of the scotophase that precedes gut purge were capable of inducing phase-shifts of the haemolymph ecdysteroid peak in neck-ligated larvae.

1984 Photoperiodic regulation of insect and molluscan hormones. Pitman, London (Ciba Foundation symposium 104), p 136–149

The pioneering work of Truman & Riddiford (1970) on the eclosion hormone was the first to demonstrate unequivocally that a circadian clock controls the release of insect neurohormone. A gated release of the prothoracicotropic hormone (PTTH), the brain neurohormone that stimulates the secretion of ecdysone by the prothoracic glands, has subsequently been demonstrated for *Manduca sexta* (Truman 1972, Truman & Riddiford 1974). The rhythmic release of these two hormones provided the physiological basis for the long-known rhythmic development of insects (Brady 1974). Meanwhile the nature of the circadian clock, or oscillation, has been studied extensively in the adult eclosion rhythm of *Drosophila pseudoobscura* by Pittendrigh and his associates (e.g. Pittendrigh 1981). Similar analyses of the nature of the clock in the large insects that can be operated upon surgically have been rather scanty, though considerable efforts were made for moth eclosion rhythm (Truman 1970, 1971). This paper summarizes our recent attempts to characterize the clock which underlies the rhythm of various developmental events and its relation to endocrine events in the saturniid moth, *Samia cynthia ricini*.

Larval–larval development

Larval–larval ecdysis in *Samia* under various light:dark regimens (see also Fujishita & Ishizaki 1981) is restricted to particular times of day (for less than 10 h periods), depending on the instar (Fig. 1). This timing of ecdysis is controlled by a circadian clock: its rhythm is abolished in constant light (LL); it free-runs in constant dark (DD); it is phase-shifted by phase-shifts in the light:dark cycle and it is generated with a fixed phase relationship to DD onset when transferred from LL to DD. Neck ligation of fourth-instar larvae under various light:dark conditions has proved that PTTH secretion is controlled by a circadian clock and that the rhythm of secretion is an immediate cause of ecdysis rhythm, as first demonstrated by Truman (1972) with *Manduca sexta*. Thus, the timing of PTTH release responsible for the formation of the next-instar larval cuticle, as assessed by neck ligation, is gated in normal light:dark cycles. This rhythm is abolished in LL, it free-runs in DD, and starts to free-run again after transition from LL to DD. Curves showing the critical period for PTTH secretion are always in parallel with ecdysis curves of intact, control larvae. The critical period for ecdysone secretion, as determined by abdominal ligation, was separated by 6 h from that for PTTH secretion.

Larval–prepupal transition

Four or five days after ecdysis the final (fifth)-instar larvae cease to eat and undergo a series of morphological and behavioural changes preparatory to pupation (see Fujishita & Ishizaki 1982a,b, Mizoguchi 1981, Mizoguchi & Ishizaki 1982). Among these, the so-called gut purge is a massive excretion of fluid faeces a few hours after the cessation of feeding (Fig. 2). The onset of gut purge is abrupt and clear-cut; hence it accurately indicates the timing of larval–prepupal transition. A remarkable feature in gut-purge rhythm is that its gate is noticeably narrower compared to the gates for larval–larval ecdysis, being confined to a period of only 3 h (Fig. 1). This high synchrony of gut purge has made it possible to analyse the nature of the clock that underlies the rhythm of larval–prepupal transition. This contrasts with larval–larval ecdysis

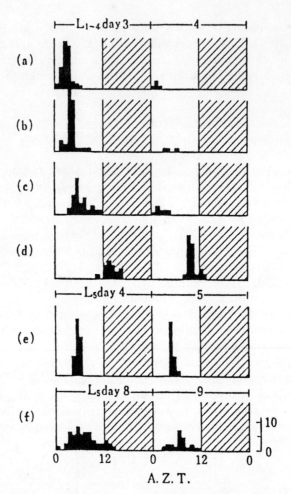

FIG. 1. Timing of larval–larval ecdysis, gut purge and pupal ecdysis of *Samia cynthia ricini* under LD 12:12. L_n, (n)th-instar larva. Larval ecdysis to the 2nd (a), 3rd (b), 4th (c) and 5th (d) instar. e, gut purge; f, pupal ecdysis. AZT, arbitrary Zeitgeber time. Vertical axis (see f) in (a), (b), (c), (d) and (f), no of animals ecdysing; vertical axis in (e), no of animals purging the gut.

rhythm, which yielded only rather ambiguous results in this kind of study, owing to its broad gates (see Fig. 6 in Fujishita & Ishizaki 1981).

By subjecting larvae to various light:dark conditions, we have characterized the nature of the clock that times the gut purge. The rhythm stops in LL conditions; it free-runs in DD; and it restarts at the transition from LL to DD. The dynamics of the clock can be adequately explained in terms of a circadian oscillation, as in many other circadian systems. Its phase-response curve,

FIG. 2. A larva of *Samia cynthia ricini* purging its gut.

obtained by application of 15 min, 500 lux light pulses to DD free-run, is of the type 0, as defined by Winfree (1970), and it resembles strikingly that obtained for *Drosophila* adult eclosion rhythm (Pittendrigh 1966). The nature of the oscillation thus defined greatly helped us to construct the experimental designs for further endocrine studies.

Neck ligation, for examining the timing of PTTH release necessary for prepupal induction, prevented gut purge, presumably due to the neural disturbance. Instead, the loss of anal proleg contractility, which occurs one day after gut purge in intact animals, served as an alternative indicator of prepupal development in neck-ligated animals (Fujishita & Ishizaki 1982a). The timing of PTTH release, as assessed by this assay after neck ligation, was again gated, indicating that a circadian clock controls the PTTH release that underlies the rhythm of prepupal induction. An important feature in this case is that the critical periods for PTTH and ecdysone secretion, as determined by abdominal ligation, are separated by 1.5 days, in contrast to the interval of only a few hours in larval–larval development (see Fig. 5, below). Another interesting fact is that light:dark changes can affect the gut-purge timing until 14–16 h before gut purge, i.e. much later than the critical period for PTTH secretion as determined above. These facts led us to examine the hormonal events associated with the clock during the day that just precedes gut purge.

An interesting result immediately emerged when we used local illumination. The photoreceptor that determines gut-purge timing was located in a broad area of the thorax, rather than in the head where almost all photoreceptors associated with the insect circadian clock reside (Truman 1976).

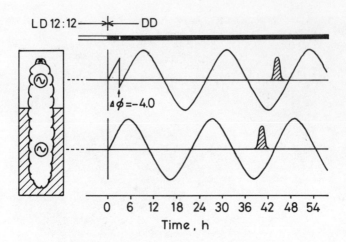

FIG. 3. Local illumination scheme to locate a photoreceptor associated with a clock that controls the timing of gut purge. When a portion containing the clock (⊝) is kept in DD, the free-running oscillation starts at DD onset (lower panel). When the photoreceptor is given a light pulse (upper panel, at arrow) the oscillation restarts immediately, giving rise to a delayed gut purge (upper panel). In each panel the gut purge is shown by the shaded peak.

Fig. 3 represents schematically the experimental design we used in this kind of study. Larvae exposed to LL were transferred to DD to allow the free-running oscillation to start. Light pulses were applied 6 h after DD onset, to bring about the maximum immediate phase-delay in gut purge. If the photoreceptor, wherever it may reside, is illuminated, the gut purge is delayed (Fig. 3, upper panel); if not, the timing of gut purge is not affected (lower panel). By this protocol we can establish the site of the photoreceptor that is associated with the circadian clock and can exclude the possible effects of light operating through non-clock processes.

The site of the photoreceptor thus disclosed (Fig. 3 of Mizoguchi & Ishizaki 1982) roughly coincided with that of the prothoracic glands (PG) of this species, which are extremely diffuse. This led us to examine the role of the PG in the timing of gut purge. Transplantation of an extraneous PG into the abdomen, followed by local illumination, yielded results consistent with the hypothesis that the PG possess the photoreceptor and the clock that presumably control the timing of ecdysone secretion (Fig. 4): when both transplanted and indigenous PG are given a light pulse, larval gut purge is delayed; if the indigenous PG alone is pulsed this delay in gut purge is not observed. The former result indicates that the clock of the transplanted PG is phase-shifted in response to light while the latter result proves that the same clock free-runs in DD so that the effects of the earlier secretion of ecdysone

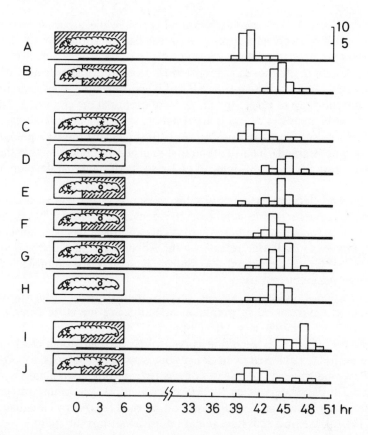

FIG. 4. Transplantation of prothoracic glands (PG) into the abdomen, followed by local illumination, to show the presence of a circadian clock in the PG that controls gut-purge timing. ★, PG. ○, control organs: brains (E, H), mesothoracic ganglia (F), and fat body (G). Unshaded boxes, exposure to light pulses; shaded boxes, shielding from the pulses. Bars indicate numbers of larvae that purged their guts. (From Mizoguchi & Ishizaki 1982.)

from the transplanted PG determines gut-purge timing, even though the secretion by the indigenous PG was delayed.

Further experiments using neck-ligated larvae to see their response to light:dark changes have decisively proved that the head is not indispensable for determining the timing of prepupal induction (M. Mizoguchi & A. Ishizaki, unpublished results). A 9h phase-shift of 'lights off' on the day that just precedes gut purge brings about a 6h phase-shift in gut purge, when larvae are reared under a normal 24h light:dark (LD) cycle. In these experiments, larvae reared under LD 16:8 were neck-ligated 6h before 'lights off' on the night that preceded gut purge, and *group A* larvae were transferred into DD immediately after ligation while *group B* larvae were transferred 9 h later. Gut purge in intact larvae subjected to the same light: dark treatments occurred with a 6 h phase difference between the two groups. Changes in the ecdysteroid titre from the haemolymph of these neck-ligated larvae, whose gut purge had been prevented, were examined by radioimmunoassay to reveal the progress of prepupal development. The titre changes in the headless A and B group larvae showed a typical increase, as in intact larvae (see Fig. 1 in Fujishita & Ishizaki 1982b), but the peak titre in group A was attained 6 h earlier than that in group B, indicating that the head is unnecessary for the light-induced phase-shifts of prepupal development at this stage.

Direct and decisive evidence for the presence in the PG of a clock that controls gut-purge timing would be the demonstration of clock-controlled release of ecdysone by the PG *in vitro*. This approach has been unsuccessful so far, however. Ecdysone release by the isolated PG subsided within 6 h of transfer to Grace's medium. A thorough search for improved culture conditions seems necessary.

Our evidence described so far reveals that the endocrine events and circadian clock involved in prepupal induction are far more complex than those involved in larval–larval development. These processes can be summarized as follows. PTTH secretion is controlled by a circadian clock, and its critical period, as assessed by neck ligation, is two days before gut purge. The critical period for ecdysone secretion, as revealed by abdominal ligation, is reached 1.5 days later, when the PG clock controls the timing of ecdysone release. The physiological significance of the dual control by circadian clocks of PTTH release and ecdysone release must await further study.

Pupal cuticle formation

Pupal ecdysis, which occurs four days after gut purge, appears rhythmic in a mixed-age population. When counted from the time of gut purge, however, the distribution of its occurrence is unimodal and its timing is not influenced by light: dark changes introduced after gut purge. Neither is the timing of PTTH secretion, responsible for the formation of the pupal cuticle two days after gut purge, affected by light: dark changes after gut purge (see Fujishita & Ishizaki 1982a). Thus, PTTH secretion required for formation of the pupal cuticle is not controlled by a light-sensitive circadian clock but occurs at a fixed time after gut purge, in contrast to the circadian clock-controlled release of PTTH in larval–larval development and in prepupal induction.

All these results on the timing of hormone secretion and overt developmental events are schematically shown in Fig. 5.

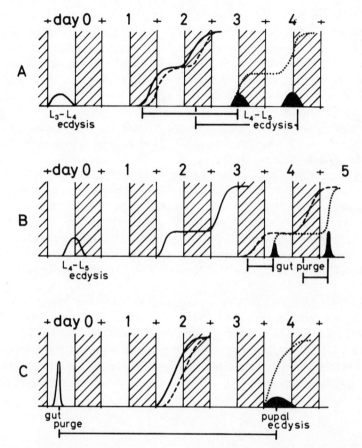

FIG. 5. Schematic representation of the overt developmental events and hormone releases during the last larval moulting (A), prepupal induction (B), and pupal moulting (C). The bimodal and sigmoidal curves represent PTTH release (——) and ecdysone release (---), and the vertical axis in each case ranges from 0 to 100%. The percentage of the animals which underwent larval ecdysis, gut purge and pupal ecdysis in untreated animals is shown by (........). The solid lines below each panel indicate the periods when animals are insensitive to light conditions for timing of the final events. (From Fujishita & Ishizaki 1982a.)

The results described here have revealed various new aspects of the relationship between hormone release and the circadian clock. The techniques used so far have been limited to ligation and organ transplantation under various light:dark conditions. More direct analyses of the hormone secretory process at a molecular level are needed for a deeper understanding of the problem, though they may not immediately provide a solution for the clock mechanism.

Recently we have isolated one of the multiple molecular forms of PTTH from *Bombyx mori* (Nagasawa et al 1984), and its amino acid sequence is now being determined. When a synthetic PTTH becomes available it will be easy to obtain the antibody against PTTH and to establish a radioimmunoassay that measures precisely the dynamics of PTTH secretion. Cloning of the PTTH gene may also be possible, by starting from the known amino acid sequence (Kakidani *et al* 1982); it is impossible to clone the PTTH gene by conventional methods in view of a supposedly minute amount of mRNA synthesized by only one pair of the PTTH-producing neurosecretory cells in the brain (Agui et al 1979).

The recent study on PTTH in *Manduca* haemolymph, using *in vitro* PTTH assay (Gilbert et al 1981), disclosed the developmental-stage-specific differentiation of PTTH in its molecular form (molecular weights of 7000 and 22 000). It is possible that the differential expression of a multiple gene family accounts for this developmental differentiation. The stage-specific differentiation in the processing of a large precursor molecule may also be a crucial problem. Characterizing the PTTH gene is an urgent task for solving these problems.

The failure to detect marked change in PTTH content in the brain during development led Gilbert et al (1981) to speculate that the key process in the regulation of PTTH release resides at the release step rather than at synthesis. Developmental-stage-specific differentiation in the pulsatile release of PTTH has also been described (Gilbert et al 1981). Detailed studies of membrane depolarization will undoubtedly become indispensable in future studies of insect hormones.

Acknowledgement

The work described here was partly supported by a grant-in-aid for Special Project Research on Mechanisms of Animal Behaviour from the Ministry of Education, Science and Culture, Japan.

REFERENCES

Agui N, Granger NA, Gilbert LI, Bollenbacher WE 1979 Cellular localization of the insect prothoracicotropic hormone: *in vitro* assay of a single neurosecretory cell. Proc Natl Acad Sci USA 76:5694-5698

Brady J 1974 The physiology of insect circadian rhythm. Adv Insect Physiol 10:1-115

Fujishita M, Ishizaki H 1981 Circadian clock and prothoracicotropic hormone secretion in relation to the larval–larval ecdysis rhythm of the saturniid *Samia cynthia ricini*. J Insect Physiol 27:121–128

Fujishita M, Ishizaki H 1982a Temporal organization of endocrine events in relation to the circadian clock during larval–pupal development in *Samia cynthia ricini*. J Insect Physiol 28:77–84

Fujishita M, Ishizaki H 1982b The role of ecdysteroids in the determination of gut-purge timing in the saturniid, *Samai cynthia ricini*. J Insect Physiol 28:961–967

Gilbert LI, Bollenbacher WE, Agui N et al 1981 The prothoracicotropes: source of the prothoracicotropic hormone. Am Zool 21:641-653

Kakidani H, Furutani Y, Takahashi H et al 1982 Cloning and sequence analysis of cDNA for porcine β-neo-endorphin/dynorphin precursor. Nature (Lond) 298:245-249

Mizoguchi A 1981 Mechanism for gut-purge timing determination in the saturniid *Samia cynthia ricini*. Iden (Tokyo) 35:80-86 [Japanese]

Mizoguchi M, Ishizaki H 1982 Prothoracic glands of the saturniid moth *Samia cynthia ricini* possess a circadian clock controlling gut-purge timing. Proc Natl Acad Sci USA 79:2726-2730

Nagasawa H, Kataoka H, Hori Y et al 1984 Isolation and some characterization of the prothoracicotropic hormone from *Bombyx mori*. Gen Comp Endocrinol, in press

Pittendrigh CS 1966 Circadian oscillation in *Drosophila pseudoobscura* pupae: a model for the photoperiodic clock. Z Pflanzenphysiol 54:275-307

Pittendrigh CS 1981 Circadian systems: entrainment. In: Aschoff J (ed) Biological rhythms (Handbook of behavioral neurobiology). Plenum Press, New York, vol 4:95-124

Truman JW 1970 Involvement of a photoreversible process in the circadian clock controlling silkmoth eclosion. Z Vgl Physiol 76:32-40

Truman JW 1971 Hour-glass behavior of the circadian clock controlling eclosion of the silkmoth *Antheraea pernyi*. Proc Natl Acad Sci USA 69:595-599

Truman JW 1972 Physiology of insect rhythms. I: Circadian organization of the endocrine events underlying the moulting cycle of larval tobacco hornworm. J Exp Biol 57:805-820

Truman JW 1976 Extraretinal photoreception in insects. Photochem Photobiol 23:215-225

Truman JW, Riddiford LM 1970 Neuroendocrine control of ecdysis in silkmoths. Science (Wash DC) 167:1624-1626

Truman JW, Riddiford LM 1974 Physiology of insect rhythms. III: The temporal organization of the endocrine events underlying pupation of the hornworm. J Exp Biol 60:371-382

Winfree AT 1970 An integrated view of the resetting of a circadian clock. J Theor Biol 28:327-374

DISCUSSION

Steel: Is gut purge actually controlled by ecdysteroids in *Samia*? You have shown that all kinds of manipulations of one phenomenon affect the other, but do you have some specific evidence that the correlation is causal?

Ishizaki: I have no evidence about whether ecdysone acts directly, for example, on the nervous system to turn on gut purge. However, Fujishita & Ishizaki (1982) have shown that if injections of sufficient ecdysone and 20-hydroxyecdysone are given to larvae no later than 18 h before the expected gut purge, they will initiate a precocious gut purge.

Steel: So it is clear that they are closely coupled, but this is not quite sufficient evidence to show that one controls the other.

Gilbert: The ecdysteroids control a tremendous series of physiological and behavioural responses, of which gut purge may be one. Several intermediary steps may be involved here, but the sequence is unknown.

Truman: Samia may be similar to *Manduca*, for which there is evidence that ecdysteroids trigger the premetamorphic behaviour of the larva. Oliver Dominick in my lab has shown that the wandering behaviour in *Manduca*, which is homologous to the gut-purge behaviour in other Lepidoptera, is regulated by ecdysone (O.S. Dominick, unpublished; Truman & Dominick 1983). When an isolated nervous system is taken from feeding *Manduca* and exposed in culture to 20-hydroxyecdysone, a programme of motor nerve activity is turned on after an appropriate latency of about 12 h. We believe that this is the neural correlate of the wandering behaviour. This and other evidence from our endocrinological experiments show that this behaviour is directly triggered by the action of ecdysone on the central nervous system (Truman & Dominick 1983).

Mordue: It is intriguing to the developmental biologist to ask why an ecdysteroid, only in this particular phase, elicits the motor pattern that gives rise to gut purge. Within only a short period earlier than this, a significant change in ecdysteroids does not elicit gut purge, and neither do the ecdysteroid peaks that occur throughout the larval stages. So we need to ask what makes the nervous system competent to respond at this particular time.

Truman: In *Manduca* another necessary feature is the disappearance of juvenile hormone. If this hormone is present at all, it will block the ability of ecdysteroids to trigger wandering behaviour. If juvenile hormone is removed early, then the behaviour may be expressed early, but only in response to ecdysone. So the juvenile hormone has a major influence on the competence of the nervous system to respond to the steroid signal.

Mordue: But in *Samia*, where we are interested in the effects of the photophase in inducing gut purge, it is important to get to grips with the precise effects of juvenile hormone. Do you still believe that juvenile hormone has any role to play in this behaviour in *Samia*, Professor Ishizaki?

Ishizaki: It is likely to be acting in a similar way to what Professor Truman has described for *Manduca*. The combined effect of ecdysone and juvenile hormone probably changes the competence of the nervous system. The juvenile hormone could be acting directly on the prothoracic gland.

Gilbert: Many studies implicate juvenile hormone in the regulation of prothoracic-gland activity (see Hiruma 1982). Presumably, before commitment for pupal development, the juvenile hormone inhibits secretion from the prothoracic gland, and after commitment it stimulates it. No data yet indicate a direct effect of juvenile hormone on the prothoracic glands. Indeed, our own work now indicates that the juvenile hormone acts indirectly on the prothoracic glands to cause the synthesis and release of another factor that activates the prothoracic gland (M.C. Gruetzmacher, L.I. Gilbert, N. Granger, W. Goodman & W.E. Bollenbacher, unpublished results). Although your *in vitro* experiments with the prothoracic glands did not work in terms of ecdysone secretion and a delay in gut purge and so on, have you ever tried to illuminate the prothoracic glands *in vitro* before returning them to the test animals?

Ishizaki: Not yet.

Giebultowicz: What do you think is happening in animals whose heads have been removed and which pupate, some after 5 days and others after 80 days? This happens with many Lepidoptera larvae, if they are ligated at the beginning of the wandering period.

Gilbert: Larvae whose heads are ligated will ultimately pupate, but they take a long time. The haemolymph ecdysteroid titre increases about 10 days after ligation, even without the head, e.g. in *Manduca*, to concentrations well beyond what would be found in the normal animal. A number of factors are involved, including prothoracicotropic and juvenile hormones in normal development. W.E. Bollenbacher and I (unpublished work) several years ago found another factor, which we believe to be a protein that transports a sterol precursor of ecdysone into the prothoracic gland, and which is also involved in timing the large ecdysteroid surge in the haemolymph. The influence of the head is interesting here. The aim, presumably, is to time all this precisely so that a whole population of insects pupates and emerges at the same time. We believe that the brain functions as a timing mechanism for insect populations that utilize these various factors but is not necessary for the prothoracic glands to secrete ecdysone ultimately.

Giebultowicz: But why do some larvae pupate much sooner than others? Is it that the prothoracic glands steadily secrete small amounts of ecdysone, until a threshold concentration is reached, at which positive feedback leads to more secretion of ecdysone?

Gilbert: That would provide a good explanation, because the prothoracic glands never stop secreting, even if it is only at a basal level.

Reynolds: It is all very well to explain the timing of pupal ecdysis in terms of a rise in the ecdysone level but the level has to come down again before the pupae ecdyse. The timing of ecdysis is critically dependent on this fall (Truman 1981). That is why the timing of prothoracic gland activity that Professor Gilbert is talking about is so important. It is needed to ensure a *sharp peak* in the ecdysteroid titre.

Ishizaki: Regardless of this endocrinological evidence, we must also remember the importance of the genetic variation intrinsic to any population of organisms. Prothoracicotropic hormone (PTTH) stimulates ecdysone release and thereby synchronizes normal development of a population. But once PTTH is deprived, it is possible that the genetic variation in the rate of the spontaneous activation of the prothoracic glands, otherwise hidden, may be unmasked, resulting in variously delayed pupation in the headless animals about which Dr Giebultowicz is asking.

Truman: You talked about larval ecdysis as being gated, but we should distinguish between primary gating (directly controlled by a circadian clock) and secondary gating (the outcome of something else being gated beforehand). The 'gating' of larval ecdysis occurs only because the release of PTTH was gated, $1\frac{1}{2}$ days previously (Truman 1972). Hence, I would consider this behaviour as secondarily gated. This distinction may be important when one considers the endocrine basis of a particular rhythm. For example, in *Manduca* there are two distinct groups of neurosecretory cells that produce eclosion hormone (Truman et al 1981): one group is in the brain and is used to regulate ecdyses that show primary gating; a totally separate group in the ventral ganglia releases hormone for non-gated ecdyses (i.e. those that are secondarily gated). Thus, it is important to clarify whether the rhythm with which one is working is primarily or secondarily 'gated'.

Sokolove: I understood the term 'gating' to refer to the final outcome. After all, if one does not know what endocrinological influences are operating, one cannot specify whether it is primary or secondary.

Truman: Yes. But if we are going to start to bring the circadian field into the realm of endocrine physiology then we must begin to think about these problems.

Professor Ishizaki showed that there is a head-critical period for the gut purge, but what is the role of the brain in timing this behaviour? Presumably, earlier in larval life, a clock in the brain can regulate the timing of PTTH release and this clock is light-sensitive. Is there some interaction between this light-sensitive brain clock and the light-sensitive clock that you believe to be in the prothoracic glands?

Ishizaki: I have no evidence yet about such an interaction. Endocrinologically, there must be some complex feedback, both positive and negative, between ecdysone and PTTH-producing cells.

Truman: Do you obtain the same kind of phase-response curve for the gut purge if you give a phase-shifting light pulse when the brain is still required as compared with when the brain is no longer required but the prothoracic glands are still sensitive to light?

Ishizaki: The phase-response curve that I showed was produced without enquiring whether the clock is involved in PTTH or ecdysone levels; we apply the light pulses presumably after PTTH secretion (as determined by neck ligation). Yet this does not necessarily mean that the PTTH is not secreted any more. Furthermore, the free-running period, as measured by introducing larvae into darkness, became progressively shorter as the dark period was prolonged. It is likely that this change in the free-running period is caused by the interaction between the free-running brain clock and the free-running prothoracic gland clock.

Pittendrigh: So would it be useful to measure a phase-response curve for animals before and after neck ligation? The curve after neck ligation would presumably be the phase-response curve for the prothoracic gland clock?

Ishizaki: After neck ligation, gut purge does not occur healthily, i.e. not in a normal fashion.

Pittendrigh: So the absence of a good assay makes it not worthwhile?

Ishizaki: Designs for appropriate experiments along your suggestion are worthwhile, of course.

Saunders: The prothoracic gland is made up of many cells. This may imply that it acts as a very complex multi-oscillator clock.

REFERENCES

Fujishita M, Ishizaki H 1982 The role of ecdysteroids in the determination of gut-purge timing in the saturniid, *Samia cynthia ricini.* J Insect Physiol 28:961-967

Hiruma K 1982 Factors affecting change in sensitivity of prothoracic glands to juvenile hormone in *Mamestra brassicae.* J Insect Physiol 28:193-199

Truman JW 1972 Physiology of insect rhythms. I: Circadian organization of the endocrine events underlying the moulting cycle of larval tobacco hornworms. J Exp Biol 57:805-820

Truman J·1981 Interaction between ecdysteroid, eclosion hormone, and bursicon titers in *Manduca sexta.* Am Zool 21:655-661

Truman JW, Dominick OS 1983 Endocrine mechanisms for the organization of invertebrate behavior. Bioscience, in press

Truman JW, Taghert PH, Copenhaver PF, Tublitz NJ, Schwartz LM 1981 Eclosion hormone may control all ecdyses in insects. Nature (Lond) 291:70-71

Circadian control of haemolymph ecdysteroid titres and the ecdysis rhythm in *Rhodnius prolixus*

C. G. H. STEEL and E. J. AMPLEFORD

Department of Biology, York University, 4700 Keele Street, Downsview, Ontario M3J IP3, Canada

Abstract. The haemolymph levels of ecdysteroids in fifth-instar *Rhodnius prolixus* show massive daily oscillations in 12 h light : 12 h dark conditions. This rhythm exhibits a temperature-compensated free-running period in constant dark. This is the first demonstration of a circadian rhythm in the blood levels of an invertebrate hormone. The rhythm is a multi-component system, since coordinated changes in rates of ecdysteroid synthesis, excretion and metabolism are all required for its production. The rhythm commences at the time of the second release of prothoracicotropic hormone (PTTH) from the brain; a function of this release of PTTH may therefore be to activate expression of the rhythm in ecdysteroids. No evidence of rhythmicity in ecdysteroid levels is seen after the first release of PTTH. The rhythm persists throughout the period of cuticle secretion. Its possible roles in synchronization of developmental events throughout the insect during this period are discussed. The final daily decrease in the titre, about 12 h before ecdysis, appears to provide a signal to the circadian system that times ecdysis in *Rhodnius*, because injection of sufficient 20-hydroxyecdysone (20–40 ng) to abolish this decrease causes a delay in the ecdysis gate on the following day.

1984 Photoperiodic regulation of insect and molluscan hormones. Pitman, London (Ciba Foundation symposium 104), p 150-169

This chapter presents evidence for a circadian rhythm in the haemolymph levels of ecdysteroids (moulting hormones) and discusses its potential significance in the regulation of physiological events. Particular attention is given to the role of this rhythm in the control of ecdysis, since ecdysis (the periodic shedding of the old cuticle) is also under circadian control, and the opportunity is thereby presented to analyse the interaction of two circadian systems at a physiological level. This system is one of the very few, but rapidly increasing, number of physiological control systems in which the formal criteria of circadian biology have been applied to the analysis of physiological control mechanisms.

Our work concerns the control of moulting in the final (fifth) instar of the blood-feeding bug *Rhodnius prolixus*. The fact that one cycle of moulting can be initiated at any time over a period of several months by allowing the insect a blood meal has resulted in the extensive use of *Rhodnius* in analysis of the physiology of insect moulting since 1930 (see Wigglesworth 1964). One of the main advantages of *Rhodnius* is the precision of timing with which physiological events unfold after their initiation at feeding. Recently, this feature has been exploited in analysis of the timing of release of neurosecretion from the brain (see Steel 1982) and in analysis of haemolymph levels of ecdysteroids during moulting (Steel et al 1982). Despite this wealth of physiological information, the importance of circadian systems has hitherto been unrecognized. We shall summarize here recent findings about the role of circadian systems in the control of physiological and behavioural events during moulting in *Rhodnius*.

Methods

We measured the ecdysteroid concentrations in haemolymph by radioimmunoassay as described previously (Steel et al 1982). In animals for which the time of ecdysis was also determined, no more than $5 \mu l$/animal of haemolymph was expressed. Removal of this small quantity of haemolymph had no measurable effect on the timing of ecdysis. We analysed the titre data statistically by non-parametric analysis of variance (Kruskal & Wallis 1952).

The behaviour of *Rhodnius* at the time of ecdysis has been described by Ampleford & Steel (1982a). Ecdysial behaviour was monitored by automated time-lapse photography at 20-min intervals, by the use of dim far-red light during the scotophase, as described by Ampleford & Steel (1982b).

Injections were given through the membrane joining the metathoracic coxa to the sternite, by means of a finely tapered, calibrated glass capillary. Decapitations were achieved with a noose of fine silk thread, and the wound was sealed with a beeswax–resin mixture.

Extracellular recordings of multi-unit electrical activity in the neurosecretory axons from the brain were obtained by the method of Orchard & Steel (1980).

The ecdysteroid titre rhythm

The titre of ecdysteroids in haemolymph smoothly increases and decreases in association with moulting when samples are taken daily between 6 and 20 days after feeding (see Steel et al 1982). A more detailed picture of the titre

was obtained by sampling groups of animals at 4 h intervals during the
decreasing portion of the curve (between Day 14 and Day 19 after feeding).
When the titre is plotted according to the interval between sampling and
ecdysis, it becomes obvious that the titre is not constant within a day (Fig. 1).
Overall, the titre is declining during this period; however, massive daily
increases in titre form daily peaks. The daily increase is approximately half
the decrease. Increases in titre appear to anticipate the time of 'lights off' (Fig.
1). On each of Days 1–3 before ecdysis (Fig. 1 inset) smaller daily increases in
titre are observed, again in association with 'lights off'. Even these smaller
increases in titre are statistically significant ($P < 0.05$). Therefore the
increases in titre at 'lights off' persist until the last 'lights off' before ecdysis.

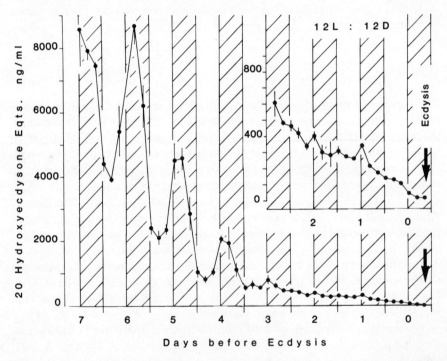

FIG. 1. Haemolymph titre of ecdysteroids before ecdysis for fifth-instar males kept on 12 h
light:12 h dark (12L:12D) at $28 \pm 0.5\,°C$. In all figures, the titre is expressed as 20-hydroxyecdy-
sone equivalents since this ecdysteroid was used throughout as the standard in the radioimmunoassay. Cross-hatched areas indicate the scotophase while clear areas represent photophase.
Points shown are means $\pm$ 1 SEM. Arrows indicate the time of ecdysis. Increases and decreases in
the titre of ecdysteroids anticipate 'lights off' and 'lights on' respectively to produce daily peaks.
The interval between peaks is about 24 h. The data for the last three days before ecdysis are
replotted in the inset on an expanded scale for ecdysteroid. Note the final 'lights off' before
ecdysis is accompanied by a *decrease* in the titre for the first and only time.

In contrast to these daily increases, the 'lights off' that immediately precedes ecdysis is accompanied by a *decrease* in the titre of ecdysteroids (see below).

The anticipatory nature of the massive increases suggested that the haemolymph titre of ecdysteroids may be modulated by an endogenous timing system. In order to demonstrate endogenous timing, the rhythm of daily peaks must be retained in the absence of light:dark cycles. Therefore, animals maintained on a 12 h L:12 h D light:dark cycle were transferred to constant dark (DD) and haemolymph samples were again taken at 4h intervals for 3.5 days in DD. Daily oscillations in ecdysteroid rhythm persist in DD (Fig. 2), with a periodicity of about 24 h. The amplitude of the rhythm

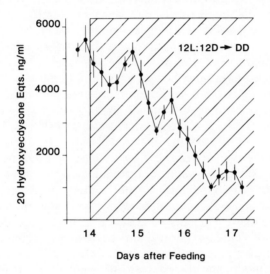

FIG. 2. Haemolymph titre of ecdysteroids for fifth-instar males transferred from 12L:12D to constant dark (DD) at $28 \pm 0.5\,°C$. Data are plotted according to days after feeding, using a three-point sliding mean. Note that peaks in the titre are still observed in DD with an interpeak interval of about 24 h.

during DD appears to decrease within about 48 h, but this observation is not surprising because the haemolymph titre represents a complex balance between numerous physiological processes (see below). The fact that daily oscillations in titre persist in DD shows that the titre is controlled by an endogenous timing system.

We then examined the effect of temperature on the free-running rhythm in DD. When animals, maintained at $24 \pm 0.5\,°C$ on a 12L:12D cycle, were transferred to DD, daily peaks were still observed, again with a periodicity of about 24 h. Thus, the free-running period of the rhythm is temperature-compensated. Since there are daily peaks in the titre of ecdysteroids, which are maintained with a free-running, temperature-compensated period, the haemolymph titre of ecdysteroids is modulated by a circadian system.

To our knowledge these data provide the first demonstration of a circadian rhythm in the blood levels of any invertebrate hormone. Two small daily peaks in haemolymph ecdysteroids are seen at the beginning of the main peak, associated with cuticle secretion in *Mamestra brassicae* (Agui & Hiruma 1982), but it is unknown whether these are circadian. Large oscillations in ecdysteroid levels are reported in *Locusta migratoria* (Girardie & De Reggi 1978) but these do not appear to be daily.

Although the rhythm in the ecdysteroid titre in haemolymph of *Rhodnius* displays superficially simple oscillating characters, closer examination reveals that it must be the product of a complex, multi-component system. The daily increases in titre are too large to be produced by changes in immunoreactivity in the radioimmunoassay that result from interconversion of ecdysteroids already in the haemolymph; hence, ecdysteroids must be secreted daily into the haemolymph. Since steroid hormones are not stored (Gilbert et al 1977), rhythmic secretion in turn implies rhythmic synthesis of ecdysone. This conclusion supports the less direct inference of Fujishita & Ishizaki (1982) and Fujishita et al (1982) that the single small ecdysteroid peak that precedes gut-purge in *Samia cynthia ricini* receives a circadian input (see also Ishizaki, this volume). By similar reasoning, the declining side of each daily oscillation in the *Rhodnius* ecdysteroid titre implies a rhythmic elimination of ecdysteroid from the haemolymph. A major factor in this rhythm is probably excretion, for massive amounts of ecdysteroid have been detected in the rectal contents of *Rhodnius* throughout the period of cuticle secretion; on Day 16 after feeding the rectum contains ~150 ng of ecdysteroid (Steel et al 1982). It is striking that the observed fall in haemolymph titre on Day 16 after feeding (~Day 6 before ecdysis in Fig. 1) requires the elimination of ~150 ng ecdysteroid from the haemolymph. These considerations imply that rhythmic excretion of ecdysteroids could adequately account for the daily decreases in their titre in haemolymph. Such a mechanism may involve rhythmic control of resorption of ecdysteroids from the lumen of the Malpighian tubules (see discussions by Maddrell & Gardiner 1980, Steel et al 1982). Certainly, Malpighian tubules are sensitive to ecdysteroids, for both stimulatory and inhibitory effects on rates of fluid secretion have been described (Gee et al 1977, Ryerse 1978, Rafaeli & Mordue 1982). It is therefore possible that rhythmic excretion of ecdysteroids may be driven by the hormone titre. Thus, coupled rhythms of synthesis and excretion of ecdysteroids appear to be the minimal requirements to explain the observed rhythm in the haemolymph. Given the complexity of these and other factors influencing haemolymph titres of ecdysteroids in insects (see Steel & Davey

1984), it is remarkable that these many factors remain synchronized in DD for long enough to produce a free-running rhythm.

In view of the large size of the daily oscillations, it may seem curious that similar rhythms have not been observed in other species; two possible explanations deserve comment. First, many curves for hormone titre are generated from single daily measurements, thereby excluding the possibility of detecting any existing rhythm. The second reason relates to the relatively long duration (about three weeks) of the moult cycle in *Rhodnius*. A rhythmic titre may assist in the maintenance of developmental synchrony throughout the insect during this extended period. Certainly, in larvae of lepidopterans such as *Calpodes ethlius* (Dean et al 1980) and *Manduca sexta* (Weilgus et al 1979), in which the main haemolymph peak associated with moulting lasts only three days, generation of a smooth titre curve has necessitated obtaining more than one measurement per day and no rhythm is apparent. Overt rhythms in the haemolymph may therefore occur only in species with longer moult cycles.

What may be the physiological significance of this ecdysteroid rhythm? It is clear that target tissues are responsive to ecdysteroid concentrations that change within less than 24 h, and hence cellular responses to a rhythmic titre may be expected. For example, specific binding of $[^3H]$20-hydroxyecdysone to nuclei of imaginal discs is essentially complete after an exposure to the hormone of only one hour, and changes in the synthetic activity of such cells are apparent within two to three hours (Fristrom & Yund 1980). Thus, epidermal cells will be influenced by the rhythm in the haemolymph. Interestingly, a decrease in the ambient titre of 20-hydroxyecdysone after a brief exposure elicits even cuticle secretion by discs (Fristrom & Yund 1980), whereas continuous exposure to the hormone fails to elicit cuticle secretion (Fristrom & Fristrom 1975). These considerations raise the novel possibility that a rhythmic titre of ecdysteroids may elicit responses from target tissues that are qualitatively different from those elicited by a non-rhythmic titre. The nervous system is a further target of ecdysteroid action in which a diversity of effects is known (see Steel & Davey 1984). Since ecdysteroids appear to modulate the excitability of many neurons (references in Steel & Davey 1984) rhythmic nervous activity may be influenced, or even driven, by the rhythm of the ecdysteroid titre. The possibility that circadian rhythms in behaviour may be related to endogenous ecdysteroid titres would appear to be an interesting avenue for future work.

Ecdysteroids and the ecdysis rhythm

The escape from the old cuticle, or ecdysis, is restricted in *Rhodnius* to certain allowed zones or 'gates' within a day, thus producing an ecdysis rhythm in the

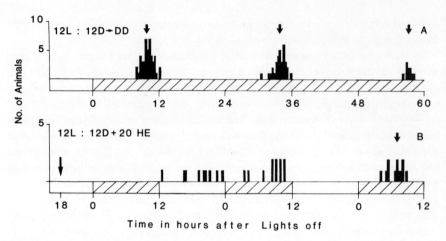

FIG. 3. (A) Time of ecdysis of fifth-instar males transferred from 12L:12D to DD during the scotophase of Day 20 after feeding. Note that gates for ecdysis persist in DD to produce a free-running rhythm with a period which is close to but not exactly 24 h. Small arrows indicate the median time of ecdysis gates. (B) Time of ecdysis for males on a 12L:12D cycle injected with 40 ng of 20-hydroxyecdysone in 1 μl distilled water at 16 h before the median time of the first ecdysis gate. The time of injection is indicated by the large arrow. Note that injection disrupts the first gate for ecdysis (normally centred at 10 h after 'lights off'). However, the effect is transient as no animals emerge outside their normal gates following the time of the expected second ecdysis gate.

whole population. This rhythm is maintained in DD (see Fig. 3A) with a temperature-compensated, free-running period of about 24 h; hence, ecdysis is timed by a circadian system (Ampleford & Steel 1982b). Therefore, in *Rhodnius*, there is both an ecdysis rhythm and a rhythm in haemolymph ecdysteroids, both of which display circadian forms of timing. During each of the seven days before ecdysis, the titre of ecdysteroids increases at 'lights off'. In contrast, the 'lights off' immediately preceding ecdysis is accompanied by a *decrease* in the titre of ecdysteroids (Fig. 1 inset). This decrease in titre could provide the circadian system that times ecdysis with the information required to determine which of the five or six available daily gates for ecdysis will be utilized by an individual insect. By contrast, several daily decreases in ecdysteroid titre are seen in *Manduca sexta* before eclosion, and their phase is temperature-sensitive; nevertheless, a similar role for these titre decreases in *M. sexta* has been postulated (see Truman, this volume, p 221-239).

We explored the potential interaction between the titre and the timing of ecdysis by injecting 20-hydroxyecdysone into pharate adult *Rhodnius* 16 h before the expected time of the first gate for ecdysis. Control injections of 1 μl of distilled water had no effect on the position of the gates for ecdysis. However, injection of 40 μg of 20-hydroxyecdysone in 1 μl distilled water resulted in a significant delay ($P < 0.05$) in the time of ecdysis for animals that would have emerged through the first gate (Fig. 3B). In addition, injection of 20-hydroxyecdysone produces a scatter in the time of ecdysis in these animals, such that many animals emerge at times of day when ecdysis is not seen in controls. However, this effect is temporary since gates are restored within 64 h of injection (Fig. 3B). The delayed ecdysis suggests that 20-hydroxyecdysone is acting to influence the timing of ecdysis. Therefore manipulation of the haemolymph titre of ecdysteroids within one day of ecdysis influences the timing of ecdysis. Such a relationship between haemolymph ecdysteroids and ecdysis would provide a mechanism for synchronizing ecdysis with the completion of prior developmental events. We are currently investigating the precise nature of this interaction between ecdysteroids and ecdysis.

Role of the brain in the rhythms of ecdysteroids and of ecdysis

There are two levels at which the brain is involved in the relationship between the ecdysteroid rhythm and the ecdysis rhythm. First, the brain appears to activate the rhythm in the ecdysteroid titre via the release of prothoracico-tropic hormone (PTTH) at the time of the 'head-critical period' (HCP) for moulting. (The HCP for moulting occurs on Day 6 after a blood meal, and decapitation after this time fails to prevent moulting; see Steel et al 1982.) Second, the brain is also necessary for expression of the ecdysis rhythm via the release of another neurohormone immediately before ecdysis; this latter hormone may be analogous to the eclosion hormone of silkmoths (Truman 1978). These two roles of the brain are discussed below.

In male fifth-instar *Rhodnius*, the main haemolymph ecdysteroid peak that produces apolysis and cuticle secretion is elicited by release of PTTH on Day 6 after feeding (Steel et al 1982). This release of PTTH is accompanied by a characteristic bursting firing pattern of the neurosecretory axons from the brain (Orchard & Steel 1980, Steel et al 1982). We monitored the relationship between this electrical activity, the changes in haemolymph ecdysteroid titre and the timing of the HCP in individual animals in the following experiment. All these parameters were measured every four hours in each of five animals for the four days that encompassed the time of PTTH release. For each animal, the electrical activity was first monitored with a suction electrode inserted through a small hole in the head capsule (upper panel, Fig. 4); a small (5 μl) sample of haemolymph was taken through the same opening, for determination of the ecdysteroid titre (centre panel, Fig. 4); the animal was then decapitated in order to determine whether or not moulting would continue in the absence of the head, i.e. whether the HCP had passed (lower

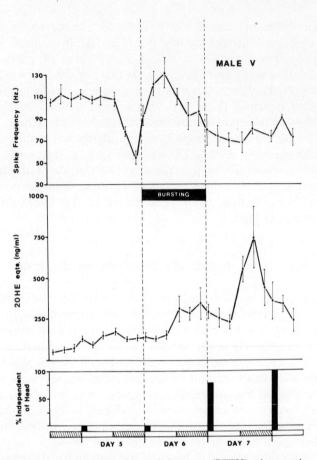

FIG. 4. Relationship between prothoracicotropic hormone (PTTH) release and commencement of the ecdysteroid titre rhythm. PTTH release (on Day 6) lasts 24 h as indicated by the duration of bursting electrical activity in the cerebral neurosecretory axons and the accompanied changes in spike frequency (upper panel), which correspond to the time at which the moulting process can no longer be prevented by decapitation, i.e. the HCP on Day 6 (lower panel; ordinate shows % of animals). The first of the daily increases in ecdysteroid titre occurs at 'lights off' on the day of PTTH release (centre panel). Note that the second daily ecdysteroid peak (Day 7) occurs after the head is no longer necessary for moulting. Maximum titres of ecdysteroids associated with cuticle secretion are not achieved until Day 14. Prior to PTTH release no rhythm in the titre is apparent. 20HE, 20-hydroxyecdysone.

panel, Fig. 4). The bursting firing pattern characteristic of PTTH release corresponds precisely with the HCP for moulting; moulting is arrested in animals decapitated before this time. By these two criteria, this release of PTTH lasts 24 h. Thus, PTTH release in *Rhodnius* is not a gated event.

The ecdysteroid titre changes dramatically during this release of PTTH.

Before the HCP, the titre displays a low and stable profile initiated orginally at feeding (Steel et al 1982). But during PTTH release, on Day 6, the titre more than doubles in association with 'lights off'. The titre then declines during the following photophase and increases again at the next 'lights off' (Day 7, Fig. 4). These constitute the first two daily oscillations in the titre which have been discussed in detail above. Thus, the circadian oscillations in titre commence at 'lights-off' on the day of PTTH release.

These findings are consistent with the classical concept of the role of PTTH as a stimulator of the prothoracic glands; however, they suggest that this stimulation involves activation of a rhythm in ecdysone synthesis. Further, it appears that the phase of the rhythm is not set by PTTH release but by the time of 'lights off' on the day of this release. This conclusion is consistent with those of Mizoguchi & Ishizaki (1982) (see also Ishizaki, this volume) that the photoreceptor for circadian influence over the ecdysteroid titre in *Samia* is located in the prothoracic glands.

It is noteworthy that oscillations in the ecdysteroid titre are not seen during the days between feeding and the HCP. The low, stable ecdysteroid titre maintained throughout this period appears to be elicited by release of PTTH for 2 h following feeding (Steel et al 1982). Thus, it is only the second release of PTTH (described above) that activates the ecdysteroid rhythm in *Rhodnius*. Clearly, there are qualitative differences in the response of the prothoracic glands to the two releases of PTTH. Possibly, different molecular species of PTTH are released on these two occasions (see Bollenbacher & Gilbert 1982).

Although the release of PTTH may activate the ecdysteroid rhythm in haemolymph, the following data show that it does not set the *Rhodnius* ecdysis gate. In contrast, in *Samia cynthia ricini*, the position of the ecdysis gate can be advanced or delayed by changes in the light:dark cycle before, but not after, the release of PTTH (Fujishita & Ishizaki 1981). Therefore, in *Samia* the position of the ecdysis gate is set at the time of PTTH release. In *Rhodnius*, 6 h phase-shifts of the environmental cycle applied before (Day 3), during (Day 6) or after (Days 9 or 12) PTTH release are all equally effective in shifting the position of the ecdysis gate (Fig. 5). Hence, the gate for ecdysis in *Rhodnius* remains labile until shortly before ecdysis, indicating that the circadian system that times ecdysis acts at a time very close to ecdysis itself (see Ampleford & Steel 1982b).

The fact that PTTH release is not important for setting the ecdysis gate does not mean that the brain is not important in the control of ecdysis. Indeed, we have found that ecdysis in decerebrate animals is random, while 'loose-brain' animals (in which all the connections of the brain with the rest of the nervous system have been severed by removal and subsequent re-implantation of the whole brain) undergo ecdysis in a gated fashion (E. J.

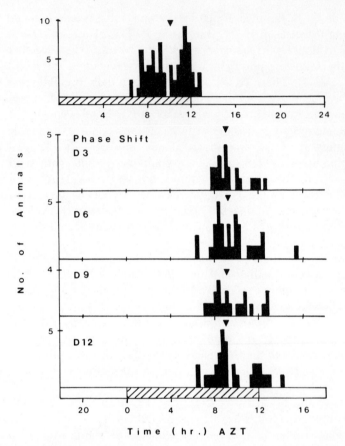

FIG. 5. Time of ecdysis for populations exposed to a 6 h phase-delay of the 12L:12D cycle at various times during the moult cycle, before, during and after PTTH release. Upper panel, no phase-shift; lower panel, phase-shift applied on Days (D) 3, 6, 9 and 12 after feeding. The light:dark cycle in the lower panel is displaced 6 h to the right to indicate the phase-shift experienced relative to the upper panel. Note that the ecdysis gates in all treatments have moved to resume their normal positions with respect to the light:dark cycle. (From Ampleford & Steel 1982b)

Ampleford & C. G. H. Steel, unpublished observations). Therefore the brain may be required either to time ecdysis or to elicit timed ecdysis. Moreover, this requirement does not depend on the nervous connections of the brain. Similar results have been described in silkmoths where eclosion in decerebrate animals is random, while 'loose-brain' moths are gated, and eclosion behaviour is triggered by the release of the eclosion hormone (Truman 1978). In *Rhodnius*, there is both histological (Steel & Harmsen 1971) and electrophysiological (Orchard & Steel 1980) evidence for the release of cerebral neurosecretory material from the corpus cardiacum at the time of ecdysis. Therefore, there may also be a neurohormonal control of ecdysis in *Rhodnius*.

Conclusions

The haemolymph titre of ecdysteroids displays daily peaks that produce a rhythm which is maintained in DD with a free-running temperature-compensated periodicity. Therefore *all* tissues are exposed to circadian inputs via the rhythm in the titre. These inputs could be important for maintaining developmental synchrony during the relatively long (three-week) cycle of moulting, and they may influence widely diverse events including cuticle formation. The rhythm in the ecdysteroid titre first appeared on Day 6 after feeding in anticipation of 'lights off' during the second release of PTTH. Although this release of PTTH is not gated, it could provide the stimulus that acts together with the environmental light:dark cycle to elicit rhythmicity in the ecdysteroid titre.

Ecdysis is also controlled by a circadian system. Therefore in *Rhodnius* there are two processes, ecdysis and the titre of ecdysteroids, which display circadian forms of timing. The haemolymph titre of ecdysteroids may provide the system that times ecdysis with the information necessary to select which ecdysis gate will be used by an individual insect: injection of 40 ng of 20-hydroxyecdysone shortly before ecdysis alters the timing and gating of ecdysis. Thus, it is very likely that these two circadian systems interact at or shortly before ecdysis, and their interaction at a physiological level therefore becomes open to experimental analysis.

Acknowledgement

Research in the authors' laboratory is supported by the Natural Sciences and Engineering Research Council of Canada.

REFERENCES

Agui N, Hiruma K 1982 Ecdysteroid titer and its critical period during larval and pupal ecdysis in the cabbage armyworm, *Mamestra brassicae* L. (Lepidoptera: Noctuidae). Appl Entomol Zool 17:144-146

Ampleford EJ, Steel CGH 1982a The behaviour of *Rhodnius prolixus* (Stål) during the imaginal ecdysis. Can J Zool 60:168-174

Ampleford EJ, Steel CGH 1982b Circadian control of ecdysis in *Rhodnius prolixus* (Hemiptera). J Comp Physiol 147:281-286

Bollenbacher WE, Gilbert LI 1982 Neuroendocrine control of postembryonic development in insects: the prothoracicotropic hormone. In: Farner DS, Lederis K (eds) Neurosecretion: molecules, cells, systems. Plenum Press, New York, p 361-370

Dean R, Bollenbacher WE, Locke M, Smith SL, Gilbert LI 1980 Hemolymph ecdysteroid levels and cellular events in the intermoult/moult sequence of *Calpodes ethlius*. J Insect Physiol 26:267-280

Fristrom D, Fristrom JW 1975 The mechanism of evagination of imaginal discs of *Drosophila melanogaster*. I: General considerations. Dev Biol 43:1-23

Fristrom JW, Yund MA 1980 A comparative analysis of ecdysteroid action in larval and imaginal tissues of *Drosophila melanogaster*. In: Hoffman JA (ed) Progress in ecdysone research. Elsevier/North-Holland, Amsterdam, p 349-362

Fujishita M, Ishizaki H 1981 Circadian clock and prothoracicotropic hormone secretion in relation to the larval–larval ecdysis rhythm of the saturniid *Samia cynthia ricini*. J Insect Physiol 27:121-128

Fujishita M, Ishizaki H 1982 Temporal organization of endocrine events in relation to the circadian clock during larval–pupal development in *Samia cynthia ricini*. J Insect Physiol 28:77-84

Fujishita M, Ohnishi E, Ishizaki H 1982 The role of ecdysteroids in the determination of gut purge timing in the saturniid, *Samia cynthia ricini*. J Insect Physiol 28:961-967

Gee JD, Whitehead DL, Koolman J 1977 Steroids stimulate secretion by insect Malpighian tubules. Nature (Lond) 269:238-239

Gilbert LI, Goodman W, Bollenbacher WE 1977 Biochemistry of regulatory lipids and sterols in insects. In: Goodwin TW (ed) International review of biochemistry, vol 14. University Park Press, Baltimore, p 1-50

Girardie A, De Reggi M 1978 Moulting and ecdysone release in response to electrical stimulation of protocerebral neurosecretory cells in *Locusta migratoria*. J Insect Physiol 24:797-802

Kruskal WH, Wallis WA 1952 The use of ranks in one-criterion variance analysis. J Am Stat Assoc 47:583-621

Maddrell SHP, Gardiner BOC 1980 The retention of amino acids in the haemolymph during diuresis in *Rhodnius*. J Exp Biol 87:315-329

Mizoguchi A, Ishizaki H 1982 Prothoracic glands of the saturniid moth *Samia cynthia ricini* possess a circadian clock controlling gut purge timing. Proc Natl Acad Sci USA 79:2726-2730

Orchard I, Steel CGH 1980 Electrical activity of neurosecretory axons from the brain of *Rhodnius prolixus*: relation of changes in the pattern of activity to endocrine events during the moulting cycle. Brain Res 191:53-65

Rafaeli A, Mordue W 1982 The responses of the Malpighian tubules of *Locusta* to hormones and other stimulants. Gen Comp Endocrinol 46:130-135

Ryerse JS 1978 Ecdysterone switches off fluid secretion at pupation in insect Malpighian tubules. Nature (Lond) 271:745-746

Steel CGH 1982 Parameters and timing of synthesis, transport and release of neurosecretion in the insect brain. In: Farner DS, Lederis K (eds) Neurosecretion: molecules, cells, systems. Plenum Press, New York, p 221-231

Steel CGH, Davey KG 1984 Integration in the insect endocrine system. In: Kerkut GA, Gilbert LI (eds) Comprehensive insect physiology, biochemistry and pharmacology, vol 8. Pergamon, Oxford, in press

Steel CGH, Harmsen R 1971 Dynamics of the neurosecretory system in the brain of an insect, *Rhodnius prolixus*, during growth and molting. Gen Comp Endocrinol 17:125-141

Steel CGH, Bollenbacher WE, Smith SL, Gilbert LI 1982 Haemolymph ecdysteroid titres during larval–adult development in *Rhodnius prolixus*: correlation with moulting hormone action and brain neurosecretory cell activity. J Insect Physiol 28:519-525

Truman JW 1978 Rhythmic control over endocrine activity in insects. In: Gaillard PJ, Boer HH
    (eds) Comparative endocrinology. Elsevier/North-Holland, Amsterdam, p 123-136
Weilgus JJ, Bollenbacher WE, Granger NA 1979 Correlations between epidermal DNA
    synthesis and hemolymph ecdysteroid titre during the last larval instar of the tobacco
    hornworm *Manduca sexta*. J Insect Physiol 25:9-16
Wigglesworth VB 1964 The hormonal regulation of growth and reproduction in insects. Adv
    Insect Physiol 2:247-336

DISCUSSION

Truman: You described the 'burst'-type firing of neurosecretory cells in *Rhodnius prolixus* on Day 6. Do these cells not fire in bursts at other times?

Steel: Yes; a similar bursting firing pattern to that I described on Day 6 (Fig. 4, p 158) is also seen immediately after feeding. This bursting activity corresponds to the *first* release of prothoracicotropic hormone (PTTH) during the moult cycle, whereas that on Day 6 corresponds to the second release (see Steel 1982).

Hardie: Does this change to a bursting pattern of firing happen in cells that are releasing PTTH; are you seeing neurosecretory spikes?

Steel: Yes; they are neurosecretory spikes, but we have no *direct* evidence that these are the cells which are producing PTTH. Detailed analyses of our electrical activity data have already been published (Orchard & Steel 1980, Steel et al 1982).

Chippendale: Have you looked for daily oscillations in ecdysteroid titres any earlier than the fifth instar?

Steel: No. Quite a lot of work is involved: we need about 10 animals per time point, every few hours, every day for several weeks, which requires very many radioimmunoassays!

Truman: You spoke of PTTH release as not being gated, and you also said that the timing of PTTH release did not control the phase of the subsequent ecdysteroid rhythm. On what evidence do you base these statements? Just because the spiking may last for almost 24 h does not mean that the onset of PTTH release is not very precisely timed by a circadian system. The onset of ecdysone secretion may then be phase-locked or time-locked to the onset of this spiking activity.

Steel: I only briefly summarized our evidence on the timing of PTTH release in *R. prolixus*, as most of it is already published. We have evidence not only from electrical activity (Orchard & Steel 1980), but also ultrastructural evidence of hormone release from the corpus cardiacum (Steel 1982) and resulting changes in the ecdysteroid titre (Steel et al 1982), as well as neck-ligation data (Fig. 4, p 158). All this evidence indicates that the release of PTTH on Day 6 lasts for 24 h. Obviously, an event that lasts 24 h cannot be considered as gated.

As for what controls the onset of this 24h release, we know nothing yet, because it is a difficult issue to address experimentally. As you know, for *Manduca sexta*, the timing of *onset* of PTTH release cannot be defined by conventional neck-ligation experiments (p377 in Truman & Riddiford 1974), so we can neither confirm nor deny your hypothetical circadian component (Truman 1972) in the onset of PTTH release using this approach.

However, the point I emphasized was that the increases in the ecdysteroid titre are associated with 'lights-off', not just on the day of PTTH release but throughout the rest of the moult cycle. Fig. 4 shows that the first of the daily increases occurs at 'lights-off' on Day 6, which is 12h after the data on electrical activity indicated that PTTH release had begun. Hence I feel that phase of the titre rhythm is related to 'lights-off', rather than to the time of onset of PTTH release. As I discussed in my paper, this view is entirely consistent with Professor Ishizaki's proposal (this volume) that the prothoracic glands contain their own photoreceptor.

Pittendrigh: In *M. sexta* there is a circadian periodicity but it is by no means as spectacular as the one Professor Steel has described. Is it possible that in all insects there is a strong pulsatile release or synthesis which is obscured by residual non-active hormone that has been metabolically changed?

Truman: Most published measurements of titres do not include multiple readings throughout the day; so daily rhythms *may* be there, but they have not been looked at. In *M. sexta* our titre data are for only about the last three days of adult development (Schwartz & Truman 1983). As Professor Steel showed for *R. prolixus*, the oscillations in *M. sexta* on the last three days are relatively small. We have not looked at earlier days in development because of problems in staging the animals.

Steel: The other side of the coin is that for several species in which it has been necessary to obtain several time-points per day in order to get a smooth titre curve throughout the moult cycle, there is no evidence of a daily rhythmicity. These are primarily animals with quite short moult cycles of 3 or 4 days or so. The moult cycle in *R. prolixus* is about 3 weeks. It is at least conceivable that a circadian rhythmicity in the titre may be a mechanism for maintaining developmental synchrony in an animal which has a very long moult cycle. One would thus not see these kinds of events in animals whose moult cycles are much shorter.

Truman: Can you phase-shift the timing of PTTH release, by shifting the photoperiod? If you were to take animals that ecdysed to the last larval instar at the same time and were to give some a 12:12 light:dark cycle and others an inverted 12:12 cycle, would PTTH release occur at the same time in both populations? This would show whether there was a clock control over PTTH release.

Steel: I don't know. We have not looked at any potential circadian involvement in the control of PTTH release yet. Your experiment requires a phase reference point for PTTH release, such as its time of onset, which is hard to define (see above).

Denlinger: Do you have any information about the juvenile hormone titre at the same time?

Steel: No; we don't know what the juvenile hormone is in *R. prolixus*.

Hodková: You said that if you artificially increase the ecdysone level you have a delay in the ecdysis gate afterwards. Do you obtain similar results if you ligate the neck or remove the brain? It is possible that this rhythm in ecdysone titre may inform the brain when it is the 'right' time to trigger ecdysis.

Steel: We have not tried those experiments.

Reynolds: Would a brain-deprived *R. prolixus* ecdyse normally anyway?

Steel: No. But animals with 'loose-brains' do undergo normal ecdysis (see p 159).

Gilbert: We can make an analogy between the ecdysteroid peak that you see in *R. prolixus* and that seen in *M. sexta* (Bollenbacher et al 1975): the components that give you the radioimmunoassay-positive material on the up-swing of the peak could be completely different from the substances present on the down-swing. On the down-swing one is really studying the rapid degradation of 20-hydroxyecdysone, and although one detects radioimmunoassay-positive material, these are presumably ecdysteroid metabolites. It is interesting that you are seeing this cyclic phenomenon which may consist in part of the degradation of the moulting hormone.

Steel: Now that we know just how enormous are the titres during the scotophase—some animals will produce 8 µg/ml in the haemolymph—we have more than enough haemolymph stored away in the freezer to do chemical analysis of which ecdysteroids exist in the haemolymph at different parts of the cycle. However, I would guess that cyclic degradation of ecdysteroids would be only one component of the overt rhythm in the blood titre.

Mordue: That high amount is quite important. The pulse of ecdysteroid may be even more potent than you think if the material present on the up-swing is biologically active and that on the down-swing is less biologically active.

Pittendrigh: Is this the only insect in which an attempt has been made to look for circadian changes in the ecdysteroid titre of the haemolymph? Have the saturniids been studied in this respect?

Truman: We have found daily steps in ecdysteroids in *M. sexta* (Schwartz & Truman 1983), but they are paltry compared with the huge peaks described by Professor Steel. All that we see in *M. sexta* is a daily modulated step-down, rather than discrete 'ups' and 'downs'.

Steel: Yes; to the best of my knowledge these results on *R. prolixus* are the first circadian oscillations that have been seen in insects or in any other invertebrate hormone, for that matter.

Mordue: The oscillations look very similar to the pulsatile release of luteinizing hormone that occurs in mammalian reproductive cycles.

Steel: Yes; the rates of change of titre within these short time-scales are quite phenomenal.

Reynolds: I am surprised that you feel it must be necessary to have both a rhythm of steroidogenesis and a rhythm of steroid metabolism. Surely either one could account for what you have seen?

Pittendrigh: I agree. All that is needed is a periodic input of ecdysone into the haemolymph against a steady aperiodic rate of removal. At the beginning the aperiodic rate of removal should be rising, then later declining.

Brady: It could also be the other way round, of course.

Steel: I find it difficult to explain our results if *either* release or degradation is continuous. The rate of decline of the ecdysteroid titre on the decreasing side can be considered as a function of the rate of ecdysteroid elimination from the haemolymph if we imagine that there is no secretion *into* the haemolymph at that time. If that rate of elimination (about $800\,\mathrm{ng\,ml^{-1}\,h^{-1}}$) is superimposed on the ascending side, on the rate at which the titre is increasing (about $600\,\mathrm{ng\,ml^{-1}\,h^{-1}}$), one would need a rate of ecdysteroid synthesis that is so enormous that I find it difficult to believe that an animal would operate that way. In other words, it seems energetically more conservative to alternate release and degradation of hormone on a daily basis.

Reynolds: The trouble is that your radioimmunoassay is probably measuring different substances on the ascending and descending phases of those peaks, so those simple calculations cannot be done.

Gilbert: Actually the data could be explained by the conjugation and deconjugation of ecdysteroids, some of which are immunoreactive and some of which are not, depending on the antiserum used. Did you find conjugated ecdysteroids in the haemolymph?

Steel: Yes, conjugation and deconjugation of ecdysteroids could be important here. Now that we have such massive amounts available, as I mentioned, we can begin to address these questions. If the conjugates are not immunoreactive (as you imply), then the 'simple calculations' to which Dr Reynolds referred just now would in fact be meaningful.

Mordue: As endocrinologists we should think not only about hormonal titres but also about receptor sensitivity. The critical part of any endocrine control system is the ability of the receptors to respond to a hormone. We know that this variability in receptivity happens classically for juvenile hormone, but we don't know enough yet about ecdysone receptors.

Pittendrigh: Is there a circadian periodicity to receptor function in vertebrates?

Mordue: There is not necessarily a *circadian* periodicity, but the ability of the hormone to turn on the receptors that respond to it is well established for certain peptides.

Sokolove: There are several instances for mammalian reproductive hormones where one hormone turns on receptors for a second hormone, for example the system involving follicle stimulating hormone and luteinizing hormone.

Brady: Is there a relationship here between these extraordinary peaks and the sensitivity of the responding system which could be revealed by what happens in constant darkness? Your results suggested that the circadian peaks were much smaller in constant darkness, so the amplitude of the rhythm was damped out. Does the responding system also show signs of having been less sensitive? Are the ecdysis gates wider?

Steel: Since we have two (probably distinct) circadian systems it is very difficult to do that kind of experiment. The way the data were plotted may be relevant here. The free-running rhythm of the titre in constant darkness was plotted in terms of days after feeding as opposed to days before ecdysis. This increases the amount of scatter in the data and reduces the apparent amplitude of the rhythm. One cannot do that experiment the other way round, since the exposure to continuous darkness necessary to get the titre rhythm to free-run would also affect the ecdysis rhythm. Hence, we would not be able to tell if any effects on (to use your example) the width of the ecdysis gate resulted from changes in the titre rhythm or from direct effects of continuous darkness on the ecdysis 'clock'.

Bowen: The daily fluctuations in haemolymph ecdysteroid titre do not necessarily imply a daily rhythm of hormone synthesis or secretion, but may instead reflect steroid clearance by way of metabolic processes or excretion. Is it possible in *R. prolixus* to sacrifice animals every few hours, remove the prothoracic glands and measure basal synthetic rates *in vitro*? This would at least tell you whether the prothoracic glands exhibit a rhythm of secretion.

Steel: Yes; this would probably be the clearest way of checking these various possibilities, but we have not done it yet.

Brady: Do any long-term mammalian cycles have such an amplitude of circadian noise superimposed on them? In this case it is 'noise' in terms of the 20-day moulting cycle, and it seems to be an extraordinary control system.

Saunders: Follett et al (1981) have some data on luteinizing hormone in the quail, which shows a daily surge following a long-day photoperiod.

Mordue: Are there any other examples of ecdysteroid titres as high as those in *R. prolixus*? Why would *R. prolixus* need such high levels when most other insects manage with substantially less?

Steel: I do not have any other examples. Our earlier titre data for *Rhodnius* was from animals taken strictly during the photophase. As I pointed out, we now realize these are the daily *minimal* levels, even though they are close to what Professor Gilbert has seen in the pupal stage of *M. sexta* (10^{-5} M). Our scotophase titres are about three-fold higher (3×10^{-5} M).

Gilbert: Since the total volume of haemolymph in *R. prolixus* is about 60 µl per animal and the total amount of ecdysteroids in R. *prolixus* is not very different from that in M. *sexta* (up to several µg) which has 20× the haemolymph volume, it is just more concentrated in R. *prolixus* (about 10^{-5}M).

Steel: Since the haemolymph titres in R. *prolixus* change at an astronomically rapid rate, one *could* propose that this fulfils a need for the saturation of receptors within a short period of time.

Goldsworthy: I perhaps rather naively thought that if titres of ecdysteroids are controlled by the light:dark cycle they would be accurately locked into that cycle. However, your data did not always show a tight locking; at least on one day the ecdysteroid titre anticipated 'lights-off', but not on others.

Steel: I do not recall such a drifting except in our very preliminary data that first indicated to us the possible presence of oscillations in titre. Otherwise there was a good locking into the light cycle.

Brady: A very steep graph like the one you showed, of course, always contains considerable room for error because slight shifts along the abscissa create large differences up and down the ordinate.

Steel: Yes. A very small lateral shift would give rise to error at a time of rapid change. This is reflected in our larger standard errors at times when the titre is changing rapidly.

Bowen: Could such shifting in ecdysteroid levels reflect the activity of a loosely coupled 'B' oscillator?

Pittendrigh: Yes.

Steel: But B oscillators are temperature-sensitive, whereas our oscillations seemed to be temperature-compensated.

Pittendrigh: But of course when the animals are entrained to a light:dark cycle the period is temperature-compensated but the phase is very temperature-sensitive.

Truman: In M. *sexta*, temperature seems to be the major cue for setting the phase of the ecdysteroid rhythm. We have not determined whether the rhythm is temperature-compensated, but I expect that it is. The question of temperature-compensation is quite separate from the ability of temperature to set the phase of a rhythm.

Steel: My comment just now related not so much to the phase of the rhythm as to the period of the free-running rhythm in the absence of an entraining light:dark cycle.

Pittendrigh: That would be temperature-compensated as long as the slave is still locked onto the pacemaker.

Steel: Yes; the question of phase is certainly intriguing and we are only just beginning to understand it.

REFERENCES

Bollenbacher WE, Vedeckis WV, Gilbert LI, O'Connor JD 1975 Ecdysone titres and prothoracic gland activity during the larval–pupal development of *Manduca sexta*. Dev Biol 44:46-53

Follett BK, Robinson JE, Simpson SM, Harlow CR 1981 Photoperiodic time measurement and gonadotrophin secretion in quail. In: Follett BK, Follett DE (eds) Biological clocks in seasonal reproduction cycles. Wright, Bristol, p 185-201

Orchard I, Steel CGH 1980 Electrical activity of neurosecretory axons from the brain of *Rhodnius prolixus*: relation of changes in the pattern of activity to endocrine events during the moulting cycle. Brain Res 191:53-65

Schwartz LM, Truman JW 1983 Hormonal control of the rates of metamorphic development in the tobacco hornworm *Manduca sexta*. Dev Biol 99:103-114

Steel CGH 1982 Parameters and timing of synthesis, transport and release of neurosecretion in the insect brain. In: Farner DS, Lederis K (eds) Neurosecretion: molecules, cells, systems. Plenum Press, New York, p 221-231

Steel CGH, Bollenbacher WE, Smith SL, Gilbert LI 1982 Haemolymph ecdysteroid titres during larval–adult development in *Rhodnius prolixus*: correlation with moulting hormone action and brain neurosecretory cell activity. J Insect Physiol 28:519-525

Truman JW 1972 Physiology of insect rhythms. I: Circadian organization of the endocrine events underlying the moulting cycle of larval tobacco hornworms. J Exp Biol 57:805-820

Truman JW, Riddiford LM 1974 Physiology of insect rhythms. III: The temporal organization of the endocrine events underlying pupation of the tobacco hornworm. J Exp Biol 60:371-382

Photoperiodic regulation of prothoracicotropic hormone release in late larval, prepupal and pupal stages of *Sarcophaga bullata*

BRIAN ROBERTS

Zoology Department, Monash University, Clayton, Victoria 3168, Australia

Abstract. Midway during the third instar, *Sarcophaga bullata* larvae cease feeding, leave the food source, and enter the post-feeding larval (PFL) stage. With specific rearing conditions (25 °C ± 0.5 °C; 16 h photophase) larvae enter the PFL stage only during the 8 h scotophase. Larvae that do not leave the food source during the first PFL temporal gate wait for the opening of the gate during the following scotophase. *In vitro* incubation techniques, specific for ecdysone secretion by isolated ring glands, have demonstrated a distinct release of ecdysone during the early hours of the scotophase. Ecdysteroid levels in the haemolymph increased shortly after. In both systems low levels of ecdysteroids were recorded at the end of the scotophase and in the early hours of the photophase. The process of pupariation is under hormonal control. High ecdysone levels were released from *in vitro*-cultured, isolated ring glands just before the formation of the red spiracular stage. The levels oscillated at 4 h intervals and decreased as the developmental events of pupariation progressed. Titres of haemolymph ecdysteroids also oscillated at 4 h intervals for some time but a distinct peak (1.0 ng/μl) was recorded 11 h after the formation of the white prepupal stage. The release of prothoracicotropic hormone may be under photoperiodic control, as a significant proportion of larvae pupariated during the scotophase. The biological significance of these events is discussed.

1984 Photoperiodic regulation of insect and molluscan hormones. Pitman, London (Ciba Foundation symposium 104), p 170-188

In holometabolic insects, the development of a rigid cuticle requires that for growth and metamorphosis to occur a new cuticle must be formed periodically and the old one shed. The moulting process is initiated by the release of the prothoracicotropic hormone (PTTH) from specific neurosecretory cells of the brain, which in turn results in the secretion of moulting hormone by the prothoracic glands (Gilbert et al 1981). The type of cuticle formed, and the developmental stage, is regulated by a third hormone, the juvenile hormone produced by the corpora allata.

In the past decade J. W. Truman and his co-workers have shown that the secretion of several of the developmental hormones of Lepidoptera, including PTTH, is controlled by photoperiodic clocks. It appears that the interaction of these clocks with the environmental photoperiod serves to restrict hormone release to a specific portion of the light:dark cycle; such a response is said to be *gated* by the photoperiod (Pittendrigh 1966). Truman (1972) and Truman & Riddiford (1974) have demonstrated the existence of specifically timed gates for larval–larval moults, together with the formation of wandering larvae and the metamorphic event of pupation in *Manduca sexta*.

Since PTTH is the hormone responsible for initiating the moulting and growth processes in all insects thus far studied, it was decided to study its release, in relation to strict rearing procedures, in the relatively large fleshfly, *Sarcophaga bullata*, an insect that is taxonomically remote from the Lepidoptera but which has been the subject of much endocrinological research.

Sarcophaga bullata is an ovoviviparous cyclorrhaphous dipteran which possesses three larval instars during which the larvae greatly increase in size and weight (Roberts 1976, Wentworth et al 1981). During the third instar the larvae feed voraciously and then leave the food, approximately midway through the instar, to enter the post-feeding larval (PFL) stage before gut-purging and pupariation. During recent years it has been shown that larval–larval moults, pre-ecdysial sclerotization of specialized larval cuticle, pupariation, formation of the pharate adult and the subsequent secretion of the adult cuticle are controlled by specifically timed releases of moulting hormone (Wentworth et al 1981, Roberts et al 1982).

To date little is known about the effects of environmental conditions on PTTH release and on consequent secretions of moulting hormone to elicit the responses outlined above. This paper specifically considers the timing of the events in relation to imposed photoperiodic rhythms that may govern the formation of the PFL stage and may influence pupariation.

Materials and methods

Living material

The ovoviviparous fleshfly *Sarcophaga bullata* (Parker) was reared in a walk-in room maintained at 25°C ± 0.5°C and with a daily photoperiod of 16 h. Adults that eclosed during the first 3 h of the photophase were supplied with sugar and water and, 96 h after eclosion, with a protein source (lamb's liver) for 24 h.

On the 12th day, 8 h after the beginning of the photophase, pregnant females were collected and larviposition was induced by squeezing of the abdomen. The progeny of each female were reared on a minimum of 125 g of fresh, sliced lamb's liver housed in individual aluminium-foil packets that were placed in separate containers. After larviposition the foil packets were lightly compressed to avoid desiccation of the food source.

Collection and observation of experimental material

The formation of the post-feeding larval and the white prepupal stages. Containers were checked hourly to determine the time and rate at which larvae left the food; those that had formed the PFL stage were counted and removed. Animals that were at the white prepupal stage were treated similarly. All recordings during the scotophase were performed under a dim red light by using a Kodak Wratten 92 filter with a 25 W bulb.

In vitro ring gland assay for PTTH. PFL and red spiracular stage larvae were placed on ice for approximately 20 min, covered with cold Grace's insect tissue-culture medium, slit posteriorly–anteriorly on the dorsal surface from the mid-region up to the mouth hooks, and quickly pinned to expose the retrocerebral complex. Ring glands were excised by cutting aortal and tracheal connections and were dissected free of surrounding tissues with extreme care to avoid touching the glands with dissection instruments. White prepupal and prepupal samples were also collected and the antero-dorsal cuticle of the first 3–4 puparial segments was excised to expose the ring glands which were removed as described above. Each ring gland was transferred to a 0.01 ml drop of Grace's medium on a small Petri-dish lid. This was then inverted as a hanging drop over a dish containing Grace's medium to minimize evaporation. After incubations at 25 °C for 2 h, 0.005 ml of fluid was sampled and radioimmunoassayed, as described previously (Bollenbacher et al 1979, Wentworth et al 1981, Roberts et al 1984). At least five measurements were made for each titre point.

Collection and extraction of haemolymph for the ecdysteroid radioimmunoassay. At selected stages of larval–pupal development, haemolymph samples were collected. For PFL and red spiracular stage larvae, the ventral anal papillae were cut and the haemolymph was carefully expressed onto parafilm. Immediately, 0.02 ml haemolymph was added to 0.2 ml of cold absolute methanol, and the extracted samples were stored at 4 °C until required. For samples of white prepupal and prepupal haemolymph, the puparium was pierced with a fine needle in the dorsal aspect of the second segment and carefully squeezed. Only larvae that had formed the white prepupal stage during the first 2 h of the photophase were used. Aliquots (0.1 ml) of the methanol extracts were quantified for ecdysteroids by radioimmunoassay as described above.

Results

Formation of the PFL stage

The temporal PFL gates. After larviposition has been induced, larvae seek crevices in the sliced liver, commence active feeding and, after two larval moults at 24 h and 44 h, enter the final instar (Roberts 1976, Wentworth et al 1981). Approximately half-way through this instar they leave the putrified liver, amass on top of the solid parts of the food source and, soon after, leave the foil packets to seek a place to pupariate.

The progeny of five individual females ($n = 327$) were observed at hourly intervals for the formation of the PFL stage. This is defined as a larva which has left the food source and cannot feed again (Fraenkel & Bhaskaran 1973).

Fig. 1 shows that the formation of the PFL stage commenced at 107 h. Under the conditions of this experiment all larvae at the 'correct' morphogenetic stage completed this event only during the scotophase. The larvae

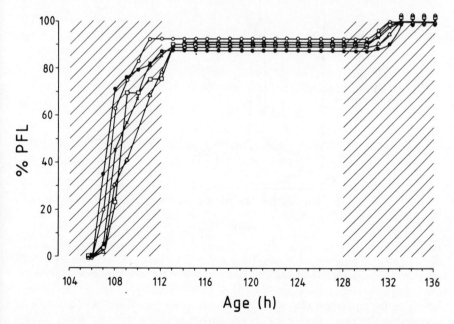

FIG. 1. The timing of entry into the post-feeding larval stage of the progeny of five females of *S. bullata* which were reared under a 16L:8D photoperiod at 25 °C.

that did not leave the food source became immobile within the foil–food package and entered the PFL stage at the subsequent scotophase, at about 130 h. All larvae were at the PFL stage by 133 h, some 3 h before the beginning of the photophase.

Activity of isolated ring glands from specifically aged larvae. Larvae were chosen from the progeny of one individual and were sampled at 10 specific times over the experimental period. These included larvae that were feeding, larvae in the food mass, larvae on top of the food source, larvae crawling up the foil packet and larvae that had left the packeted food source.

Ring glands from larvae that were feeding showed low activity. In contrast, larvae that were on the food surface, but not actively feeding (approximately 107 h), showed high ring-gland activity with a secretion of over 1.4 ng ecdysone. Ring glands from larvae that were in the process of leaving the foil–food packet or that had left the food source (108 to 114 h) showed little activity (Fig. 2).

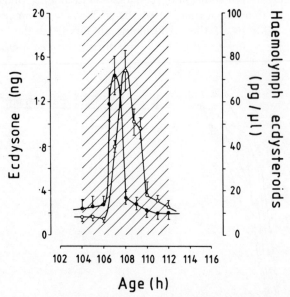

FIG. 2. The activity of ring-gland ecdysone (solid circles) and haemolymph ecdysteroids (open circles) during the temporal post-feeding larval gate observed during the scotophase. Each point represents the mean (bar : standard error), based on at least five individual measurements.

Levels of haemolymph ecdysteroids. The progeny of a different female were sampled at the times described above. In larvae that remained in the food in the early hours of the scotophase the levels of moulting hormone proved to be minimal. Approximately half-way through the scotophase, while larvae were crawling up the inner sides of the foil container, the concentrations of ecdysteroids in the haemolymph increased to a peak of approximately 75 pg/μl at 108 h. In the established PFL stage (110–114 h) the levels of moulting hormone were reduced (Fig. 2).

The formation of the white prepupal stage

After leaving the food source larvae seek a place for pupariation—in this case, amongst leaves of paper towelling. The progeny of 20 individual females ($n = 1247$) were checked hourly and the time of formation of the immobile white prepupal stage was recorded. The progeny of the majority of females (85%) showed no definite response to the photoperiodic gate, although many (55%) showed that formation of the white prepupal stage was more common during either the first or the second scotophase. In contrast, the progeny of three females showed clear-cut gated responses to photoperiod (Fig. 3); most of them initiated and completed white prepupal formation during the scotophase or the very early hours of the photophase.

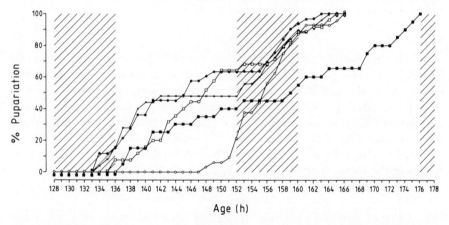

FIG. 3. The temporal formation of the white prepupal stage of progeny of five females.

Ring-gland activity in vitro

The activity of the ring glands was assessed *in vitro* during the periods before and after the white prepupal stages (Fig. 4). During the late hours of the PFL stage the synthesis of ecdysone by the ring glands was minimal, but as larvae approached the red spiracular stage, ecdysone synthesis increased, reaching a

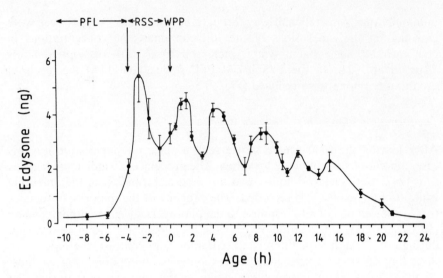

FIG. 4. Ecdysone secretions by ring glands (RG) *in vitro*. Ring glands were obtained from the post-feeding larvae, prepupal and pupal stages of *S. bullata*. PFL, post-feeding larvae; RSS, red spiracular stage; WPP, white prepupal stage. Each point represents the mean (bar: 1 standard error), based on at least five individual measurements.

maximum of over 5 ng ecdysone during the first third of the red spiracular stage (-3 h). This proved to be the maximal rate of secretion observed in this study. After this initial increase, the rate of ecdysone synthesis by the ring glands oscillated, producing three significant peaks, of decreasing amplitude, at approximately 4 h intervals. By 21 h after the white prepupal stage, gland activity had returned to the low, early PFL-stage levels. The significant peaks of ring-gland activity at -3 h, 1 h and 9 h correlated temporally with the three peaks in the haemolymph titre (see Fig. 5).

Haemolymph titre of ecdysteroids during late larval and prepupal development

Ecdysteroid levels in the PFL stage were extremely low (<0.02 ng/μl) but began to increase as the animals approached the red spiracular stage (Fig. 5). Midway through the red spiracular stage (-2 h) the ecdysteroid titre in the haemolymph peaked at approximately 0.4 ng/μl, but then dropped so that at the formation of the white prepupal stage the level was only about 0.15 ng/μl haemolymph. Two hours after the formation of the white prepupal stage the haemolymph titre of ecdysteroids increased to a level comparable with that of the mid-aged red spiracular stage. Shortly thereafter (4 h after the white

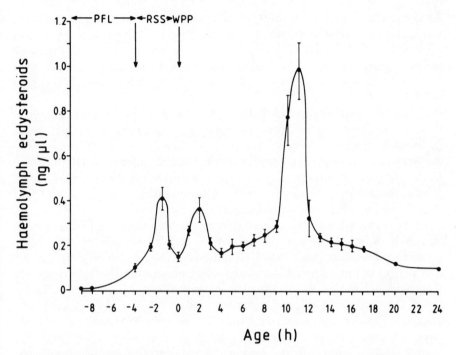

FIG. 5. The haemolymph titre of ecdysteroids during the post-feeding larval and prepupal stages of *S. bullata*. Details as for Fig. 4.

prepupal stage) the titre in the haemolymph decreased again to 0.18 ng/μl and remained at this level for several hours. It was during this period that apolysis was observed in the anterior segments of prepupae. From 6–9 h after the white prepupal stage the haemolymph titre of ecdysteroids began to increase, and by 10 h it had increased dramatically, peaking at 1 ng/μl at 11 h. By 13 h the titre had decreased to 0.2 ng/μl, after which time it dropped gradually to approximately 0.1 ng/μl, 24 h after the white prepupal stage. Of particular interest was that each peak in the titre was approximately 3 h in duration and, except for the absence of a peak 6 h after the white prepupal stage, the peaks occurred approximately every 4 h, as noted for ecdysone secretion by the ring glands.

Discussion

In these experiments, the conditions of rearing all developmental stages of the flesh-fly, *S. bullata*, were strictly controlled and require some discussion.

As insect development depends on temperature stability, the temperature was continually monitored and the photophase critically controlled at 16 h light: 8 h dark (16L:8D). These conditions were chosen specifically because the photophase is some 2.5 h longer than the diapause-inducing day-lengths reported (Denlinger 1972, Roberts & Warren 1976) for Sarcophagidae reared at 25 °C.

Only adults that emerged in the first 3 h of the photophase were chosen for these experiments. A number of studies have been made on emergence rhythms of dipterous insects, and it is now accepted that the emergence rhythm in flies is entrained by photoperiod and thermoperiod (Beck 1980). Under the experimental conditions a daily emergence maxima occurred 1–3 h after the beginning of the photophase. This choice of animals produced adults that showed synchronous reproductive cycles.

On eclosion, adults were offered only commercial sugar and water for the first 96 h of development, the carbohydrate being necessary for oocyte maturation (Wilkens 1968). At 96 h, thinly sliced lamb's liver was offered for a 24 h period to initiate vitellogenesis and egg maturation (Wilkens 1969). In this study and another (Wentworth & Roberts 1984) 4 h was found sufficient for all the females to utilize the protein source. When compared to females offered a protein source shortly after eclosion for a longer period, say 3–4 days, this procedure synchronized the vitellogenic cycle.

In *S. bullata*, embryonic development occurs within a sac-like uterus, and at 25 °C eggs hatch in the uterus by the end of the 11th day of female adult life; but, in the absence of a suitable source for larviposition, larvae are not deposited (Denlinger 1972). In this study pregnant females were collected 8 h after the beginning of the photophase on Day 12 and their larvae were extruded, by squeezing, onto fresh, sliced lamb's liver, which resulted in synchronously aged larvae.

Under these conditions the synchronous populations of adult females and developing embryos were exposed to the same photoperiodic conditions. This was obligatory as, in *Sarcophaga* spp., the phase that is sensitive to the photoperiod is during the embryonic and the early larval stages (Saunders 1971, Denlinger 1972).

Truman & Riddiford (1974) have shown that during the first part of the fifth instar, larvae of *Manduca sexta* feed continuously but that, by half-way through the instar, and within a few hours during the scotophase, feeding ceases, the gut is cleared and larvae transform into the wandering stage. In *Sarcophaga*, larvae began to leave the food during the scotophase at 107 h, with 50% of those at the PFL stage that were committed for the first temporal gate achieving this commitment by 108 h. Approximately 90% of all larvae entered the PFL stage and those that did not waited for the subsequent gate to open during the following scotophase.

In nature the significance of such photoperiod-entrained behaviour is obvious. For example, larvae may be deposited on a carcass and may develop within its confines. The establishment of the PFL stage, before sunrise, would be a distinct advantage to the larvae because predators, particularly carrion-eating birds, would not be active at that time.

The results of *in vitro* culturing of prothoracic glands were directly correlated with the PTTH activity of the neurosecretory cells (Bollenbacher et al 1979). In the experiments reported here, the ring glands were active for 2 h approximately midway through the scotophase, soon after ecdysteroid levels in the haemolymph had increased. The radioimmunoassay results corroborate the findings presented by Truman & Riddiford (1974) who report that for *M. sexta* a release of PTTH, during the scotophase and of about 3.5 h duration, is responsible for the transformation to wandering larvae.

The study of the formation of the white prepupal stage in relation to photoperiod proved interesting in that the progeny of many flies showed sensitivity to the photoperiod at some time during the scotophase. In fact, a small percentage showed an almost total response (Fig. 3) in that the white prepupal stage was completed in the scotophase or during the early hours of the photophase.

For over a decade it has been considered that the stage of the life-cycle that is sensitive to photoperiod never extends to the whole of development. In *Sarcophaga* spp. the embryos, within the maternal uterus, are particularly sensitive (Denlinger 1972). The larvae then remain sensitive throughout their development (Saunders 1971), but become insensitive at the time of puparium formation. The results I have presented in this paper would appear to nullify the previous findings. However, I consider the formation of the white prepupal stage to be a continuing effect of photophase gained during the sensitive stages, particularly because I cannot suggest any significant biological advantage for gated puparium formation—especially for an insect that, in nature, may be several inches beneath the soil surface. This aspect of pupariation certainly warrants further study.

The fluctuating ecdysteroid titres and ring-gland activity (Roberts et al 1983) have not been observed previously during the red spiracular and early prepupal stages of Diptera (Shaaya & Karlson 1965, Ohtaki et al 1968, Seligman et al 1977, Briers & De Loof 1980, Wentworth et al 1981). However, similar fluctuations over a longer period have been observed for the larval–pupal development of *Calpodes ethlius* (Dean et al 1980). The physiological significance of these repeated peaks is not clear, but the characteristic morphological and behavioural changes during this developmental period suggest that these peaks may be important in *Sarcophaga* development.

The results reported here relate to mixed progeny red spiracular and white prepupal stages which formed only during the first 2 h of the photoperiod. The first surge in the ecdysteroid titre, several hours before the white prepupal stage, may be involved in the progressive tanning of the cuticle between and around the posterior spiracles to form the red spiracular stage. This sclerotization may be analogous to the pre-ecdysial tanning of the mandibular mouth hooks and the anterior and posterior spiracles of *Sarcophaga*, which are produced by moulting hormone (Roberts et al 1982). This peak may also be involved in initiating pupariation, since the white prepupal stage occurs approximately 1–2 h after this peak.

The second ecdysteroid peak occurred several hours after the white prepupal stage, when the puparium was orange-red, and just before apolysis of the anterior segments of the animal. This increase immediately preceded the brown coloration of the puparium that represents cuticular sclerotization, which is initiated by moulting hormone (Karlson & Sekeris 1976). The second peak may well also be responsible for puparium sclerotization.

The third and largest peak in haemolymph ecdysteroids occurred 11 h after the white prepupal stage and was temporally similar to those previously reported for whole-body extracts of *Sarcophaga* (Briers & De Loof 1980, Wentworth et al 1981). It is presumably important for the completion of apolysis, the secretion of the pupal cuticle and the completion of puparial tanning.

The analysis of ecdysone biosynthetic acitivity of the ring glands indicated that fluctuating ring-gland activity contributes significantly to the haemolymph titre of ecdysteroids, but that not all the surges in ecdysteroid titre may be correlated. Although the peaks in ring-gland activity and ecdysteroid titre differed quantitatively, there were excellent temporal correlations at −3 h, 1 h and 9 h. The quantitative discrepancy between ring-gland activity and ecdysteroid titres was initially perplexing, but recent studies with *M. sexta* prothoracic glands indicate that the apparent gland activity and the titres of ecdysteroids in the haemolymph do not always correlate quantitatively (L. I. Gilbert, personal communication). The principal temporal difference between *in vitro* ring-gland activity and ecdysteroid titre is the peak of ring-gland activity at 4–5 h, which is not accompanied by a concomitant increase in the ecdysteroid titre. In *Drosophila* a similar lack of correlation has recently been reported between ring-gland activity *in vitro* and the ecdysteroid titre of whole-animal extracts (Redfern 1983).

The oscillations in the synthesis of ecdysone by ring glands *in vitro* and the apparent resulting oscillatory fluxes in the ecdysteroid titre were only detected because ring-gland activity and ecdysteroid titre were measured at hourly intervals. This unexpected finding poses new questions about how ring-gland activity ultimately regulates development, and suggests that the endocrine control of insect post-embryonic development is more complex than previously thought and that it may be under photoperiod control entrained during the sensitive phase. In view of the daily photophase of 16L:8D it would appear that the animals divided the 24 h period into 4 h time-blocks, as demonstrated by the ring-gland and haemolymph oscillatory fluxes. There seems to be a neuroendocrinological basis for these oscillations, involving the photoperiod, the brain and the mode of PTTH release. The results reported here clearly show the importance of photoperiodic effects on hormonal releases. I consider that these preliminary experiments will lead to further interesting studies.

Acknowledgements

I thank Professor L. I. Gilbert and Dr W. E. Bollenbacher of the Biology Department, University of North Carolina, Chapel Hill, for their collaboration. I also thank Dr S. L. Wentworth for her comments and criticism of this manuscript. This research was supported by National Institutes of Science grants (AM-30118 and NS-18791) to Professor Gilbert and Dr Bollenbacher respectively, and a Monash University grant (SC 18/82) to Dr Roberts.

REFERENCES

Beck SD 1980 Insect photoperiodism. Academic Press, London, p 60

Bollenbacher WE, Agui N, Granger NA, Gilbert LI 1979 *In vitro* activation of insect prothoracic glands by the prothoracic hormone. Proc Natl Acad Sci USA 76:5148-5152

Briers T, De Loof A 1980 The molting hormone activity in *Sarcophaga bullata* in relation to metamorphosis and reproduction. Int J Invertebr Reprod 2:363-372

Dean RL, Bollenbacher WE, Smith SL, Locke M, Gilbert LI 1980 Haemolymph ecdysteroid levels and cellular events in the intermoult/moult sequence of *Calpodes ethlius*. J Insect Physiol 26:267-280

Denlinger DL 1972 Induction and termination of pupal diapause in *Sarcophaga* (Diptera: Sarcophagidae). Biol Bull (Woods Hole) 142:11-24

Fraenkel G, Bhaskaran G 1973 Pupariation and pupation in cyclorrhaphous flies (Diptera): terminology and interpretation. Ann Entomol Soc Am 66:418-422

Gilbert LI, Bollenbacher WE, Agui N, Granger NA, Sedlak BJ, Gibbs D, Buys CM 1981 The prothoracicotropes: source of the prothoracicotropic hormone. Am Zool 21:641-653

Karlson P, Sekeris CE 1976 Control of tyrosine metabolism and cuticle sclerotization by ecdysone. In: Hepburn HR (ed) The insect integument. Elsevier, Amsterdam, p 145-155

Ohtaki T, Milkman RD, Williams CM 1968 Dynamics of ecdysone secretion and action in the fleshfly *Sarcophaga peregrina*. Biol Bull (Woods Hole) 135:322-334

Pittendrigh CS 1966 The circadian oscillation in *Drosophila pseudoobscura* pupae: a model for the photoperiodic clock. Z Pflanzenphysiol 54:275-307

Redfern CPF 1983 Ecdysteroid synthesis by the ring gland of *Drosophila melanogaster* during late-larval, prepupal and pupal development. J Insect Physiol 29:65-71

Roberts B 1976 Larval development in the Australian flesh fly *Tricholioproctia impatiens*. Ann Entomol Soc Am 69:158-164

Roberts B, Warren MA 1976 Diapause in the Australian flesh fly *Tricholioproctia impatiens.*
Aust J Zool 23:563-567

Roberts B, Baker M, Kotzman M, Wentworth SL 1982 A possible role of ecdysteroids in
pre-ecdysial tanning in larvae of *Sarcophaga bullata* (Diptera: Sarcophagidae). J Insect Physiol
28:123-127

Roberts B, Gilbert LI, Bollenbacher WE 1984 *In vitro* activity of dipteran ring glands and
activation by the prothoracicotropic hormone. Gen Comp Endocrinol, in press

Saunders DS 1971 The temperature-compensated photoperiodic clock 'programming' development and pupal diapause in the flesh-fly, *Sarcophaga argyrostoma.* J Insect Physiol 17:801-812

Seligman M, Blechl A, Blechl J, Herman P, Fraenkel G 1977 Role of ecdysone, pupariation
factors and cyclic AMP in formation and tanning of the puparium of the flesh fly, *Sarcophaga
bullata.* Proc Natl Acad Sci USA 74:4697-4701

Shaaya E, Karlson P 1965 Der Ecdysonetiter wahrend der Insektenentwicklung. II: Die
Postembryonale Entwicklung der Schmeissfliege *Calliphora erythrocephala* Meig. J Insect
Physiol 11:65-69

Truman JW 1972 Physiology of insect rhythms. I: Circadian organization of the endocrine events
underlying the moulting cycles of the larval tobacco hornworm. J Exp Biol 57:805-830

Truman JW, Riddiford LM 1974 Physiology of insect rhythms. III: The temporal organization of
the endocrine events underlying pupation of the tobacco hornworm. J Exp Biol 60:371-382

Wentworth SL, Roberts B, O'Connor JD 1981 Ecdysteroid titres during postembryonic
development of *Sarcophaga bullata* Sarcophagidae: Diptera. J Insect Physiol 27:435-440

Wentworth SL, Roberts B 1984 Ecdysteroid levels during adult reproductive and embryonic
developmental stages of *Sarcophaga bullata* (Sarcophagidae: Diptera). J Insect Physiol, in
press

Wilkens JL 1968 The endocrine and nutritional control of egg maturation in the fleshfly
Sarcophaga bullata. J Insect Physiol 14:927-943

Wilkens JL 1969 The endocrine control of protein metabolism as related to reproduction in the
fleshfly *Sarcophaga bullata.* J Insect Physiol 15:1015-1024

DISCUSSION

Denlinger: The second release of ecdysone (60–70h after pupariation),
which is involved in initiation of adult development in *Sarcophaga bullata*, is
much broader than the release at pupariation. Have you looked for cycling
during that interval?

Roberts: Yes, in my paper with Wentworth et al (1981), but not in this respect
in *S. bullata.* Are you thinking of oscillating ecdysteroid titres?

Denlinger: Yes; I thought it might be even more pronounced in that broader
second pulse.

Roberts: Yes, this would be an interesting experiment to do. Is it at this age
(i.e. 60–70h after the white prepupal stage) that you extract the ring glands?

Denlinger: We have not done that.

Pittendrigh: In the genus *Drosophila*, the only species in which pupariation is
gated is *D. victoria*, (Rensing & Hardeland 1967). If the light:dark cycle is
shifted by 6h, some of the pupation events, instead of being in one night, are

shifted to the next night. This also persists in constant darkness. How common, in Diptera and other insects, is it for pupariation to be gated?

Roberts: I don't know.

Page: Some mosquitoes have a rhythm in pupation (Nayar 1967, Jones & Reiter 1975).

Saunders: I believe that *Drosophila lebanonensis* has gated ecdysone-specific puffing patterns in the salivary gland chromosomes, that lead apparently to puparium formation (Eeken 1974).

Pittendrigh: Rensing (1967) also states that there is a circadian gating of puparium formation in *D. melanogaster* but I am very sceptical about that. We have failed to find such a rhythm in either *D. melanogaster* or *D. pseudoobscura*.

Roberts: I believe that Rensing (1967) alludes to a cyclic change in nucleolar volume and in some other cellular components, including RNA synthesis.

Denlinger: I have never come across a gated rhythm of puparium formation in 6 or 7 other *Sarcophaga* species, including a strain of *Sarcophaga bullata*. But we have never tested our strains at the long day-length that Dr Roberts has used (LD 16:8). We use LD 15:9 as our longest day-length.

Saunders: Daniel Gibbs and I (unpublished observations, 1972) did an extensive experiment on *S. argyrostoma* at Stanford. We collected newly formed puparia continuously through the 24-h period and we found no gating of puparium formation. There are some spectacular larval rhythms in leaving the food however, particularly in the Trypetid fruit flies (Causse 1974).

Denlinger: There is a close synchrony within a single batch of *Sarcophaga* larvae: all the larvae within one small container seem to leave at the same time, while those in a neighbouring container may leave at a very different time (unpublished observations).

Saunders: It would be useful to do these experiments in a big mixed-aged population like the *Drosophila* bottle. One would probably find some strong peaks.

Goldsworthy: I understand that when you measure ring-gland activity you are assuming that this indicates the activity of the gland before it was excised, and that this reflects the PTTH activity at that time. If you, then, do not get a correspondence between that activity and the ecdysteroid levels in the haemolymph how do you interpret that? Do you say that the measured activity is not a true reflection or that there is no PTTH associated with that peak?

Roberts: Several ecdysteroid peaks were clearly evident in ring gland cultures *in vitro*. In haemolymph samples one peak just prior to the major peak was missing. Perhaps ecdysteroids were sequestered and accumulated, and were later released to result in the large peak. Redfern (1983) also finds the same peak missing in *Drosophila*. He and I were amazed at the similarity of our results.

Goldsworthy: Your explanation might be acceptable if you were considering a small peak, but since this is a large peak it doesn't seem to be as convincing.

Roberts: It is a small peak that is missing. Published work (Zdarek & Fraenkel 1972) has indicated that the large peak (11 h) results in apolysis and in secretion of the pupal cuticle. My technique for removal of the pupal brain involved cutting the puparium from above the mouthparts to the dorsal aspect of the 4th or 5th segment. This revealed that apolysis occurred as early as four hours after the formation of white prepupa.

Goldsworthy: I was intrigued that you have to squeeze the animal to get blood out of it and that you sometimes damage the anterior end of the animal. Does the prothoracic gland contain any large quantities of stored ecdysteroid? Can you get falsely high levels in the haemolymph because of damage in this way?

Roberts: I was not using the same animals for the ring-gland experiments and the haemolymph experiments. The timing of haemolymph removal did not allow this, so the two sets of results were from two sets of animals. A small cut in the anal papillae was used to obtain pure haemolymph, without any contaminating cells or any broken fat body. If the haemolymph is expressed onto parafilm, as I described, it is very easy to pipette up and put into the radioimmunoassay tubes.

Gilbert: We should remember, when dealing with a titre, that the titre results not only from the synthetic activity of the ring gland but also from the catabolic capacity of the organism. It is quite possible that at a particular stage the rate of catabolism will exceed the rate of synthesis, which will result in a drastic decrease in the ecdysteroid titre. The ring gland may continue to be active but this may not be reflected in an ecdysteroid peak. Redfern (1983) suggests that for *Drosophila* there is an extra-ring-gland source of ecdysteroids which explains the large ecdysteroid peak at a time when the ring-gland activity is apparently very low. So a change in the catabolic rate might explain the data.

Goldsworthy: But to explain a large peak in this way one would need a dramatic decrease in the rate of removal or inactivation of ecdysteroids.

Gilbert: Yes; or, as I said, a source of ecdysteroids other than the ring gland.

Denlinger: But the ring gland is required for the initiation of adult development: if it is removed, the fly cannot initiate development.

Roberts: The activity of ring glands in *S. bullata* occurred about an hour before the ecdysteroid activity was noted in the haemolymph. The post-feeding larvae had intermediate amounts of ecdysteroids. In those larvae leaving the aluminium foil container, the ring-glands had lost practically all activity. I agree that the ring gland is necessary for the establishment of post-feeding larvae, the events of the moult cycle and the numerous events of pupariation.

Truman: From what we heard earlier, in the papers by Professors Steel and Ishizaki about the ability of the prothoracic glands to go through intrinsic bouts of activity, I would be worried about concluding that a peak of ring-gland activity necessarily corresponds to a peak of prothoracicotropic hormone (PTTH) secretion. Are you intending to measure the PTTH levels directly by exposing prothoracic glands or ring glands to haemolymph extracts and then measuring the stimulation of ecdysteroid secretion? It would be useful to do this, to be absolutely sure of the time of PTTH secretion.

Roberts: We have developed a *Sarcophaga* dose–response protocol, and consequently it would be possible to do this. We stumbled across this gated behavioural response because the gland that I use as the receptor gland is taken from an organism that has left the food source. There is a period of about 12–24 h when the ring glands from these maggots show only basal levels when incubated *in vitro*, making them an ideal target for stimulation by brain extracts. They can, in fact, be stimulated to secrete an 11-fold increase in ecdysone.

Bowen: In relation to the lack of coincidence between the fluctuations in titre and the ring-gland activity, might it be useful to compare whole-body extracts with haemolymph titres? If they coincide, this would indicate that tissue uptake could account for the apparent differences, as Scheller et al (1981) found in the swallowtail. In *Manduca*, at least, whole-body extracts assayed during pupal–adult development do coincide with the haemolymph titres, so this could be something worth checking for in *Sarcophaga*.

Roberts: We have tried this, but not since we have made the breeding activities more stringent, so we would need to repeat it. Sherry Wentworth has been analysing the puparium and whole-body extracts for ecdysteroids. In young prepupae the puparium has the epidermis adhering to it, which shows a tremendous amount of ecdysteroid activity.

Pittendrigh: It is important to distinguish where the hormone is, in these assays—whether it is in the ring gland or in the haemolymph. An analogous case in vertebrates is quite striking. Reppert et al (1981) measured oxytocin and vasopressin in the serum, and found no measurable circadian periodicity but, on the other side of the blood–brain barrier, in the cerebrospinal fluid, there was a spectacular rhythm in each of these peptides.

Reynolds: The gating of leaving of the food is interesting. You said that the 10% of larvae that take the second gate for leaving the food were inactive for 24 h on the surface of the food before they left it. Does this imply that leaving the food is separately gated from finishing feeding?

Roberts: Yes, it would imply this.

Reynolds: In that case, does the peak in ecdysteroids gate the finishing of feeding or the leaving of the food?

Roberts: That is a good question. I would say that the larvae can measure time so precisely that perhaps those that have not finished their 'commitment' to feeding will not leave the food even if the environmental cue is favourable.

They would complete their commitment to feeding and leave the feed when the favourable photoperiodic cue occurred 24 h later.

Truman: Perhaps for them to respond to ecdysone there needs to be a fall in juvenile hormone. It is possible, therefore, that the fall in juvenile hormone is what turns off feeding. The later ecdysteroid pulse would then cause the animals to leave the food.

Reynolds: That would be very different from *Manduca*.

Roberts: By selecting the time of eclosion of adult females we can vary the percentage of larvae leaving the food during the same scotophase between 50 and 100%. This point relates to something in David Saunders's paper (this volume) about a certain population getting another shot of day-length. Once the larvae have left the food I believe they are committed to pupariation. Those that remain on the food get an extra photophase pulse.

Reynolds: Perhaps a good way to look at the timing of puparium formation would be to select 'gate-two' larvae that are leaving the food. When one does this with *Manduca* there is a much tighter timing of subsequent events.

Roberts: We could easily do that. As I said before, it is a question of selecting the time of emergence of the parents.

Saunders: Have you tried standard experiments such as changing the relationship between the photoperiod and the age of the animal, or transferring cultures into continuous darkness or continuous light? For example, in constant darkness the gating may not persist.

Roberts: No.

Denlinger: It seems a strange maladaptation for a fly to wait another day on a food source after it has finished feeding. After all, carrion feeders and other scavengers are a real threat. The life-cycle strategy seems to be geared towards feeding rapidly and then quickly escaping underground to pupariate.

Roberts: I don't agree. Maggots that have not completed feeding would be protected, for example, by the skin and carcass of the carrion. During the night they would leave the carcass in relative safety from predators (e.g. birds) to seek a place in the soil for pupariation.

Steel: You implied generally that because certain endocrine events occur during the scotophase they were under what you referred to as photoperiodic control. How good an argument is that?

Roberts: My own work is not directly on rhythms, but since I observed an almost 100% response for the formation of post-feeding larvae, I must assume that this behaviour is under the control of the scotophase. It could be that 'lights-off' initiates the response, but I doubt this, as the activity of the ring gland plus the haemolymph was noted during the scotophase.

Steel: But this work was done on a light:dark cycle and you are simply saying that the endocrinological activity occurs during the night. This does not necessarily imply any underlying circadian or rhythmic form of control, although the correlation is certainly suggestive. Have you done any experiments to see if there is any endogenous timing mechanism for that system?

Roberts: No.

Saunders: We have done some preliminary experiments to check this in *S. argyrostoma* by changing the phase-relationship between the light:dark cycle and the age of the larvae. We find no consistent relationship between the light cycle and the rush of larvae out of the meat; sometimes they come out in the dark and sometimes they come out in the light from different cultures, depending on where the culture starts from in the light:dark cycle. It looks to me as though this behaviour is not a gated event. We have also placed cultures in constant light, but find no clear evidence for free-running rhythmicity. Experiments in constant darkness have not been done.

Gilbert: But you are each considering a different species, so it may be unfair to extrapolate results from one to the other.

Denlinger: While we are discussing endocrine events in *Sarcophaga* I might point out the interesting differences in juvenile hormone, from puparium formation onwards, between short-day and long-day flies (Walker & Denlinger 1980). Short-day, (diapause-destined) flies have a very high juvenile hormone activity, detected in whole-body homogenates, at the time of puparium formation. The amount falls several hours later, and then rises again, cyclically, every 24 h for several days. Puparium formation does not occur at any specific time of day. The first peak of the cycle coincides with puparium formation, but can occur during the scotophase or the photophase. With the long-day flies we have been unable to detect any cycles at all.

Chippendale: Do you have evidence for the presence of juvenile hormone in the haemolymph at these times?

Denlinger: Yes; the same type of pattern was reflected in the haemolymph.

Bowen: What was the frequency of these assays?

Denlinger: We have not tried the hourly assays that Dr Roberts has done, but have used 6 h intervals.

Reynolds: Dr Roberts, I am puzzled that you can detect these four-hourly cycles of ecdysteroid titre in a population of animals if puparium formation is not gated. The curves that you obtained for cumulative puparium formation showed a lot of temporal variation.

Saunders: But the synchrony of white puparium formation is very precise, and therefore it allows one to synchronize accurately the development of the insects.

Roberts: The formation of the white prepupa provides a precisely staged and clearly identifiable experimental animal.

REFERENCES

Causse R 1974 Etude d'un rythme circadien du comportement du prenymphoses chez *Ceratitis capitata* Wiedenmann (Diptera Trypetidae). Ann Zool Ecol Anim 6:475–498

Eeken JCJ 1974 Control of the cellular response to β-ecdysone in *Drosophila lebanonensis*. I: Experimental puff induction and its relation to puparium formation. Chromosoma (Berl) 49:205-217

Jones MDR, Reiter P 1975 Entrainment of the pupation and adult activity rhythms during development in the mosquito *Anopheles gambiae*. Nature (Lond) 254:242-244

Nayar JK 1967 Endogenous diurnal rhythm of pupation in a mosquito population. Nature (Lond) 214:828-829

Redfern CPF 1983 Ecdysteroid synthesis by the ring gland of *Drosophila melanogaster* during late-larval, prepupal and pupal development. J Insect Physiol 29:65-71

Rensing L 1967 Aspects of the circadian organization of *Drosophila*. In: Medioni J (ed) Die zeitliche Verteilung tierischer Aktivitat. Masson, Paris

Rensing L, Hardeland R 1967 Zür Wirkung der circadien Rhythmik auf die Entwicklung von *Drosophila*. J Insect Physiol 13:1547-1568

Reppert SM, Autman HG, Swaminathan S, Fisher DA 1981 Vasopressin exhibits a rhythmic daily pattern in cerebrospinal fluid but not in blood. Science (Wash DC) 213:1256-1257

Scheller K, Wohlfahrt TA, Koolman J 1981 Different ecdysteroid titers in spring and summer generations of the swallowtail, *Iphiclides podalirius*. Naturwissenschaften 68:45

Walker GP, Denlinger DL 1980 Juvenile hormone and moulting hormone titres in diapause and non-diapause destined flesh flies. J Insect Physiol 26:661-664

Wentworth SL, Roberts B, O'Connor JD 1981 Ecdysteroid titres during postembryonic development of *Sarcophaga bullata* Sarcophagidae : Diptera. J Insect Physiol 27:435-440

Zdarek J, Fraenkel G 1972 The mechanism of puparium formation in flies. J Exp Zool 179:315-324

Reproductive endocrinology and photoperiodism in a terrestrial slug

P. G. SOKOLOVE, E. J. McCRONE, J. van MINNEN and W. C. DUNCAN

Department of Biological Sciences, University of Maryland Baltimore County (UMBC), 5401 Wilkens Avenue, Catonsville, Maryland 21228, USA

Abstract. Photoperiodic control of reproductive development has been studied in the hermaphrodite slug, *Limax maximus*. It has been shown that slug maturation can be triggered by long-day light cycles or by implants of brains or cerebral ganglia from animals exposed to long days. Similar treatments have also been shown to increase spermatogonial proliferation, as revealed by incorporation of [^{3}H]thymidine into gonad DNA. These findings indicate that release from the cerebral ganglia of one or more gonadotropic factors is promoted by long days. Stimulation of [^{3}H]thymidine incorporation by homogenates of a small area of cerebral ganglion points to a specific cluster of neuroendocrine cells as the likely source of active factor. Since growth of the penis, albumen gland and gonad occurs rapidly in immature slugs implanted with fragments of mature gonads, the existence of gonadal hormone(s) can be presumed, and neurohormones from the cerebral ganglia probably act indirectly *via* the gonad to promote reproductive tract development. Long-day photoperiods have also been found to promote expression of a circadian locomotor rhythm at about the time that slugs reach the female phase of development. Whether reproductive hormones play a role in this behavioural transformation remains to be determined.

1984 Photoperiodic regulation of insect and molluscan hormones. Pitman, London (Ciba Foundation symposium 104), p 189-203

Endocrine centres that control development and function of pulmonate reproductive systems have been studied in a variety of slugs and snails. However, relatively few investigations have focused on environmental factors that might influence seasonal maturation in these animals, and only recently have molluscan physiologists begun to examine specifically the role of photoperiod in the regulation of pulmonate reproduction (see, for example, Enée et al 1982, Bohlken & Joosse 1982). Thus, although it has long been recognized that photoperiodic regulation of seasonal reproductive states is important in an impressive variety of animals from insects to mammals, our understanding of photoperiodic regulation of molluscan systems is still in its infancy.

A major objective of our work has been to elucidate the endocrine pathways and processes that govern photoperiodically controlled reproductive development in a single molluscan species, the giant garden slug, *Limax maximus*. In *L. maximus* we have been able to show that seasonal reproductive maturation is robustly photoperiod-dependent. Our results have demonstrated that the development of reproductive tract organs is directly or indirectly mediated by one or more hormones released from cells located in the central nervous system in slugs exposed to long-day photoperiods. Currently, we are in the process of identifying the source(s) of such hormone(s) and we hope to study, ultimately at the cellular level, the events and physiological processes that link environmental photoperiod to reproductive hormone synthesis, or secretion, or both. This paper reviews what we have learned so far about the role of photoperiod in slug reproductive development and about the organization of the endocrine system that regulates slug maturation.

Methods

Animal maintenance. Slugs (*L. maximus*) were hatched in the laboratory and maintained in an environmental chamber in refrigerator storage boxes at $15 \pm 0.5\,°C$ on 8 h light : 16 h dark (LD 8 : 16) light cycles. Maturation was induced in some animals by moving storage boxes to another environmental chamber with a light cycle of LD 16 : 8. Details of maintenance procedures are provided elsewhere (Sokolove & McCrone 1978).

Implantation methods. Details of the methods for removal and implantation of brains, cerebral ganglia or gonads have been reported previously (Sokolove & McCrone 1978, McCrone & Sokolove 1979, McCrone et al 1981). In general, brains (or cerebral ganglia) were obtained from long-day-triggered slugs in the male- or female-phase of maturation. All the recipient animals were short-day juveniles, and all the donor organs were implanted into the posterior haemocoel.

Gonadal incorporation of [³H]thymidine. Proliferation of spermatogonia in response to long-day photoperiods, implanted cerebral ganglia, or injections of slug haemolymph or homogenates of cerebral ganglion tissue was monitored *in vivo* by pulse labelling with [³H]thymidine. Autoradiographs of sectioned gonads and scintillation counting of the nucleic acid fraction of gonadal tissue, which had been extracted by hot acid hydrolysis, were used to follow spermatogonial synthesis of DNA. (For details of the assay procedure see Melrose et al 1983.) Generally, homogenate or blood was injected daily over 5 days into immature slugs, and gonadal incorporation of [³H]thymidine was assayed on Day 7. In implantation experiments, the assay was done one week after organ implantation.

Organ indices. To determine relative growth of reproductive organs after various experimental treatments, we used reproductive organ indices. Slugs were weighed and sacrificed, and reproductive organs (usually the gonad, penis and albumen gland) were removed and weighed. Reproductive organ indices were then calculated as the ratio of organ wet weight to total slug weight $\times 10^3$.

Circadian locomotor activity. Locomotor activity of individual slugs was measured in miniature wheels as described previously (Sokolove et al 1977). Event-recorder data were counted visually to obtain hourly totals, and free-runs were analysed by the χ^2 periodogram method (Sokolove & Bushell 1978) to determine period estimate, mean hourly activity and presence or absence of significant periodicity.

Results and discussion

Photoperiodic response

In the field, *L. maximus* undergoes a transition from the immature juvenile to the male phase of sexual development—marked by growth of the gonad and penis—between mid-May and late July. Later, during August, mature sperm are released from the gonad into the hermaphrodite duct, and the albumen gland and other female accessory sex organs develop. The same protandrous sequence of hermaphrodite development can be induced in laboratory-reared juvenile slugs by a transfer from short-day (LD 8:16) to long-day (LD 16:8) light cycles (Sokolove & McCrone 1978). This photoperiodic response occurs in blinded as well as normal animals (McCrone & Sokolove 1979), but blinded slugs are relatively insensitive to long-day red (>600 nm) light cycles (Sokolove et al 1981).

Reproductive tract development

Slugs raised on short-day photoperiods remain immature indefinitely and can serve as recipients for exogenously derived tissues and organs from long-day (i.e. maturing) or short-day (immature) donors. Using short-day slugs as recipients, we found that implanted whole brains or cerebral ganglia from

long-day donors can produce normal reproductive tract development, while
brains or cerebral ganglia from short-day donors have no effect (McCrone &
Sokolove 1979, McCrone et al 1981). These results indicate that the brains
and, in particular, the cerebral ganglia of slugs exposed to LD 16:8 light
cycles produce a 'maturation hormone' that promotes reproductive development.

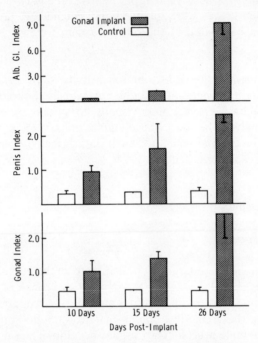

FIG. 1. Rapid, early growth of reproductive organs—albumen gland (Alb. Gl.), penis and
gonad—of *Limax maximus* following implantation of mature (female-phase) gonad fragments.
Recipients and controls were short-day, immature slugs maintained throughout on LD 8:16.
Mean (±SD) reproductive organ indices (see text) are shown for separate groups of three or four
recipients sacrificed at different times after implantation.

Spermatogonial proliferation

Next, we monitored spermatogonial proliferation in a developing gonad by
measuring *in vivo* incorporation of [^{3}H]thymidine into gonadal DNA. Again,
we were able to demonstrate an effect either of long days or of implanted
long-day cerebral ganglia: gonadal incorporation of label increased markedly
about four weeks after exposure of immature slugs to long-day light cycles
and about one week after implantation of cerebral ganglia from long-day
donors (Sokolove et al 1983). We also showed that spermatogonial incorpora-

tion of label could be stimulated by injections of haemolymph (blood) from long-day, but not short-day, animals (Melrose et al 1983). Thus, production, or secretion, or both, of a specific, blood-borne 'male gonadotropic factor' seems to be stimulated by long-day exposure.

Although the circumstantial evidence would suggest that male gonadotropic factor and 'maturation hormone' are identical, we have no direct evidence. It could be argued that more than one brain-derived hormone is secreted as a result of long-day treatment, and that full reproductive development (of which spermatogonial proliferation is only a part) is coordinated by factors from numerous neuroendocrine centres. Until male gonadotropic factor has been isolated and used to promote the entire maturational sequence, the issue must remain unresolved.

Identification of cells that produce male gonadotropic factor

More precise localization of the neuroendocrine cells that produce male gonadotropic factor is clearly desirable for the eventual study of the physiological effects of inductive photoperiods at the cellular level. One approach we have used is to subdivide the cerebral ganglia into small regions and then to test homogenates of each region separately for male gonadotropic factor activity by injection of homogenate into immature animals. The results of such an experiment are shown in Table 1.

TABLE 1 *In vivo* [³H]thymidine labelling of slug gonad after injection with extracts of different parts of brain

Extract injected[a]	[³H]Thymidine incorporation (d.p.m./mg gonad)	Total protein per dose (µg)	Specific activity (d.p.m./mg.µg prot)
Whole cerebral ganglion	6437 ± 309[b]	134.8	48 ± 22
Area Z	7383 ± 695	16.4	450 ± 42
Remaining cerebral ganglion	2912 ± 844	114.4	25 ± 7
Saline control	2120 ± 465	—	—

[a] Except for controls, each injection contained 0.4 animal equivalent (a.e.) of tissue (for example, 1 cerebral ganglion = 0.5 a.e. cerebral ganglia).
[b] Mean ± SEM; $n = 5$ in each group of test animals.

In this experiment long-day cerebral ganglia were separated, and the male gonadotropic factor activity in one ganglion was compared to that in a portion of the other ganglion. After obtaining preliminary data, we chose to examine specifically a small region of cerebral ganglion ('area Z') containing numerous, large ($\sim$70 μm diameter) cells that border the cerebral commissure. Our results showed that area Z contained as much male gonadotropic factor as an entire cerebral ganglion and that the specific activity of area Z homogenate was almost 10-fold higher than that of whole cerebral ganglion homogenate. The cells in area Z are, therefore, likely to be the cellular source of male gonadotropic factor.

Although area Z somata are not stained by 'classical' histological methods for neurosecretion (i.e. paraldehyde–fucsin, alcian blue–alcian yellow), electron microscopy indicates that Z cells are true neurosecretory cells, since they contain numerous elementary granules and active Golgi zones. Recently, C. R. Marchand demonstrated in our laboratory (unpublished results) that area Z cells stained selectively with anti-somatostatin, and electron micrographs of the immunoreactive regions of cytoplasm revealed that these areas were rich in elementary granules. Thus, anti-somatostatin may be able to cross-react with presumptive male gonadotropic factor, or with some closely associated antigen. Further experiments are in progress to examine this intriguing possibility.

Gonadal control of accessory sex organ and gonad growth

Considerable evidence suggests that growth of male and female reproductive organs in terrestrial pulmonates is under the control of the gonad, or ovotestis (Abeloos 1943, Laviolette 1954, Runham et al 1973). When *L. maximus* are castrated before long-day exposure, growth of reproductive organs such as the penis is abolished (McCrone & Sokolove 1979). Subsequent implantation of an immature gonad leads to the rapid development of accessory sex organs in such slugs, even if they are no longer exposed to long days (E. J. McCrone, unpublished). This suggests that the brain can be photoperiodically triggered in the absence of a gonad.

Development of accessory sex organs also takes place after implantation of small pieces of mature gonad, although recipient slugs are maintained exclusively on short days. In intact (uncastrated) recipients such implants promote growth not only of the accessory sex organs but also of the gonads (Fig. 1). Thus, the development of both accessory sex organs and gonads appears to be under the direct control of gonadal hormone(s).

This result raises an important question about the true function of male gonadotropic factor. If gonadal hormone acts to promote gonad growth (i.e. cell proliferation), male gonadotropic factor may stimulate spermatogonial proliferation indirectly via the gonad, and the primary physiological function of male gonadotropic factor may be to stimulate secretion of gonadal hormone. Such a model can be rigorously tested only *in vitro*, however, and an appropriate *in vitro* system has yet to be developed.

Further evidence for direct control of accessory sex organ development via the gonad is provided by a recent preliminary experiment in which small gonad explants were incubated *in vitro* with immature albumen glands. Incorporation of [³H]thymidine into albumen-gland DNA was significantly greater in albumen glands cultured for one week with mature (female-phase) gonad explants than in those cultured alone (E. J. McCrone, unpublished). If confirmed, this finding is important not only because it shows a direct effect of a presumptive gonadal hormone, but also because it offers the possibility of testing whether secretion of that hormone is stimulated by male gonadotropic factor.

Endocrine pathways in L. maximus

We have postulated a simple scheme showing the pathways for endocrine control of photoperiodically stimulated reproductive tract growth and function in *L. maximus* (Fig. 2). In a number of respects this scheme is similar to the general one for pulmonates suggested by Boer & Joosse (1975), but there are some differences. For example, the central nervous system is not shown as producing separate male and female neuroendocrine products, since *L. maximus* brains at any stage of development promote the same male–female development sequence when implanted into immature slugs.

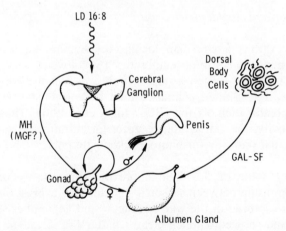

FIG. 2. Schematic diagram showing the organization of the reproductive endocrine system in *L. maximus*. Long-day light cycles (LD 16:8) trigger neurosecretion of maturation hormone (MH) and/or male gonadotropic factor (MGF) from cerebral ganglia. The gonad responds by secreting separate male (♂) and female (♀) hormones that promote development of accessory sex organs such as the penis and albumen gland [and possibly even of the gonad itself]. Biosynthesis of galactogen in the albumen gland is regulated by a galactogen-synthesis stimulating factor (GAL-SF) secreted by dorsal body cells.

The gonad is shown here as an intermediate endocrine organ that secretes separate male and female sex hormones. The concept of separate gonadal hormones derives from the fact that in *L. maximus* the development of male and female accessory sex organs is temporally separated. Direct evidence to support this view is, however, lacking. It is equally possible that there are significant differences in target organ sensitivity so that, for example, a low titre of gonad hormone might result in development of male accessory sex organs while a higher titre causes rapid growth of female accessory sex organs.

Dorsal bodies, which typically lie atop the cerebral ganglia, have been shown to play a major part in controlling the development of accessory sex organs in some pulmonates (Geraerts & Algera 1976, Wijdenes & Runham 1976). In *L. maximus* dorsal body cells are not organized as a coherent organ but are scattered as individual cells in the connective tissue sheath that surrounds the brain. The product of these cells appears not to control growth of female accessory sex organs as it does in other pulmonates, but a factor originating in dorsal body cells (which we have called galactogen-synthesis stimulating factor or GAL-SF) has been shown to regulate polysaccharide biosynthesis in the albumen gland (van Minnen et al 1983, van Minnen & Sokolove 1983).

Photoperiodism and circadian behaviour

L. maximus exhibits a circadian locomotor rhythm under conditions of constant darkness and constant temperature (Sokolove et al 1977). Slugs can be entrained or phase-shifted by light : dark cycles in the absence of their optic tentacles, but blinded animals cannot be entrained in light cycles of wavelengths greater than 600 nm (Beiswanger et al 1981). Thus, at least for spectral sensitivity, the extraocular receptor for entrainment appears similar to the extraocular pathway for photoperiodic light perception (see Sokolove et al 1981).

In reviewing some of the data in previous reports, we discovered an apparent relationship between seasonal state and the expression of circadian activity. Slugs captured in the wild in August and September were typically more active and showed a much clearer pattern of circadian activity than animals captured from May to July. To see whether this might be related to changes in reproductive state, we attempted to follow both free-running locomotor behaviour and sexual development in groups of slugs that had been photoperiodically stimulated.

Four groups of short-day slugs, each group derived from the same egg clutch, were transferred at time zero to an LD 16 : 8 light cycle. Free-running

activity and entrained locomotor activity of individual animals were monitored on slug 'running wheels' at more or less regular intervals during the next
10 months. At the same time, while some animals were being monitored for
activity, others from the same group were sacrificed and their reproductive
organ indices were determined. A few (20%) of the sacrificed slugs had just
completed a locomotory assay at the time of sacrifice. Results of the
experiment are shown, in part, in Fig. 3. A more complete description of the
findings will be presented elsewhere.

It is apparent from Fig. 3 that not all animals were rhythmic when tested.
Before week 6, none of the 28 animals tested was rhythmic in its locomotor
behaviour and only about 40% (11 out of 28) were rhythmic during the
following 10 weeks. In most cases mean activity levels before week 16 were
extremely low so that it was difficult or impossible to tell whether slugs during
this period were truly arrhythmic or simply dormant. After week 16,
however, activity levels increased and almost all the slugs expressed a clear
rhythm. By weeks 21–25, 100% of the 17 slugs tested expressed a robust
circadian locomotor rhythm, whereas none of the short-day controls showed
any signs of rhythmic behaviour.

Mean reproductive indices for gonad, penis and albumen gland all increased in long-day-stimulated slugs as expected; the gonad and albumen
gland data are shown in Fig. 3. Gonad (and penis) enlargement preceded
growth of the albumen gland by about 5 to 10 weeks. Because circadian

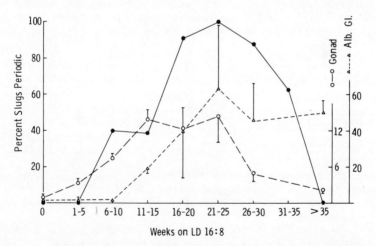

FIG. 3. Effect of long days (LD 16:8) on reproductive organ growth and circadian locomotor
behaviour. Short-day slugs were placed on LD 16:8 at time zero and assayed for free-running
locomotor activity at various times thereafter. Numbers assayed ranged from 5 to 22 animals in
each time period. Mean (±SEM) gonad and albumen gland indices are shown for groups of 3 to 8
slugs sacrificed during the same time periods.

activity is first observed at about the same time that rapid development of the albumen gland is initiated, the expression of circadian behaviour may, in some way, be linked specifically to female-phase development. Clearly, the circadian activity peaks when albumen gland enlargement is maximal.

An important question concerns the part played by photoperiod in the transition from juvenile, dormant and non-rhythmic animals to mature, active and periodic animals. In the foregoing experiment all slugs were exposed to long days, and it is possible that the behavioural change itself is long-day-dependent. We feel, however, that the observed changes in locomotor behaviour are more likely to result from the internal, hormonal alterations that occur during maturation.

Since it is possible to induce reproductive tract development in the absence of long days by brain or gonad implants, we can readily test whether or not expression of behavioural rhythmicity is photoperiod-dependent. Preliminary trials with brain-implanted, short-day, juvenile slugs already suggest that the expression of rhythmicity in *L. maximus* is hormonally governed, but further work is necessary to determine what (neuro)endocrine product(s) and organ(s) play a key role in the transformation of behaviour.

Acknowledgements

This work was supported in part by research grants from the National Science Foundation (PCM 81-10191) and the National Institutes of Health (AL 16259). Special thanks are due for the excellent technical assistance provided by Anne Alberg and Inge Rever.

REFERENCES

Abeloos M 1943 Effets de la castration chez un mollusque, *Limax maximus* L. C R Hebd Séances Acad Sci 216:90-91

Beiswanger CM, Sokolove PG, Prior DJ 1981 Extraocular photoentrainment of the circadian locomotor rhythm of the garden slug *Limax*. J Exp Zool 216:13-23

Boer HH, Joosse J 1975 Endocrinology. In: Fretter V, Peak J (eds) Pulmonates. Academic Press, London, p 245-302

Bohlken S, Joosse J 1982 The effect of photoperiod on female reproductive activity and growth of the freshwater snail *Lymnaea stagnalis* kept under laboratory conditions. Int J Invertebr Reprod 4:213-222

Enée J, Bonnefoy-Claudet R, Gomot L 1982 Effet de la photopériode artificielle sur la reproduction de l'Escargot *Helix aspersa* Mull. C R Séances Acad Sci Ser III Sci Vie 294:357-360

Geraerts WPM, Algera LH 1976 The stimulating effect of the dorsal-body hormone on cell differentiation in the female accessory sex organs of the hermaphrodite freshwater snail, *Lymnaea stagnalis*. Gen Comp Endocrinol 29:109-118

Laviolette P 1954 Rôle de la gonade dans le déterminisme humoral de la maturité glandulaire du tractus genital chez quelques gastéropodes Arioniae et Limaeidae. Bull Biol Fr Belg 88:310-332

McCrone EJ, van Minnen J, Sokolove PG 1981 Slug maturation hormone: *in vivo* evidence for long-day stimulation of secretion from brains and cerebral ganglia. J Comp Physiol 143:311-315

McCrone EJ, Sokolove PG 1979 Brain–gonad axis and photoperiodically stimulated sexual maturation in the slug, *Limax maximus*. J Comp Physiol 133:117-123

Melrose GR, O'Neill MC, Sokolove PG 1983 Male Gonadotrophic factor in brain and blood of photoperiodically stimulated slugs. Gen Comp Endocrinol 52:319-328

Runham NW, Bailey TG, Laryea AA 1973 Studies of the endocrine control of the grey field slug, *Agriolimax reticulatus*. Malacologia 14:135-142

Sokolove PG, Beiswanger CM, Prior DJ, Gelperin A 1977 A circadian rhythm in the locomotor behavior of *Limax maximus*. J Exp Biol 66:47-64

Sokolove PG, Bushell WN 1978 The chi-square periodogram: its utility for analysis of circadian rhythms. J Theor Biol 72:131-160

Sokolove PG, Kirgan J, Tarr R 1981 Red light insensitivity of the extraocular pathway for photoperiodic stimulation of reproductive development in the slug, *Limax maximus*. J Exp Zool 215:219-223

Sokolove PG, McCrone EJ 1978 Reproductive maturation in the slug, *Limax maximus*, and the effects of artificial photoperiod. J Comp Physiol 133:317-325

Sokolove PG, Melrose GR, Gordon TM, O'Neill MC 1983 Stimulation of spermatogonial DNA synthesis in slug gonad by a factor released from cerebral ganglia under the influence of long days. Gen Comp Endocrinol 50:95-104

van Minnen J, Sokolove PG 1983 Galactogen synthesis stimulating factor in the slug, *Limax maximus*. In: Lever J, Boer HH (eds) Molluscan neuro-endocrinology. North-Holland, Amsterdam, p 153-159

van Minnen J, Wijdenes J, Sokolove PG 1983 Endocrine control of galactogen synthesis in the albumen gland of the slug, *Limax maximus*. Gen Comp Endocrinol 49:307-314

Wijdenes J, Runham NW 1976 Studies on the function of the dorsal bodies of *Agriolimax reticulatus* (Mollusca; Pulmonata). Gen Comp Endocrinol 29:545-551

DISCUSSION

Gilbert: In normal development, how high can the reproductive organ index be in *Limax maximus*?

Sokolove: The penis index can reach 15–20, and the albumen gland index, in a fully mature adult, can be over 100. The gonad index typically peaks at a value of 15–20 and then begins to decline.

Brady: Is the locomotor rhythm merely reflecting the functional activity level?

Sokolove: I do not really know. The change in overt rhythmicity during maturation may reflect a general increase in activity level, and there may be an unexpressed rhythm in immature slugs and during early stages of development. I am interested in the change in the locomotor rhythm because it shows an apparent effect of reproductive hormones on behaviour. Whether an increased locomotor rhythm indicates simply an increase in general activity level rather than a sudden expression of rhythmicity is unclear at present.

Brady: Is the effect on inducing the rhythm due to the brain implant, or due to the brain implant's effect on the gonads? Have you implanted mature gonads?

Sokolove: We have done that experiment only very recently, and do not yet have the results.

Goldsworthy: When you have switched on the reproductive activity in intact animals, through a long-day regime, what happens if you switch them back to short days?

Sokolove: It depends on how many weeks of long days that they have seen. If they have seen 1–3 weeks of long days and we switch them back to short days they do not mature; but if they have seen 4 weeks or more of long days then they go on to mature.

Goldsworthy: It seems strange that you can implant a long-day brain which is then permanently switched towards producing maturation.

Sokolove: This result is correct. The system is apparently very robust and, once turned on, is on permanently.

Pittendrigh: I recall that Earl Segal (1961) demonstrated an annual rhythm of reproductive activity in *Limax* kept for several years in an incubator under constant photoperiodic conditions.

Sokolove: Segal (1961) tested *Limax flavus* on LD 11:13 and LD 13:11 and saw no photoperiodic effect whatsoever—that is, no difference between the long-day and the short-day groups. But he did apparently see an annual rhythm in egg laying. *L. maximus* has an approximately annual life-cycle, and we can keep this species alive in the lab for a maximum of about 1½ years. If Segal collected the related species, *L. flavus*, from the wild at a specific time, it is quite possible that *L. flavus* simply produced eggs approximately one year after he began the experiment, and then again about one year later. Perhaps *L. flavus* is reproductively insensitive to photoperiodic stimulation, or perhaps 11 hours of light is past the critical photoperiod for stimulation of maturation. In *L. maximus* we can trigger maturation by long days at any time, and we don't see any indication of an annual cycle in either long-day or short-day animals.

Giebultowicz: How big are the neurons that presumably release the maturation hormone, and could you record from them?

Sokolove: They are about 50–70 μm in diameter, and we can record from them fairly easily.

Giebultowicz: Can you see any neurohaemal type of organ?

Sokolove: No. Using injections of lucifer yellow dye, we have followed the axonal branching pattern of a few of these cells. Some branches cross over the midline, and one major branch goes all the way through the pedal-cerebral connective and exits via one of the pedal nerves. But there seems to be no organized neurohaemal organ.

Mordue: The cells seem to take a long time before they begin to exert an effect. Are they refractory? Do you know whether they are turned on immediately but take three weeks to produce hormones, or whether three weeks of stimulation is needed before they start producing hormones?

Sokolove: We have not done a systematic examination of this either histologically or physiologically, so I can't answer the question.

Bowen: When you say that long days induce *release* of the neurosecretion, do you also mean that they induce *synthesis?*

Sokolove: They probably induce both synthesis and release. We have looked at long-day and short-day blood, and we have seen an increase in titre after long-day stimulation. Similarly, from experiments with brain homogenates we have found more hormone activity in long-day than in short-day brains.

Bowen: If you keep the slugs on short days do they ever become periodic?

Sokolove: No; they don't.

Denlinger: Do you have information on the chemical nature of the sex hormones in your slugs or in other systems?

Sokolove: No. Dr Joosse (this volume) has studied that subject more than we have at present. Given the small piece of gonad tissue that is able to elicit a full response, I suspect that the hormone is not a stored peptide but is more likely to be a steroid, which is being synthesized by the tissue.

Steel: You said that you needed to keep these animals on about 20 weeks of LD 16:8 in order to elicit some of these responses. But presumably these circumstances would not be encountered in the field?

Sokolove: That is true. We are not even sure that 16h is the critical photoperiod; it could be that 12h is already past their critical photoperiod, and that a 12-h day is a long day. Animals that are kept on long days for 4 weeks and then returned to short days still mature, sometimes more rapidly than animals kept on long days through to the end of reproductive development.

Steel: Your so-called 'area Z' seemed to be substantially larger than the area that contains the putative neurosecretory cells. What else might be in that area?

Sokolove: There are not many other organized clusters. Occasional small cells can be seen in the area and there are large tracts that form the cerebral connectives. Dr Joosse (this volume) also has information about cells in that region but I am not sure whether they are identical to the ones we call Z cells.

Joosse: Above these area Z cells you find the dorsal body hormone-producing cells. So you first have to show that that is not the hormone that matures the gonad. The dorsal body hormone has been shown to have an action on the reproductive system in your experimental animal.

Sokolove: I agree. The dorsal bodies in many pulmonates are organized into relatively tight clusters that sit on the dorsal surface of the cerebral ganglia. In *L. maximus*, the dorsal body cells are scattered throughout the brain-sheath connective tissue and can even be found in the connective tissue in the sub-oesophageal ganglia. Our studies with homogenates of suboesophageal ganglia have given no indication of gonadotropic hormone activity in those ganglia. However, the 'dorsal body' cells are fewer in number there, so the titres are bound to be lower.

Gilbert: Is the brain homogenate heat-stable?

Sokolove: No; it is heat-sensitive.

Gilbert: When you implant brains does the response of the host depend on whether the donor of the brain is in the male or the female phase?

Sokolove: No.

Gilbert: Is the level of this hormone constant throughout the entire time?

Sokolove: We have not titred the level of activity in the brain homogenates. We have done whole-brain or cerebral ganglia implants and we see no difference in their ability to stimulate reproductive maturation. We are now removing and homogenizing brains at various times during the maturational sequence to see whether there is a difference in titre. We are also assessing blood titres during maturation.

Page: Do you know where the photoreception for the photoperiodic time measurement is taking place?

Sokolove: No; except that there are many light-sensitive cells in the brain. We have recorded intracellularly and shown that certain cells are responsive to illumination (unpublished observations). We have also looked at the action spectrum for a few of those cells and found them to be insensitive to red-light stimulation above 600 nm (unpublished observations). We know that the photoreception in *L. maximus* is extraocular because if we remove the optic tentacles we still get a photoperiodic response and we still see a biological rhythm. Neither entrainment of the rhythm nor the photoperiodic response takes place if we use red-light cycles.

Page: But, if the eyes are present, isn't the action spectrum for both entrainment and the photoperiodic response expanded?

Sokolove: Yes. There is an input from the eyes but it is not obligatory.

Page: How well does the brain survive after the implant? Is it possible to implant a short-day brain and then to put the animal in a long-day photoperiod to induce a long-day response?

Sokolove: Yes. We have been trying to do that experiment for some time but have been held up by intermittent failure of our environmental chambers. We are currently repeating the experiment.

Joosse: *L. maximus* is a very important animal in which to study the site of photoreception in the brain, although the work is indeed very laborious. If I understand correctly, when you have an activated brain and you cauterize different parts of it and implant it, you can find the output from the brain, but this does not mean that you have found the site of photoreception.

Sokolove: That is correct. We chose to examine area Z on the basis of some preliminary microcautery experiments. Our results, incidentally, argue circumstantially against dorsal bodies being involved in the gonadal response because the response can be abolished by localized microcautery, whereas the dorsal body cells in *L. maximus* are distributed throughout the entire brain connective tissue.

Joosse: Are the maturation hormone neurons in *L. maximus* in the same place as the growth hormone cells identified by Wijdenes et al (1980) in *Arion hortensis*?

Sokolove: Those authors do not believe so.

Pittendrigh: I recall that there is some evidence of photoperiodic control of reproductive activity in *Aplysia*.

Sokolove: Yes. Marvin Lickey (1968) has done some work on the seasonal changes in circadian activity, and Strumwasser et al (1969) have reported a seasonal effect on egg-laying behaviour in this species. But to my knowledge there have been no controlled experiments on reproduction under artificial photoperiodic conditions.

Pittendrigh: Since the pacemakers are in the eyes of *Aplysia* (see e.g. Jacklet 1969) the system is apparently very different from *L. maximus*.

Sokolove: I agree. It surprises me that explicit photoperiodic experiments with *Aplysia* have not been tried. This species would be a prime candidate for such experiments, given that it may be seasonal in its reproductive activity.

REFERENCES

Jacklet JW 1969 A circadian rhythm of optic nerve impulses recorded in darkness from the isolated eye of *Aplysia*. Science (Wash DC) 164:562-564

Lickey ME 1968 Seasonal modulation and non-24-hour entrainment of a circadian rhythm in a single neuron. J Comp Physiol Psychol 66:712-716

Segal E 1961 Discussion section. In: Biological clocks (Cold Spring Harbor Symp Quant Biol, vol 25) p 504-505

Strumwasser F, Jacklet JW, Alvarez RB 1969 A seasonal rhythm in the neural extract induction of behavioral egg-laying in *Aplysia*. Comp Biochem Physiol 29:197-206

Wijdenes J, van Minnen J, Boer HH 1980 A comparative study on neurosecretion demonstrated by the alcian blue-alcian yellow technique in three terrestrial pulmonates (Stylommatophora). Cell Tissue Res 210:47-56

Photoperiodicity, rhythmicity and endocrinology of reproduction in the snail *Lymnaea stagnalis*

J. JOOSSE

Biological Laboratory, Vrije Universiteit, De Boelelaan 1087, Postbox 7161, 1007 MC Amsterdam, The Netherlands

Abstract. Sexual maturation and the start of female reproductive activity in *Lymnaea stagnalis* are accelerated by long-day photoperiods (16 h light per 24 h). In adult snails, long-day conditions enhance ovipository activity, compared to medium-day (12 h light per 24 h) and short-day (8 h light per 24 h) photoperiods. Starved snails and snails kept at low temperature (8 °C) continue egg laying in a long-day photoperiod. In these conditions the release of the female gonadotrophic dorsal body hormone is low. However, the neurosecretory caudodorsal cells, which produce the ovulation- and oviposition-inducing hormone (caudodorsal cell hormone, CDCH) can still be activated. Long-day snails are more sensitive to CDCH; ovulation and oviposition take a shorter time. Induction of egg laying in specimens collected in the field starts six weeks before and persists six weeks after spontaneous egg laying, which occurs most frequently in June and July. The caudodorsal cells show a clear diurnal rhythm in synthesis and release of CDCH. This rhythm is synchronized by the eyes. There are indications of a rhythmicity in steroid synthesis in the Sertoli cells and in the cellular release of the secretory product from the albumen gland cells. Egg laying in laboratory conditions takes place during the light phase of the day. In the field, oviposition occurs nearly exclusively in the afternoon.

1984 Photoperiodic regulation of insect and molluscan hormones. Pitman, London (Ciba Foundation symposium 104), p 204-220

The simultaneously hermaphrodite freshwater snail *Lymnaea stagnalis* has been studied for many years in our department. Our research programme is primarily focused on the endocrine and neuroendocrine centres, their function and the nervous and hormonal pathways of information to these centres. In this paper I shall describe the effects of the photoperiod on female reproductive activity, the role of the endocrine centres that control this activity, and rhythmicity in organs related to female reproductive activity.

The animals are bred in the laboratory in a semi-automatic breeding system, consisting of tanks with continuous water refreshment, at a temperature of 20 °C, and under a medium-day photoperiod (12 h light : 12 h dark). The diet consists of fresh lettuce leaves and the fish food Tetraphyll, alternately. The amount of food supplied is restricted, which keeps egg-laying activity relatively low and apparently, therefore, favours body growth. The life-span of the snails under these conditions is about 10 months. During experiments the snails are kept individually in perforated polythene beakers, placed in tanks with continuous water refreshment, and fed lettuce in excess. Pond snails copulate frequently, but isolated snails are capable of internal self-fertilization. Thus, for egg laying, copulation is not conditional. However, acceptance of semen accelerates the maturation of the female accessory organs and the onset of egg laying in juvenile specimens in the male protandric phase (van Duivenboden 1983). After female maturation the snails show a continuous copulatory and ovipository activity in laboratory conditions.

The natural habitat of *L. stagnalis* is in freshwater lakes and ditches. In natural conditions the snails hatch from July to September. When the shell height is about 20 mm the snails start egg laying, and in early autumn egg laying stops. Oogenesis continues at a low rate. In contrast, spermatogenesis is blocked at the meiotic stage at temperatures below 8 °C. Therefore, from November until the end of March no sperm is produced (Joosse 1964, Joosse & Veld 1972). In June, egg laying is resumed. The snails die at an age of 12–14 months.

Structure and functioning of the reproductive system

The ovotestis consists of about 25 acini. Oocytes mature in follicles in vitellogenic areas, which are surrounded by spermatogenic areas where spermatogenesis occurs (Fig. 1). The hermaphrodite spermoviduct gives rise to separate female and male ducts, each with accessory sex organs. At ovulation oocytes (up to 200) are transported to the carrefour region of the spermoviduct where fertilization takes place. Then the egg cells are packaged one by one into eggs in the pars contorta. Each egg cell is surrounded by perivitellin fluid (rich in proteins and galactogen) and egg membranes. In the oothecal gland, egg-mass formation occurs. During oviposition the egg mass is fixed to a substrate. This complex programme takes about 2 h at 20 °C and involves various secretory processes, as well as ciliar and muscular activities (Dogterom et al 1983a). It is probably directly controlled by the genital nervous plexus (Fig. 2; see de Jong-Brink & Goldschmeding 1983).

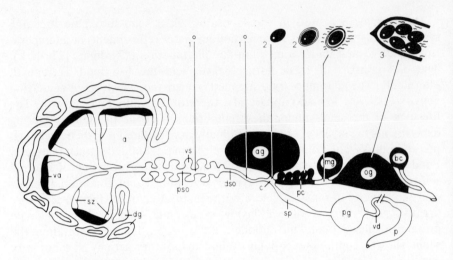

FIG. 1. The various stages of egg-mass formation in *Lymnaea stagnalis*. Oocytes mature in vitellogenic areas (va) in the acini (a) of the ovotestis. (1) After ovulation the oocytes are transported via the proximal (pso) to the distal spermoviduct (dso), where fertilization takes place. (2) During egg formation, each egg cell is surrounded by secretion from the albumen gland (ag) and by two egg membranes secreted by the pars contorta (pc). (3) The egg mass is formed by addition of secretory products from the muciparous (mg) and oothecal glands (og). bc, bursa copulatrix; c, carrefour; dg, digestive gland lobes; p, penis; pg, prostate gland; sp, spermduct; sz, spermatogenic zone; vd, vas deferens; vs, vesiculae seminales. (From Dogterom et al 1983a, reproduced with permission.)

Endocrine control of female reproductive activity

The endocrine control of female reproductive activity in *L. stagnalis* has been studied in detail (see Joosse & Geraerts 1983, Geraerts & Joosse 1984). The endocrine dorsal bodies, attached to the cerebral ganglia (Fig. 2), produce the dorsal body hormone. This hormone stimulates vitellogenesis and the cellular differentiation, growth and synthetic activity of the female accessory sex organs. The neuroendocrine caudodorsal cells (CDC) are located in the cerebral ganglia in two groups adjacent to the intercerebral commissure, which is the release site of the caudodorsal cell hormone (CDCH). This hormone induces ovulation, stimulates the female reproductive tract to egg and egg-mass formation probably by activating the genital nervous plexus, and induces egg-laying behaviour probably by activating and inhibiting nerve cells in various ganglia that control muscular activity related to the egg-laying behaviour (Fig. 3). Centres in the lateral lobes (small ganglia connected to the cerebral ganglia) accelerate the onset of puberty and enhance female reproductive activity by activating the dorsal bodies and

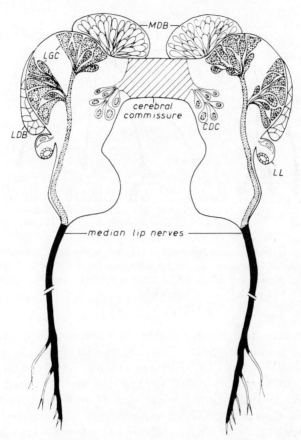

FIG. 2. Diagrammatic transverse section through the cerebral ganglia of *L. stagnalis*. LGC, light green cells; CDC, caudodorsal cells; LL, lateral lobes; MDB and LDB, mediodorsal and laterodorsal bodies. The periphery of the median lip nerves is the neurohaemal area of the LGC. The periphery of the cerebral commissure is the neurohaemal area of the CDC.

CDC. There are also indications for steroid synthesis in the Sertoli cells. However, the functional significance of this hypothetic gonadal hormone is still unknown (see below).

During reproductive periods dorsal body hormone seems to be released continuously. Long-term stimulating effects on egg laying, such as an increase in food supply (Scheerboom 1978), high temperature (Joosse & Veld 1972) and a long-day photoperiod (Bohlken & Joosse 1982), will certainly increase dorsal body activity, thus enhancing the production of ripe oocytes and egg-mass material.

In the short term, oviposition can rapidly (within 2 h) be induced by a

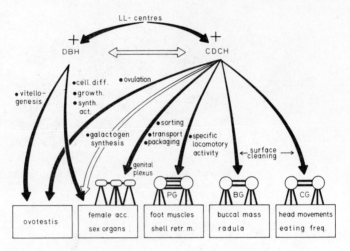

FIG. 3. Schematic presentation of the endocrine control of female reproductive activity in *L. stagnalis*. For details, see text. LL, lateral lobes; DBH, dorsal body hormone; CDCH, caudodorsal cell hormone; cell diff., cell differentiation; synth. act., synthetic activity; PG, pedal ganglia; BG, buccal ganglia; CG, cerebral ganglia.

change from dirty to clean water, and by the addition of oxygen to the water. These stimuli activate the CDC, which are usually electrically silent (i.e. in the resting state). Active CDC discharge with a series of synchronous action potentials in all the CDC, lasting 30–60 min (i.e. the 'active state': Kits 1980, de Vlieger et al 1980), during which CDCH is released (Kits 1981) by exocytosis (Roubos et al 1982). Subsequently, the CDC become inexcitable, but exocytotic activity continues, although at a lower level (the 'inhibited state'). This state lasts about 5 h; then the CDC enter the resting state again. Short-term stimuli appear to activate CDC very rapidly: within 5 min after application neural discharges start (Kits 1980). The long-term stimuli mentioned above also change the excitability, but in a less direct way (see below).

Effects of photoperiod

Photoperiodic effects on sexual maturation

Breeding of pond snails at three different photoperiods (short days, 8 h light : 16 h dark, LD 8 : 16; medium days, LD 12 : 12; and long days, LD 16 : 8), at a temperature of 20 °C, from egg masses produced by medium-day snails, shows that spontaneous egg laying occurs at all photoperiods but starts two weeks earlier under long-day conditions (Bohlken & Joosse 1982). Thus, in contrast to *Limax maximus* (Sokolove & McCrone 1978, Sokolove, this volume) female sexual maturation, as such, in *L. stagnalis* is not photoperiod-dependent, but only accelerated in long-day conditions. Since *Lymnaea* is simultaneously hermaphrodite, with a short protandric period, the same conclusion will hold for the development of the male activity.

Photoperiodic effects on egg laying

Adult snails bred and maintained in laboratory culture conditions (about 800 snails per tank) at three different photoperiods show clear differences in egg production. The ratios of numbers of eggs produced at the short-, medium- and long-day photoperiods are 1:3:21 (see Fig. 4). Thus, in mass-culture conditions the long-day photoperiod, compared to the other photoperiods, has a strong stimulating effect on egg production (Bohlken & Joosse 1982).

Interaction of photoperiodic effects with feeding regimen and temperature

Transfer of snails from mass culture to isolated conditions causes important changes. After isolation, egg production increases rapidly and considerably at all three photoperiods (Fig. 4), due to a higher oviposition frequency (within one week) and a gradual increase (after three weeks) in the size of egg masses. The increase in egg production at the short- and medium-day photoperiods, however, is much higher (about 45 and 25 fold, respectively) than the increase at the long-day photoperiod (about 4 fold). Consequently, the ratios of egg production at the short-, medium- and long-day photo-periods are 1:1.2:2.3 in isolated conditions (S. Bohlken & J. Joosse, unpublished results).

Which factor(s) might cause the difference? The snails were kept isolated in the water of the breeding tanks in which they had lived before, so effects of changes in the composition of the water can be excluded. Isolated specimens are prevented from copulation. However, there are no indications that male sexual activity inhibits egg laying. Absence of direct contact with other snails cannot be excluded as a possible factor. The most relevant factor, however, will be the accessibility to food. Isolated specimens are always in the direct neighbourhood of food (lettuce), whereas in the breeding tanks food is periodically absent. Scheerboom (1978) has shown, in similar experimental conditions, that food supply, food consumption and assimilation of food, as well as egg production, are linearly and positively related. This suggests that in *L. stagnalis* the stimulating effect of long-day conditions dominates when food is scarce.

To further test this hypothesis, we studied the effects of medium- and

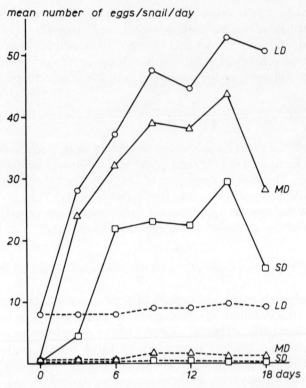

FIG. 4. Egg production of snails in mass culture conditions (dotted lines), compared to that of snails transferred to isolated conditions (solid lines) in the same tank at three different photoperiods. LD, MD, SD, long-, medium-, and short-day snails, respectively.

long-day photoperiods on egg laying in starved snails (S. Bohlken & J. Joosse, unpublished results). Medium-day snails ceased egg-mass production within one week after the onset of starvation, and they all survived a six-week starvation period. The long-day snails continued to produce egg masses, which became extremely small. After three weeks, mortality started and at the end of the experiment nearly all long-day snails had died. These results prove that in *L. stagnalis* during severe adverse conditions, such as food deprivation, it is the photoperiod that primarily determines whether oviposition will occur.

Interaction of this photoperiodic effect with temperature has also been studied. Previous experiments have shown that below about 12 °C egg production of medium-day snails stops (Joosse & Veld 1972). Fig. 5 shows the results of an experiment in which we studied the effect of a transfer from 20 °C

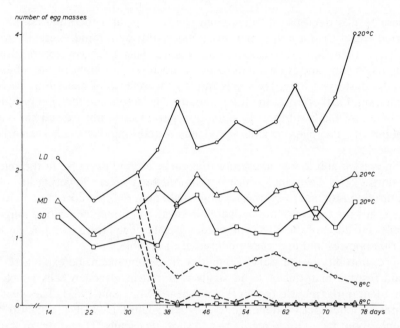

FIG. 5. Mean number of egg masses per snail per period of four days produced by groups of snails ($n = 40$) during acclimation to isolated conditions and three different photoperiods for 34 days. Thereafter 20 specimens of each group were transferred to 8 °C, while the others remained at 20 °C. In contrast to medium-day (MD) and short-day (SD) snails, the long-day (LD) snails continued to produce egg masses at 8 °C.

to 8 °C on egg laying of adult snails, adapted to various photoperiods. The medium- and short-day snails produced a very low number of egg masses for three weeks and then stopped egg laying completely. The long-day snails continued egg laying throughout the entire experimental period (six weeks), although at a lower level compared to the snails at 20 °C. There was no mortality in this experiment. Thus, the stimulating effect of the long-day photoperiod overrides the inhibiting effect of low temperatures.

To analyse the role of the endocrine centres in the interaction between these environmental factors, we require additional information. Medium-day snails, after three days of starvation or maintenance at low temperature (6 °C) have a reduced synthetic activity in the albumen gland (measured by the incorporation of labelled glucose into polysaccharides). This decrease reaches the low level characteristic of that in animals without dorsal bodies (Veldhuijzen & Cuperus 1976). The inactivation of the albumen gland is also apparent from studies on the enzyme galactogen synthetase in this gland. The activity of this enzyme falls by 70% after 24 h of starvation in medium-day snails.

These results demonstrate that pond snails, kept at a medium-day photo-period, react to starvation and low temperature by a rapid decrease in the activity of the female accessory sex organs. This decrease occurs also in long-day snails, and is apparent from the decrease in weight of the albumen glands of starved long-day snails due to the release of secretions for egg formation. Furthermore, the total amount of galactogen in the eggs produced by long-day snails during the starvation period does not exceed the mean amount of galactogen in albumen glands of fed long-day snails (van Elk & Joosse 1981).

Starvation and low temperature thus cause a rapid decrease in the release of dorsal body hormone, which is followed by a severe lowering in oocyte maturation rate and in synthesis of egg-mass material. In short- and medium-day snails the CDC are not activated in these conditions, but in the long-day snails activation of the CDC still occurs, because egg laying continues as long as ripe oocytes and egg-mass material are available.

The mortality of the starved long-day snails remains to be explained. The main reserve material of pond snails is stored in glycogen cells which are abundant in the mantle region (Hemminga & Maaskant 1983). The glycogen stores are photoperiod-dependent: long-day snails have a glycogen store that is only about 20% that in medium- and short-day snails. Therefore, in starved long-day snails the glycogen stores will be depleted much earlier than in snails kept at the other photoperiods. At low temperature the metabolic activity is low and, therefore, long-day snails can survive longer.

Photoperiodic effects on the reactivity of the reproductive system

Studies on the time schedule of the successive stages of egg-mass production after CDCH injections (in the form of intercerebral commissure extract) at 20 °C, and in a medium-day photoperiod, revealed the following latencies: ovulation within 10–20 min; egg formation, 20–30 min; egg-mass formation, 60–90 min; and oviposition within about 120 min. At long-day photoperiod all stages start 10 min earlier (Dogterom et al 1983a).

In dose–response studies of the reactivity of medium- and long-day snails to CDCH injections, the minimum dose for the ovulation response of long-day snails was lower compared to medium-day snails (Dogterom et al 1983b). Apparently, the gonad and the female tract of long-day snails are more sensitive to CDCH.

After oviposition the snails are unable to react to CDCH injections. This refractory period is shorter in long-day snails (6–12 h) compared to medium-day snails (12–18 h). These differences must be caused by an increased release, in long-day snails, of dorsal body hormone, or CDCH, or both (Dogterom et al 1983a).

Spontaneous egg laying and reactivity to CDCH in snails living in field conditions

In the field, spontaneous oviposition of pond snails in freshwater ditches (25 km from Amsterdam) was observed from the end of May until mid-September, with the highest frequency in June and July. During this period the water temperature in the Netherlands is usually above the minimum temperature (12–14 °C) for spontaneous egg laying, even at a medium-day photoperiod.

Induction of egg laying in more than 50% of field specimens, by injections of CDCH, was found from six weeks before until six weeks after the period of spontaneous egg laying (G. E. Dogterom & R. Thijssen, unpublished results). Since dorsal body activity also starts earlier in the spring than CDC activity, in snails under natural conditions (Joosse 1964), the reactivity of snails to CDCH may be determined by dorsal body hormone. Furthermore, activation of the CDC, so that they release neural discharges, may depend on short-term stimuli such as oxygen concentration, water quality and food consumption.

Photoperiodic effects on the CDC

As mentioned above, the CDC are usually in the resting state. Experimentally applied electrical stimulation of CDC in isolated central nervous systems may initiate an afterdischarge of the cells. This stimulation is more successful in long-day snails than in medium-day snails, suggesting that the threshold for a change from the resting to the active state of the CDC is lower in long-day snails (de Vlieger et al 1980). Unfortunately no quantitative data are available for the effect of the photoperiod on the excitability of the CDC after a change from dirty to clean water.

In starving medium-day snails the CDC are hyperpolarized (ter Maat et al 1982). Apparently, oviposition in these snails stops because of some kind of block in the transition from the resting to the active state of the CDC. Starved long-day snails continue ovipository activity. Preliminary studies of the CDC in these animals showed that their membrane potential is not different from that of starved medium-day snails (de Vlieger et al 1983).

Rhythmicity

A clear diurnal rhythm in the activity of the CDC, as well as in that of the growth-hormone-producing light green cells in the cerebral ganglia of *L.*

stagnalis, has been demonstrated by Wendelaar Bonga (1971) on the basis of quantitative electron microscopical investigations in field specimens collected in June. Release of CDCH and light green cell hormone shows a rapid increase a few hours before sunset and is probably correlated with the change in light intensity. The release activity remains high for about 6 h. Synthetic activity (formation of elementary granules) in the cell bodies of the CDC and the light green cells is high during the night and low during the day.

These results were confirmed by Roubos (1975). Moreover, Roubos showed that the rhythm of the CDC neurosecretory activity is synchronized by the natural light : dark cycle via the eyes (Fig. 6). The information from the eyes probably reaches the CDC via a nervous pathway. The diurnal rhythmicity of the light green cell activity is not affected by blinding of the snails.

The diurnal rhythm in the activity of the CDC is less clear in snails collected in the field in autumn. Moreover, in medium-day snails kept in laboratory conditions the rhythm is not very pronounced (Wendelaar Bonga 1971). These observations point to a stimulatory influence of long-day conditions on CDC rhythmicity.

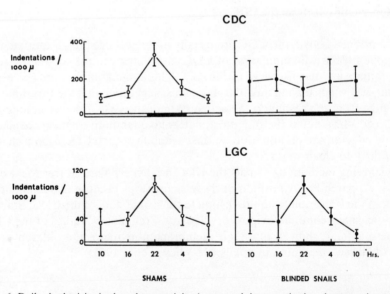

FIG. 6. Daily rhythmicity in the release activity (measured, by quantitative electron microscopy, from the number of exocytosis figures, or indentations, in the neurohaemal areas) of the neuroscretory caudodorsal cells (CDC) and light green cells (LGC) of snails kept in natural long-day conditions. In blinded snails the rhythmicity of the CDC is no longer synchronized. Each mean (and standard deviation) is derived from five snails; (after Roubos 1975).

Gonadal steroid synthesis

The steroidogenic activity of the ovotestis and the digestive gland of *L. stagnalis* was measured by de Jong-Brink et al (1981) *in vitro*, during a 24h cycle, from the conversion of pregnenolone into progesterone. The highest values were measured from 21.00 to 03.00 h. A distinct correlation was found between the diurnal activity of these steroid-synthesizing enzymes and the extensiveness of the smooth endoplasmic reticulum in Sertoli cells carrying spermatids and in Sertoli cells after spermiation. De Jong-Brink et al (1981) suggest that the Sertoli cells are responsible for the steroid production. Since, in Basommatophora, there is no evidence for an endocrine control of the accessory sex glands by the gonad, these steroids must have an intragonadal role.

Diurnal activity of the albumen gland

Release of secretory material by the albumen gland has to be differentiated into the release of secretion products via exocytosis by the glandular cells into the intraglandular ducts (cellular release) and the release of secretory material from the gland during egg formation (glandular release). Cellular release shows a diurnal rhythmicity in long-day snails, with a narrow peak near midnight (3 h after the start of darkness). The concomitant increase in secretory activity of the albumen gland cells is less distinct, but also reaches a maximum during the dark period (de Jong-Brink et al 1982).

Ovipository activity

In laboratory conditions isolated snails show oviposition mainly during the light phase: medium-day snails produce 84% of their egg masses during this period, and long-day snails produce 87%. The long-day snails show no clear preference for the first or second half of the light period.

Observations on egg laying in semi-field conditions in June revealed no oviposition at all between 07.00 and 12.00 h. The majority of the egg masses were produced between 15.00 and 19.00 h (Thijssen 1983).

Preliminary experiments on diurnal changes in the reactivity of the snails to injected ovulation hormone (CDCH) were done on snails in laboratory conditions (long-day isolated snails) and in semi-field conditions in June. The snails in the semi-field conditions showed a high response in the afternoon and early evening, whereas the laboratory snails showed a decreased reactivity during the dark period (Thijssen 1983).

Acknowledgements

I am highly indebted to Drs W. P. M. Geraerts and A. ter Maat for critical reading of the manuscript, to Mr R. van Elk for drawing Fig. 4, to Dr E. W. Roubos for composing Fig. 6, and to Mrs T. Laan for typing the manuscript.

REFERENCES

Bohlken S, Joosse J 1982 The effect of photoperiod on female reproductive activity of the freshwater pulmonate snail *Lymnaea stagnalis* kept under laboratory breeding conditions. Int J Invertebr Reprod 4:213-222

de Jong-Brink M, Goldschmeding JT 1983 Endocrine and nervous regulation of female reproductive activity in the gonad and the albumen gland of *Lymnaea stagnalis*. In: Lever J, Boer HH (eds) Molluscan neuro-endocrinology. North-Holland, Amsterdam, p 126-131

de Jong-Brink M, Schot LPC, Schoenmaker HJN, Bergamin-Sassen MJM 1981 A biochemical and quantitative electron-microscope study on steroidogenesis in ovotestis and digestive gland of the pulmonate snail *Lymnaea stagnalis*. Gen Comp Endocrinol 45:30-38

de Jong-Brink M, Koop HM, de Roos WF, Bergamin-Sassen JM 1982 Regulation of secretory activity in the albumen gland of the pulmonate snail *Lymnaea stagnalis* (L.). Int J Invertebr Reprod 5:207-219

de Vlieger TA, Kits KS, ter Maat A, Lodder JC 1980 Morphology and electrophysiology of the ovulation hormone producing neuro-endocrine cells of the freshwater snail *Lymnaea stagnalis* (L.). J Exp Biol 84:259-271

de Vlieger TA, Lodder JC, Joosse J, van Elk R 1983 Egg-laying and excitability of the ovulation hormone producing caudo-dorsal cells (CDC) in *Lymnaea stagnalis* starved at different photoperiods and in parasitically infected snails. In: Lever J, Boer HH (eds) Molluscan neuro-endocrinology. North-Holland, Amsterdam, p 182-183

Dogterom GE, Bohlken S, Joosse J 1983a Effect of the photoperiod on the time-schedule of egg-mass production in *Lymnaea stagnalis*, induced by ovulation hormone injections. Gen Comp Endocrinol 49:255-260

Dogterom GE, Bohlken S, Geraerts WPM 1983b A rapid *in vivo* bioassay of the ovulation hormone of *Lymnaea stagnalis*. Gen Comp Endocrinol 50:476-482

Geraerts WPM, Joosse J 1984 Freshwater snails (Basommatophora). In: Wilbur KM (ed) The mollusca (7), reproduction. Academic Press, New York, p 141-207

Hemminga MA, Maaskant JJ 1983 Regulation of glycogen metabolism in *Lymnaea stagnalis*. In: Lever J, Boer HH (eds) Molluscan neuro-endocrinology. North-Holland, Amsterdam, p 167-169

Joosse J 1964 Dorsal bodies and dorsal neurosecretory cells of the cerebral ganglia of *Lymnaea stagnalis* L. Arch Néerl Zool 15:1-103

Joosse J, Veld CJ 1972 Endocrinology of reproduction in the hermaphrodite gastropod *Lymnaea stagnalis*. Gen Comp Endocrinol 18:599-600

Joosse J, Geraerts WPM 1983 Hormones. In: Wilbur KM, Saleuddin ASM (eds) The mollusca (4), physiology part 1. Academic Press, New York, p 317-406

Kits KS 1980 States of excitability in ovulation hormone-producing neuroendocrine cells of *Lymnaea stagnalis* (Gastropoda) and their relation to the egg-laying cycle. J Neurobiol 11:397-410

Kits KS 1981 Electrical activity and hormone output of ovulation hormone-producing neuro-endocrine cells in *Lymnaea stagnalis* (Gastropoda). In: Salanki J (ed) Neurobiology of invertebrates—mechanisms of integration. Akadémiai Kiadó, Budapest, Hungary, Adv Physiol Sci 23:34-54

Roubos EW 1975 Regulation of neurosecretory activity in the freshwater pulmonate snail *Lymnaea stagnalis* (L.) with particular reference to the role of the eyes. Cell Tissue Res 160:291-314

Roubos EW, Boer HH, Schot LPC 1982 Peptidergic neurones and the control of neuroendocrine activity in the freshwater snail *Lymnaea stagnalis*. In: Farner DS, Lederis K (eds) Neuro-secretion, molecules, cells, systems. Plenum, New York, p 119-127

Scheerboom JEM 1978 The influence of food quantity and food quality on assimilation, body growth and egg production in the pond snail *Lymnaea stagnalis* (L.) with particular reference to the haemolymph glucose concentration. Proc Kon Ned Akad Wet C81:184-197

Sokolove PG, McCrone EJ 1978 Reproductive maturation in the slug, *Limax maximus*, and the effects of artificial photoperiod. J Comp Physiol 125:317-325

ter Maat A, Lodder JC, Veenstra J, Goldschmeding JT 1982 Suppression of egg laying during starvation in the snail *Lymnaea stagnalis* by inhibition of the ovulation hormone-producing caudo-dorsal cells. Brain Res 239:535-542

Thijssen R 1983 Reproductive activities of the pond snail *Lymnaea stagnalis* under field conditions. In: Lever J, Boer HH (eds) Molluscan neuro-endocrinology. North-Holland, Amsterdam, p 181-182

van Duivenboden YA 1983 Transfer of semen accelerates the onset of egg-laying in female copulants of the hermaphrodite freshwater snail *Lymnaea stagnalis*. Int J Invertebr Reprod 6:249-257

van Elk R, Joosse J 1981 The UDP-galactose 4-epimerase of the albumen gland of *Lymnaea stagnalis* and the effects of photoperiod, starvation and trematode infections on its activity. Comp Biochem Physiol 70B: 45-52

Veldhuijzen JP, Cuperus R 1976 Effects of starvation, low temperature and the dorsal body hormone on the *in vitro* synthesis of galactogen and glycogen in the albumen gland and the mantle of the pond snail *Lymnaea stagnalis*. Neth J Zool 26:119-135

Wendelaar Bonga SE 1971 Formation, storage and release of neurosecretory material studied by quantitative electron microscopy in the freshwater snail *Lymnaea stagnalis* (L.). Z Zellforsch 113:490-517

DISCUSSION

Goldsworthy: You said that you saw rhythms in the histological appearance of the light green cells, but not in the caudodorsal cells (CDC), in blinded snails. Is the effect of long days on oviposition seen also in blinded animals?

Joosse: Oviposition does occur mainly in the light phase of the day but we have not studied the rhythmicity of egg laying in blinded animals.

Chippendale: Are you now investigating the chemical nature of the caudo-dorsal cell hormone (CDCH)?

Joosse: Yes; we have been trying to isolate it for many years, but the quantities are minute. The dorsal body hormone, the growth hormone and the ovulation hormone are all peptides. The ovulation hormone has a relative molecular mass of 4700, which is nearly identical to that of *Aplysia* (4385). The amino acid composition and sequence of this hormone in *Aplysia* have been determined (Strumwasser et al 1980). The ovulation hormone of *Lymnaea* has an isoelectric point of 9.3, but that of the dorsal body hormone is about 3.5 so they are easily separable (Joosse & Geraerts 1983).

Pittendrigh: Have any of the *Lymnaea stagnalis* hormones been sequenced?

Joosse: No. The amount of ovulation hormone in one *Aplysia* is 10000 times more than in one *Lymnaea*.

Gilbert: What is the role of thyrotropin releasing hormone (TRH) in molluscs?

Joosse: There are reports of immunoreactive TRH in the dark green cell type in *Lymnaea* (Grimm-Jørgensen 1983). We tested TRH and did not find any effect on the sodium flux of *Lymnaea*. We have found a completely different centre for the endocrine control of sodium transport across the body wall. This factor is released by the cerebral ganglia (de With & van der Schors 1983).

Goldsworthy: I believe that you regard the activity of the CDC and the dorsal bodies as being under some gross control from the lateral lobes. Are these lobes responsible for the long-day effect on oviposition?

Joosse: The lateral lobes are interesting centres adjacent to the cerebral ganglia. Their effects on female reproductive activity are exactly the same as those of long-day conditions: the lateral lobes induce earlier female maturation and enhance female reproductive activity. When the lobes are removed in medium-day snails, and one tries to adapt the snails to three different photoperiods (short- , medium- and long-day) the different patterns of egg production that arise are completely identical to those of the unoperated controls, except that the levels are all lower in snails without lateral lobes, which is consistent with the known lateral-lobe effect. Thus, the photoperiod effect is not transduced via the lateral lobes (see Joosse & Geraerts 1983).

Reynolds: Your study of exocytotic profiles indicated that release of CDCH was still occurring more than two hours after the initial surge. Yet the postulated blood titre had already returned to basal levels at that time.

Joosse: These levels were not basal but they were lowering. The half-life of CDCH is shorter than 30 min, which might explain why its continued release is necessary, even during decreasing levels. The mechanism of exocytosis in the absence of action potentials is not yet understood.

Reynolds: Do you think that the continued release of CDCH has a physiological role after two hours?

Joosse: As long as these cells are releasing they cannot be activated electrically. This means that these phenomena also determine the duration of the inhibited state of the cells. So, in long-day conditions, when the release is more rapid, the inhibited state is shorter. In addition, there is a lot to be done internally in the animal after an egg mass has been produced. It is very strange that the animal does not have a good coordination between the number of oocytes ovulated and those packaged in the egg mass. After oviposition one can find, in the female tract, up to 80 egg cells which are not packed. These are then transported to the bursa copulatrix where they are hydrolysed. Such activities could be controlled by CDCH. Moreover, CDCH stimulates the synthesis of new egg-mass material, particularly the perivitellin fluid. It makes sense for this to happen immediately after oviposition.

Mordue: You said that the CDC are synchronous, and that a hundred cells can fire together. You have information about the number and duration of exocytotic profiles. Do the cells empty and have to fill up again completely? Is pulsatile release involved?

Joosse: The amount of hormone in the cerebral commissure and the CDC together is about 130 OIU (ovulation-inducing units). During egg laying, about 70 OIU disappears from this system; concomitantly, about the same amount of 70 OIU appears in the blood (Geraerts et al 1984). This amount is clearly much more (70×) than needed for the induction of ovulation. As soon as release starts, transport and synthetic activity begin in the cells.

Mordue: In many insect systems, release of neurosecretory hormones is not synchronous, as it is in your system. Once you have established the composition and size of the hormone molecule it should be possible to determine the quantities of peptide released. Eventually you should be able to say how many peptide molecules are in each granule. This would be most useful. This has been done for acetylcholine release but there are not many systems where this type of calculation has been possible for peptides.

Joosse: Yes. It is a useful system for such studies, but we need to know first the structure of the molecule. We can now keep the nervous systems of inactive animals in physiological saline, at a pH controlled by CO_2, for a long time. If we add a cyclic AMP derivative the whole system becomes activated and we can monitor the bursting activity. This means that we can study, say, 5 or 10 min of release activities in a controlled way. This will enable us to study biosynthetic activity, and the relative molecular mass and composition of the materials both stored in the cells and after release. Dr W.P.M. Geraerts has now found that four different peptides are released by these cells (Geraerts et al 1984).

Hodková: You said that long days stimulate the release of the ovulation hormone and that food stimulates the release of dorsal body hormone. Are these two activities somehow coupled? For example, under a short photo-period, is the production of dorsal body hormone low even if the food supply is very high?

Joosse: It is likely that both endocrine centres will be interrelated. We have not yet studied the electrical characteristics of the ovulation hormone cells in animals without the dorsal body hormone. A gonadal hormone may also be involved. We are now trying to study the effects of possible gonadal steroids on these endocrine cells in the brain.

Brady: It always surprises me that in molluscs, unlike insects, so much of what one would loosely call the brain is involved with hormonal control. Has any animal other than *Lymnaea* invested such a high proportion of its central neurons in the hormonal system?

Joosse: I don't know. The great advantage of molluscan systems for studying this question is that the cells of one type tend to be grouped together in identifiable places in constant numbers. About four years ago we thought there were about 10 cell types but now our neurocytochemical studies have revealed about 30 different peptidergic cell types. However, some of these have a neurotransmitter function and some have a neuroendocrine function.

Goldsworthy: I wonder whether Dr Brady's question is prompted from an artificial basis. In the mollusc, neurosecretory cells are scattered profusely throughout the nervous system. Yet the same arrangement exists in insects and is simply ignored because its study is too difficult! Dr Joosse has been considering here only the endocrine cells and not the non-endocrine neurons.

Joosse: We now have much to study about the relationship of the endocrine cells to other 'common' neurons. We are currently very interested in the so-called ring neuron. This innervates caudodorsal (endocrine) cells as well as motor centres in the pedal ganglia (ter Maat & Jansen 1984). In *Aplysia* much more is known than in *Lymnaea* about functions of non-peptidergic cells (Kandel 1979).

REFERENCES

de With ND, van der Schors RC 1983 Neuroendocrine aspects of sodium and chloride metabolism in the pulmonate snail *Lymnaea stagnalis*. In: Lever J, Boer HH (eds) Molluscan neuro-endocrinology. North-Holland, Amsterdam, p 208-212

Geraerts WPM, Van Asselt A, ter Maat A, Hogenes TM 1984 Studies on the release activities of the neurosecretory caudo-dorsal cells of *Lymnaea stagnalis*. In: Hoffmann JA, Porchet M (eds) Biosynthese metabolisme mode d'action des hormones d'invertebres. Springer, Heidelberg, in press

Grimm-Jørgensen Y 1983 Possible physiological roles of thyrotropin releasing hormone and a somatostatin-like peptide in gastropods. In: Lever J, Boer HH (eds) Molluscan neuro-endocrinology. North-Holland, Amsterdam, p 21-28

Joosse J, Geraerts WPM 1983 Hormones. In: Wilbur KM (ed) The mollusca (4), physiology part 1. Academic Press, New York, p 317-406

Kandel ER 1979 Behavioural biology of *Aplysia*. W.H. Freeman, San Francisco

Strumwasser F, Kaczmarek LK, Chiu AY, Heller E, Jennings KR, Viele DP 1980 Peptides controlling behaviour in *Aplysia*. In: Bloom FE (ed) Peptides: integrators of cell and tissue function. Raven Press, New York, p 197-218

ter Maat A, Jansen RF 1984 The egg-laying behaviour of the pond snail: electrophysiological aspects. In: Hoffmann JA, Porchet M (eds) Biosynthese metabolisme mode d'action des hormones d'invertebres. Springer, Heidelberg, in press

Physiological aspects of the two oscillators that regulate the timing of eclosion in moths

JAMES W. TRUMAN

Department of Zoology, NJ-15, University of Washington, Seattle, WA 98195 USA

Abstract. The rhythm of adult eclosion in the moth *Manduca sexta* is influenced by two circadian systems. One, the G system, is located in the moth brain. It is sensitive to light and it free-runs under constant conditions. During the circadian gates, the G system is thought to excite the brain centres that release an eclosion hormone whereas during the intergate period the G system inhibits these centres. The output of the second system, the E system, is manifest in a daily modulation in the levels of the steroid hormone ecdysteroid. The clock for the E system is a circadian clock that is *not* located in the brain and is temperature-sensitive. The E system, acting through the declining levels of ecdysteroid, appears to excite the eclosion hormone centres. The behaviour of the eclosion rhythm as the result of the interaction of these two oscillators has many points of similarity with that determined for the coupled oscillator model in *Drosophila* spp.

1984 Photoperiodic regulation of insect and molluscan hormones. Pitman, London (Ciba Foundation symposium 104), p 221-239

Light and temperature are the two environmental cues that most commonly are used for *zeitgebers*. For the eclosion rhythm of *Drosophila* spp. it has been postulated that light and temperature can interact with different components of the insect's circadian system (Pittendrigh 1981). The time of ecdysis can be faithfully modelled as the interaction between two oscillators: a driver oscillator that is light-sensitive and a driven, damped oscillator that is temperature-sensitive and that triggers the ecdysial event itself.

Recent experiments with the moth *Manduca sexta*, a species that is sensitive primarily to temperature (Lockshin et al 1975), have indicated that light and temperature interact with two physiologically separate and perhaps mutually exclusive components of the insect's circadian system. These components are each circadian oscillators, and they are good candidates for the two oscillators postulated on the basis of the *Drosophila* rhythm.

The role of the brain in gating eclosion—the G system

Studies on adult eclosion of various species of silkmoths first indicated that this behaviour was regulated by a brain-centred system (Truman & Riddiford 1970, Truman 1972). Transplantation of the brain between species that had different eclosion times resulted in transplantation of the respective eclosion gates. This gating system, along with the photoreceptor that receives the light information for its entrainment, resides in the protocerebral area of the brain and it triggers the behaviour through the release of a peptide hormone—eclosion hormone (Reynolds & Truman 1980). For ease in discussion, I have termed this brain-centred system that gates the release of eclosion hormone the 'G system'.

Ecdysteroids, the preparatory behaviour and the E system

Studies on the eclosion of both flies and moths have indicated that other factors besides the gating clock play a role in regulating eclosion. In *Drosophila*, flies rendered arrhythmic by rearing them in constant light are still capable of eclosing at the end of metamorphosis although their distribution relative to the 24h day is random (Pittendrigh & Skopik 1970). Consequently, eclosion can still take place even in the absence of the rhythmic input of the gating clock. Other studies on the fly show that the gating clock can be phase-shifted by light pulses at any time during metamorphosis and even back in the early larval stages (Zimmerman & Ives 1970). Thus, the gating clock is running through most of the life of the insect but it triggers behaviour only at one time—at the end of metamorphosis. These observations suggest that additional influences besides the G system are required for the triggering of eclosion behaviour.

The fact that eclosion behaviour occurs only at a specific time at the end of metamorphosis does not necessarily mean that release of eclosion hormone is confined to this time. Indeed, in the moth *M. sexta* sensitivity to eclosion hormone does not appear until the day of eclosion (Reynolds et al 1979), so hormone could be released, potentially, during the time of the gate on every day of development but the insect would be responsive to it, and hence eclose, only on the last day. However, as seen in Fig. 1, blood samples taken from insects at various times during the last 4 days of adult development failed to show any significant eclosion-hormone activity except during the gate on the last (18th) day of development. Thus, the gating of eclosion reflects the underlying gating of the release of eclosion hormone. Examination of the levels of eclosion hormone at the release sites in the corpora cardiaca showed that suprathreshold levels of hormone have accumulated by

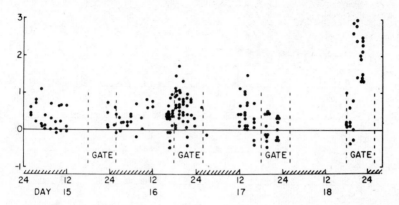

FIG. 1. Blood titres of eclosion hormone during the last 4 days of adult development in *Manduca sexta*. Each point represents a single measurement for eclosion hormone activity using the isolated wing assay (Reynolds & Truman 1980). The threshold for hormonal activity is a score of about 1. The time corresponding to the eclosion gate is indicated for the last 4 days of development. Significant levels of hormone appear during the gate only on the last (18th) day of development.

about Day 12 of development (Truman et al 1981). Thus, even before the last day of adult development, the endocrine system has sufficient eclosion hormone and the gating clock is running but, nevertheless, eclosion hormone is not released.

The developmental competence to release eclosion hormone appears to be conveyed through the ecdysteroid titre. This was first indicated by the experiments of Slama (1980) on *Tenebrio*. He demonstrated that this beetle would not ecdyse until the circulating ecdysteroids that initiated the moult subsequently declined to low levels. Subsequent experiments on *M. sexta* confirmed that ecdysteroids play a prominent role in the timing of ecdysis in insects (Truman 1981, Truman et al 1983). In this moth, treatment with exogenous steroid at any time up to about 12 h before the release of eclosion hormone delayed eclosion. The extent of the delay was dose-dependent and the maintenance of high ecdysteroid levels by steroid infusions blocked ecdysis for as long as the infusions were maintained. The time at which steroid treatments ceased to be effective in delaying eclosion coincided with a normal drop in the circulating levels of ecdysteroids. This evidence suggests that the drop in circulating ecdysteroids is the cue responsible for allowing eclosion to occur. I have referred to the system that regulates the timing of the ecdysteroid decline as the 'E system'.

The timing of eclosion in *Manduca* is a function of inputs from both the G (gating) and the E systems. This is best seen in experiments in which graded doses of the ecdysteroid, 20-hydroxyecdysone, were injected into developing

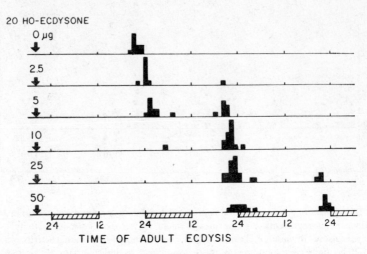

FIG. 2. The effects of injection of various doses of ecdysteroid (arrows) per insect on the time of adult eclosion in *Manduca sexta*. [Dosages are given as the total dose per insect.]

Manduca about 26 h before their normal time of eclosion. As shown in Fig. 2, increasing dosages of 20-hydroxyecdysone delayed eclosion in a saltatory fashion such that the insects 'jumped' from gate to gate. Importantly, the steroid treatment defined not only the gate that the insect selected but also the time of emergence within the gate (*i.e.* whether the insect emerged early or late in the gate).

The ability of the ecdysteroid titre to influence the timing of eclosion provides an interesting complication in that the E system itself has a circadian component. Late in adult development of *Manduca*, events such as the digestion of the pupal cuticle (Truman et al 1983), the appearance of sensitivity to eclosion hormone (Reynolds et al 1979) and the death of selected muscles (Schwartz & Truman 1983) and neurons (J. W. Truman & L. M. Schwartz, unpublished results) each occur at a characteristic time relative to the day–night cycle. Since many of these events take place before the release of eclosion hormone, the G system, acting through eclosion-hormone release, could not be involved in their timing. Declining levels of circulating ecdysteroids have been implicated in the control of all these events. Thus, since these developmental changes were phase-locked to particular times of day, the endocrine signal that controls them, the ecdysteroid decline, must also be phase-locked to time of day.

Unlike eclosion hormone, which is released as a discrete pulse, the ecdysteroids are present in the blood throughout development (Bollenbacher et al 1981). To investigate the possibility of a circadian modulation of the titre, we took blood samples at 3 h intervals during the last 4 days of adult development and measured the ecdysteroid titre by radioimmunoassay. Throughout this period the titre declined by a series of discrete, daily steps with the levels staying relatively stable during the night, followed by a decline during the day (Schwartz & Truman 1983). The basis for the rhythm—whether it is due to a daily modulation in the rate of ecdysteroid synthesis or in the rate of steroid metabolism—is unknown at present. The various developmental events seem to be triggered as the titre falls below particular levels (Schwartz & Truman 1983).

An indirect monitor of a particular phase of the steroid decline in *Manduca* has been provided by the *preparatory behaviour* (J. W. Truman, unpublished). This behaviour occurs approximately 8–10 h before adult eclosion. It lasts for 1 to 2 h and involves a marked increase in the frequency of rotary movements of the abdomen. At its termination the attachments between the old and new cuticles have been loosened. The time of onset of the preparatory behaviour is ecdysteroid-dependent and can be delayed in a continuous fashion by the injection of graded doses of 20-hydroxyecdysone. Another indication of the steroid regulation of the behaviour comes from studies on isolated abdomens (J. W. Truman, unpublished). When isolated 3 days before the normal time of eclosion, these abdomens will nevertheless display the behaviour, but they will do so about 12 h early. Importantly, this treatment also causes a precocious decline in the abdominal ecdysteroid titre (Schwartz & Truman 1983). Injection of steroid into these abdomens then results in a dose-dependent delay in behavioural onset. Thus, the insects appear to be committed to perform the preparatory behaviour after the ecdysteroid titre declines below a certain threshold level. We have used the behaviour as a marker for the time of occurrence of this threshold.

A number of features of the preparatory behaviour are especially important to the present discussion. *Manduca* that were debrained early in adult development nevertheless showed the preparatory behaviour at the appropriate time of day when they finished metamorphosis 14 to 16 days later (J. W. Truman, unpublished). Thus, unlike eclosion, the timing of this behaviour is regulated by a clock that resides outside the brain.

The dominant and perhaps exclusive *zeitgeber* for entrainment of the preparatory behaviour rhythm is temperature. Manifestly, when developing *Manduca* were exposed to a 12L:12D light:dark cycle and to a 12 h 25 °C:12 h 27 °C temperature cycle, which were at various phase relationships to each other, the timing of the preparatory behaviour was essentially phase-locked to the temperature step-up, irrespective of the phase of the superimposed light cycle. In contrast to the preparatory behaviour, the timing of eclosion in *Manduca* was a function of the photoperiod cycle as well as the temperature cycle. Thus, the eclosion of *Manduca* is similar to that of *Drosophila* (Pittendrigh 1960) in that both light and temperature are effective in setting the phase of the eclosion peak, but it differs from the fly in that there was no 'forbidden phase', relative to the light cycle, that the eclosion distribution could not occupy.

Although temperature sets the phase of the preparatory behaviour, this behaviour is not a passive response to a temperature transient. Indeed, animals transferred to constant light and constant temperature showed a preparatory behaviour rhythm that free-ran for at least four cycles (i.e. as long as the experiments were run).

Thus, using the preparatory behaviour as a marker for the decline in the ecdysteroid titre, one can make the following conclusions about the E system: it is influenced by a circadian oscillator that is primarily (or exclusively) temperature-sensitive; and it is located outside the brain. The locus of the E clock is not yet known but a likely candidate would be the prothoracic glands that secrete ecdysteroids.

Interactions between the G and E systems in determining the time of eclosion

A working model has been devised to describe the interaction of the two circadian systems in timing eclosion. For the sake of example, I have formulated the model in terms of explicit physiological mechanisms (Fig. 3).

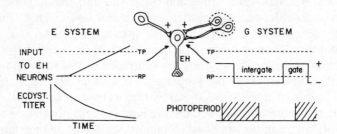

FIG. 3. Schematic representation of the inputs that regulate the activity of the eclosion hormone neurons (EH). Excitation provided by the E system increases as the blood ecdysteroid level drops. The input from the G system is set by the light:dark cycle and is excitatory during the gate and inhibitory between gates. The hypothetical effects of these respective inputs on the membrane potential of the EH cell are indicated. RP, resting potential; TP, threshold potential.

Obviously, many of these explicit features may need to be revised as more information is gained about this system. I have postulated that the cells that produce eclosion hormone (the EH cells) in the brain of the moth are acted on by both the G and the E systems. The effects of the E system are mediated through ecdysteroid-sensitive neurons that excite the EH cells. As the ecdysteroid level drops these ecdysone-sensitive neurons become active and their level of excitatory input onto the EH cells is inversely proportional to the ecdysteroid titre. When the ecdysteroid titre has declined to a sufficiently low level, the excitation from these cells drives the EH cells above their threshold, resulting in release of eclosion hormone.

The input from the G system is mediated through a separate neural network whose output is represented as a square wave: during the period of the eclosion gate the G system input to the EH cells is excitatory, while during the intergate period the input is inhibitory. The maximum level of the excitatory input from the G system is assumed to be subthreshold because the gating clock does not evoke release of eclosion hormone when the ecdysteroid titre is high (and hence when there is no E system input). Consequently, even at its level of maximum excitation the G system input cannot drive the EH cells above threshold unless this input is combined with the rising ramp of excitation provided by the E system.

The studies by Pittendrigh & Skopik (1970) on the gating of *Drosophila* eclosion compared the eclosion of flies under arrhythmic conditions (in constant light) with those that were gated. An interesting feature of this analysis was that the gating influence was able either to advance or to delay eclosion relative to its expected time on the basis of developmental age alone. The interaction of the G and E systems accounts for these advances and delays in the timing of eclosion (Fig. 4). Under conditions of constant light, the G system input is assumed to be zero, and the insects eclose according to their developmental age as mediated through the E system (ecdysteroid decline). The superposition of the G system can then cause early eclosion when the excitatory input during the gating phase is added to a subthreshold E system input. Alternatively, a delay in eclosion could come about because, in insects that are 'ready' to ecdyse between gates, the suprathreshold excitatory input from their E system would be at least partially counteracted by inhibitory inputs from the G system to keep the EH cells from releasing eclosion hormone.

Relationship to the coupled oscillators in *Drosophila*

The formal analysis of the eclosion rhythm in *Drosophila* suggested that the rhythm is regulated by two oscillators arranged in a hierarchical manner in which an endogenous, light-sensitive driver oscillator is coupled to a damped, temperature-sensitive driven oscillator (Pittendrigh 1981). The latter oscillator then triggers ecdysis. The E and G systems that influence eclosion in *Manduca* are both based on self-sustained circadian oscillators that are primarily sensitive to temperature and light respectively. Both have a direct input into the eclosion-hormone release centres and I have not had to

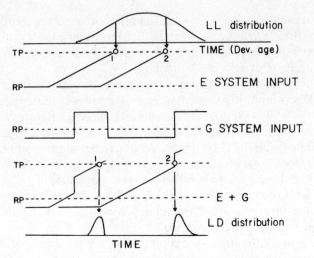

FIG. 4. Interaction of the E and G system to regulate the timing of eclosion under constant light (LL) and under light:dark (LD) conditions. Under LL conditions the G system is not operating and the time of ecdysis is determined only by developmental age (top) and hence the E system input. The E system input is indicated for two insects that are early (1) and late (2) in the distribution. Under LD conditions the G system is operating and its input adds to that of the E system to advance the ecdysis of 1 and delay that of 2. In this way the LL distribution is divided into two gates. Other abbreviations as in Fig. 3.

postulate any direct interaction between the two oscillators as such. Obviously, however, a search for physiological evidence for direct interaction is in order. It is not yet clear whether these apparent differences between the fly and the moth systems are substantive.

The interaction of the G and E systems in *Manduca* can account for many of the behaviours of the eclosion rhythm that have been described in *Drosophila*. 'Gating bias', as originally described for eclosion in *Drosophila* (Pittendrigh & Skopik 1970), is clearly due to the interaction of ecdysteroid with the G system (Fig. 2). A reason for initially postulating coupled oscillators in the fly was the appearance of transients after the insects were given a phase-shifting light pulse (Pittendrich et al 1958). *Manduca* that are entrained to a 12 L (27 °C):12 D (25 °C) cycle and then subjected to a shifted light cycle (while temperature is maintained at 27 °C) required up to 6 days to attain a new steady state (J. W. Truman, unpublished). When both light and temperature were shifted at the same time, then a new steady state occurred after only one cycle. In terms of the G and E systems, one would expect that simultaneous shifts in both light and temperature would shift both systems. By contrast, the shift of only the light cycle would immediately reset the G

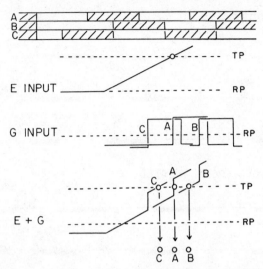

FIG. 5. Interaction of the E and G cycles during a stable photoperiod (A) and the first cycle after a 6h phase-delay (B) or a 6h phase-advance (C). Since only light is shifted the E system input would stay the same in all three cases. The G input for only the first full cycle after the shift is shown. It is assumed that the G clock shifts immediately but that the interaction with the E input during the first cycle prevents a full delay (B) or a full advance (C). For further explanation see text. Abbreviations are as in Fig. 3.

clock but not the E clock. As seen in Fig. 5, under delaying conditions the unshifted phase of the declining ecdysteroid titre would result in sufficient excitation to produce release of eclosion hormone before the first shifted G gate (B in Fig. 5). Hence, a full delay would not be expressed. Similarly, under a phase-advance condition (C in Fig. 5), the earlier G gate would be faced with a lower level of ecdysteroid-induced excitation, thereby resulting in a later ecdysis than that expected on the basis of the G shift alone.

An initial test of the importance of the E system in the generation of transients is shown in Fig. 6. *Manduca* were subject to light-cycle delays of 6 or 12h. Under this treatment, the insects showed essentially no shift in eclosion time on the first cycle of the shift. I have interpreted this to mean that the E system input accumulated to the point that ecdysis was triggered, even outside the gate. In order to reduce the E system input, replicate groups of insects were injected with a constant amount of 20-hydroxyecdysone. The 6- and 12h-shifted groups subsequently showed shifts in the major distribution of eclosion of about 6 and 12h respectively. These results suggest that in *Manduca* the light shift immediately resets the G system but that this resetting is normally masked by the strong input from the E system.

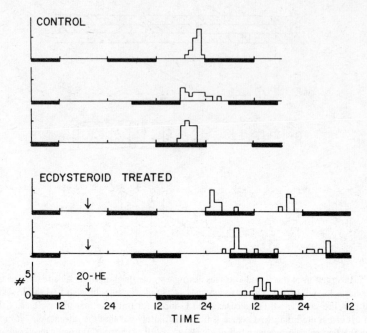

FIG. 6. Effect of ecdysteroid treatment in allowing *Manduca* to respond immediately to a shift in photoperiod. Insects were maintained at 12 L (27 °C) : 12 D (25 °C). On Day 17 of development they were placed in constant temperature (27 °C) and maintained in the same photoperiod or given a 6 or 12 h delay. The control group was uninjected; the ecdysteroid-treated group received 5 μg 20-hydroxyecdysone per animal, at the time indicated. The ecdysteroid treatment allowed the insects to follow immediately the shift in photoperiod.

Future directions

We have, as yet, only begun to explore the *Manduca* system in a preliminary fashion and numerous questions need to be answered. The two oscillators in this system have been described as light-sensitive and temperature-sensitive but we have not excluded the possibility that each clock may have some sensitivity to the other modality. While temperature is the main *zeitgeber* for entraining the E system, we cannot yet exclude a feeble sensitivity to light. It should be noted that one candidate for the locus of the E clock, the prothoracic glands, has been shown to be photosensitive in the moth *Samia cynthia ricini* (Mizoguchi & Ishizaki 1982). Similarly, since we have studied the behaviour of the brain clock, so far, only in insects that have their prothoracic glands, we cannot determine how sensitive the brain clock might be to temperature. The possibility of direct interaction between the two clocks, beyond the postulated mutual input onto the centres that release eclosion hormone, is unexplored.

A second point of caution is that although the interaction of these two centres can account for transients after phase shifts, this does not necessarily mean that the E and G clocks cannot show transient behaviour on their own. We have not yet been able to study either clock isolated from the influence of the other. This needs to be done in order to obtain a clear indication of the rhythmic properties of each component.

Acknowledgements

Unpublished results reported in this paper were supported by grants from the National Science Foundation and the National Institutes of Health.

REFERENCES

Bollenbacher WE, Smith SL, Goodman W, Gilbert LI 1981 Ecdysteroid titer during larval–pupal–adult development of the tobacco hornworm, *Manduca sexta*. Gen Comp Endocrinol 44:302-306

Lockshin RA, Rosett M, Srokose K 1975 Control of ecdysis by heat in *Manduca sexta*. J Insect Physiol 21:1799-1802

Mizoguchi A, Ishizaki H 1982 Prothoracic glands of the saturniid moth *Samia cynthia ricini* possess a circadian clock controlling gut purge timing. Proc Natl Acad Sci USA 79:2726-2730

Pittendrigh CS 1960 Circadian rhythms and the circadian organization of living systems. Cold Spring Harbor Symp Quant Biol 25:159-184

Pittendrigh CS 1981 Circadian organization and the photoperiodic phenomena. In: Follett DE, Follett BK (eds) Biological clocks in seasonal reproductive cycles. Wright, Bristol, p 1-35

Pittendrigh CS, Bruce VG, Kaus P 1958 On the significance of transients in daily rhythms. Proc Natl Acad Sci USA 44:965-973

Pittendrigh CS, Skopik SD 1970 Circadian systems. V: The driving oscillation and the temporal sequence of development. Proc Natl Acad Sci USA 65:500-507

Reynolds SE, Taghert PH, Truman JW 1979 Eclosion hormone and bursicon titres and the onset of hormonal responsiveness during the last day of adult development in *Manduca sexta* (L). J Exp Biol 78:77-86

Reynolds SE, Truman JW 1980 Eclosion hormones. In: Miller TA (ed) Neurohormonal techniques in insects. Springer, New York, p 196-215

Schwartz LM, Truman JW 1983 Hormonal control of the rates of metamorphic development in the tobacco hornworm *Manduca sexta*. Dev Biol 99:103-114

Slama K 1980 Homeostatic function of ecdysteroids in ecdysis and oviposition. Acta Entomol Bohemoslov 77:145-168

Truman JW 1972 Physiology of insect rhythms. II: The silkmoth brain as the location of the biological clock controlling eclosion. J Comp Physiol 81:99-114

Truman JW 1981 Interaction between ecdysteroid, eclosion hormone, and bursicon titers in *Manduca sexta*. Am Zool 21:655-661

Truman JW, Riddiford LM 1970 Neuroendocrine control of ecdysis in silkmoths. Science (Wash DC) 167:1624-1626

Truman JW, Rountree DB, Reiss SE, Schwartz LM 1983 Ecdysteroids regulate the release and action of eclosion hormone in the tobacco hornworm, *Manduca sexta* (L). J Insect Physiol, in press

Truman JW, Taghert PH, Copenhaver PF, Tublitz NJ, Schwartz LM 1981 Eclosion hormone may control all ecdyses in insects. Nature (Lond) 291:70-71

Zimmerman WF, Ives D 1970 Some photophysiological aspects of circadian rhythmicity in *Drosophila*. In: Menaker M (ed) Biochronometry. National Academy of Sciences, Washington DC, p 381-391

DISCUSSION

Gilbert: Are you assuming that the prothoracic glands in the tobacco hornworm, *Manduca sexta*, are secreting at Day 16; and, if they are, what triggers them to stop secreting and then to degenerate?

Truman: There is a complication in that the prothoracic gland undergoes histolysis late in development but no one has pin-pointed the time at which it occurs in *M. sexta*. Larry Schwartz and I have shown that these glands are still secreting ecdysone late in adult development (Schwartz & Truman 1983). When the abdomen of a developing adult *M. sexta* is isolated on Day 15 of development, the remainder of the development of the abdomen is accelerated and compressed into two days rather than three. Injection of ecdysteroids into such abdomens counteracts this effect so that the subsequent development takes the normal three days or even longer. Thus, the rate of development is sensitive to the presence of ecdysteroids. We then implanted a pair of prothoracic glands into the abdomens of another group of animals on Day 2 of development. When they subsequently reached Day 15, we isolated their abdomens, each of which contained a prothoracic gland implant. The remaining development of these fragments was normal. I have concluded from these experiments that the prothoracic glands are secreting ecdysone as late as Day 15. This secretion seems not to be regulated by the nervous system, and may reflect some sort of autonomous control by these glands, perhaps involving feedback effects of the ecdysteroid titre. The prothoracicotropic hormone is definitely not involved in prothoracic gland regulation at this time in development.

Gilbert: Isn't the ecdysteroid titre about the same on the day before the critical day?

Truman: Ecdysteroid levels show about a half-life decrease every day.

Gilbert: Have you looked at the morphology of the prothoracic glands *in situ*?

Truman: No.

Steel: Did you say that your model required that the declining ecdysteroid titre was insensitive to shifts in the light:dark cycle? Do you have evidence for that?

Truman: Yes. In *M. sexta* the ecdysteroid titre appears completely insensitive. The titre was monitored indirectly by using the preparatory behaviour as a marker.

Steel: But could you not measure the titre directly?

Truman: Yes, we could. A direct measurement would be much more laborious but we shall clearly have to do it. By using the behavioural marker we can at least tell when would be the best time or under which conditions we could expect the differences in titre to be greatest. Then we can better select our times for doing the radioimmunoassays.

Steel: In the development of your model I understand that you wanted to find an interpretation for the 'jumping gate' phenomenon. We can induce jumping gates with ecdysteroid injection in *Rhodnius*, but only with extremely high doses (100 ng) that the normal animal never sees just prior to ecdysis (unpublished observations). What haemolymph titres would result from the doses you are using?

Truman: Our doses are in the form of single injections, but in related studies we have done infusions. One can use an infusion as low as less than 30 ng $g^{-1}h^{-1}$ to block ecdysis for as long as a week. The insects then take the next ecdysis gate after the infusion is terminated. These are reasonable physiological doses, but they are only effective by infusion, rather than by single injection. Most of our experiments involve administration by injection because we don't have enough infusion pumps.

Steel: Do you always see this jumping phenomenon, even at the lowest doses?

Truman: Yes, under the environmental conditions that we are using. One would think that the relative importance of the E (ecdysteroid) system to the G (gating input) system would be a function of temperature. This is because we think that temperature not only sets the phase of the decline in the E system but also that it controls the rate at which the ecdysteroids decay.

Pittendrigh: How can an *arrhythmic* decline of ecdysteroids in the E system have a *phase*?

Truman: One can pick a specific concentration of ecdysteroids and ask when that concentration is attained under conditions of a temperature cycle or after release of the insects into constant conditions. We think that when a specific point in the titre is reached this occurs at a fixed phase either of the entraining temperature cycle or relative to the entry into free-running conditions. This conclusion is based primarily on the observation that certain developmental events that are directly triggered by the declining ecdysteroid titre occur at specific times of day, as I elaborated in my paper.

Mordue: In your model (Fig. 3, p 226) is it necessary for the neurons in the E system and in the G system to be different?

Truman: No.

Mordue: It seems to be quite possible that the change in ecdysone levels affects the G system just as well as it affects the E system.

Truman: Yes; the G system could be ecdysone-sensitive. My model shows one possibility that is relatively simple to test—that the neuroendocrine output and the two inputs are in separate sets of cells. Obviously the eclosion hormone cells themselves might be steroid-sensitive and the threshold for their firing might depend on ecdysteroid levels.

Page: It looks as though your model would not be able to handle the asymmetry in transients seen in different phase-shifts. What do you think?

Truman: It can handle them.

Pittendrigh: But you stressed the point that the transients that you were considering were symmetrical.

Truman: In the example that I gave, the transients were symmetrical but this is not an obligatory part of the model. The studies on *Drosophila* eclosion show very nicely that the number of transient cycles is not fixed but is rather a function of ambient temperature (Pittendrigh 1981). This temperature dependence feature is a natural product of the *M. sexta* model. The ease with which the animal can follow a phase-shift in the photoperiod depends on the slope of the E system function. If the slope is steep, then the insect will not be able to follow readily a shift in the G system, and a number of cycles will be required before the shift in the rhythm in complete. If the slope is shallow, then the rhythm is better able to follow the shift in the G system and a new steady state will be established quite rapidly. The data from *M. sexta* suggest that the slope of the E system is a function of the decline in circulating ecdysteroids. Under lower temperatures one would expect the rate of decline in the ecdysteroid titre to be slower and, therefore, the E system slope to be shallower. Consequently, phase-shifts should be accomplished much faster at cooler temperatures than at warmer temperatures. This happens in *Drosophila*, but we have not yet tested it in *M. sexta*.

Reynolds: Is it possible that the gating system is not important at all at the high temperature?

Truman: The importance of the gating system is certainly reduced. In the experiments that I discussed in which a light and a temperature cycle were presented to the insects at various phases relative to one another, the preparatory behaviour followed the temperature cycle very closely. The timing of the eclosion behaviour was also strongly influenced by temperature, but a weak effect of photoperiod was also seen. One would expect that at lower temperatures the E system effect should be weaker, for the reasons outlined above, and photoperiod should play a more dominant role in determining the time of eclosion. We intend to try these experiments.

Ishizaki: You mentioned debrained animals. Could you explain that in more detail?

Truman: The debrained animals were maintained under a light:dark cycle with a superimposed temperature cycle of 2°C. The operation was done two days after pupal ecdysis. We looked at the onset of the behaviour on Day 18 of development, which is the only day that it is shown. The behaviour occurred at its proper time of day even in the animals that had been debrained for almost three weeks. The brain is obviously not needed for the timing of this behaviour. We have not yet determined if brainless animals will show a free-running preparatory behaviour rhythm when placed in constant conditions.

Gilbert: Is there any difference in this between males and females?

Truman: We think there is a slight difference in their ecdysteroid decline but the differences are not statistically significant.

Gilbert: Is your model likely to be a general one for Lepidoptera? In some, ovarian ecdysone secretion starts just before emergence, and one would expect a higher titre in females.

Truman: Ovarian ecdysteroids leading to different ecdysteroid titres in males and females are one possible mechanism to generate sex differences in the time of ecdysis. Is the phase of the driver oscillator in *Drosophila* sex-independent, Professor Pittendrigh?

Pittendrigh: Very nearly, but not entirely, and not enough to explain the differences in the ecdysteroid titre.

Truman: We think a similar system is working in the saturniid moths. These moths differ from *M. sexta* in that they pupate above ground. Their eclosion rhythm is very light-sensitive and does not show the temperature sensitivity seen in the rhythm of *M. sexta*. The effect of temperature, as transmitted through the E system, is much weaker in the saturniids. This would explain why in these moths we can complete phase-shifts in one cycle (J. W. Truman, unpublished) rather than in the six or seven cycles needed by *M. sexta*.

Gilbert: An insect like *Galleria* in a beehive should act like *M. sexta*.

Pittendrigh: I have been trying to relate your model, Professor Truman, to the facts, as I know them, for the *Drosophila* system. There is, of course, no reason why *M. sexta* and *Drosophila* species should be the same in all details, but I suspect that both of us expect (or hope for!) some major similarities. We clearly do agree that several aspects of the gating phenomena, including transients, call for some two-oscillator system. On the other hand, the model you have developed for *M. sexta* is quite unable to accommodate the *Drosophila* behaviour in one major respect: your gating oscillator for *M. sexta* is directly coupled to the light. I assume therefore that it is also the temperature-compensated pacemaker of the system. In *Drosophila* species the light-coupled oscillator (pacemaker) is definitely *not* responsible for gating; it drives a temperature-dependent slave that gives the gating signal. I have provided detailed evidence for this (Pittendrigh 1981). There are other differences— especially in the need to invoke a gate that is several hours wide in each insect.

Truman: I have talked about the gating clock, but what is actually triggering eclosion? In my model we are looking at one final output pathway that has two rhythmic inputs to it: one input is correlated with the steroid decline, and the other is rhythmic, the nature of which is not understood, although we think of it as a positive–negative input. In this model we cannot talk about a driver and a driven component, or a master and a slave: both oscillators are endogenous. But the way they interact could be mimicked by a driver/driven or a master/ slave system.

Pupal diapause in *Manduca sexta*

Bowen: From the viewpoint of classical endocrinology and clock biology, more is known about pupal diapause than any other type of photoperiodically controlled dormancy. I would like to discuss some of my own results on *Manduca sexta*. Much is known about the endocrinology of this species' development and metamorphosis but very little is known about its clock biology, although many of its hormonal responses are under the control of photoperiod. The insect enters a pupal diapause in response to short days experienced by the developing larva. This is a classical pupal diapause in the sense that short-day-reared animals, after undergoing pupal ecdysis, show very low but detectable amounts of ecdysteroids in the haemolymph. The developing long-day animals, in contrast, show a large peak of ecdysteroids (approx. 4 µg/ml haemolymph) that ultimately culminates in adult emergence about three weeks after larval–pupal ecdysis. We measured ecdysteroid titres in the haemolymph during the first few days of pharate adult development in long-day-reared (non-diapausing) animals. We also measured the *in vitro* basal rates of ecdysteroid synthesis by prothoracic glands removed at various times from diapausing and non-diapausing animals. The prothoracic gland activity was determined using the same animals from which haemolymph samples were taken. After dissection, the prothoracic glands were incubated for two hours in Graces' medium. The ecdysteroids present in the incubation medium were then measured by radioimmunoassay.

As development proceeded in the non-diapausing animal, there was a gradual increase in the haemolymph ecdysteroid titre (measured every 3 h) until about the middle of Day 3, when there was a very large increase. We assume that this increase is related to the release of prothoracicotropic hormone (PTTH). The rate of ecdysone synthesis by the prothoracic glands of developing animals preceded the increase in haemolymph titre by about one day. The changing synthetic capacity of the prothoracic glands is more than sufficient to explain the increase in haemolymph titre, and it appears that the prothoracic glands are being turned on in non-diapausing animals. In diapausing animals, on the other hand, basal synthetic activity in the prothoracic glands did not increase at all and actually fell somewhat as diapause proceeded. This suggests that short-day diapause induction somehow prevents the prothoracic glands from being turned on in the pupa. We know that PTTH is present in the diapausing animal in amounts comparable to those in the non-diapausing animal. We believe that the release of PTTH is being inhibited in diapause. However, PTTH is not the only endocrinological component of the pupal diapause response in *M. sexta*. The prothoracic glands of short-day-reared animals seem to be refractory to PTTH stimulation. We incubated prothoracic glands of both non-diapausing and diapausing animals with PTTH, and compared their rates of ecdysteroid synthesis. The synthetic response to PTTH of non-diapausing, Day 0 pupal prothoracic glands is rapid and acute and forms the basis of our *in vitro* bioassay for PTTH. The diapausing Day 0 glands incubated with PTTH, on the other hand, do not respond as well; their maximum synthetic capacity is about one-third that of the non-diapausing glands. As diapause proceeds this difference becomes more apparent until, by Day 23, the diapausing glands are incapable of responding to PTTH at all. Thus, short days experienced by the larva appear to effect two responses which form the basis of diapause in the pupa: (1) PTTH release is inhibited and (2) the prothoracic glands are rendered refractory to PTTH stimulation.

Reynolds: Did your diapause-inducing conditions induce 100% diapause?

Bowen: No; approximately 90%.

Reynolds: So at the early times you could not distinguish diapausing pupae morphologically, whereas later on you could do so?

Bowen: I could not distinguish diapausing from non-diapausing pupae morphologically on Days 0, 1 and 2, but by Day 3 they can be differentiated. Of course one can differentiate long- from short-day-reared animals earlier than Day 3 of pupal life, on the basis of ecdysone synthesis *in vitro*, by the prothoracic glands, and on the basis of ecdysteroid titres in the haemolymph.

Reynolds: Did you look at titres of ecdysteroids before pupation?

Bowen: Yes. We have measured ecdysteroid titres as well as juvenile hormone synthesis *in vitro* by the corpora allata in both short- and long- day-reared fifth (or final) instar larvae. There seem to be hardly any differences in the ecdysteroid titres between the two sets of animals. But there are differences between long- and short-day-reared animals in the ability of the corpora allata to make juvenile hormone III (but not JH I, which we measure concurrently). Photoperiodic or seasonal time-measurement might well involve juvenile hormone. Indeed, this hormone may be connected to the hour-glass component of seasonal time-measurement, which could involve the build up of an allatotropin or allatohibin.

Mordue: Do we have any evidence from other manipulations of the endocrine system that the prothoracic glands can be made refractory in this way? *M.*

sexta is clearly very different from the corn borer, in which the prothoracic glands keep going all the time.

Bowen: I believe that this refractory phenomenon has been observed before (e.g. Agui 1975) but a good interpretation has not come forward.

Denlinger: Are you certain that the prothoracic gland does indeed become activated at the initiation of adult development, or could those ecdysteroids be coming from some non-prothoracic gland cells?

Bowen: I have no data on this. We do know, however, that diapausing prothoracic glands do not degenerate.

Giebultowicz: I have done an experiment that has nothing to do with regulation of diapause, but it involved the isolation of *M. sexta* abdomens at 8 and 24 h after pupation. I found that they were capable of development up to the adult stage, although slowly. For curiosity, I tried the same experiment with short-day animals, and found that they were not really able to develop (although I followed them only for 30 days; perhaps they can develop later on). They certainly could not develop at the rate that long-day animals can. The difference between long- and short-day animals must be not only in the endocrine glands themselves but also in the peripheral tissues. Perhaps only long-day animals have ecdysteroids stored in inactive forms.

Gilbert: I believe that is true. Besides the difference between diapausing and non-diapausing pupae in the ability of the prothoracic glands to respond to PTTH, which Dr Bowen just described, there are obviously other physiological factors. For example, the amount of wax on the cuticle of a diapausing pupa compared to that on a non-diapausing pupa is quite different (Bell et al 1975). Other biochemical parameters also differ, as we have seen by doing synthetic experiments on different proteins, with different degrees of labelling (unpublished information). Dr Giebultowicz's observation is surprising: an isolated abdomen (taken before the critical time for PTTH release and ecdysone synthesis by the prothoracic glands) will develop with no PTTH and little ecdysone from the prothoracic glands. Did males and females behave similarly? The ovary is the only other source I could think of for ecdysteroids.

Giebultowicz: Males and females seem to react similarly; I couldn't detect any differences.

Gilbert: People talk about oenocytes making ecdysone in some insects (e.g. Romer et al 1974), but in *M. sexta* we have never been able to show that they do.

Giebultowicz: The most interesting thing is that the long-day abdomen would develop but the short-day one would not.

Gilbert: In the corn borer system (see Chippendale, this volume) the insect maintains diapause, I believe, by a superabundant synthesis of a particular hormone whereas, in the pupal diapause in *M. sexta*, the shut-off of a particular hormone is involved. Each of these provides an example of the ingenuity of insects.

REFERENCES

Agui N 1975 Activation of prothoracic glands by brains *in vitro*. J Insect Physiol 2:903-913
Bell RA, Nelson DR, Borg TK, Caldwell DL 1975 Wax secretion in non-diapausing and diapausing pupae of the tobacco hornworm, *Manduca sexta*. J Insect Physiol 21:1725-1729
Pittendrigh CS 1981 Circadian organization and the photoperiodic phenomena. In: Follett BK, Follett DE (eds) Biological clocks in seasonal reproductive cycles. Wright, Bristol, p 1-35
Romer F, Emmerich H, Nowock J 1974 Biosynthesis of ecdysones in isolated prothoracic glands and oenocytes of *Tenebrio molitor in vitro*. J Insect Physiol 20:1975-1987
Schwartz LM, Truman JW 1983 Hormonal control of the rates of metamorphic development in the tobacco hornworm *Manduca sexta*. Dev Biol 99:103-114

A hormonal basis for the photoperiodic control of polymorphism in aphids

JIM HARDIE

Agricultural Research Council Insect Physiology Group, Imperial College at Silwood Park, Ascot, Berks SL5 7DE

Abstract. In temperate climates summer generations of aphids are parthenogenetic and viviparous, thus undergoing a type of reproduction that is maintained under long-day conditions. As day-length decreases towards autumn, sexual forms develop and give rise to over-wintering eggs. Several lines of research indicate that juvenile hormone is involved in the induction of the various polymorphic forms associated with this seasonal alternation. This paper centres on the production of the parthenogenetic and sexual females in two aphid species. *Aphis fabae* is a host-alternating species (heteroecious) while *Megoura viciae* can complete its life-cycle on one species of host plant (autoecious). Topical application of natural juvenile hormones and their analogues can mimic the effects of long days under short-day conditions, and recent experiments with precocenes (anti-juvenile hormone compounds) have shown the reverse effect, i.e. mimicking of short days under long-day conditions. Attempts to identify aphid juvenile hormones have revealed only juvenile hormone III and, while long-day-reared *M. viciae* contain higher titres than short-day aphids, the titres are very low. Evidence for neuroendocrine involvement is reviewed, as is evidence for juvenile hormone control of male production in *Myzus persicae*.

1984 Photoperiodic regulation of insect and molluscan hormones. Pitman, London (Ciba Foundation symposium 104), p 240-258

This paper relates mainly to two aphid species: the black bean aphid, *Aphis fabae*, and the bean and vetch aphid, *Megoura viciae*. Both species exhibit a seasonal alternation between parthenogenetic and sexual modes of reproduction but their life-cycles differ in that *A. fabae* migrates between a woody, winter host plant and a herbaceous, summer host (*heteroecy*; Fig. 1a) while *M. viciae* may remain on one plant species throughout the year (*autoecy*; Fig. 1b). The long-day, parthenogenetic forms are viviparous and can be termed *viviparae*; they are also referred to as *virginoparae* as they give birth to progeny that continue to reproduce parthenogenetically. Virginoparae occur both as winged (*alate*) and non-winged (*apterous*) adults, depending on environmental conditions such as temperature, nutrition and degree of

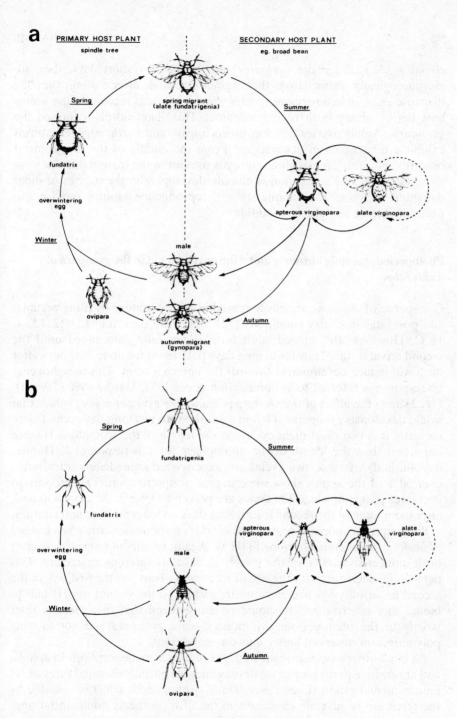

FIG. 1. Life-cycles of (a) *Aphis fabae* and (b) *Megoura viciae*.

crowding. Sexual females (*oviparae*) are induced by short days, they are morphologically distinct from the virginoparae and, after mating, they lay diapause eggs. In heteroecious species winged migrants recolonize the winter host before giving birth to the oviparae. This alate morph is termed the *gynopara*. Aphid ovaries develop precociously, and parthenogenetic forms exhibit a telescoping of generations. From the middle of the fourth instar onwards, not only are daughter embryos present in the maternal ovaries but the grand-daughter generation is already developing in the ovaries of older daughter embryos. This unique style of reproduction ensures rapid multiplication during favourable conditions.

Photoperiod, juvenile hormone and wing development in the gynopara of *Aphis fabae*

Gynoparae of *A. fabae* are easily reared in the laboratory by using prenatal and postnatal short-day conditions (12h light:12h dark; i.e. LD 12:12) at 15 °C. However, the winged adult form is not fully determined until the second larval instar. Transfer to long days (LD 16:8) for up to four days after birth will induce development towards the apterous form. This morphogenetic response is referred to as apterization (Lees 1977, Hardie 1980a, 1981a). Fig. 2 shows the effect of transferring presumptive gynoparae (i.e. aphids that would develop as gynoparae if left in short days) to two long-day cycles (more correctly it is two short-night cycles, as the length of the scotophase is more important than the length of the photophase for this response; J. Hardie, unpublished). If these two cycles are experienced immediately after birth, over 60% of the aphids show some degree of apterization. This proportion decreases progressively as the cycles are perceived later in development and, after the middle of the second instar, long days no longer induce apterization.

Presumptive gynoparae reared in short days respond similarly when treated topically with juvenile hormone I (JH I). Again, treatment immediately after birth induces over 60% of the insects to develop apterous characters. This percentage decreases with the age at treatment. Thus, on the first day of the second instar only 5% become apterized while on the second day JH fails to induce any apterization. It should be emphasized that these results refer strictly to the photoperiodically induced alate gynopara and not to wing polymorphism observed under long-day conditions.

As in all other insects investigated, JH regulates metamorphosis in aphids, and at sensitive periods of larval development artificially elevated titres of JH induce juvenilization (Lees 1980). This morphogenetic effect is revealed by the retention of juvenile characters in the fifth (normally adult) instar and, when maximal, the effect results in the appearance of fifth-instar, super-

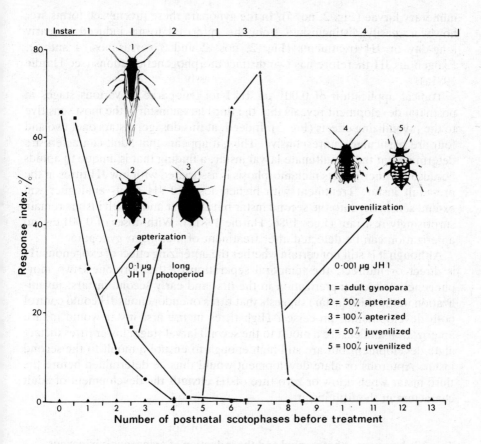

FIG. 2. Morphogenetic effects of long photoperiods and juvenile hormone on the gynoparae of *A. fabae*. Exposure of presumptive gynoparae to two long-day cycles before return to short days induces apterization (solid squares). Topical application of 0.1 μg JH I has a similar effect (solid circles). Apterized individuals may show a variety of forms intermediate between the fully apterous (3) and the alate (1) aphid; one such intermediate is shown (2) which is rated as 50% apterized (Lees 1977, Hardie 1981a). The response index refers to the percentage of insects that showed some degree of apterization. Also shown is the degree of juvenilization induced in gynoparae by a single treatment with 0.001 μg JH I on each day of larval development (solid triangles). The fifth-instar (normally adult) insects were graded into five categories based on the retention of larval characters (Lees 1977, 1980, Hardie 1981a). A normal alate (1) is termed 0% response; a fifth-instar, supernumerary larva (5) is 100% response; an aphid showing 50% response (4) is also depicted. The response index for juvenilization is based on the mean percentage response (see Lees 1977). As presumptive gynoparae are more sensitive to night-length than to day-length (J. Hardie, unpublished), the number of scotophases experienced before treatment is used as a measure of development: it is equal to the day of development minus one.

numerary larvae (Fig. 2, no. 5). In the gynopara these juvenilized forms are, however, easily distinguished from the apterized forms induced by early long-day or JH treatments (Fig. 2, nos. 2 and 3 versus nos. 4 and 5). Exogenous JH therefore has two distinct morphogenetic actions (see Hardie 1981a).

Topical application of 0.001 μg JH I to gynoparae at various stages in postnatal development reveals that the third larval instar is the most sensitive to the juvenilizing effects (Fig. 2). Indeed, at this dosage, instars one, two and four are particularly unresponsive. Thus, it appears that adult characters are determined in the penultimate larval instar, a finding that is unique to aphids because in other insects metamorphosis is associated with low JH titres in the pre-adult instar. Treatment with higher doses of JH or its analogues will extend sensitivity into the second instar but the first and fourth instars remain surprisingly resistant (Lees 1980, Hardie 1981a). With doses of 0.001 μg, no apterization can be detected after treatment of first-instar gynoparae.

Although it is still not certain whether the apterizing effect of exogenous JH is direct or indirect, the temporal separation of the hormone's two morphogenetic effects (apterization in the first and early second instars; juvenilization in the third instar) suggests that titres of endogenous JH could control both developmental processes. High titres in the first instar would induce apterization and ensure a moult to the second larval stage; lower titres dictate alate development but are still high enough to ensure a moult to the second instar. Apterous or alate development would thus be determined before the third instar when a low or zero titre of JH ensures the development of adult characters in the fifth instar.

Juvenile hormone, photoperiod and the induction of oviparous/viviparous intermediates and viviparous morphs

Mittler et al (1976) demonstrated that gynoparae of both *Myzus persicae* and *A. fabae*, when reared from the fourth instar onwards on plants treated with a JH analogue (kinoprene), produced winged progeny with parthenogenetic ovaries. Under normal short days, apterous oviparae with gamic ovaries were expected to develop. These observations were later extended to show that topical application of natural insect JHs had similar effects on *A. fabae* and on *M. viciae* (where an alate gynopara is not obligatory; see Fig. 1b) (Lees 1978, Hardie 1981b). It appears that the treatment with JH or its analogues of fourth-instar larvae or recently adult short-day aphids stimulated the development of wings and other alate structures in the presumptive oviparous embryos; simultaneously, embryonic germaria within these embryos were diverted towards the parthenogenetic rather than the gamic type. A variety of external characters was seen, ranging from fully alate forms (Fig. 3a) to forms that had a sclerotized pterothorax but no wings. Their ovaries could also be intermediate between parthenogenetic and gamic in that some ovarioles contain embryos while others contain haploid, yolky eggs (Fig. 3b). By using timed applications of JH, and observing sequential batches of progeny, it was shown that the embryos most sensitive to this treatment were not the largest ones, just pre-parturition, but those at a slightly earlier stage of development which appeared to be almost fully determined as oviparae or viviparae (Hardie 1981b).

Although the fully alate forms, containing only embryos, were close in appearance to normal alate viviparae (produced by crowding in long-day conditions and by short days in heteroecious aphid species), they were frequently rendered sterile by embryo retention; many also possessed oviparous features. These alates were clearly abnormal in several respects and can be included in the category of JH-induced oviparous/viviparous intermediates together with the forms with more obviously intermediate characters (e.g. ovaries with embryos and haploid eggs; see Hardie 1981b). Similar oviparous/viviparous intermediate forms have been induced under more natural conditions when photoperiod or temperature are close to being critical. They are also seen at switch-over points in the progeny sequence induced by the reversal of the photoperiod from short to long days (or *vice versa*) (see Hardie 1980b, Searle & Mittler 1982). Embryos in the final stages of determination as oviparae or viviparae are probably subjected to unbalanced hormonal conditions in the maternal haemolymph, and this state may be mimicked by JH treatment.

During the study of single, topical treatments with JH of fourth-instar and adult gynoparae of *A. fabae* I noticed that while a batch of oviparous/viviparous intermediates were produced close to the beginning of reproductive life, a small batch of apparently normal viviparae appeared at the end. The position of these aphids in the progeny sequence was correlated with the time of treatment (Hardie 1981b). Thus, JH can induce normal viviparae, in presumptive ovipara-producers, but their position in the progeny sequence suggests that in *A. fabae* their embryonic development is influenced at a much earlier stage than those that develop into oviparous/viviparous intermediates. In order to test this hypothesis, JH was applied daily to gynoparae during the first, second and fourth instars (the third instar was avoided because of its sensitivity to the juvenilizing effect of JH; any insects apterized by early JH treatment were rejected). The resulting adults, although sometimes retaining some larval characters, were capable of parturition, but they produced fewer oviparae and many more viviparae than did fourth-instar or adult gynoparae that received only a single dose. Indeed, in certain treated individuals no oviparae were born, but only a few

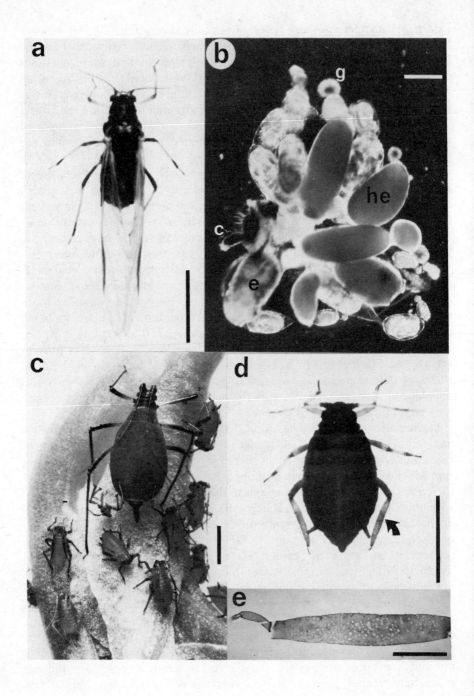

oviparous/viviparous intermediates and a large batch of normal viviparae (J. Hardie & A. D. Lees, unpublished).

Although oviparous/viviparous intermediates could be induced by topical applications of kinoprene or JH I onto fourth-instar or adult *M. viciae* ovipara-producers, no normal viviparae were observed (Lees 1978, J. Hardie & A. D. Lees, unpublished). Daily treatments with JH I, as described above with *A. fabae*, were also unsuccessful in inducing presumptive, oviparous embryos to develop into normal viviparae. However, when short-day aphids were reared on kinoprene-treated beans, during prenatal, first, second and fourth instars and during adult development, 13% (6/46) of the 'ovipara-producers' gave birth to normal apterous viviparae (Fig. 3c). Control aphids produced only oviparae (J. Hardie & A. D. Lees, unpublished).

Thus, by judicious manipulation of the dosage of JH or its analogues it is possible in both *A. fabae* and *M. viciae* to induce embryos within the mother to develop as normal, viable, parthenogenetic morphs under short-day conditions. This is the type of development that normally occurs in long photoperiods.

Photoperiod, precocene and the induction of oviparae

If the effect of exogenous JH is to mimic long-day conditions by acting directly on the embryos, allatectomy should produce short-day effects under long-day conditions. Surgical allatectomy has not proved possible in aphids but recently Hales & Mittler (1981) have shown that precocene III (6-methoxy-7-ethoxy-2,2-dimethylchromene) has an anti-JH effect on *M. persicae* and that it induces precocious adult development. Similar results have been obtained with *A. fabae* and *M. viciae* (J. Hardie, unpublished).

FIG. 3. Effects induced by juvenile hormone, kinoprene and precocene in *A. fabae* and *M. viciae*. (a) A fully alate oviparous/viviparous intermediate with parthenogenetic ovaries (i.e. containing only embryos) induced by topical application of JH I to a fourth-instar, short-day gynopara of *A. fabae*. Control gynoparae produced only apterous oviparae. Scale bar = 1 mm. (b) A 'mixed' ovary of an oviparous/viviparous intermediate containing both embryos and haploid, yolky eggs. This result is induced either by JH I treatment as in (a) or by precocene III treatment of the fourth-instar, long-day alate virginopara, as in (d). Ovaries of oviparae contain only haploid eggs, viviparae only embryos. Scale bar = 20 μm. c, cauda; e, embryo; g, germaria; he, haploid egg. (c) Apterous vivipara of *M. viciae* with progeny. This female was induced by rearing her short-day mother on kinoprene-treated beans; control mothers produced only oviparae. Scale bar = 1 mm. (d) Ovipara-like morph of *A. fabae* induced by precocene III treatment of a fourth-instar, long-day, alate virginopara. Note the swollen metathoracic tibiae (arrow; see e). Control aphids produced only apterous virginoparae. Scale bar = 1 mm. (e) Hind tibia of an ovipara-like aphid induced by precocene III in long days (as in d). Note the presence of scent plaques which release the sex pheromone. Scale bar = 20 μm.

Chemical allatectomy has also been used in an attempt to induce the production of oviparous females in *A. fabae* (J. Hardie, unpublished). Under normal circumstances only winged viviparae give rise to oviparae in this species, an event which is initiated by transferring them from long to short photoperiods (Hardie 1980b). In order to test the effect of allatectomy on polymorphism 1.0 μg of precocene III was applied to early, fourth-instar virginoparae that had been crowded under long-day conditions, to induce wing formation. These aphids moulted through to the winged adult but often produced very few progeny. However, many of these developed into oviparous-like adults with short, swollen, hind tibiae bearing scent plaques (pheromone-release sites specific to oviparae; Fig. 3d and e) and with ovaries containing both embryos and haploid, gamic eggs (Fig. 3b). Control treatments resulted in adults that produced only the expected apterous viviparae with parthenogenetic ovaries. Precocene III was also applied to adult apterous virginoparae of *M. viciae* reared in long days, and apparently normal oviparae were induced, but in only two out of 38 treated mothers. These results demonstrate that the photoperiodic response is reversed by precocene III.

Neurosecretion and the regulation of polymorphism by the corpus allatum in
M. viciae

By applying supplementary illumination over localized areas Lees (1964) was able to show that the photoperiodic receptor of *M. viciae* lay in the brain immediately below the mid-dorsum region of the head capsule. Johnson (1963) had previously reported that, in other aphid species, this part of the brain contained at least two groups of neurosecretory cells (Group I and Group II cells), which appeared to correspond to the median neurosecretory cells described for other insects. Similar cells were found in *M. viciae* (Pagliai & Morselli 1970, Steel 1977) and microcautery techniques revealed that ablation of the Group I cells prevented the production of virginoparae; long-day females with brain lesions switched from the production of virginoparous progeny to oviparae. This result is normally associated with the reversal of the photoperiod from long to short (Steel & Lees 1977). In addition, brain regions lateral to the Group I cells were also necessary for normal photoperiodic function, as damage to these areas simulated the effect of Group I cell ablation even when the Group I cells were histologically normal. It was proposed that these lateral regions contained the photoperiodic receptor and clock which controlled the rate of release of neurosecretory hormone from the Group I cells. This hormone, provisionally termed 'virginoparin' (Steel 1976), was believed to be directly released onto developing embryos and thus to promote their development as virginoparae.

As the effects of topically applied JH and its analogues on short-day ovipara-producers, described above, were so strikingly similar to the proposed action of 'virginoparin', and because the median neurosecretory cells are known to regulate the activity of the corpus allatum in other insects (e.g. McCaffery 1976), it seemed not unreasonable to search for a relationship between the corpus allatum (a single fused body in most aphids), the photoperiodic regime and the Group I cells. Such a relationship was found in *M. viciae* between the corpus allatum volume and the photoperiod in that 20-day-old adult apterae reared in long days (i.e. virginopara-producers) had significantly smaller corpora allata than did short-day aphids (i.e. ovipara-producers; Table 1). Corpora allata of long-day aphids, cauterized in the

TABLE 1 Corpus allatum volumes measured in adult apterae of *M. viciae* 20 days after final ecdysis

Treatment[a]	Corpus allatum volume ± SEM (μm^3)	n
Long-day-reared	18 390 ± 1193	11
Long-day-reared; sham cautery	20 939 ± 1513	14
Long-day-reared; successful cautery	30 495 ± 3031	10
Short-day-reared	32 283 ± 1917	10

[a] Long-day-reared insects were virginopara-producers; short-day-reared were ovipara-producers. Sham-operated controls continued to produce virginoparae, while successful cautery indicates a switch to ovipara production before Day 20.

region of the Group I cells and which had switched from the production of virginoparae to oviparae, were significantly larger than normal or sham-operated long-day aphids. Indeed, the corpora allata of successfully cauterized long-day aphids were similar in size to short-day ovipara-producers. These results suggest that photoperiodic control of the female morph in *M. viciae* has at least three components, the lateral regions possibly containing the photoperiodic receptor and/or clock, the Group I cells and the corpus allatum which may well be the final effector organ. The Group I cells may have an allatotropic function. It is also noteworthy that there appears to be an inverse relationship between corpus allatum volume and activity if, as proposed earlier, long days induce high titres of JH.

Juvenile hormone titres in *M. viciae*

So far the evidence that photoperiod controls the titre of JH derives from the results of topical application of natural JHs and their analogues and from measurement of corpus allatum volume. However precisely the topical application can simulate long-day effects, there is always the possibility that the action is indirectly associated with regulatory effects on the aphid's own endocrine system. More direct evidence for this theory would come from direct measurement of haemolymph titres of JH under controlled photoperiodic conditions. Owing to the small size of the aphids, haemolymph analysis is impracticable but whole-body extraction procedures have been attempted. Bioassays using the *Galleria* wax test and an aphid metamorphic assay based on the work of Lees (1980) have both proved unsuccessful (J. Hardie, unpublished). Chemical measurements of JH titre, in collaboration with investigators at Zoecon Corporation USA, have provided some features of interest (J. Hardie et al unpublished). Thus, JH III was consistently detected (albeit at low levels) in whole-body extracts of *M. viciae*. Levels of JH III were 0.28 ng/g fresh weight or less. A much lower level (close to the limit of detection, 0.01–0.02 ng/g) of material that co-eluted with JH 0, I and II was also detected in one sample. There was a significant difference between the mean titres recorded in long-day-reared and in short-day-reared adult apterous *M. viciae* shortly after ecdysis $(0.15 \pm 0.03[\text{SEM}] \, \text{ng/g}$ and $0.06 \pm 0.01 \, \text{ng/g}$, respectively; $P < 0.05$). Whether this difference is large enough to account for development of embryos as virginoparae under long-day conditions remains unclear. The occurrence and involvement of another, as yet unidentified, juvenile hormone in *Megoura* is not inconceivable. Indeed, the chemistry of JHs in the hemiptera is not yet understood (see Feldlaufer et al 1982).

Juvenile hormone and sex determination in aphids

In many aphid species males, like oviparae, are induced by short days. Sex determination is of the XX:X0 type and thus takes place at the single maturation division of the parthenogenetic egg, just after ovulation. Female embryos are determined as oviparae or virginoparae during later embryonic development.

After rearing *M. persicae* on kinoprene-treated plants under controlled photoperiodic conditions, Mittler et al (1979) showed that male production was either reduced or entirely prevented and that there was a corresponding increase in the numbers of female progeny. More recently, Hales & Mittler (1981) reported the appearance of a few males born to long-day *M. persicae* females treated with precocene III. These two lines of evidence again suggest that JH titres and photoperiod are linked, male determination occurring in short-day, low-JH conditions while long days and high titres of JH promote development of female eggs. This hypothesis and the role of JH in controlling the differentiation of relatively advanced female embryos into oviparae or viviparae are compatible for an individual parthenogenetic egg, as there would be a temporal separation of the two developmental pathways (i.e. during the maturation division JH titres determine the sex of the egg; if the egg develops as a female embryo, then at some later stage JH titres determine her to be an ovipara or a vivipara). However, certain complexities arise because of the telescoping of generations and the variety of life-cycles exhibited by different aphid species. Certainly it seems premature to propose a simplistic hormonal control theory to cover the determination of both sex and female type (i.e. vivipara or ovipara); but target-sensitivity changes and differential responses to changing JH titres may provide explanations for some of these complexities.

Discussion

During the past six or seven years progress has been made in understanding hormonal control of the polymorphism associated with the seasonal alternation of parthenogenetic and sexual modes of reproduction in aphids. This alternation is environmentally dictated, usually by day-length. Various lines of research indicate that in *A. fabae*, *M. viciae* and *M. persicae* (species having heteroecious or autoecious life-cycles) JH is of major importance; but the conclusive evidence is still lacking. High JH titres may be associated with the long-day, parthenogenetic part of the life-cycle, and low JH titres with the short-day, sexual phase. The dual function of JH, in both the metamorphosis and the appearance of adult polymorphic forms, is well known in other insects, such as ants, bees and termites, and the two functions are compatible because of different critical periods of determination for the developmental pathways concerned (see Nijhout & Wheeler 1982). However, this dual control in aphids may have further complexities owing to precocious ovulation and embryonic development during the larval instars of the mother. For example, JH titres must be low or zero during the third-instar larva; otherwise metamorphosis would be affected. But, in long days, ovulation and embryogenesis continue at this time without the subsequent production of males or oviparae. It is interesting that the third instar is shorter than the other three larval instars (in *A. fabae* alate virginoparae, the third instar lasts for 2 days, the first and second for 3 days and the fourth for 5 days at 15 °C). It may also be significant that adult characters are determined in the third, penultimate larval instar, and not in the pre-adult instar as in other insects. In parthenogenetic aphids the grand-daughters begin to develop in the embryos of the fourth-instar (pre-adult) mother.

The photoperiodic regulation of JH titres, which in turn control nonmetamorphic phenomena, is found in other insects. For example, long days are associated with high JH titres and with non-diapause adults in *Leptinotarsa decemlineata* (de Kort et al 1981). In contrast, larval diapause in *Diatraea grandiosella* is induced by long days and high JH titres, which also maintain the diapause state (Chippendale 1982). In *Oncopeltus fasciatus* and *Hippodamia convergens* photoperiod appears to regulate JH titres, which in turn coordinate migration and reproduction (Rankin & Riddiford 1978, Rankin & Rankin 1980).

Acknowledgements

I thank Professor A. D. Lees for invaluable advice, and Jane Price for technical assistance and artwork.

REFERENCES

Chippendale GM 1982 Insect diapause, the seasonal synchronization of life cycles, and management strategies. Entomol Exp Appl 31:24-35

de Kort CAD, Khan MA, Bergot BJ, Schooley DA 1981 The JH titre in the colorado beetle in relation to reproduction and diapause. In: Pratt GE, Brooks GT (eds) Juvenile hormone biochemistry. Elsevier/North-Holland, Amsterdam, p 125-134

Feldlaufer MF, Bowers WS, Soderlund DM, Evans PH 1982 Biosynthesis of the sesquiterpenoid skeleton of juvenile hormone 3 by *Dysdercus fasciatus* corpora allata *in vitro*. J. Exp Biol 223:295-298

Hales DF, Mittler TE 1981 Precocious metamorphosis of the aphid *Myzus persicae* induced by the precocene analogue 6-methoxy-7-ethoxy-2,2-dimethylchromene. J Insect Physiol 27:333-337

Hardie J 1980a Juvenile hormone mimics the photoperiodic apterization of the alate gynopara of aphid, *Aphis fabae*. Nature (Lond) 286:602-604

Hardie J 1980b Reproductive, morphological and behavioural affinities between the alate gynopara and virginopara of the aphid, *Aphix fabae*. Physiol Entomol 5:385-396

Hardie J 1981a Juvenile hormone and photoperiodically controlled polymorphism in *Aphis fabae*: postnatal effects in presumptive gynoparae. J Insect Physiol 27:347-355

Hardie J 1981b Juvenile hormone and photoperiodically controlled polymorphism in *Aphis fabae*: prenatal effects on presumptive oviparae. J Insect Physiol 27:257-265

Johnson B 1963 A histological study of neurosecretion in aphids. J Insect Physiol 9:727-739

Lees AD 1964 The location of the photoperiodic receptors in the aphid *Megoura viciae* Buckton. J Exp Biol 41:119-133

Lees AD 1977 Action of juvenile hormone mimics on the regulation of larval–adult and alary polymorphism in aphids. Nature (Lond) 267:46-48

Lees AD 1978 Endocrine aspects of photoperiodism in aphids. In: Gaillard PJ, Boer HH (eds) Comparative endocrinology. Elsevier/North-Holland, Amsterdam, p 165-168

Lees AD 1980 The development of juvenile hormone sensitivity in alatae of the aphid *Megoura viciae*. J Insect Physiol 26:143-151

McCaffery AR 1976 Effects of electrocoagulation of cerebral neurosecretory cells and implantation of corpora allata on oocyte development in *Locusta migratoria*. J Insect Physiol 22:1081-1092

Mittler TE, Nassar SG, Staal GB 1976 Wing development and parthenogenesis induced in progenies of kinoprene-treated gynoparae of *Aphis fabae* and *Myzus persicae*. J Insect Physiol 22:1717-1725

Mittler TE, Eisenbach J, Searle JB, Matsuka M, Nassar SG 1979 Inhibition by kinoprene of photoperiod-induced male production by apterous and alate viviparae of the aphid *Myzus persicae*. J Insect Physiol 25:219-226

Nijhout HF, Wheeler DE 1982 Juvenile hormone and the physiological basis of insect polymorphisms. Q Rev Biol 57:109-133

Pagliai AMB, Morselli I 1970 Aspects of neurosecretion in parthenogenetic and amphigonic females of *Megoura viciae* Buckt. (Hom Aphid). Boll Zool 37:169-172

Rankin SM, Rankin MA 1980 The hormonal control of migratory flight behaviour in the convergent ladybird beetle, *Hippodamia convergens*. Physiol Entomol 5:175-182

Rankin MA, Riddiford LM 1978 Significance of haemolymph juvenile hormone titer changes in timing of migration and reproduction in adult *Oncopeltus fasciatus*. J Insect Physiol 24:31-38

Searle JB, Mittler TE 1982 Embryogenesis and oogenesis in alate virginoparae, gynoparae, and oviparae of the aphid *Myzus persicae*, in relation to photoperiod. J Insect Physiol 28:213-220

Steel CGH 1976 Neurosecretory control of polymorphism in aphids. In: Luscher M (ed) Phase and caste determination in insects: endocrine aspects. Pergamon Press, Oxford, p 117-130

Steel CGH 1977 The neurosecretory system in the aphid *Megoura viciae* with reference to unusual features associated with long-distance transport of neurosecretion. Gen Comp Endocrinol 31:307-322

Steel CGH, Lees AD 1977 The role of neurosecretion in the photoperiodic control of polymorphism in the aphid *Megoura viciae*. J Exp Biol 67:117-135

DISCUSSION

Denlinger: Is it possible to dissect out the embryos of *Megoura viciae* and apply juvenile hormone (JH) directly? Can you culture them outside the female?

Hardie: I hope to attempt *in vitro* work very shortly. At the moment one cannot say whether the JH has a direct effect or not.

Ferenz: In many insects the corpus allatum volume is not so nicely correlated with any events. It is often a bad measure. Did you try to dissect out the corpora allata and to measure JH biosynthesis *in vitro*?

Hardie: No; it is virtually impossible because the glands are too small.

Chippendale: Can you rule out the possibility that the JH titre was so low because the hormone had degraded between the time you collected the aphids and the time that the chemical assay was done?

Hardie: No, we can't rule that out entirely. We use an internal standard and can measure percentage recovery. But if the hormone was degraded during extraction we would not know to what extent.

Gilbert: How much JH did you have to apply?

Hardie: In the bioassay devised by Tony Lees (1980) 2 ng of juvenile hormone I (JH I) is required for a 50% response; 20 ng of juvenile hormone III (JH III) is required. Thus, to collect enough JH III for a single treatment at this level we would need to extract about 100 g of adult *M. viciae.* To get the effects on photoperiodic polymorphism one needs about 0.1 µg (Hardie 1981a).

Goldsworthy: You seem to have shown that there is some relationship between the neurosecretory cells and the activity of the corpus allatum. It is also possible that your application of these rather large amounts of JH could affect the activity of the neurosecretory cells. Could the relationship work in the opposite direction? In the locust, for example, exogenous JH can cause massive release of neurosecretion (McCaffery 1973). If the same thing was happening in the aphid would it fit in with your interpretation?

Hardie: Because I don't know whether the action of JH is direct or indirect I have tried to approach it from different angles to see whether I could obtain predictable results. So far this has been successful e.g. with precocene treatment. We cannot measure haemolymph hormone titres because of the small size of the insects, so we may be as close as we are going to get. Perhaps if someone identifies the juvenile hormone in *Rhodnius* or another hemipteran then we could try again to see whether this molecule is present in long- and short-day-reared aphids.

Gilbert: I believe that people in Bill Bowers's laboratory have identified the juvenile hormone from the corpora allata in *Dysdercus in vitro* (Feldlaufer et al 1982). The problem, of course, is whether the *in vitro* culture really reflects exactly what happens *in vivo.* Would you be prepared to speculate that the hemipteran juvenile hormone is probably a different molecule from any of the homologues identified in other groups?

Hardie: Yes; I think it must be. We have found JH III but only in very small amounts.

Hodková: Precocene is known also to have an anti-feedant action in some insects. Thus, some effects of precocene may be mediated by suppression of feeding rather than by inhibition of the corpus allatum. Did you observe any anti-feedant effects in aphids?

Hardie: Yes; the aphids tended to wander rather than to settle. But one cannot starve an aphid and produce the sexual female in long days.

Joosse: To me, the fact that the neurohormone is released in the region where the embryos are present suggests that there is a synergistic action of the neurohormone and the juvenile hormone. I agree with Graham Goldsworthy that when you apply only juvenile hormone it may be difficult to interpret because the JH will first have an action on the release of the neurohormone and then it can act on the embryos.

Hardie: Yes; this is possible. I have presented the results obtained, and I cannot rule out an indirect action such as the one you suggest.

Joosse: Can you apply a homogenate of the brain?

Lees: Yes; one could do this, but it has not yet been looked at thoroughly.

Steel: Our observations on neurosecretion in *Megoura* (Steel 1977) indicated that the quantity of stainable neurosecretory material that was stored in the brain was really very small. Consequently, the use of brain homogenates might not be a feasible experimental approach and would be fraught with difficulties.

Joosse: It is very difficult, from staining procedures alone, to suggest how sensitive the organs might be. One is dealing with minute amounts, perhaps, but the selectivity may be enormous.

Steel: I agree. Dr Hardie, when you apply JH topically to the P generation (mother) of aphids, which generation shows the morphological change?

Hardie: It is the next (G1) generation.

Steel: Do you see any effect on the G2 generation?

Hardie: Normally the affected Gl animals, with mixed ovaries, are infertile, so they never produce the next (G2) generation.

Steel: Could precocene be used to produce a chemical allatectomy, and could you remedy the presumed JH deficiency resulting from that by topical application of JH?

Hardie: The problem with that is that very few aphids responded—only 2/38 that I have done so far—so the 'rescue' experiment would be difficult. In an ovulation assay, however, I have managed to use precocene to prevent or to slow down ovulation and embryogenesis and then, by using juvenile hormone, I have been able to 'rescue' that successfully (J. Hardie unpublished). That is a totally different type of assay, but it is the only evidence I have, apart from the precocious adult development, that precocene has an anti-JH effect.

Steel: The JH is being applied to animals that are not endocrinologically incompetent, and which are capable of secreting their own juvenile hormone. This extra load of JH interacts, no doubt, with the animal's own juvenile hormone, amongst other things. It is therefore difficult to ascribe the effects that you see to direct effects of the applied juvenile hormone on the embryos.

Hardie: Yes, but until one can test the tissue of interest *in vitro*, this is all we can do. I do realize the limitations of topical application of JH.

Mordue: The precocenes have, unfortunately, turned out not to be as effective universally as we had been expecting initially. Occasionally, precocene treatment to insects will cause such a large release of JH when the corpus allatum collapses that a juvenilizing effect is observed (Miall & Mordue 1980). The 2/38 animals that responded to precocene in your experiments, Dr Hardie, may not have lacked JH, but may have reacted to a pulse of JH as the glands collapsed.

Hardie: I do have evidence that precocenes I and II (but not III) induce juvenilizing effects in aphids. They don't produce any anti-JH effect that I can find.

Gilbert: In the absence of the identification of the juvenile hormone in these animals, and in the use of a quantity of juvenile hormone deemed 'physiological' in another insect, even the putative *in vitro* studies will, at best, probably give you 'pharmacological' results.

Hardie: Yes; this may prove to be so. Although we have found small amounts of JH III, we do know that JH II, JH I and JH 0 are juvenile hormone analogues as far as the aphid is concerned. Perhaps even JH III is such, as well. Maybe what we are really looking for is an unknown hormone.

Ferenz: In the carabid beetle, *Pterostichus nigrita*, there is a similar story in the neurosecretory cells and the corpus allatum, although it is a little more complicated. The female carabid beetles need both short and long days for them to reach maturity (Ferenz 1977). We found that the corpora allata (after dissection and bioassay) have a low JH biosynthetic activity in short days and, when the beetles are transferred into long days, this activity increases immediately, from 0.8 to $1.8 \mu mol\, JH\, h^{-1}\, pair^{-1}$ (Ferenz 1981). We can replace the complicated procedure of short-day and long-day treatment just by topical application of JH ($5 \times 50 \mu g$ ZR 515 within 20 days). The implantation of active corpora allata is not sufficient to induce egg production; they do not synthesize enough JH. We have also examined the brain, and can make some correlations with corpora allata activity and photoperiod (Hoffmann 1970). Immature animals, kept in long days straight after eclosion, have very small amounts of stainable material in their median neurosecretory cells. There is no transport of neurosecretory material and the corpora allata are completely inactive. In short days, neurosecretory material is synthesized in the brain but there is nearly no transport of this material; as a result, probably, the corpora allata have a low activity. After transfer from short days to long days there is still a strong biosynthesis of neurosecretory material and, in addition, a strong transport along the nervi corporis allati I, resulting in a high activity of the corpora allata. We assume that the median neurosecretory cells make a neurohormone, perhaps an allatotropin, which regulates the corpus allatum activity. The biological clock system that measures day-length probably influences synthesis and release of this allatotropin.

Hardie: This is similar to what I am proposing for the aphids, although I cannot remove the corpora allata, in the way that you do, and assay for activity.

Steel: An obvious problem with the hypothesis that the role of brain neurosecretion is that of an allatotropin is that so far there is no evidence that the neurosecretory cells in *Megoura* go anywhere near the corpora allata.

Hardie: No; this is true.

Gilbert: Where do they go?

Steel: I have followed them down only through the circumoesophageal connectives into the thorax and into the nerve cord. After that they are so fine that one loses track of them. We did some cautery experiments in which I attempted to disrupt the connections between the corpora allata and the brain (Steel & Lees 1977). These did not affect the ability of the animal to respond to changes in day-length.

Hardie: We don't know where the endings of these axons are in *M. viciae*. I have used the electron microscope to try to trace them through the ventral nerve cord but I could find hardly any evidence of neurosecretory axons there, even when I used serial, thick, longitudinal sections through the nerve cord. Bruce Johnson, who did a lot of early work on aphid neurosecretion (Johnson 1963), was surprised at this but he had always simply assumed that the various neurosecretory nerves had come from the nerve cord. Certain neurosecretory nerves can be detected clearly, elsewhere, with the electron microscope.

Mordue: I understood that the cautery which finally produced a response was acting through the corpora allata. Did you ablate the lateral part of the brain?

Hardie: I have not followed up cautery with the type of autopsy that Dr Steel has used to find out exactly where the damage had occurred. I used the physiological effect, i.e. a switch in the morph of the progeny, to prove an effective cautery.

Goldsworthy: I would be careful about assuming, just because one can trace axons down a long way, that there are not release sites *en passant*.

Hardie: Yes; if the hormone were released into the haemolymph, it could indeed have an effect on the corpus allatum. Although it would seem strange, teleologically, for the axons to extend down to the posterior end of the aphid to release a factor that is affecting the corpus allatum at the anterior end.

Ferenz: If it is true that the neurosecretory cells produce an allatotropic factor that activates the corpora allata, there might be no ultimate need for the nerve tracts to enter the corpora allata. In locusts we have just found an allatotropic factor that is apparently released into the blood from the brain via the corpora cardiaca. We can extract this factor from the brain and from the corpora cardiaca and incubate it together with the corpora allata, and we see a stimulation of 15–20 fold in the activity of the corpora allata (Ferenz & Diehl 1983). This material thus need not go along the nerve tracts into the corpora allata to be effective.

Joosse: Neurohaemal areas regenerate very well, so sectioning of the nerves is not a helpful technique for studying neuroendocrine functions. When you treat the long-day animals with precocene, to remove the corpora allata, and then expose them to long days, you could perhaps easily study the effect of the neurohormone alone.

Hardie: Yes; this could be done as long as I could get a more predictable response to the precocenes.

Joosse: That would not be necessary; you could check that later on.

Brady: Have you or Professor Lees tried to do parabiosis experiments on aphids to test for these blood-borne hormonal effects?

Lees: I could not do parabiosis experiments with long- and short-day insects, as the response cannot be seen for 12 or so days—that is, after the progeny have been born. This is too long a period to keep a parabiotic pair alive. After about five days, embryo productivity usually declines drastically.

REFERENCES

Feldlaufer MF, Bowers WS, Soderlund DM, Evans PH 1982 Biosynthesis of the sesquiterpenoid skeleton of juvenile hormone III by *Dysdercus fasciatus* corpora allata *in vitro*. J Exp Zool 223:295-298

Ferenz HJ 1977 Two-step photoperiodic and hormonal control of reproduction in the female beetle, *Pterostichus nigrita*. J Insect Physiol 23:671-676

Ferenz HJ 1981 Effect of the photoperiod on corpus allatum activity in vitro in the beetle *Pterostichus nigrita* F. Experientia (Basel) 37:1211-1212

Ferenz HJ, Diehl I 1983 Stimulation of juvenile hormone biosynthesis in vitro by locust allatotropin. Z Naturforsch C Biosci 38:856-858

Hardie J 1981 Juvenile hormone and photoperiodically controlled polymorphism in *Aphis fabae*: postnatal effects in presumptive gynoparae. J Insect Physiol 27:347-355

Hoffmann HJ 1970 Neuro-endocrine control of diapause and oocyte maturation in the beetle, *Pterostichus nigrita*. J Insect Physiol 16:629-642

Johnson B 1963 A histological study of neurosecretion in aphids. J Insect Physiol 9:727-739

Lees AD 1980 The development of juvenile hormone sensitivity in alatae of the aphid *Megoura viciae*. J Insect Physiol 26:143-151

McCaffery AR 1973 Relationship of the corpus allatum to the neurosecretory system in locusts. J Endocrinol 57:li-lii (abstr)

Miall RC, Mordue W 1980 Precocene II has juvenile-hormone effects in 5th instar *Locusta migratoria*. J Insect Physiol 26:361-364

Steel CGH 1977 The neurosecretory system in the aphid *Megoura viciae*, with reference to unusual features associated with long-distance transport of neurosecretion. Gen Comp Endocrinol 31:307-322

Steel CGH, Lees AD 1977 The role of neurosecretion in the photoperiodic control of polymorphism in the aphid *Megoura viciae*. J Exp Biol 67:117-135

Environmental signals, the neuroendocrine system, and the regulation of larval diapause in the southwestern corn borer, *Diatraea grandiosella*

G. MICHAEL CHIPPENDALE

Department of Entomology, 1-87 Agriculture Building, University of Missouri, Columbia, Missouri 65211, USA

Abstract. Some of the timed physiological processes and behavioural events on which the southwestern corn borer, *Diatraea grandiosella*, depends for its year-by-year survival are described. This insect enters a facultative diapause as a fully grown larva. Diapausing larvae are characterized by the retention of a moderate titre of juvenile hormone in their haemolymph. Topics considered include the role of day-length and temperature in the induction, maintenance and termination of diapause, and the relationship between the intensity of diapause and the titre of juvenile hormone in the haemolymph. Possible roles for juvenile hormone in regulating the availability of prothoracicotropic hormone and in stimulating the synthesis of selected proteins in the fat body of pre-diapausing larvae are also considered. The accumulation of nutrient reserves, including proteins, in advance of diapause confers adaptive advantage, but has received little study. Some evidence implicating juvenile hormone in the control of the distinctive behaviour displayed by last-instar, pre-diapausing larvae on their host plants is also presented. Insect diapause is a complex changing state which can occur in the egg, larval, pupal or adult stage. While considerable advances have been made in our understanding of insect diapause in recent years, much additional research is needed to determine fully the respective functions of the receptors, the clock system and the effectors in the control of diapause.

1984 Photoperiodic regulation of insect and molluscan hormones. Pitman, London (Ciba Foundation symposium 104), p 259-276

Our understanding of the regulation of insect diapause is restricted because of the limited information available about the characteristics of systems that measure seasonal time in insects. The presence of receptors to discriminate changing environmental signals, a clock system, and effectors to control the developmental response are the minimum requirements for an insect to measure seasonal time (Beck 1980, Saunders 1982, Page 1982). The clock appears to be centred in the brain, and neurosecretion seems to be the first-order effector, but the organization and operation of the time-measuring system remain to be determined (Saunders 1981).

Diapause is a genetically controlled state of developmental arrest that enables insects to survive during seasons that are unsuitable for their growth and development, and to synchronize their populations with the available food (Danilevskii 1965, Beck 1980). Using day-length and temperature as primary cues, insects accurately time the onset and termination of their diapause. A facultative diapause begins after sensitive pre-diapausing stages have been exposed to inductive conditions. This time-lag between the determination and the onset of diapause indicates that insects store environmental information (Goryshin & Tyshchenko 1973).

Since numerous requirements that follow a chronological sequence are necessary for insects to complete their diapause, the state of diapause may be classed as a syndrome (de Wilde 1970). Specific requirements differ between species, between different geographical populations of the same species, and between embryonic, larval, pupal and adult diapause. For example, information available about the over-wintering requirements of a Missouri population of the southwestern corn borer, *Diatraea grandiosella* Dyar, reveals the complex ecological, behavioural and physiological adaptations that contribute to diapause. The year-by-year survival of this insect depends on its ability to: time the onset of its larval diapause; accumulate reserve nutrients; suppress gametogenesis; cease feeding; complete pre-diapause behavioural patterns; decrease its water content; reduce its oxygen consumption; maintain a low metabolic rate; develop some cold hardiness; complete diapause development; and time the termination of its diapause and the resumption of its morphogenesis (Chippendale & Reddy 1973, Takeda & Chippendale 1982). Here, I shall review some recent findings about the regulation of the diapause of this pyralid moth.

Effect of day-length and temperature on the southwestern corn borer's diapause

The southwestern corn borer uses day-length and temperature to programme the induction and termination of its diapause. A photothermogram has established the relationship between day-length, including civil twilight, temperature accumulation above a developmental temperature zero of 17 °C, and the seasonal programming of generations of a southern Missouri population of the southwestern corn borer (Takeda & Chippendale 1982). The insect completes two generations and a partial third generation each year and survives in diapause from September to May.

Southwestern corn borers were obtained from southern Missouri in 1980 and reared on an artificial medium under constant temperatures and day-lengths. They showed a stable critical photoperiod in the ecological range of about 15 h light per day at 23, 25 and 30 °C. An intermediate percentage of diapause was found at 20 °C in larvae exposed to day-lengths of 16 h or longer (Kikukawa & Chippendale 1983) (Fig. 1A). The critical photoperiod in the

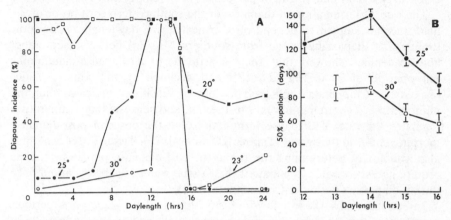

FIG. 1. Photoperiod response curves of a laboratory colony of the southwestern corn borer originally collected from southern Missouri in 1980 (36 °N latitude). (A) Diapause induction. (B) Diapause development. Each point represents data from about 50 larvae. Vertical bars show days to 30% and 70% pupation (from Kikukawa & Chippendale 1983, reproduced with permission).

physiological range was about 9 h light per day at 25 °C and about 13 h light per day at 30 °C. The insect, therefore, displays a short day–long day, or type III response curve, at 25 °C and 30 °C, and a long day, or type I response curve, at 20 °C and 23 °C, with the exception that long days induce some diapause at 20 °C (Beck 1980).

When the southwestern corn borer was reared under a temperature cycle, the incidence of diapause showed a positive correlation with the duration of the low-temperature phase and its coincidence with the scotophase. A thermoperiod of 18 °C (12 h) : 36 °C (12 h) under constant darkness also induced a high incidence of diapause (Chippendale et al 1976). Recent findings have shown a 100% incidence of diapause when larvae were reared under a 20 °C (12 h) : 30 °C (12 h) thermoperiod in constant darkness, even though the mean temperature (25 °C) induced less than 10% diapause (Kikukawa 1983).

The rate of diapause development of the southwestern corn borer is more temperature-dependent than is diapause induction, yet both processes are under photoperiodic control and appear to use a similar time-measuring system (Takeda & Chippendale 1982). Fig. 1B shows the rate of diapause development, expressed as days to 50% pupation, under different photoperiods at 25 °C and 30 °C. Diapause development occurred faster at 30 °C than at 25 °C (Kikukawa & Chippendale 1983). The critical photoperiod was not sharply defined, but was in the same range as that for diapause induction. It fell between 14 and 16 h light per day at both temperatures.

The rate of termination of diapause of the southwestern corn borer in the field does not appear to depend on a critical spring day-length. A periodic sampling of diapausing larvae from southern Missouri between September and December showed that their sensitivity to a diapause-maintaining photoperiod of 30 °C LD 12 h:12 h had declined by the winter solstice (Takeda & Chippendale 1982). This loss of sensitivity indicates that the photoperiodic requirement is met in the fall, and suggests that temperature regulates the rate of diapause termination and the onset of post-diapause morphogenesis in the spring (Tauber & Tauber 1976). Tissue water content is also a factor in determining the timing of post-diapause pupation. Larvae require access to water to pupate if their tissue water falls below about 55% during diapause (Reddy & Chippendale 1973).

Insects generally show a low-intensity threshold for their photoperiodic responses which, therefore, include some twilight and are not influenced by changing levels of solar illumination (Withrow 1959, Saunders 1982). When the southwestern corn borer was exposed to an inductive photoperiod of 30 °C LD 14 h:10 h in which different light intensities were used in the photophase, a threshold intensity of $0.15\,\mu\mathrm{W\,cm}^{-2}$ white-light energy was obtained for diapause induction (Kikukawa 1983). This low threshold of sensitivity correlates with the larvae spending their late instars within the stalks of their host plants, and having their sensitivity for diapause determination extend throughout the larval period (Chippendale & Reddy 1973). The spectral sensitivity of the photoperiodic response has not been determined.

Juvenile hormone and the southwestern corn borer's diapause

Juvenile hormone (JH) has been implicated in the control of the larval diapause of a few lepidopterous insects (see review by Chippendale 1983). For example, diapausing southwestern corn borers retain some activity within their neuroendocrine system and a moderate titre of JH in their haemolymph. The first clue about the presence of elevated titres of JH in diapausing larvae came from the observation that spotted larvae moult into pigment-free or immaculate larvae at the onset of diapause, and that pigment-free larvae may undergo further stationary moults during diapause. Subsequently, several lines of evidence indicated a role for JH in the southwestern corn borer's diapause, but specific diapause-associated functions remain to be determined (Chippendale 1983).

The titre of JH in the haemolymph of southwestern corn borers that were programmed for non-diapause and for diapause has been compared by using the *Galleria* wax test (Yin & Chippendale 1979a). To conduct this bioassay, we took pooled samples of 0.25 to 1.5 ml haemolymph from 3 to 60 larvae between 19 and 190 days of age (Fig. 2A). The results showed that last-instar,

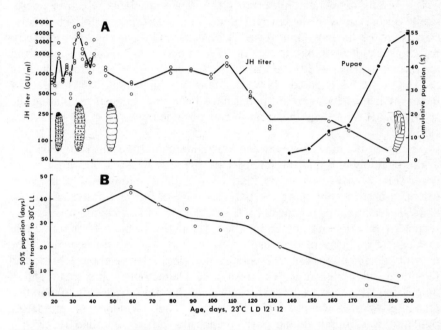

FIG. 2. Juvenile hormone (JH) titre in the haemolymph of the southwestern corn borer related to the onset and intensity of diapause, and the rate of post-diapause pupation. (A) JH titre estimated by the *Galleria* wax test (1 *Galleria* unit ~ 2.6 pg JH equivalents). Each point represents a separate assay. An ecdysis from a spotted to a pigment-free morph shows that diapause has begun. The pupation rate is also shown (from Yin & Chippendale 1979a, reproduced with permission). (B) Change in diapause intensity expressed as days to 50% pupation after larvae had been transferred from 23 °C LD 12 h:12 h to 30 °C in constant illumination (from Takeda & Chippendale 1982, reproduced with permission).

pre-diapausing larvae, in contrast to last-instar, non-diapausing larvae, retained a high JH titre which reached a maximum of about 4300 *Galleria* Units (GU) per ml near the end of their feeding period. After larvae had entered diapause and ecdysed into the pigment-free morph their JH titre remained between 700 and 1500 GU/ml during early and mid-diapause. Their

JH titre then declined and reached a mean titre of 70 GU/ml at 190 days of age, which is the threshold titre for pupal apolysis.

A chemical assay was conducted to examine the number and ratio of JH homologues present in the haemolymph of diapausing southwestern corn borers (Bergot et al 1976). Relatively large, pooled samples of haemolymph were used. The results showed that early diapausing larvae contained mean titres of 0.83 ng/ml JH I, 2.55 ng/ml JH II and 1.03 ng/ml JH III. JH II is, therefore, the main homologue present.

The results of allatectomies, corpora allata transplants, electron microscopic observations of the corpora allata, and measurements of JH esterase activity in the haemolymph of pre-diapausing and diapausing southwestern corn borers indicated that the rate of JH secretion from the corpora allata and the rate of hydrolysis of JH contribute to the regulation of the circulating titre of JH (Yin & Chippendale 1979a,b, Mane & Chippendale 1981). Cerebral factors that may be neurohormonal have been implicated in regulating the activity of JH esterase in the haemolymph of some insects (e.g. see Jones et al 1981).

A relationship may exist between the maintenance of a substantial JH titre in the haemolymph and the intensity of diapause in the southwestern corn borer (Fig. 2A,B) (Takeda & Chippendale 1982). The intensity of diapause was measured by obtaining the pupation rate of larvae transferred from a diapause-maintaining regime of 23 °C LD 12 h : 12 h to a diapause-accelerating regime of 30 °C in constant illumination. Using this technique, we found that the highest intensity of diapause was at 60 days of age. Subsequently, the intensity declined gradually, revealing a correlation between the JH titre and the intensity of diapause. The results of allatectomies and treatment of diapausing larvae with a JH mimic indicated that JH is necessary to maintain diapause (Yin & Chippendale 1979a). A high incidence of premature pupation was found among early diapausing larvae that had received a bilateral allatectomy. By contrast, diapause was prolonged in larvae that received a single application of the JH mimic ZR-1662 (ethyl-10-methoxy-3,7,11-trimethyl-2,4-dodecadienoate, 0.03 μg/larva).

Role of interactions within the neuroendocrine system on the southwestern corn borer's diapause

Interactions within the cerebral neuroendocrine system may regulate the southwestern corn borer's diapause and development. Since intact nervi corporis allati are required for the corpora allata of diapausing larvae to retain their capacity to secrete JH, the glands are under cerebral control (Yin & Chippendale 1979a). In turn, JH may 'feed back' on to the cerebral neurosecretory system to regulate the production, the release, or both, of prothoracicotropic hormone (PTTH) (Chippendale & Yin 1976).

Repeated topical applications of a JH mimic caused diapausing southwestern corn borers to undergo stationary ecdyses and to revert to the spotted morph, but a head ligature prevented this response (Yin & Chippendale 1979a). If JH activates the prothoracic glands directly, head-ligatured larvae should have undergone stationary ecdyses. The result therefore suggests that tissues in the head, or tissues in the thoraco-abdomen which interact with those in the head, serve as a target for JH. Larvae that had been given a head ligature may not have responded to the JH mimic because their PTTH-producing system was not activated. The moderate titre of JH present in the haemolymph of diapausing larvae may, then, inhibit the synthesis or transport of PTTH, or its release into the haemolymph. Such a role for JH was demonstrated in last-instar larvae of the tobacco hornworm, *Manduca sexta*, where the presence of JH in the haemolymph prevents the secretion of PTTH and the onset of the pupal moulting cycle (Nijhout 1981).

Since PTTH controls the secretion of ecdysone, additional information about the origin, nature and function of this neurohormone is required to increase our understanding of the regulation of larval and pupal diapause. Recently, some progress has been made in determining the characteristics and site of release of PTTH. A polypeptidic PTTH has been partially purified from the brain of the silkworm, *Bombyx mori* (Nagasawa et al 1979, Kingan 1981), and a specific neurosecretory cell in each half of the brain of *M. sexta* has been identified as the site of synthesis of PTTH. In addition, the corpora allata, rather than the corpora cardiaca of *M. sexta*, are thought to be the primary release sites for PTTH (Agui et al 1979, Carrow et al 1981). These workers have also developed new *in vitro* assays for PTTH which should be useful for further investigations into the diapause-related functions of this neurohormone.

Effect of juvenile hormone on the southwestern corn borer's fat body

Since biosynthesis is suppressed in diapausing insects, the accumulation of nutrient reserves in advance of diapause confers on the insect an adaptive advantage and, therefore, warrants further study. Research on storage and lipid-carrying proteins has been largely restricted to non-diapausing insects, where the emphasis has been placed on proteins that accumulate in advance of metamorphosis (Wyatt & Pan 1978, Roberts & Brock 1981). Although an increase in soluble proteins occurs in the fat body of last-instar, non-diapausing southwestern corn borers, pre-diapausing larvae accumulate larger amounts of protein. The maximum mean titre of soluble proteins was

2.2 mg/fat body in pre-diapausing larvae, compared with 1.6 mg/fat body in non-diapausing larvae. Since the increase in weight of the fat body during the last instar results primarily from storage of lipid, proteins showed an apparent decrease when measured as μg/mg fat body (Turunen & Chippendale 1980).

Juvenile hormone may stimulate the synthesis of selected proteins in the fat body of last-instar, pre-diapausing southwestern corn borers. Topical applications of JH II or a JH mimic (ZR-1662) had most obvious effects on the sequestration of a low relative molecular mass (low M_r) protein, which has been named the diapause-associated protein (Brown & Chippendale 1978), and a high M_r protein fraction (lipoprotein 8-9; see Fig. 3 and Turunen & Chippendale 1980). Larvae treated with JH II appeared to accumulate relatively more diapause-associated protein than lipoprotein 8-9, whereas the reverse appeared to happen for larvae treated with ZR-1662.

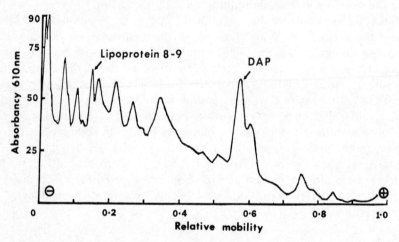

FIG. 3. Proteins of the perivisceral fat body of newly diapaused larvae of the southwestern corn borer separated by disc electrophoresis in 7% acrylamide, and stained with Coomassie blue. DAP, diapause-associated protein (from Turunen & Chippendale 1980, reproduced with permission).

The diapause-associated protein has been purified from the fat body of diapausing southwestern corn borers by gel filtration and chromatofocusing (J. W. Dillwith & G. M. Chippendale, unpublished results). Automated cation-exchange chromatography showed that the protein contains the residues of 17 amino acids, and calibrated gel filtration and dissociating electrophoresis showed that the protein has an M_r of about 35 000. The protein is unusual in containing relatively large amounts of the aromatic acids tyrosine (24 residues/molecule) and phenylalanine (12 residues/molecule). An antibody to the purified protein was raised in rabbits, and its specificity for the protein has been determined (J. W. Dillwith & G. M. Chippendale, unpublished results). The availability of the purified protein and its antibody opens the door to additional investigations into the role of the protein. The pattern of synthesis and use of the protein suggest that it serves as a storage protein during diapause when the rate of protein synthesis is low. The specific function of the protein, however, remains to be determined (Turunen & Chippendale 1979).

A complex pattern of lipoproteins is present in the fat body and haemolymph of the southwestern corn borer (Turunen & Chippendale 1981). One of these, lipoprotein 8-9, is found in larvae, pupae, and adults, and is released *in vitro* from the fat body of diapausing larvae. The released fraction is made up of at least two proteins of similar electrophoretic mobility and M_r, and it corresponds to the major lipoprotein fraction in the haemolymph. Lipoprotein 8-9 is the major protein fraction in the haemolymph of diapausing larvae, and may be a significant carrier of neutral and polar lipids, even though it contains only 3–5% lipid. The protein components of lipoprotein 8-9 have apparent M_r values of about 5.2×10^5 and isoelectric points of 5.5 and 5.65, and they have aspartate, glutamate, tyrosine and phenylalanine as their principal amino acids (Turunen & Chippendale 1981). The lipoprotein has characteristics in common with very high density lipoproteins isolated from Lepidoptera, and with storage proteins isolated from Lepidoptera and Diptera (Gilbert & Chino 1974, Munn et al 1971, Kramer et al 1980). Its origin, nature and fate require further study.

Diapause-associated behaviour of the southwestern corn borer

Insects frequently show distinctive behaviour as they prepare for diapause. This behaviour appears to be regulated by environmental signals that are linked to diapause determination and that operate through the insect's neuroendocrine system. For example, pre-diapausing southwestern corn borers show a behavioural pattern that is strictly associated with the onset of diapause, and that confers adaptive advantages (Chippendale 1978). Each fully grown larva descends to the root zone of its host plant, excavates a cell in the base of the stalk, prepares an exit hole for the adult, and may girdle the stalk. Larvae cannibalize each other while making these preparations. Typically, a single larva survives to occupy the over-wintering niche, even though each host plant can support the growth of several larvae. Short days, low temperatures, and host-plant senescence appear to be the primary signals controlling this behaviour.

Some evidence has been obtained to implicate JH in the regulation of this pre-diapause behaviour of the southwestern corn borer (Chippendale 1978). Since last-instar larvae retain a high JH titre throughout the entire pre-diapause period (Fig. 2A), JH may potentiate rather than release this behaviour. Further study is needed to determine whether a specific JH titre correlates with the onset of pre-diapause behaviour, and whether the removal of corpora allata and the application of JH to allatectomized larvae prevents and restores the behaviour, respectively (Truman & Riddiford 1977).

Conclusion

This paper has reviewed some recent studies about the regulation of the larval diapause of the southwestern corn borer. Since diapause is a complex changing state, it needs to be studied at several levels to be fully understood. A thorough study of an insect's diapause therefore requires that research should include the ecology, behaviour, physiology and biochemistry of pre-diapausing, diapausing and post-diapausing individuals. The genetics of diapause also requires much additional study. In addition, the responses of insects to experimental photoperiodic and temperature regimes should be compared with actual occurrences in the field.

To date, there are insufficient data available to integrate the respective functions of the exteroreceptors and proprioreceptors, the clock system and the effectors into a unified theory about the regulation of insect diapause and seasonal time-measurement. For example, additional research is needed into the transduction of environmental signals, the role of proprioception in the regulation of diapause and the organization and operation of the clock that measures seasonal time. Further research is also needed into the diapause-related functions of neurohormones, juvenile hormone and ecdysteroids. Additional comparative studies examining the regulation of egg, larval, pupal and adult diapause should also be undertaken.

Acknowledgements

This paper is a contribution from the Missouri Agricultural Experiment Station, paper no. 9353. Research summarized from my laboratory was supported in part by grants from the US National Science Foundation, currently PCM78-22488 A01. I gratefully acknowledge the contributions of my present associates, J. W. Dillwith, S. Kikukawa and K. Cassatt, and my former associates to the studies described here.

REFERENCES

Agui N, Granger NA, Gilbert LI, Bollenbacher WE 1979 Cellular localization of the insect prothoracicotropic hormone: *in vitro* assay of a single neurosecretory cell. Proc Natl Acad Sci USA 76:5694-5698

Beck SD 1980 Insect photoperiodism. Academic Press, New York

Bergot BJ, Schooley DA, Chippendale GM, Yin C-M 1976 Juvenile hormone titer determinations in the southwestern corn borer, *Diatraea grandiosella*, by electron capture-gas chromatography. Life Sci 18:811-820

Brown JJ, Chippendale GM 1978 Juvenile hormone and a protein associated with the larval diapause of the southwestern corn borer, *Diatraea grandiosella*. Insect Biochem 8:359-367

Carrow GM, Calabrese RL, Williams CM 1981 Spontaneous and evoked release of prothoracicotropin from multiple neurohemal organs of the tobacco hornworm. Proc Natl Acad Sci USA 78:5866-5870

Chippendale GM 1978 Behavior associated with the larval diapause of the southwestern corn borer, *Diatraea grandiosella*: probable involvement of juvenile hormone. Ann Entomol Soc Am 71:901-905

Chippendale GM 1983 Regulation of growth and development–larval and pupal diapause. In: Downer RGH, Laufer H (eds) Endocrinology of insects. AR Liss, New York, p 343–356

Chippendale GM, Reddy AS 1973 Temperature and photoperiodic regulation of diapause of the southwestern corn borer, *Diatraea grandiosella*. J Insect Physiol 19:1397-1408

Chippendale GM, Yin C-M 1976 Endocrine interactions controlling the larval diapause of the southwestern corn borer, *Diatraea grandiosella*. J Insect Physiol 22:989-995

Chippendale GM, Reddy AS, Catt CL 1976 Photoperiodic and thermoperiodic interactions in the regulation of the larval diapause of *Diatraea grandiosella*. J Insect Physiol 22:823-828

Danilevskii AS 1965 Photoperiodism and seasonal development of insects. Oliver and Boyd, Edinburgh

de Wilde J 1970 Hormones and the environment. Mem Soc Endocrinol 18:487-513

Gilbert LI, Chino H 1974 Transport of lipids in insects. J Lipid Res 15:439-456

Goryshin NI, Tyshchenko GF 1973 Accumulation of photoperiodic information during diapause induction in the cabbage moth, *Barathra brassicae* L. Entomol Rev (Engl Trans Entomol Obozr) 52:173-176

Jones G, Wing KD, Jones D, Hammock BD 1981 The source and action of head factors regulating juvenile hormone esterase in larvae of the cabbage looper, *Trichoplusia ni*. J Insect Physiol 27:85-91

Kikukawa S 1983 Geographical adaptations and seasonal time measurement of the southwestern corn borer, *Diatraea grandiosella*. PhD thesis, University of Missouri

Kikukawa S, Chippendale GM 1983 Seasonal adaptations of populations of the southwestern corn borer, *Diatraea grandiosella*, from tropical and temperate regions. J Insect Physiol 29:561-567

Kingan TG 1981 Purification of the prothoracicotropic hormone from the tobacco hornworm, *Manduca sexta*. Life Sci 28:2585-2594

Kramer SJ, Mundall EC, Law JH 1980 Purification and properties of manducin, an amino acid storage protein of the haemolymph of larval and pupal *Manduca sexta*. Insect Biochem 10:279-288

Mane SD, Chippendale GM 1981 Hydrolysis of juvenile hormone in diapausing and non-diapausing larvae of the southwestern corn borer, *Diatraea grandiosella*. J Comp Physiol 144:205-214

Munn EA, Feinstein A, Greville GD 1971 The isolation and properties of the protein calliphorin. Biochem J 124:367-374

Nagasawa H, Isogai A, Suzuki A, Tamura S, Ishizaki H 1979 Purification and properties of the prothoracicotropic hormone of the silkworm, *Bombyx mori*. Dev Growth & Differ 21:29-38

Nijhout HF 1981 Physiological control of molting in insects. Am Zool 21:631-640

Page TL 1982 Extraretinal photoreception in entrainment and photoperiodism in invertebrates. Experientia (Basel) 38:1007-1013

Reddy AS, Chippendale GM 1973 Water involvement in diapause and the resumption of morphogenesis of the southwestern corn borer, *Diatraea grandiosella*. Entomol Exp Appl 16:445-454

Roberts DB, Brock HW 1981 The major serum proteins of dipteran larvae. Experientia (Basel) 37:103-110

Saunders DS 1981 Insect photoperiodism—the clock and the counter—a review. Physiol Entomol 6:99-116

Saunders DS 1982 Insect clocks. 2nd edn. Pergamon Press, Oxford

Takeda M, Chippendale GM 1982 Environmental and genetic control of the larval diapause of the southwestern corn borer, *Diatraea grandiosella*. Physiol Entomol 7:99-110

Tauber MJ, Tauber CA 1976 Insect seasonality: diapause maintenance, termination, and postdiapause development. Annu Rev Entomol 21:81-107

Turunen S, Chippendale GM 1979 Possible function of juvenile hormone-dependent protein in larval insect diapause. Nature (Lond) 280:836-838

Turunen S, Chippendale GM 1980 Proteins of the fat body of non-diapausing and diapausing larvae of the southwestern corn borer, *Diatraea grandiosella*: effect of juvenile hormone. J Insect Physiol 26:163-169

Turunen S, Chippendale GM 1981 Relationship of lipoproteins present in the larval haemolymph of the southwestern corn borer, *Diatraea grandiosella*, to feeding and diapause. Comp Biochem Physiol B Comp Biochem 70:759-765

Truman JW, Riddiford LM 1977 Invertebrate systems for the study of hormonal effects on behavior. Vitam Horm 35:283-315

Withrow RB 1959 A kinetic analysis of photoperiodism. In: Withrow RB (ed) Photoperiodism and related phenomena in plants and animals. Am Assoc Adv Sci Publ 55:439-471

Wyatt GR, Pan ML 1978 Insect plasma proteins. Annu Rev Biochem 47:779-817

Yin C-M, Chippendale GM 1979a Diapause of the southwestern corn borer *Diatraea grandiosella*: further evidence showing juvenile hormone to be the regulator. J Insect Physiol 25:513-523

Yin C-M, Chippendale GM 1979b Ultrastructural characteristics of insect corpora allata in relation to larval diapause. Cell Tissue Res 197:453-461

DISCUSSION

Mordue: Your paper reminds us that diapause, rather than being a stage of quiescence, is an essential stage in the life-cycle of many insects. It allows the animal to make a range of changes in its biochemistry, physiology and behaviour, so allowing the necessary changes in metabolism to take place.

Ferenz: You measured juvenile hormone (JH) titres, and JH esterase activities in the haemolymph. Did you also measure JH biosynthesis by the corpora allata to see how it related to the JH titres?

Chippendale: No. Recently we have been devoting our attention to the fat body of the southwestern corn borer as a possible target for JH, and to the binding of JH to proteins in the haemolymph. We have not cultured the corpora allata of diapausing larvae and measured their rate of JH biosynthesis.

Ferenz: You are talking about binding proteins: but any lipoprotein that you can find in the haemolymph is probably a binding protein for JH. Or do you have a really distinct JH binding protein?

Chippendale: We have found a protein with a low relative molecular mass (M_r) in the haemolymph of the southwestern corn borer, which shows a high affinity for JH, much like the one present in the tobacco hornworm, *Manduca sexta* (Kramer et al 1976). JH also binds to a high M_r lipoprotein fraction present in the haemolymph, but not to all lipoproteins that are present (Turunen & Chippendale 1981).

Bowen: Do you find the diapause-associated protein anywhere else in the animal besides the fat body?

Chippendale: We have found that the protein accumulates only in the fat body of last-instar prediapausing larvae (Brown & Chippendale 1978). We are presently studying its distribution using the diapause-associated protein antibody, and have found that it can be detected immunologically in the larval haemolymph (J.W. Dillwith & G.M. Chippendale, unpublished work).

Mordue: What temperatures do the animals face in the winter? Is it possible that the diapause-associated protein is related to cold-hardiness?

Chippendale: The southwestern corn borer is found only at latitudes below about 38°N which have relatively mild winters. In Missouri, diapausing larvae show only moderate cold-hardiness (Chippendale & Reddy 1974). We have considered a role for the diapause-associated protein in cold-hardiness, but we have no evidence to support such a function.

Hodková: It seems that diapause induction is associated with a sharp increase in JH titre. What happens if you maintain, artificially, a high JH titre long before diapause normally occurs, so that the naturally occurring prediapause increase in JH titre is covert? Is diapause induced under these conditions? Perhaps this increase, and not the high JH titre itself, is a feedback signal necessary for diapause induction.

*Chippendale:*We have not examined the effect of JH treatments on early instar prediapausing southwestern corn borers. We have treated larvae that are already in diapause with a JH mimic and thereby significantly delayed their rate of pupation. We have also found that about 70% of non-diapausing larvae, treated early in their last instar with a JH mimic, enter a diapause-like state (Yin & Chippendale 1979).

Brady: How much is the difference in response between the diapausing and the non-diapausing corn borers due to the JH titre and how much is due to the dynamics of the change over these very different time-scales: one of 19 days (non-diapause) and one of 200 days (diapause)?

Chippendale: The JH titre present in last-instar southwestern corn borers appears to be very important in regulating their developmental programme. We measured JH titres in non-diapausing larvae reared at 30 °C and in diapausing larvae reared at 23 °C. The JH titre in the haemolymph of last-instar non-diapausing larvae drops off to about 140 *Galleria* Units/ml within 6 h of the ecdyses, and remains low (Yin & Chippendale 1976). Last-instar prediapausing larvae, by contrast, retain a relatively high titre of JH (Yin & Chippendale 1979). Additional data from larvae reared under long days (non-inductive) and short days (diapause-inductive) at the same temperature would be valuable to rule out temperature effects, but such data are not available. We should also keep in mind that the JH titres were obtained from pooled samples of haemolymph of relatively large numbers of corn borers, not from individuals.

Truman: The high concentration of aromatic amino acids in the diapause-associated protein reminds me of other insect storage proteins such as calliphorin and manducin, compounds that John Law now calls arylphorins (Telfer et al 1983). How does your protein compare with these proteins in M_r and aromatic content?

Chippendale: An important difference is that the diapause-associated protein of the corn borer has a low M_r of about 35000 (Turunen & Chippendale 1980) compared with the hexameric storage proteins, which have M_r values of about 500000 (Roberts & Brock 1981). Both contain high levels of tyrosine and phenylalanine, which make up about 12% of total amino acids of the diapause-associated protein (J. W. Dillwith & G. M. Chippendale, unpublished work) and about 20% of those of calliphorin and manducin (Munn et al 1971, Kramer et al 1980). The diapause-associated protein could be another kind of storage protein for aromatic amino acids.

Truman: What happens to the concentration of the diapause-associated protein as diapause progresses?

Chippendale: Our electrophoretic studies have indicated a gradual but not a complete loss of the diapause-associated protein from the fat body during diapause (Brown & Chippendale 1978). We have not yet used the antibody to the protein to measure the change in titre of the protein during diapause.

Gilbert: Storage proteins that have been found in other insects, including Lepidoptera, have also been found in non-diapausing larvae. They are sequestered in late larval life by the fat body, and utilized during pupal–adult development. So I doubt that this diapause-associated protein is analogous to those other storage proteins.

Pittendrigh: What do we know about the half-life of JH molecules? Have you had cause to look at JH titres throughout the day, in a way comparable to Colin Steel's observations on ecdysone titres? Is there any daily variation of JH levels?

Chippendale: We have measured the half-life of JH I incubated *in vitro* in the plasma of the southwestern corn borer, and found it to be about 44 min in diapausing larvae. This half-life was longer than that in non-diapausing larvae (Mane & Chippendale 1981). At present it is uncertain how this finding relates to the rate of JH hydrolysis *in vivo*. We have also shown that early diapausing larvae that were injected with 20-hydroxyecdysone at various intervals after receiving a head ligature required 17 days to complete a normal pupal ecdysis, suggesting that a very low rate of hydrolysis was occurring in their haemolymph (Chippendale & Yin 1976). Our measurements of JH titre for the corn borer were obtained using pooled samples of haemolymph taken during the photophase on different days (Yin & Chippendale 1979).

Mordue: Is there any evidence about JH perturbation on a daily basis?

Gilbert: No. The reason that one can do that type of experiment with ecdysteroids is that there is a good radioimmunoassay for ecdysteroids, in which purification of the ecdysteroids is not necessary. There is no comparable assay for JH. The only assay that works on tissue extracts of JH requires the hormone to be extensively purified before the radioimmunoassay is done. Nevertheless, if this were done, the data on JH would probably be similar to the data on ecdysteroids. A number of investigators, including Nijhout & Williams (1974), postulated that JH in some way inhibits secretion of prothoracicotropic hormone (PTTH). How would you then account for the stationary moults that occur in the corn borer? I understood that during this period of diapause there was a rather constant titre of JH. If this titre is inhibiting PTTH secretion, how can you also have moulting during that time?

Chippendale: About the only way to account for the stationary moults in the southwestern corn borer is to assume that the JH titre is a critical factor. At times the JH titre of some diapausing larvae may be sufficiently high to activate their PTTH-producing system, thus resulting in larval moults (Chippendale & Yin 1976). We do not have information about the JH titre of individual larvae.

Mordue: These stationary moults are interesting. In insect development it is notable that embryonic moults take place without any increase in size.

Gilbert: There are also insects that, under certain conditions, can moult along with a *decrease* in size, e.g. *Trogoderma glabrum* (Beck 1972).

Saunders: Do the southwestern corn borers feed during these moults? I believe that the sugar-cane borer, *Diatraea saccharalis*, has stationary moults, and they also feed during this time (B.J.R. Philogène, unpublished results, 1983).

Chippendale: Diapausing southwestern corn borers do not feed. Larvae that moult during diapause inevitably show some decrease in size.

Saunders: This strategy seems to have a very high cost, doesn't it?

Chippendale: Yes; we are puzzled and cannot think of a good reason for the southwestern corn borer to undergo these stationary moults. Yagi & Fukaya (1974) have also shown that diapausing larvae of the rice-stem borer, *Chilo suppressalis*, may have stationary moults. Recently we found that diapausing southwestern corn borers obtained from Mexico moulted more frequently than did those from Missouri (Kikukawa 1983). Perhaps the moulting provides a clue about the evolution of diapause in these stem borers (Kikukawa 1983). There may be selection against stationary moulting, especially at more northerly locations, because moulting requires that larvae draw upon their reserves.

Reynolds: I can think of an adaptive reason for undergoing stationary moults: it may be useful in avoiding fungal diseases. Zacharuk (1973) has shown in wireworm larvae that invasion by entomophagous fungi during a moult cycle sometimes fails to kill the insect because the larva escapes the fungus by leaving the cuticle behind. The fact that the diapausing corn borers are underground, where they might be particularly susceptible to disease, may be relevant to this explanation.

Masaki: Stationary moulting is rather common among diapausing larvae. But this kind of moulting occurs only when the animals are kept in short days at high temperatures—that is, in an abnormal combination of photoperiod and temperature. This kind of stationary moult does not occur under natural hibernating conditions, does it?

Chippendale: We have studied stationary moulting of diapausing larvae in our laboratory colony of the southwestern corn borer at 20, 23, 27 and 30°C (Chippendale & Yin 1976). The highest number of moults occurred at the lower temperatures. We have not studied moulting in larvae in their overwintering sites in corn plants, but I would guess that moulting does occur in the natural habitat.

Gilbert: A laboratory temperature of 20°C is still fairly warm compared to a Missouri winter!

Masaki: You mentioned the Mexican strain of the southwestern corn borer, which shows a much lower incidence and intensity of diapause. It would be worth trying to compare the JH titres and the measurements made on the diapause-associated protein with those from the Missouri strain. By what mechanism is the *intensity* of diapause controlled in different strains?

Chippendale: We have not compared possible mechanisms involved in controlling the intensity of diapause in the Mexican and Missouri strains of the southwestern corn borer. Comparisons of the titres of JH and the diapause-associated protein between the two strains could provide useful information, but are not available. Up to now, we have found a critical photoperiod for the Mexican strain which accounts for the seasonal programming of its diapause, and we have shown a few other day-length and temperature effects (Kikukawa & Chippendale 1983).

Giebultowicz: You mentioned that the removal of the corpora allata and the cutting of the nerve between the brain and the corpora allata had the same effect of breaking diapause and lowering the JH titre. For many Lepidopteran larvae it is believed that there is an allatotropic factor released from the brain. Would you suggest that your insects do not have this factor, but, rather that there is some kind of nervous or local neurosecretory effect? Did you try to transplant the brain into larvae that were programmed not to have diapause, to see if you could stimulate the corpora allata to produce JH?

Chippendale: We have obtained preliminary results about how the brain of the southwestern corn borer controls the corpora allata solely from sectioning the nervi corporis allati and transplanting brains (Yin & Chippendale 1979). Intact nervous connections between the brain and the corpus allatum appear to be required for JH secretion to be maintained. We found that severing the nervi corporis allati of early diapausing larvae had the same effect as allatectomy; i.e. 67% of the treated larvae pupated prematurely. We have suggested that the corpora allata are stimulated by neural impulses from the brain, but we have not ruled out the presence of an allatotropin. However, in the kind of experiment you mentioned, we found no evidence for an allatotropin when brains from last-instar prediapausing larvae were transplanted into last-instar non-diapausing larvae (Yin & Chippendale 1979).

Goldsworthy: I understood that of your allatectomized animals, at least 30% of them still went into diapause.

Chippendale: No; they did not go into diapause; 33% *remained* in diapause. Early diapausing corn borers were allatectomized and 67% pupated (Yin & Chippendale 1979).

Goldsworthy: But, even so, it would seem that there is not necessarily any absolute relationship between JH titre and diapause.

Chippendale: No; this result is not absolute, but we believe that a 67% premature pupation rate in 30 days is sufficiently significant to indicate that JH is involved (Yin & Chippendale 1979).

REFERENCES

Beck SD 1972 Growth and retrogression in larvae of *Trogoderma glabrum* (Coleoptera:Dermestidae). 3: Ecdysis and form determination. Ann Entomol Soc Am 65:1319-1324

Brown JJ, Chippendale GM 1978 Juvenile hormone and a protein associated with the larval diapause of the southwestern corn borer, *Diatraea grandiosella*. Insect Biochem 8:359-367

Chippendale GM, Reddy AS 1974 Diapause of the southwestern corn borer, *Diatraea grandiosella*: low temperature mortality and geographical distribution. Environ Entomol 3:233-238

Chippendale GM, Yin C-M 1976 Endocrine interactions controlling the larval diapause of the southwestern corn borer, *Diatraea grandiosella*. J Insect Physiol 22:989-995

Kikukawa S 1983 Geographical adaptations and seasonal time measurement of the southwestern corn borer, *Diatraea grandiosella*. PhD thesis, University of Missouri

Kikukawa S, Chippendale GM 1983 Seasonal adaptations of populations of the southwestern corn borer, *Diatraea grandiosella*, from tropical and temperate regions. J Insect Physiol 29:561-567

Kramer KJ, Dunn PE, Peterson RC, Seballos HL, Sanburg LL, Law JH 1976 Purification and characterization of the carrier protein for juvenile hormone from the hemolymph of the tobacco hornworm, *Manduca sexta* Johannson (Lepidoptera: Sphingidae). J Biol Chem 251:4979-4985

Kramer SJ, Mundall EC, Law JH 1980 Purification and properties of manducin, an amino acid storage protein of the haemolymph of larval and pupal *Manduca sexta*. Insect Biochem 10:279-288

Mane SD, Chippendale GM 1981 Hydrolysis of juvenile hormone in diapausing and non-diapausing larvae of the southwestern corn borer, *Diatraea grandiosella*. J Comp Physiol 144:205-214

Munn EA, Feinstein A, Greville GD 1971 The isolation and properties of the protein calliphorin. Biochem J 124:367-374

Nijhout HF, Williams CM 1974 Control of moulting and metamorphosis in the tobacco hornworm *Manduca sexta* (L.): cessation of juvenile hormone secretion as a trigger for pupation. J Exp Biol 61:493-501

Roberts DB, Brock HW 1981 The major serum proteins of dipteran larvae. Experientia (Basel) 37:103-110

Telfer WH, Keim PS, Law JH 1983 Arylphorin, a new protein from *Hyalophora cecropia*; comparisons with calliphorin and manducin. Insect Biochem 13:601-614

Turunen S, Chippendale GM 1980 Fat body protein associated with the larval diapause of the southwestern corn borer, *Diatraea grandiosella*: synthesis and characteristics. Comp Biochem Physiol B Comp Biochem 65:595-603

Turunen S, Chippendale GM 1981 Binding of juvenile hormone, methoprene, and hydroprene to haemolymph proteins of larvae of the southwestern corn borer, *Diatraea grandiosella*. Insect Biochem 11:429-435

Yagi S, Fukaya M 1974 Juvenile hormone as a key factor regulating larval diapause of the rice stem borer, *Chilo suppressalis* (Lepidoptera: Pyralidae). Appl Entomol Zool 9:247-255

Yin C-M, Chippendale GM 1976 Hormonal control of larval diapause and metamorphosis of the southwestern corn borer, *Diatraea grandiosella*. J Exp Biol 64:303-310

Yin C-M, Chippendale GM 1979 Diapause of the southwestern corn borer *Diatraea grandiosella*: further evidence showing juvenile hormone to be the regulator. J Insect Physiol 25:513-523

Zacharuk RY 1973 Penetration of the cuticular layers of Elaterid larvae (Coleoptera) by the fungus *Metarrhizium anisopliae*, and notes on a bacterial invasion. J Invert Pathol 21:101-106

Concluding general discussion

Models, hormone titres and clocks

Mordue: Transduction of the photoperiodic signal into mechanisms that affect the regulation of development in insects and molluscs is remarkably subtle. An insect, for example, uses juvenile hormone (JH) and ecdysones to regulate its normal development. Yet it can use the same hormones, but in completely different ways, to elicit diapause. In addition, there is a regulated programme of development, dependent on both JH and ecdysone, to control normal moulting and metamorphosis. But in some insects, at the same time, the insect uses these hormones, as normal development is proceeding, to induce either diapause or polymorphism, or both.

Gilbert: The only exception to the dogma that hormone deficiency results in diapause is in the embryonic diapause of the silkworm, where there is a presumed diapause hormone from the suboesophageal ganglion of the mother.

*Pittendrigh:*Professor Mordue said that diapause was being 'regulated' (and this is a strong word) by the same set of hormones in different ways. What is the evidence, for any given case, that the hormonal changes that we see are *causes* and not *correlates*?

Reynolds: That is an extremely important point. It is too easy for us endocrinologists, because we can measure these changes in hormone titres, to assume that the titres must be vital in controlling development. It is remarkable that in an insect like *Tenebrio* one can isolate the abdomen and it will go through the same sequence of developmental and hormonal changes, and in the same time, as it would if one had not isolated it (Delbecque et al 1978). We normally assume that the central nervous system controls changes in hormone titre, but here it is clear that the normal course of development, including changes in hormone titre, is very resistant to perturbation.

Saunders: But how central is this decision about whether an insect enters diapause or not? In *Manduca sexta*, Dr M.F. Bowen and I (unpublished results, 1983) have done some experiments in which we can transplant the brain only (without corpora cardiaca or corpora allata) from a fifth-instar long-day animal into the abdomen of a fifth-instar short-day animal. This reprogrammes its development and makes it develop without a diapause. This result suggests that the diapause/non-diapause decision is primarily brain-centred.

Reynolds: That decision about diapause must be central, but a lot of the programming of changes in hormone titre during subsequent development

277

must nevertheless be rather peripherally regulated, perhaps as a result of interplay between many systems. We should be searching for some kind of central switch that can be thrown in these photoperiodic decisions so that everything else then takes care of itself.

Sokolove: An analogy, from the neurophysiological point of view, would be a central walking programme. For example, an insect has six legs which have to be coordinated when it walks. For this purpose a central locomotion programme is built into the nervous system. But if the insect eats a lot, it weighs more, and peripheral receptors are needed to allow it to compensate for that weight by modifying the central programme in an appropriate fashion.

Pittendrigh: In insects where there is a relatively sharp critical day-length for inducing diapause, as in many Lepidoptera, is anything known about the state of the endocrine system on the two sides of that critical day-length? What is the signal for inducing diapause at the endocrine level?

Gilbert: Dr Bowen has been trying to find out if there are any endocrine differences between larvae destined to enter pupal diapause and those destined not to do so because they have been subjected to different light:dark regimes.

Bowen: Bell et al (1975) have looked at the diapause intensity of *M. sexta* raised under different photoperiods within the inductive range. Longer photoperiods induce a diapause of longer duration than do shorter photoperiods.

Mordue: In adult *Pyrrhocoris* and *Leptinotarsa spp.*, under short days, the endocrine effects are quickly and readily brought about and switched off. Perhaps the adult system uses a different mechanism than that used for larvae.

Truman: But even insect endocrinologists only know about the *output* of the system. The physiological mechanisms behind summation of photoperiodic information and measurements of day-length are as much 'black boxes' to endocrinologists as they are to people studying photoperiodism.

Mordue: How does your model system, Dr Veerman, help the endocrinologist to discover more about these mechanisms?

Veerman: One could perhaps try to apply the model (see this volume, p 48) to various well investigated insect species to see what it reveals about differences, for instance, in their counter systems. Dr Vaz Nunes has applied our model to three species of insect, *Megoura viciae*, *Sarcophaga argyrostoma* and *Pieris brassicae*, and she believes that it fits these insects (Vaz Nunes 1983). There are differences not only in the parameters of the hour-glass but also certain differences in how the counter, according to our model, operates in these insects. For instance, *Megoura*, from the model, has a somewhat different counter from the ones in *Sarcophaga* and *Tetranychus*, which are similar to each other. The circadian influence, which is interpreted in a resonance way in this model is completely absent in *Megoura*, very strong in *Sarcophaga* and less so in *Tetranychus*.

Mordue: How well does your model predict resonance experiments for different categories of insects?

Veerman: We have to start with certain experiments that have been done with a particular species in order to fix the parameters that are necessary for us to use the model in the first place. Then we can apply it to new experiments. It has not been applied yet very much beyond the spider mite and the preliminary trials for these three insects that I have mentioned.

Sokolove: Surely the results of Dr Saunders on *Sarcophaga* were more than sufficient for you to be able to set parameters and to predict the photoperiodic behaviour of the system, Dr Veerman? The astounding aspect of your work is the close correlation between the model predictions and the actual experimental data. How well, operating from a minimal number of experiments in Dr Saunders's case, can you reproduce the circadian surface?

Veerman: The model has very little 'noise' for *Tetranychus*, largely because the photoperiodic responses are almost always all or nothing for these mites. The noise is larger for other animals. As far as we know, we can now produce those circadian surfaces with the model, at least for *Sarcophaga* and *Tetranychus*.

Sokolove: That's very impressive. How does one build a summation system physiologically? I see a problem in the sort of model that Dr Saunders presented, where there is a quantal input every so often until a threshold is reached. That works on short time-scales in nervous systems where large signals give rise to intracellular events, and the threshold is reasonably well defined. For events with a slow time-course, it does not work well, however, because there is noise both in the threshold itself and in the event that is approaching threshold. The chances of mistriggering become very high if the difference between the mean signal level and the mean threshold is anywhere near the range of the noise. The model bothers me because it does not allow one to say that, after a precise number of events, something will definitely occur. There is too much chance for error in timing, so that a response may occur a day or two earlier or later.

Mordue: But within this kind of model one should examine the effect of photoperiodic cues in one set of environmental stimuli. Other stimuli must also be summated and integrated before there is a response. For *Rhodnius* the classic signal for hormone release is feeding, which is a single, relatively simple event, but many other insects, such as *Manduca*, require a summation of various stimuli.

Reynolds: Even in *Rhodnius*, the summation of stimuli may be important. It is known that a sub-threshold meal can cause release of some ecdysone, although the insect does not go on to moult (Wigglesworth 1955).

Steel: Actually there is only indirect evidence that ecdysteroids might be released in such circumstances. For example, if *Rhodnius* is fed non-nutritious meals, these cause morphological activation of the epidermal cells, but the cells soon regress again to their condition before feeding (Beckel & Friend 1964).

Chippendale: I think that it is vital to study the various components of the receptor–clock–effector system in one insect, while recognizing that no insect is a perfect model. For example, *M. sexta* has been used extensively for endocrinological studies, and we are beginning to learn more about its pupal diapause (e.g. Bell et al 1975, Denlinger & Bradfield 1981). Further study of the seasonal programming of the life-cycle of this insect could provide valuable information about how its receptor, clock and effector system are integrated.

We have heard about the likely convergent evolution of the photoperiodic response (Pittendrigh et al, and Masaki, this volume) and we should be careful about making generalizations. For example, even within one family of moths, differences have been found in the hormonal control of the larval diapause of the southwestern corn borer, *Diatraea grandiosella*, and the European corn borer, *Ostrinia nubilalis* (Chippendale & Yin 1979, Bean & Beck 1980).

Mordue: In molluscs, too, we need to examine the transduction of the signal into an endocrine event. In *Lymnaea* one can use photoperiod to stimulate identifiable cells, some of which respond quickly to environmental cues such as feeding and oxygen supply (see Joosse, this volume). The simplicity of the molluscan neurophysiology means that it offers the possibility of much more detailed study than has been possible so far in most insects.

Joosse: Nevertheless, my neurophysiological colleagues say that even when one injects a stain into a molluscan neuron that normally never reacts to light, then that neuron *will* become reactive to light. So all neurons are possible receptors for the light signal. It is therefore very difficult to locate the important photoperiodically sensitive spot, even in molluscs.

Concluding comments

Pittendrigh: Our task in this symposium was to discuss photoperiodic regulation of insect and molluscan hormones. In fact, our discussion seems to have focused on two somewhat separate topics: (1) the role of photoperiod in diapause induction and termination; and (2) endocrine correlates of the diapause and non-diapause states. There has been, I think, some implicit assumption that an endocrine cue initiates or causes diapause, but is there any real evidence for that? Are we sure that a change in photoperiod, in causing the onset of diapause, does so via an endocrine agent? What leaves me still sceptical on this issue is the marked contrast between the timing phenomena we have discussed (the sharp restriction of ecdysis, eclosion or gut purge to some particular time of day; or the precision of the photoperiodic time-measurement itself) and the very gradual changes in ecdysteroid titre, for example, that Jim Truman (this volume) has described for *Manduca sexta*. How does the insect extract a well defined time-cue from such gradual and noisy change? Is some of the timing taking place in receptor organs, or is it related to the times at which competence for certain events appears? On the other hand, the spectacular pulsatile changes in ecdysteroids that Colin Steel (this volume) reports from *Rhodnius prolixus* are what one would expect if hormones were to mediate the sharp timing of events. Why are Professor Steel's observations so unique? I am reminded here of some remarkable observations recently from Reppert et al (1981): in mammals both somatostatin and vasopressin show no periodicity in the general circulation but manifest a spectacular daily pulse in the cerebrospinal fluid. Is it possible that some comparable compartmentalization exists in insects—that sharply timed hormone pulses do in fact occur somewhere to account for sharp timing—and we are missing them?

*Mordue:*The different target tissues may respond at different times, with different affinities for different levels of ecdysteroids. Certain events may be triggered immediately when the ecdysteroid or other hormone levels first begin to rise; other events may take place later and the relevant target tissues may require considerably more hormone. The residence time of the hormone on the receptor may also be relevant. The concept of different tissues responding in different ways to the same hormone is certainly one that is not unfamiliar to the endocrinologists amongst us.

*Truman:*Perhaps Larry Schwartz's results on the last half of adult development in *Manduca sexta* are relevant to the precision of hormonal timing of development. This work showed that the rate of development is controlled by the ecdysteroid titre (Schwartz & Truman 1983): if the titre declines too rapidly, the developmental sequences speed up and are compressed in time. If the animal is supplemented with exogenous ecdysteroids then development is slowed down and, even at moderate hormone levels, can be stopped altogether. The rate of development is inversely proportional to the dosage of applied steroid. Also, as the animal develops, it becomes progressively more sensitive to a particular dosage of hormone. These two relationships may act to maintain tissue coordination during the long period of adult development. For example, consider what would happen if two tissues were slightly out of synchrony late in development. The tissues would be exposed to the same ecdysteroid concentration, but the more mature tissue would be more affected, and hence more retarded by the steroid than the less mature tissue. Consequently, in this way the less mature tissue would have a chance to catch up, and synchrony would eventually be re-established. If the normal slow decline in the ecdysteroid titre is replaced by an abrupt fall in the titre, then the developmental synchrony between various tissues becomes disrupted.

Reynolds: One does not know the extent to which events that are precisely timed are triggered by factors other than ecdysteroids but which are dependent on them. In *M. sexta*, ecdysis and post-ecdysial tanning, which are precisely timed, are probably not directly dependent on the ecdysteroid titre but depend on peptide hormones—eclosion hormone and bursicon —the release of which depends on the ecdysteroid titre itself. Detailed titres of eclosion hormone and bursicon in single cannulated animals have shown us that each hormone is released in massive single pulses (Reynolds et al 1979).

*Pittendrigh:*That does give a discrete signal but the timing of that signal still seems to depend on a somewhat variable overall ecdysone titre.

Reynolds: In the case of events that are subject to circadian timing the release of eclosion hormone is independently gated.

Steel: It is an attractive idea that release of peptide hormone into the haemolymph could be a much more precisely timed phenomenon than, say, steroid hormone release simply because the peptide hormones are part of the nervous system and therefore 'linked in' to the environment more directly.

Gilbert: Although the ecdysteroid levels, for example, may indeed be generally 'fuzzy', as Professor Pittendrigh implied, we should remember that the titre is not measured for ecdysone only but for all the ecdysteroids that have radioimmunoassay activity. If one could analyse separately the moulting or the pre-moulting hormone or a host of metabolites, one might find much sharper peaks than we are used to seeing.

Pittendrigh: Do the radioimmunoassay techniques use monoclonal antibodies?

Gilbert: No, the antibodies are polyclonals; nobody yet has reported suitable monoclonal antibodies. But even monoclonals would not necessarily produce better results, although they would give more uniformity among different laboratories!

*Sokolove:*We have heard little about hormonal effects on the clock. Professor Truman at this symposium has been relatively provocative in pointing out that hormones are major mediators of circadian organization, as opposed to merely being outputs. We have not heard anything about the effect on either phase or period of prothoracicotropic hormone (PTTH), ecdysteroids or eclosion hormone release. If there is no effect, then the clock is not just temperature-compensated but is also relatively insensitive to some striking hormonal changes.

Truman: There is definitely a strong effect of ecdysteroids on the phase of eclosion hormone secretion. People interested in diapause have focused on the syndrome itself. We have not returned to the earlier stages, the ones that David Saunders mentioned, during which the animal is gathering the photoperiodic information to make its decision. We need to know the phase of PTTH release, and of ecdysone secretion under different photoperiods, and the titres of JH secretion under long-day and short-day conditions in otherwise identical animals. Without these background data we cannot even begin to guess at possible endocrine mechanisms. If we want to understand the physiology of diapause induction, we need to return to the point where the people studying photoperiod tell us that the induction is taking place, and then we can look at the final outcome.

Chippendale: Available methods for measuring JH titre have been adequate for our work up to now. However, it would be very worthwhile to study circadian patterns in JH titre once a suitable assay becomes available.

Gilbert: Many of us are simply ignorant of the field. As endocrinologists we answer questions such as what is the structure of PTTH; where does it come from; what is its mode of action? Many data buried in the endocrinological literature have yet to be studied in terms of what time of day the experiments were done, and under what conditions a particular organism was raised. This symposium has shown, for me, the importance of conditioning of the experimental organism.

Joosse: Perhaps it is wrong to hope that work on hormones will reveal the form of signal that the nervous system usually shows. People working on clock mechanisms and timing in the nervous system know that signals are integrated by networks of nerve cells, and the sharp signal of the output reflects the final decision. In the hormonal systems, however, one rarely finds examples of short surges such as the luteinizing hormone peak that triggers ovulation in the vertebrates, and the ovulation hormone peak in *Lymnaea*, as we have shown. For very complex events, such as the development of an embryo in a mammal, or diapause in insects, not one but many events are involved. Increasing amounts of one hormone may cause different reactions in different tissues, e.g. increased storage of reserves, increased ionic exchange and changes in eating activity. The number of targets is numerous and each reacts at its own pace to the change in concentration of that hormone. So I am not surprised that diapause induction, for example, requires gentle fluctuations of hormone levels. We should not expect to see sharp points.

With reference to Professor Pittendrigh's comment on vasopressin, we should remember that in vertebrates the endocrine system in the periphery is separated from that in the central nervous system by the blood–brain barrier. This explains why effects of vasopressin in the brain are very different from those in the periphery. Such differences might also occur in insects, which also have a blood–brain barrier. In molluscs it has been shown that complex activities, such as egg laying, are controlled by neurosecretory cells which release three or four different peptides, each with different functions. Discouragingly for us, this may also be true for some types of neurohormone-producing cells, such as those that produce PTTH.

Page: The output side of this system, where photoperiodicity is controlling some physiological response, seems to be complex. It may be a mistake to attempt to understand the system by working backwards from the output side. The photoperiod provides such a well defined stimulus that it should be possible to follow it into the nervous system, through the clock, and then to the output.

Bowen: But behaviour has been used as an assay by clock biologists for years, and this 'downstream' approach has been very valuable.

Page: That approach may well have hindered clock biologists in efforts to understand the physiological and molecular mechanism of the clock. Other investigators have moved away from the behavioural approach, which is so complicated, and are now making rapid progress. For example, Arnold Eskin (1979), using the isolated eye of *Aplysia*, has been attempting to follow the light information into the nervous system, step by step, and has made significant progress in identifying important physiological processes and molecules in the entrainment pathway.

Steel: We have just been considering what endocrinologists might be doing to answer questions that the clock biologists are producing, but the other side of the problem is equally fascinating. It is very difficult to translate models of clock behaviour into physiologically testable systems. I would like to see clock biologists generate models that make physiologically testable predictions.

Mordue: The endocrinological approach cannot be considered as just an 'on or off' mechanism. Many dynamic events are intertwined and then a cue occurs and produces a new and different dynamic equilibrium. The problem is to identify what the dynamic equilibrium is when the cue comes along.

In this final discussion we have not gone into detail about the genetic approach described by Dr Lankinen and Professor Masaki in their work on *Drosophila* and crickets: this is an area that should become a very active research interest in the future.

Despite Professor Joosse's hesitation about the value of the identifiable neurons present in molluscs (p 280), I do believe that they offer several advantages. Jim Truman has described, tentatively, identifiable eclosion hormone cells. In addition, the possible presence of a photoperiodic receptor in the prothoracic glands, as detailed by Professor Ishizaki, needs to be examined in detail. Perhaps recognizable cell types there can be influenced by a photoperiodic stimulus. In my opinion, these topics in particular would benefit from experiments that combine the endocrinological and the biological clock approaches.

REFERENCES

Bean DW, Beck SD 1980 The role of juvenile hormone in the larval diapause of the European corn borer, *Ostrinia nubilalis*. J Insect Physiol 26:579-584

Beckel WE, Friend WG 1964 The relation of abdominal distension and nutrition to molting in *Rhodnius prolixus* (Ståhl) (Hemiptera). Can J Zool 42:71-78

Bell RA, Rasul CG, Joachim FG 1975 Photoperiodic induction of the pupal diapause in the tobacco hornworm, *Manduca sexta*. J Insect Physiol 21:1471-1480

Chippendale GM, Yin C-M 1979 Larval diapause of the European corn borer, *Ostrinia nubilalis*: further experiments examining its hormonal control. J Insect Physiol 25:53-58

Delbecque J-PA, Delachambre J, Hirn M, De Reggi M 1978 Abdominal production of ecdysterone and pupal–adult development in *Tenebrio molitor* (Insecta, Coleoptera). Gen Comp Endocrinol 35:436-444

Denlinger DL, Bradfield JY 1981 Duration of pupal diapause in the tobacco hornworm is determined by number of short days received by the larva. J Exp Biol 91:331-337

Eskin A 1979 Circadian system of the *Aplysia* eye: properties of the pacemaker and mechanisms of its entrainment. Fed Proc 38:2573-2579

Reppert SM, Autman HG, Swaminathan S, Fisher DA 1981 Vasopressin exhibits a rhythmic daily pattern in cerebrospinal fluid but not in blood. Science (Wash DC) 213:1256-1257

Reynolds SE, Taghert PH, Truman JW 1979 Eclosion hormone and bursicon titres and the onset of hormonal responsiveness during the last day of adult development in *Manduca sexta* (L). J Exp Biol 78:77-86

Schwartz LM, Truman JW 1983 Hormonal control of the rates of metamorphic development in the tobacco hornworm *Manduca sexta*. Dev Biol 99:103-114

Vaz Nunes M 1983 Photoperiodic time measurement in the spider mite *Tetranychus urticae* Koch. PhD thesis, University of Amsterdam

Wigglesworth VB 1955 The role of the haemocytes in the growth and moulting of an insect, *Rhodnius prolixus* (Hemiptera). J Exp Biol 32:649-663

Index of contributors

*Entries in **bold** type indicate papers; other entries refer to discussion contributions*

*Non-participating co-author.

Indexes compiled by John Rivers

287

Subject index